EDI DEVELOPMENT STUDIES

The Adaptive Economy

Adjustment Policies in Small, Low-Income Countries

Tony Killick

The World Bank
Washington, D. C

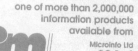

Copyright © 1993
The International Bank for Reconstruction
and Development / THE WORLD BANK
1818 H Street, N.W.
Washington, D.C. 20433, U.S.A.

The Economic Development Institute (EDI) was established by the World Bank in 1955 to train officials concerned with development planning, policymaking, investment analysis, and project implementation in member developing countries. At present the substance of the EDI's work emphasizes macroeconomic and sectoral economic policy analysis. Through a variety of courses, seminars, and workshops, most of which are given overseas in cooperation with local institutions, the EDI seeks to sharpen analytical skills used in policy analysis and to broaden understanding of the experience of individual countries with economic development. Although the EDI's publications are designed to support its training activities, many are of interest to a much broader audience. EDI materials, including any findings, interpretations, and conclusions, are entirely those of the authors and should not be attributed in any manner to the World Bank, to its affiliated organizations, or to members of its Board of Executive Directors or the countries they represent.

Because of the informality of this series and to make the publication available with the least possible delay, the manuscript has not been edited as fully as would be the case with a more formal document, and the World Bank accepts no responsibility for errors.

The material in this publication is copyrighted. Requests for permission to reproduce portions of it should be sent to the Office of the Publisher at the address shown in the copyright notice above. The World Bank encourages dissemination of its work and will normally give permission promptly and, when the reproduction is for noncommercial purposes, without asking a fee. Permission to copy portions for classroom use is granted through the Copyright Clearance Center, 27 Congress Street, Salem, Massachusetts 01970, U.S.A.

The backlist of publications by the World Bank is shown in the annual *Index of Publications*, which is available from Distribution Unit, Office of the Publisher, The World Bank, 1818 H Street, N.W., Washington, D.C. 20433, U.S.A., or from Publications, Banque mondiale, 66, avenue d'Iéna, 75116 Paris, France.

Tony Killick is Senior Research Fellow at the Overseas Development Institute, London, United Kingdom.

Library of Congress Cataloging-in-Publication Data

The adaptive economy : adjustment policies in small, low-income countries
/ Tony Killick.
     p. cm.—(EDI development studies).
   Includes bibliographical references (p.).
   ISBN 0-8213-2125-0
   1. Structural adjustment (Economic policy)—Developing countries.
I. Title. II. Series.
HC59.7.K4817 1993
338.9'0091724—dc20   92-14469
                              CIP

EDI Catalog No. 400/058

CONTENTS

FOREWORD

The *Adaptive Economy* was prepared for use in Senior Policy Seminars organized by the National Economic Management Division of the World Bank's Economic Development Institute (EDI). It discusses in relatively nontechnical terms the principles of adjustment policy with special reference to small, low-income countries. The book will be of interest to practitioners, teachers, and students of development economics.

Amnon Golan
Director
Economic Development Institute

ABBREVIATIONS AND ACRONYMS

CFA	Communauté Financière Africaine
EPZ	export processing zone
f.o.b.	free on board
GATT	General Agreement on Tariffs and Trade
GDP	gross domestic product
IDS	Institute for Development Studies
IFC	International Finance Corporation
IFI	International financial institution
IMF	International Monetary Fund
NIC	newly industrializing country
NTB	nontariff barrier
OECD	Organisation for Economic Co-operation and Development
ODI	Overseas Development Institute
OPEC	Organization of Petroleum Exporting Countries
R&D	research and development
REXR	real effective exchange rate
RXR	real exchange rate
SAL	structural adjustment loan
SLIC	small, low-income country
SSA	Sub-Saharan Africa
UNCTAD	United Nations Conference on Trade and Development
UNICEF	United Nations Children's Fund
UNIDO	United Nations Industrial Development Organization
WIDER	World Institute for Development Economics Research

PREFACE

In 1988 the Economic Development Institute (EDI) of the World Bank commissioned me to prepare a volume of essays on structural adjustment for use in its policy seminars on this subject. The original intention was for a modest collection, but as the work proceeded I became dissatisfied with my scheme. Increasingly I realized that what was needed most was a book that would set the explosion of adjustment programs that occurred in the 1980s into the context of the long-term process of economic development and the structural changes intrinsic to it.

This volume is therefore grounded on the not particularly controversial premise that all economies at all times need to adjust or adapt to changing circumstances if they are to achieve a reasonable pace of development. Adjustment is thus not viewed as a phenomenon of the late twentieth century, nor as separate from or preliminary to the struggle for economic development. The book, therefore, sets out to clarify the forces to which economies need to respond; the attributes that contribute to an economy's capacity to adjust; the difficulties that stand in its way; and, above all, how policy can facilitate this.

Although the book is addressed to readers with some grounding in economics, I have tried to make it accessible to a wide readership. Thus, the presentation is largely nontechnical, although informed by recent developments in theory and empirical research. The particular target audience is economists working for or advising government departments and agencies, but it is also intended for teachers and students of development economics. The reference list provides useful sources for further study.

Taken collectively, developing countries are so disparate, with widely differing characteristics and constraints, that attempting a text valid for all of them is impractical. The composition of their imports and exports, the size of their economies, and their stage of development all have a major bearing on the nature of their adjustment problems and opportunities. This book therefore concentrates on small, low-income countries (SLICs). This may seem restrictive, but actually covers most of Sub-Saharan Africa (the principal exception being Nigeria), plus such countries as Bolivia, the Dominican Republic, Haiti, Honduras, Morocco, Myanmar, Papua New Guinea, and Sri Lanka. With a slightly more liberal interpretation, this list can be expanded to include Bangladesh and Nepal. We are therefore dealing with a high proportion of developing countries, focusing on those with the most fragile economic base upon which to respond to changing needs. Moreover, the illustrative material is not confined to this group. I have drawn upon whatever country experiences illustrate the point under discussion, so long as the examples are relevant to the SLICs' circumstances.

I have accumulated a large number of debts in preparing this book. The chief of these is to Peter Knight of EDI and his predecessor, Suman Bery, for their encouragement and support and for their patience in allowing the project to expand as it did. Although financed by EDI, the view offered here is an independent one. I have benefited from information and advice provided by the World Bank, but I have throughout expressed my own opinions on the often contentious issues addressed. It follows that the Bank and its staff do not necessarily agree with the views expressed.

Next I must thank Matthew Martin and Moazzam Malik, who at various times helped me enormously in preparing materials for writing and revising this text, and who almost always managed to make discreet sense of my often vague or inconsistent directions. Matthew Martin is co-author of chapter 8. Equally fervent gratitude is offered to Jane Kennan, who worked all hours and with great skill to bring the manuscript to a state fit to be given to a publisher, and who has helped in many other ways. Thanks are due also to Margaret Cornell and Alice S. Dowsett for their skillful editorial work. Tribute should be paid to the admirable support of Graham Hurford and his colleagues in the library of the Overseas Development Institute, without which using the wide range of sources listed would have been impossible. I have had the benefit of helpful comments on various drafts from staff members of EDI and other World Bank departments, anonymous referees, colleagues at the Overseas Development Institute, and a host of others too numerous to list individually. However, special thanks go to Malcolm McPherson of Harvard University for reading the entire manuscript and making a host of trenchant criticisms and constructive suggestions. I am most grateful to them all, but am alone responsible for the final result.

T.K.

Overseas Development Institute, London

1

INTRODUCTION

During the 1970s and well into the 1980s, the world became a more dangerous—and for many a more hostile—place in which to pursue the goal of development. Instability increased in world markets for goods, capital, and foreign exchange. Capital movements saw enormous swings, the debt problem surfaced, and the exchange rates of the leading currencies fluctuated widely with much overshooting, to the detriment of many developing countries. In 1973-74 and 1979-80 the world price of petroleum, saw huge real increases, and then a large decline in the later 1980s. World market conditions for many of the primary products exported by developing countries deteriorated, and the countries faced increasing difficulty in maintaining the momentum of expanding manufactured and nontraditional exports to the advanced economies of the Organisation for Economic Co-operation and Development (OECD). Underlying some of these developments were recessions among the OECD countries, which were particularly marked in the early 1980s, and a more persistent slow-down in the growth trend compared to that achieved in the 1960s and early 1970s.

The severity and persistence of this deterioration in the world economic climate forced upon developing country governments—and on those who make decisions about the allocation of external assistance—the question of what policy changes they should adopt in response to these new realities. In some cases, the urgent need to find solutions was intensified by natural or manmade disasters such as famine or war. For many developing countries the 1980s was the decade of adjustment, and this reorientation of policies thrust to the fore questions about how economies can be made more flexible and how they should respond to the changes in the wider economic environment.

A further dimension of the change in the policymaking climate was a renewed interest in economies' structural characteristics as governments realized that the deterioration was not merely temporary, and that fundamental adaptations were therefore needed to minimize the potential damage to economic progress. How to use policy instruments to achieve a more flexible economic structure became a key, and largely new, issue to which existing textbooks offer few ready answers. These questions remain high on the agenda.

At the same time, academics and policymakers have reappraised the role of the state in economic life, and have increasingly realized that just as markets fail, so do governments. From this intellectual shift and the accumulated evidence underlying it, the belief has emerged that many past policies have been mistaken, involving heavy costs and producing perverse results. This belief added to the impulses for a re-examining policies within developing countries.

One response to the global deterioration, particularly to the second oil shock of 1979-80, was the World Bank's decision to introduce a new type of credit in support of medium-term programs of structural adjustment. It was a term that readily took hold in policy circles, and structural adjustment considerations came to dominate discussions about developing country policies in the 1980s. In due course, the World Bank added sectoral adjustment credits and new Structural Adjustment and Enhanced Structural Adjustment facilities operated jointly by the International Monetary Fund (IMF) and the World Bank to its structural adjustment lending. Other development and aid agencies added the term to their own language, and developing country governments quickly learnt the language. Many of them had little alternative. The 1980s saw a veritable explosion of the policy conditionality associated with the Bank and Fund's stabilization and adjustment lending, so that today few developing countries exist, particularly in Africa and Latin America, that have not at some time adopted adjustment programs supported by these institutions.

However, this book is not primarily about the adjustment policies of the Fund, the Bank, and other aid donors. Rather, it attempts to go back to more basic questions about the relationship between structural adaptation and long-run economic development, about what determines the flexibility of an economy and how policy can contribute to increasing this, and about an economy's adaptation to shocks and trends that are beyond national policymakers' control.

Chapter 2, therefore, surveys the types of change to which economies have to adapt over time. This involves exploring the relationship between structural transformation and long-run development and the forces underlying this, as well as the various shocks to which national economies have had to respond. Chapter 3 then examines the attributes of a flexible economy and their determinants and compares the view of the nature of adjustment taken there with the view adopted by the Fund and the Bank. The next two chapters are about principles of policy. Chapter 4 focuses on broad strategic questions, including the roles of the market mechanism and the state, while chapter 5 takes a more detailed look at the policy instruments available for promoting flexibility and the criteria that governments may use to choose between alternative policies.

Chapter 6 then looks in some detail at one specific policy instrument central to the adjustment process, the real exchange rate, exploring its determinants and effectiveness and emphasizing the complexities involved in using it to good effect. Chapter 7 employs a rather different focus, reverting to the question of the respective roles of the state and of markets, and addressing it in the context of policies of adaptation for the agricultural and manufacturing sectors. Having earlier identified the development of the financial system as one of the "enabling" aspects of structural transformation, facilitating flexibility and development in other parts of the economy, chapter 8 is devoted to financial policy issues. Here too much of the discussion concerns striking the difficult balance between the liberalized development of financial markets and their promotion and regulation by the state.

The final two chapters set the process of economic adaptation in broader context. Chapter 9 is concerned with global economic aspects. It raises the question of whether adjustment in a single country is feasible, that is, whether the global economic environment is consistent with the adjustment efforts of individual countries, given industrial country practices and policies on trade and finance. This leads to consideration of the IMF and World Bank's adjustment conditionality, stating the positive case for this, but also emphasizing its rather severe practical limitations.

Chapter 10 is concerned with the domestic context. It considers the likely impact of economic adaptation on the poor, stressing its large potential benefits for the long-term, but also drawing attention to ways in which it can endanger the poor in the shorter term and how to minimize these risks. The book concludes with a topic that emerges from the preceding chapters as of crucial importance: the political management of change. It suggests that politics can often constitute an obstacle to flexibility, but that the resulting poor economic performance is apt to set countervailing forces in motion, and that political and economic structures cannot be divorced from one another.

2

ECONOMIC DEVELOPMENT AND STRUCTURAL FLEXIBILITY

The economic aspects of development concern increasing people's material welfare. This, in turn, can be thought of as the product of three interrelated factors: the efficiency with which existing resources are employed; the growth of productive resources over time; and the ways in which the resulting output and income are distributed among the factors of production and different income groups. Underlying and influencing these basic determinants of welfare is a certain social and economic structure. It is this structure—how it changes and the relationship of these changes to economic development—that is the subject of this chapter.

The Meaning of Structure

Given its central importance for this study, we will first clarify the idea of structure. The three alternative ways to compute national accounts provide an entry point. Thus, we can think of the structure of production, represented by industrial origin accounts, which is probably the most common meaning given to the structure of an economy. In addition to the obvious sectors of agriculture and industry, we might also mention the financial system as of particular importance in an economy's structure. When focusing on the balance of payments, reclassifying the productive sectors into those producing tradeable and nontradable goods and services can also be useful. Second, we can think of the factoral composition of value added, the availability at a given time of labor, enterprise, capital, and natural resources. Third, we can think of the composition of demand, or of the sources and uses of resources, as a dimension of structure, particularly the breakdown of resource uses between consumption, saving, and investment.

National accounting aggregates, however, give us only part of the picture. There is a more elusive, but very important, aspect of an economy's structure that can be loosely called its institutional base.

Included in this is the political system; the legal framework and the agencies for its enforcement; established patterns of social organization and control, including the existence and freedoms of special interest organizations like trade unions; the agencies of public administration; and the physical infrastructure that provides transport and communications. Demographic variables can also be counted in, including the population's age and dependency characteristics, and the degree of urbanization.

In short, when we talk of an economy's structure, we are referring to aspects that are in some sense basic, long-lasting, and underpinning the more transitory aspects of economic life. By implication, structural variables are mostly somewhat deep-seated and normally change only gradually.

Despite a long-standing debate between the neoclassical and structuralist schools, we do not yet have an adequate theory to describe the connections between development and structural change. However, a well-established fact, both historically and through cross-country studies, that long-term regularities are apparent in the way an economy's structure changes as per capita incomes rise. Other types of change also occur in response to shocks and other influences. This chapter explores the relationships between development and structural change, the causes of these connections, and additional claims upon an economy's adaptability. It then elucidates the features that contribute to an economy's flexibility, before turning briefly to discussions of structural adjustment policies in the broader context provided here.

Long-Term Structural Trends

Beginning with the relationships between long-run development and structural change, we will first examine the changes that occur during development to the structure of production, before turning to other aspects of structural change.

The Structure of Production

Much of what we know about the relationships between economic growth and structure is derived from the work of Simon Kuznets. His study of the patterns of modern economic growth in the industrialized countries (Kuznets 1965)—meaning growth from about the mid-eighteenth century—generated a series of historical generalizations about changes that occur during the process of modernization that remain generally valid today. Kuznets' historical observations are strongly consistent with cross-country observations of the differences between countries at various levels of per capita income, with which the name of Hollis Chenery is also associated. Table 2.1 summarizes the results of some of this work.

Table 2-1. The Economic Structures of Low-, Middle-, and High-Income Countries

Indicator	Low-income countries	Middle-income countries[a]	High-income countries
As a percentage of GDP			
1. Gross domestic saving	9	20	26
2. Investment	14	23	26
3. Trade: Exports	16	23	23
Imports	21	26	23
4. Food consumption	39	29	15
5. Agriculture	48	23	7
6. Manufacturing	10	18	28
7. Services	31	38	47
As a percentage of merchandise exports			
8. Primary products (nonfuel)	71	42	28
9. Manufactures	7	20	61

Note: The figures for low-income countries relate to countries with actual per capita incomes of below US$300, and the figures for high-income countries relate to countries with actual per capita incomes greater than US$4,000 (both in 1980 U.S. dollars). The figures for middle-income countries are predicted values for a country with a per capita income of US$1,000.

a. Predicted value only, based on an assumed population of 20 million people.

Source: Syrquin and Chenery (1989, table 3).

Some of the main observations, most of which are illustrated in table 2-1, are as follows:

- As per capita income rises, the share of agriculture in both total output and employment falls.
- At the same time, the share of industry (mainly mining and manufacturing) in output and employment rises and, within it, the share of manufacturing rises relative to mining.
- Manufacturing tends to start with relatively simple consumer goods, such as processed foods and clothing, gradually shifts to the production of heavy capital goods, and proceeds finally to microelectronics and other hi-tech products.
- The service industries tend to grow in importance relative to GDP and total employment.
- Dependence on trade—high ratios of imports and exports to GDP—also tends to diminish with rising per capita income. This is a result of the enlargement of the national economy as development proceeds, rather than being intrinsic to development as such, for there is a strong negative correlation between economy size and trade ratios. Since a high proportion of developing countries (and almost all African countries) have small economies, they also tend to be heavily dependent on trade.[1]
- Parallel with the changes in productive structure, the share of primary products in total exports diminishes as growth proceeds. This feature of international trade in turn affects the rate of transformation of the domestic economy, as the decline of primary production in GDP is slower in countries whose commodity exports are large relative to total production.

Two qualifications are necessary here. First, although manufacturing tends to go through the phases described above, this tendency is quite weak statistically because of the influence of exports and of import substitution. The pattern of manufacturing within any one country will be strongly affected by any comparative advantage that the country may have established on world markets, and by domestic policies relating to protection and import substitution.

Second, the tendency for the share of manufacturing to rise as incomes go up has weakened with time. A recent study by the World

---

1. When measurements are adjusted for economy size, cross-country comparisons actually suggest that a country tends to increase its trade relative to GDP as incomes rise. This explains the figures in table 2-1, which show larger exports relative to GDP at middle and high per capita income levels.

Bank (1987) actually suggests an inverted-U relationship, with the share of manufacturing first rising and then, after a per capita income of around US$8,000, falling (figure 2-1). The study goes on to point out, however, that this result may be due, in part at least, to the classification as services of a variety of activities associated with manufacturing that were formerly undertaken within manufacturing companies, but are now contracted out to more specialized enterprises. In any case, among low-income countries, figure 2-1 reinforces the strong presumption that manufacturing will be of increasing importance for many years as their economies develop.

What is implicit in these observed regularities is that growth is associated with a diversification of production. An increasingly wide range of manufactured products and services will augment a productive structure previously dominated by agriculture and, in some cases, mining. Specialization in production and in distribution will increase as demand within the economy becomes more diverse. The same trends will be observed within sectors. For example, in agriculture output will become less dominated by the production of starchy foods and other basics, and resources will be shifted into the production of meat and horticultural and other "luxury" foods, particularly to meet the needs of the towns as urbanization proceeds. Within the rural economy, off-farm activities of various kinds will become more important as sources of income and employment, relative to income derived directly from farming. By implication, informal activities will decline relative to total economic activity.

Another approach to analyzing changes in the structure of production during development is to divide output into tradable and nontradable goods and services. Tradables consist of all goods that do or can enter into trade as exports or imports; thus, the domestic production of such goods covers both exports and import substitutes. Nontradables consist of everything else. As a very rough approximation, one can think of tradables as largely made up of the total output of agriculture, mining, and manufacturing, plus certain service industries such as tourism and shipping. Note a tradable does not actually have to be traded, it must merely be capable of being exported or imported. The most important nontradables are the construction industry, certain

Figure 2-1 Relationship between GDP Per Capita and the Share of Manufacturing Value Added in GDP in Selected Economies, 1984

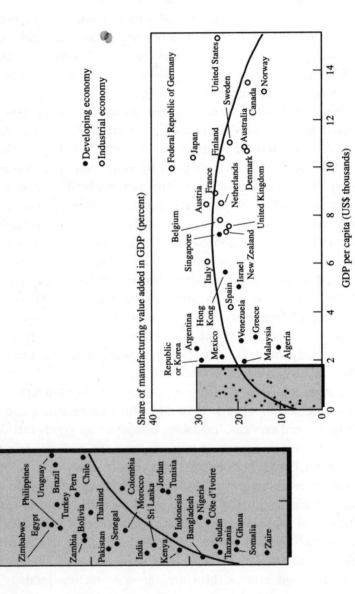

Source: World Bank 1987.

utilities, and various government and other services, such as health, education, defence, and domestic service.

This is a distinction of some importance for our study. As it will show, balance of payments difficulties are the largest single motive for adopting adjustment policies in developing countries. Such adjustments almost certainly require the relative transfer of resources out of nontradables into tradables, to boost exports and reduce import requirements. The ability to do this with reasonable ease is therefore an important attribute. At the same time, some evidence shows that the importance of tradables in total output tends to diminish as development proceeds, chiefly as a result of the relative rise in services already noted. (See Chenery, Robinson, and Syrquin 1986, especially table 3.7. This shows an 8 percent increase in the share of nontradables in total value added between early and late stages of development, with a corresponding reduction in the share of tradables.)

However, the distinction between these two categories of output is elusive, for it is difficult to think of any good or service that is not tradable at all. Thus, defence can be traded, as is illustrated by the use of mercenaries from other countries. Adjoining countries already trade electric power and water. Education is traded as evidenced by the large number of fee-paying students from developing countries studying in Western universities. Many other examples exist. Moreover, a modern economy has so many intersectoral linkages that the output of agriculture and industry will depend crucially on inputs from nontraded sectors, thus further weakening the distinction. It is therefore best to think of tradability as a quality possessed by almost all outputs, but in varying degrees. So when we talk of shifting resources from nontradables to tradables we mean moving from outputs that do not enter much into trade to those that make up the bulk of exports and imports.

In addition to those summarized above, we can also make generalizations concerning financial development. Goldsmith, in a series of studies of relationships between the development of the economy's financial and real sectors, has focused on this aspect. He too has employed both historical and cross-country methods. From these he has been able to establish another inverted-U relationship: at the earlier stages of development, the financial system grows substantially faster than both GDP and wealth before leveling off or declining beyond some level of per capita income. He uses a financial interrelations ratio as a measure of this, defined as the ratio of the value of all financial instruments to the total value of wealth in the economy. Table 2-2 shows the general pattern that he observed.

Table 2-2. Financial Interrelations Ratios, Selected Countries and Years

India		Japan		United States	
Period	*Ratio*	*Period*	*Ratio*	*Period*	*Ratio*
1876-1913	0.15	1886-1913	0.62	1881-1912	0.77
1914-39	0.24	1914-40	1.41	1913-39	1.11
1951-75	0.39	1956-75	0.93	1940-55	1.18
				1956-75	0.92

Source: Goldsmith (1983).

All three countries revealed rising ratios in the earlier periods. This trend persisted throughout in the case of India, a country with low per capita incomes, whereas it declined in both Japan and the United States in the later years, when most modernization had already been achieved. During the earlier stages, the value of agricultural land and livestock diminishes relative to the total value of all assets, while bank deposits, holdings of government-issued debt, and other financial claims increase their share. This process of financial deepening starts with the commercial banks and the monetization of economic activity. After a time, however, more specialized financial institutions—insurance companies, building societies, pension funds, and savings banks—attain increasing importance, and the financial sector thus experiences the diversification of output noted earlier for other parts of the productive structure.

Other aspects of structural change

Aside from the regularities just described concerning the productive structure, we should also note others relevant to our purposes. First, and unsurprisingly, the ratio of domestic saving to GDP tends to rise with per capita income. At low levels of average income most of it is consumed. This has a depressing effect on investment, and hence on economic growth (what used to be called the poverty trap), but developing countries have in the past been able to augment their own saving by attracting finance from the rest of the world, and can thus sustain higher investment levels. As incomes grow the savings ratio rises, the gap between saving and investment narrows, and, in the general case, is finally reversed, so that the country ultimately becomes a net exporter of capital.[2] The first and second lines of table 2-1 show this trend at work, although it does not show high-income countries as capital exporters, perhaps because of the large-scale capital imports of the United States in recent years.

A related structural feature is the tendency for the availability of capital to rise relative to labor during the process of development. This is true both of inanimate capital—buildings, machines, the transport network, and so on—and of human capital, or the income-earning skills of the labor force. These capital:labor ratios are difficult to measure directly, but one rough and ready proxy that is sometimes used for the employment of inanimate capital is energy use (although there is also a large consumption element in this). This is illustrated in table 2-3, which shows the industrialized countries using over forty times as much energy per head of the population as low-income countries.

As regards human capital, the skilled proportion of the labor force rises with per capita income, as modern knowledge becomes more widely disseminated within society. Another widely observed feature is progressive urbanization of the population. Thus, the World Bank (1990b, table 31) establishes the proportion of the population living in urban areas in low-income, middle-income, and OECD countries in 1988 to have been 25, 58, and 77 percent respectively (the figure for low-income countries excludes India and China). This urbanization is largely the result of the industrialization already noted, but is also often encouraged by a pro-urban bias in the delivery of government services and in other aspects of policy.

---

2. It is with this in mind that economists have referred to the heavy importations of capital by the United States in the 1980s and 1990s as perverse.

Table 2-3. Energy Use by Different Groups of Countries, 1989
(kilograms of oil equivalent)

Type of economy	Energy used per head of population
Low-income economies	124
Lower-middle-income economies	888
Upper-middle-income economies	1,890
OECD countries	5,182

Note: India and China are excluded from the low-income countries.
Source: World Bank (1991, table 5).

Changes in the institutional basis of economic activity are another structural element very important during development, even though it cannot be reduced to statistics. By the institutional base we mean the norms, rules, and compliance procedures that constrain the behavior of individuals in society, and also the organizations that enforce the rules. As the economy becomes more complex, and production more specialized, the institutional base has to become more sophisticated, defining property rights, enforcing contracts, encouraging invention, and in other ways anticipating or accommodating changing demands, thereby facilitating structural change and reducing its costs. Unfortunately, we cannot go much beyond this very general description because institutional arrangements vary greatly from country to country, even at comparable levels of development, and no common pattern of development is evident (for further reading on this subject see a special issue of *World Development* on institutions and development 17(9), September 1989; Ostrom, Feeny, and Picht 1988, especially chapter 6 by David Feeny; Morris and Adelman, 1988, who are, however, chiefly concerned with influences on income distribution).

Finally, we should mention changes in the size distribution of income, although the empirical basis for generalization about this is quite weak. (Ram 1988 briefly reviews recent literature on this topic). The chief hypothesis here is Kuznets' suggestion that there is an inverted-U relationship between per capita income and income inequality, as conventionally measured by the Gini coefficient: as poor countries begin to raise average incomes, inequality first tends to rise, but after some critical level of per capita income, then begins to fall. A number of econometric studies have found some support for this hypothesis. None finds very strong support, however, no doubt partly because of poor data, but also presumably because many other factors besides stage of development will influence the size of the Gini, not least the sociopolitical system and the policies pursued.

Explaining the Regularities

Our next task is to clarify the forces underlying the regularities we have observed above, particularly with respect to the productive structure. The consumer's preferences provide the most obvious starting point.

The Sovereignty of the Consumer

A now rather old-fashioned idea in economics is that the consumer is sovereign. This is a way of saying that, subject to technical and resource constraints, it is the preferences of consumers in the expenditure of their money incomes that ultimately determine what shall be produced. When demand for a product is lively, consumers will be willing to pay a high price for it, and this will induce supplies onto the market. The opposite will happen with a product that consumers no longer desire very much. This idea is old-fashioned because it oversimplifies reality, for example, by ignoring the role of advertising in manipulating demand and other influences from the side of supply, but it does help explain the long-run changes in productive structure noted earlier, primarily because there are observed regularities in patterns of demand that broadly match the shifts in the productive mix.

The best-known such regularity is expressed in Engel's Law, which states that the proportion of income spent on food diminishes as income increases. This is one of the most robust of empirical generalizations about economic life. It is reflected in the fourth line of table 2-1, which shows the share of food in GDP diminishing steadily as per capita income rises.[3] Given this, the long-run tendency for the share of agriculture in total output to diminish is hardly surprising.

---

3. Within the general trend described by Engel's Law there is a further well-established tendency as incomes rise: the demand for certain types of food such as meat and bread grows relative to the demand for such starchy staples as cassava and

One can go beyond Engel's Law to offer a rather richer set of generalizations about consumption patterns. Cross-country studies reveal
a remarkably universal pattern of consumer preferences, apparently
valid across varied economic and cultural differences (see Clements,
Suhm, and Theil 1979; Finke, Rosalsky, and Theil 1983; Theil and
Seale 1987). Figure 2-2 sets out unweighted means of income elasticities of demand for various categories of consumption calculated for
thirty countries based on 1975 data.[4] The countries varied from the
very poor (India) to the very rich (the United States), and the use of
unweighted means can be justified by the limited dispersion of the
country results around the means in figure 2-2.

Figure 2-2 reveals the following:

- Engel's Law is confirmed, with an income elasticity for food of
  well below one. With a mean elasticity of 0.46, a 10 percent rise
  in income will induce less than a 5 percent rise in food expenditures.
- The income elasticities for beverages and tobacco, and clothing
  and footwear, are around unity, that is, demand grows at about
  the same pace as income.
- Housing (represented by gross rent and fuel), household furnish-
  ings, medical care, transport and communications, and recreation
  all have income elasticities well above unity. Significantly, most
  of these items are produced in various service industries, and this
  can be related to the long-run tendency for the share of the
  services sector in GDP to grow. Unfortunately, the system of
  classification used does not bring out the general tendency for
  income elasticities for manufactured goods, taken together, also
  to have relatively large values.
- Although the above generalizations are valid for the complete
  sample of countries, poor and rich, there are also some important

---

maize (Bennett 1954). Conversely, there is a relative shift back to low-quality staples
when living standards deteriorate, as has occurred in many African countries in recent
years.

4. The income elasticity of demand measures the proportionate increase in demand
for an item resulting from a given proportionate increase in income, holding all other
variables constant. It is thus a measure of the sensitivity of the demand for an item to
changes in income.

Figure 2-2. Mean Income Elasticities of Demand for Thirty Countries, Selected Commodity Groups, 1975

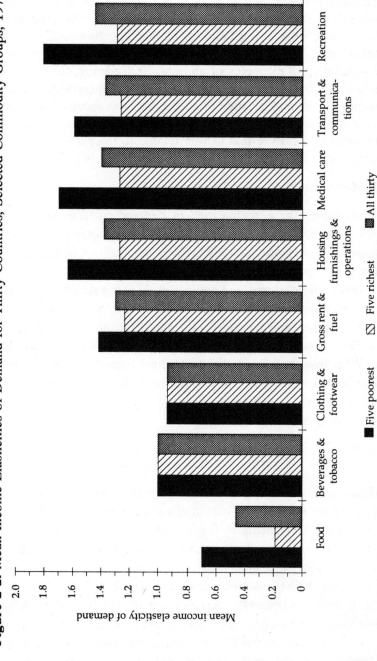

Notes: The five poorest countries are India, Pakistan, Sri Lanka, the Philippines, and Thailand. The five richest are Germany, France, Denmark, Luxembourg, and the United States.

Source: Finke, Rosalsky, and Theil (1983, table 1).

differences between them. The income elasticity for food is much lower in wealthy countries than in poor countries. The same tendency is true, in varying degrees, of housing, furniture, private medical care, transport and communications, and recreation. Paradoxically, no examples of an opposite tendency, for elasticities to rise with income, are recorded. How can there be a general tendency for income elasticities to decline with income? The answer is that the income elasticity of household saving increases with income, a feature that can be related to the earlier observation of higher savings rates in rich countries than in poor.

The Influences of Trade and Technology

Notwithstanding these regularities in demand patterns and their conformity to the shifts in the pattern of production noted earlier, statistically speaking they provide only a partial explanation of the fall of the primary sectors and the rise of manufacturing and services. **International trade patterns** and policies also exert a strong influence, for trade frees domestic producers of tradables from the confines of the domestic market, and the ability to import means that production abroad satisfies much demand. The explanatory power of trade is large partly because world trade has had a long-term tendency to grow faster than world output, as shown by the following ratios of the growth of world trade relative to the growth of world GDP (World Bank 1991, tables A6, A9):

1965-73	1.84	1980-89	1.16
1973-80	1.48	**1965-89**	**1.48**

Paradoxically trade also provides an important negative explanation, for a country's pattern of industrialization is also affected by its policies on and achievements in import substitution. With growth in import substitution the domestic economy expands to meet more of the demands of local consumers, as well as producers' demands for capital goods for the expansion of productive capacity.

However, while trade and the opportunities for specialization within it greatly loosen the ties between demand patterns and domestic production, in the end the demand patterns reassert themselves through their influence on world prices and the profitability of different categories of trade. Note the large differences in the rates of growth of world export volumes by commodity group set out in Table 2-4. Although these are the joint outcome of technical, price, and income changes, they nonetheless conform to expectations based on long-term trends in demand patterns. As the table shows, world trade in agricultural products and metals is expanding less rapidly and trade in manufactures much more rapidly than total world trade. Unfortunately, data on trade in services are not as good and some services are largely nontradable, but trade in services has certainly become an important part of total commerce between nations. According to one estimate (UNCTAD 1988b, chapter 11, box 12), world receipts in respect of service transactions in 1986 amounted to nearly US$1,000 billion, equivalent to about half the value of merchandise trade.

Engel's Law, and a similar tendency for nonfood primary products to display small—and probably declining—income elasticities of world demand is a grave problem for the SLICs with which this book is chiefly concerned, for they are heavily dependent on primary product exports and are selling on markets with generally small income elasticities of demand (see Bond 1987 for estimates of income elas-

Table 2-4. Growth of World Export Volumes by Commodity Group, 1965-88 *(percentage per annum)*

				1965-88	
Commodity	*1965-73*	*1973-80*	*1980-88*	*Growth*	*Relative to all exports*
Food	4.6	6.8	3.3	4.87	0.84
Non-food agriculture	3.1	0.9	5.3	3.2	0.56
Metals and minerals	6.8	8.6	0.3	5.0	0.88
Fuels	8.7	0.5	-2.2[a]	2.5[a]	0.44
Manufactures	10.7	6.1	5.3	7.4	1.30
ALL EXPORTS	8.7	4.6	3.7	5.7	1.00

Notes: "World" as used in the title corresponds to the World Bank's "Total Reporting Economies."

a. 1980-87.

Source: World Bank (1990b, table A8).

ticities of demand for primary commodities). Specializing in items for which demand grows at least in line with world income is healthier.

Technological progress is another potent influence on patterns of change in productive structures, and one of growing importance because of the accelerating pace of technological advances. Indeed, one of the challenges of adaptation SLICs face in the late twentieth century is to reduce the technology gap between themselves and both industrial and more advanced developing countries. UNIDO (1989b, p.2) has described the consequences of productive advances for manufacturing:

> In the advanced industrial countries, where technological developments in industry have been concentrated, new products are continuously introduced which either substitute or supplement existing products. New production processes are being applied which have higher productivity and/or different factor proportions, higher flexibility and different economies of scale. In place of some materials traditionally supplied by developing countries, new materials are being introduced. These innovations in turn lead to changes in production costs, quality, timing, etc. and thus to changes in the competitive system both at the micro and macro-economic level.

Technological progress has, of course, occurred in all branches of production. Its influence on structure might, therefore, be regarded as random or neutral. In practice this is not the case, however, because some branches of production have proved able to benefit more from technological developments than others. Specifically, this helps to explain the rise of manufacturing relative to agriculture, for there is a well-established, long-run tendency for productivity growth to be more rapid in the former.

Yet here again the hidden hand of demand is pulling some of the levers. Technological progress is not an autonomous given, independent of market forces. Rather it—and the investments in research and development that underlie it—is highly sensitive to market conditions, and the high income elasticities of demand for manufactures relative to those for agricultural products certainly help to explain the more rapid improvements in productivity in industry.

Interactions

The increased diversity of demand and output, along with the influence of technical progress, have the further effect of increasing the structural complexity of economies, the extent of linkages between the various sectors of production, and the increased use of intermediate goods within the economic system. Indeed, investigators have found that this increased demand from producers for intermediates is statistically an important reason for the relative growth of the industrial and some service sectors. Thus, both final and intermediate demand are important.

The variables traced also interact with each other in other ways. We have already noticed from table 2-1 how saving and investment tend to rise proportionately to GNP as per capita income goes up, and have mentioned the trend for inanimate and human capital to grow relative to unskilled labor. This too has implications for the productive structure, facilitating the development of activities that make intensive use of skilled labor and/or inanimate capital, and leading to a movement of resources out of traditional lines.

The growing availability of capital also has implications for a country's pattern of international trade. According to standard trade theory, a country will have a comparative advantage in goods requiring proportionately large inputs of factors of production that are in abundant supply (and therefore relatively cheap) within the economy. On this basis, a country at the earliest stages of development might be expected to export agricultural and other traditional products that require little capital and few modern skills, then proceed to the export of the simpler types of manufactured consumer goods on the basis of limited capital and plentiful semiskilled labor, and finally graduate to more sophisticated manufactured goods and services that make heavy use of both physical capital and skills. Such a model is in line with the results of Balassa's (1979) research. He found that differences in countries' physical and human capital endowments largely explained intercountry differences in the structure of exports. As a result, he suggested a "stages" approach to comparative advantage, according to which the structure of exports changes with the accumulation of these two types of capital. Such an approach fits well with the pattern of structural transformation observed earlier and helps to explain the relative growth of industrial exports shown in table 2-1.

Another consequence of the increasing complexity and specialization that marks the modern economy is the separation of saving and investing. In an economy dominated by small-scale agriculture, petty trade, and other informal enterprises, a large share of investment is undertaken directly by those who save for this purpose. As the demands of production grow more complex and require more capital, and as the saving capacities of other households grow with income, banks and similar institutions increasingly have to mediate between savers and investors. Hence the financial deepening cited earlier as a feature of economic growth and the increasing diversity of financial institutions.

We are not, of course, suggesting any kind of historical determinism in presenting these various generalizations about how economic structures change during development. Individual countries can deviate markedly from the general pattern, and the fact that much development and industrialization has already occurred itself conditions the likely future patterns of development. Nonetheless, the patterns of change observed during twenty to thirty years conform quite closely to those first identified from Kuznets' research into the eighteenth and nineteenth century histories of the now industrialized economies. In any case, what we are chiefly concerned about conveying here is that long-run economic change can be understood in stimulus and response terms. Economic structures alter radically in the course of development, responding to the opportunities—and warning signals— generated by changing patterns of consumer and producer demand, evolving factor proportions and technologies, and shifting comparative advantages. A key question that remains is whether these patterns are best regarded as more or less incidental and automatic outcomes of the development process or whether causality is involved, running from structural change to development.

The Question of Causality

Lurking beneath the question of causality is another: how do we perceive developing economies as working? In the neoclassical traditions of economists who stress the efficiency of market mechanisms, structural change is a consequence of growth, a gradual response brought about fairly smoothly through price signals, the mobility of factors between alternative uses, and entrepreneurs' ability to exert foresight and anticipate future needs in the search for maximum rates of return on their capital. After all, regularities in income elasticities are hardly secrets. The stress placed above on the power of final demand to determine shifts in the productive structure is consistent with this neoclassical view.

However, we have also drawn attention to the rather intimate interrelations between various aspects of structural transformation, which at least suggest that disentangling cause from effect will be difficult, and that it may be unwise to take too simple a view. We shall also be referring later to features of developing economies that will stand in the way of smooth adaptation—imperfect information flows, dualistic markets, the influence of traditional value systems, and social structures—by creating bottlenecks and discouraging large responses to price incentives.

We have, moreover, already referred to the increased specialization and diversification that is part of development and underlies the structural changes we have been examining. This specialisation further illustrates the difficulties of disentangling cause from effect because, while it might be seen as a more or less passive response to increasingly sophisticated demands on the part of consumers and producers, specialization has additional advantages: it permits greater exploitation of technical and managerial economies of scale and the development of purpose-designed equipment and skills, and generally creates larger benefits from learning by doing. These kinds of reasons are why people have viewed trade as an "engine of growth." Depending on how important we believe such benefits to be, establishing whether production is responding to demand or demand is growing because of the benefits of specialization becomes difficult.

So while much structural transformation is doubtless a more or less automatic response to changing demands and opportunities, believing that to some extent the causality runs in the opposite direction is also reasonable. Some changes, at least, can be thought of as enabling, that is, permitting and encouraging a rate of growth that would otherwise be frustrated.

Industrialization. Belongs in the enabling category, particularly if the alternative is specialization in agricultural production. Balance of payments considerations provide one reason for this. A country that tries to develop using agriculture as the leading sector must earn enough from its agricultural exports to meet the growing domestic demand for manufactures through imports. Moreover, it must do so in the face of generally low world income elasticities of demand for agricultural products, which as we have seen lead to only slowly expanding world demand and a declining share of agriculture in trade. This is not an impossible task, and Australia and New Zealand are often cited as examples of countries that have successfully pursued such a path. In both these countries, however, agriculture makes up only a modest part of total GDP (4 percent in Australia and 8 percent in New Zealand in 1989), while manufacturing is much larger (15 percent and 17 percent, respectively). Even if this is not an impossible development path, it is certainly a difficult one, as many struggling primary product exporting countries can attest.

In addition to the balance of payments case, manufacturing has recorded a superior ability to generate technological advances, to take advantage of the economies of scale that are such a feature of modern production economics, and to stimulate growth in other parts of the economy through its purchases of inputs and production of capital and intermediate goods.

None of these considerations is an argument for neglecting the primary sectors. For one thing, the well-being of agriculture and mining is likely to be crucial to the success of industrialization. They will be supplying the raw materials for much of manufacturing; agriculture will also be a source of capital and labor; and in countries where the bulk of the population still lives in rural communities, agriculture will be the main source of domestic demand for the manufactured consumer goods being produced. Moreover, sluggish world demand notwithstanding, the performance of the mining and agricultural sectors is also liable to make a crucial difference to the availability of the foreign exchange that manufacturing will need in the earlier stages of industrialization, producing minerals and cash crops for export as well as foodstuffs that would otherwise have to be imported. A substantial number of SLICs, particularly in Africa, have suffered badly from the consequences of neglecting agriculture. Indeed, agricultural stagnation has been a chief source of Africa's economic difficulties in recent years.

Thus, the argument is for a balanced expansion of the various sectors, not for a single-sector strategy. Moreover, a country will only reap the developmental advantages of manufacturing if its industry is efficient in international terms. The argument does not point toward a hot-house fostering of industry behind high protective barriers with scant regard to competitive efficiency (see chapter 7).

The investment ratio. One may also think of a rising investment ratio as one of the enabling aspects of structural transformation, including larger investments in human skills. In the sense that investment in productive capacity must precede output from that capacity, the causality must run from investment to growth, although an expanding economy is likely to stimulate further investment. One of the advantages of economies with high investment rates is that they are better able to take advantage of technological advances, for much technology is "embodied" in fixed or human capital. Quite apart from investments in factories, farms, wholesaling, retailing, and the infrastructure, of at least equal importance are investments in education and training and in the creation of research capacities. That development is investment-led is perhaps the least controversial of our enabling changes, so long as we do not fall into the mistake of thinking that investment is the unique determinant of growth.[5]

Financial deepening. Financial deepening, considered in more depth in chapter 8, is another of the structural changes that one can think of as enabling accelerated development. The financial system, and the money it creates, is unique in the extent to which it affects the rest of the economy, for money is the only product that can be traded against all other products. The interest rates that emanate from financial markets also have far-reaching effects on the economy as a whole (Shaw 1973, p.3).

Chapter 8 describes a number of ways in which one might expect the development of the financial system to promote the expansion of

---

5. Some of the earlier literature on development, under the influence of the Harrod-Domar growth model or Rostow's historical model of development, tended to place undue stress on investment as the determinant of growth. As experience showed us that far more was involved, some later writers have tended to down-play investment too much.

the rest of the economy. By reducing risks and losses of liquidity and by offering a financial reward it will encourage saving, or that part of saving that enters the financial system. This, in turn, will encourage greater capital formation, as will the reduced risks, greater liquidity, and improved availability of capital in the quantities intending investors desire. The same factors will also discourage capital flight—the exportation of domestic saving for investment overseas—and encourage inflows from the rest of the world. In addition, if we agree that not everyone is equally equipped to put savings to productive use, the financial system's development is likely to raise the average returns achieved from investment by providing a mechanism whereby entrepreneurs have access to the savings of others for productive investment. Moreover, on the neoclassical model, a well-functioning capital market will ensure that investible resources will be put to the uses that promise the highest rates of return.

Some cautions are again in order, however. For one thing, externalities, monopoly power, and other conditions that drive wedges between private and social valuations are well-known reasons why the workings of private markets may not maximize social rates of return. Another reason for caution is that the connections between financial deepening and the rest of the economy are complex, with various interactions, so that we need to be wary about imputing any one-way causality. Goldsmith's (1983) research into the behavior of the financial interrelations ratio, reported earlier, by no means indicates any rigid or simple relationship, and he was very reticent about imputing causality. However, more recent econometric tests provide some support for a causality that runs from financial to "real" development, so that developing countries whose financial systems have been a leading sector in development have experienced more rapid growth than those with lagging financial systems (Jung 1986). Interestingly, and consistent with Goldsmith's ratios quoted earlier, the evidence suggests that beyond some level of income causality becomes reversed, with financial development becoming demand-led.

The picture that emerges implies that economies flexible enough to accommodate the structural transformations that accompany, and promote, long-run development are at an advantage. Before exploring how to promote this flexibility, however, additional reasons exist for placing value on this characteristic and it is to these we turn next.

Coping with the Unexpected

An economy faces interacting, long-run patterns of change that require responses, whether automatic or policy-induced. However, it is not these that were responsible for the emphasis multilateral and bilateral agencies placed on structural adjustment in recent years. Rather, this has been due to a need to respond to relatively short-term, or unexpected, changes that have occurred in the overall economic environment.

These additional reasons are often expressed in terms of the need for economies to adjust to shocks of various kinds. We need to be careful about this language, however. The dictionary defines a shock as "a sudden and violent effect tending to impair the stability of something." A number of the factors we discuss below fall well within such a definition, but others do not. Some are more in the nature of trends. This is more than a quibble. If an economy is required to adjust to an adverse trend this necessity can be expected to persist over a period of years, but in most cases will not involve very large changes in any one year. By contrast, a shock is likely to be more severe, but of shorter duration.

Influences from the Outside World

In an increasingly interdependent world, developing countries cannot avoid being strongly influenced by what happens in the rest of the globe, particularly in the industrialized OECD countries. The pace of expansion of the latter economies strongly affects their demand (and tolerance) for imports from developing countries. Trends within their capital and foreign exchange markets and in international markets strongly influence the availability of international capital to developing countries, the terms upon which it can be provided, and the degree of exchange rate stability among major currencies. A number of such influences have turned against developing countries in the past, meaning that they had to pursue their economic goals in a more hostile world environment. This, in particular, led to so much attention being paid to the need for these countries to adjust to the new realities.

Table 2-5 shows some of these trends and their effects. Line 1, which records the growth rates of the industrial countries, shows that after 1981 growth was somewhat slower than in the preceding decade, and exhibited substantial fluctuations around the trend. The difference from the period average is not large, but the general opinion is that the faster growth rates achieved in the 1960s and 1970s are unlikely to be repeated in the future. This slow-down could have adverse implications for the developing countries, although for 1982-89 as a whole the growth of world trade—the chief mechanism through which the growth performance of the industrial countries impinges upon the developing world—held up well, proceeding at about the same pace as for the preceding decade, and actually faster relative to GNP growth. It was, however, an unstable trend, with large year to year fluctuations (column 11). The overall resilience was all the more striking given the spread of protectionism (described in chapter 9) and the dampening effect of the increased volatility of major currency exchange rates, which increased the costs and uncertainties of trade and added to protectionist pressures in the industrial countries (see de Grauwe 1988, who found that close to 20 percent of the observed slow-down in trade among the industrial countries since the early 1970s could be attributed to increased exchange rate variability).

The large movements in the price of petroleum since the early 1970s have been another major source of disturbance, and here the word shock is wholly appropriate, for the major changes were both sudden and violent. First prices quadrupled in 1973-74. This was followed by a gradual decline in real oil prices, that is, when deflated by an index of manufactured goods' prices, before another major jump in 1979-81 when prices doubled. Then in 1985-86 they declined significantly, leaving the real price in 1990 at only about a third of the 1982 peak and not much above the 1972 level. Finally came Iraq's invasion of Kuwait and a brief near-doubling in the nominal price of oil during the third quarter of 1990. Not surprisingly, these swings had major implications for both oil-importing and oil-exporting countries. The 1979-81 shock hit oil-importing developing countries particularly hard, and many of them found a high proportion of their export earnings being absorbed by the cost of oil, although they were beneficiaries of the price decline after 1985.

Table 2-5. External Shocks in the 1980s: Indicators for Small Low-Income Countries and Sub-Saharan Africa

Indicator	Average 1972-81 (1)	1982 (2)	1983 (3)	1984 (4)	1985 (5)	1986 (6)	1987 (7)	1988 (8)	1989 (9)	Average 1982-89 (10)	Mean annual deviation[a] (11)
1. GNP growth in industrial countries (% p.a.)	3.5	0.5	2.7	4.4	3.3	3.0	3.4	4.1	3.0	3.0	25.0
2. Growth in world trade volume (% p.a.)	5.2	-1.6	2.9	8.8	3.3	4.9	6.5	9.1	7.2	5.1	68.9
3. Total capital flows (US$ billion)[b]											
Small low-income countries	—	9.4	8.0	6.2	6.6	7.5	8.2	10.1	11.0	8.4	16.1
Sub-Saharan Africa	—	8.2	6.6	3.9	3.7	5.8	6.2	7.5	7.6	6.2	20.8
4. World real interest rates[c], deflated by											
Industrial country inflation rate	0.1[d]	5.8	4.5	6.6	4.7	3.3	4.3	4.7	5.2	4.9	15.1
Developing country export price changes	-1.6[d]	19.8	17.9	17.2	14.2	24.2	-2.3	5.4	5.2	12.4	60.7
5. Terms of trade changes (% p.a.)											
Small low-income countries	8.7	-12.7	10.0	6.4	-13.0	-0.1	2.1	18.3	0.8	1.0	772.5
Sub-Saharan Africa	9.2	-8.3	9.2	5.0	-9.9	2.8	—	12.4	-1.9	0.9	687.5
6. Import volume changes (% p.a.)											
Small low-income countries	0.7	—	-3.7	3.1	3.8	1.1	-0.1	4.8	1.3	1.3	151.0
Sub-Saharan Africa	0.9	-7.1	-10.1	-5.1	0.4	1.6	-0.4	0.8	—	-2.6	143.8

— Indicates figure is zero, or less than 0.05 of a percentage point.
p.a. = per annum
Note: Sub-Saharan Africa (SSA) excludes Nigeria and South Africa.
a. Mean annual deviations, 1980-87, ignoring signs, expressed as a percentage of mean in column (10).
b. Net external borrowing, as defined by the IMF.
c. LIBOR.
d. 1975-79.
Source: IMF (1990, Statistical Appendix); except for item 4, first entry, United Nations (1987, table A.9 and 1990 table A3, but with second entry deflated by IMF index of developing country export unit values

Figure 2-3 shows a serious decline in the real price of non-oil primary products on world markets during the 1980s. The slower growth among the OECD countries was probably the strongest influence on this, but other factors were also involved. As noted in the previous section, structural changes are occurring in the patterns of industrial country production and demand that are tending to reduce their income elasticity of demand for primary products. Technological change is also tending to dampen demand in many cases by reducing the primary material content of finished output. On the supply side, however, many exporting countries faced great balance of payments pressure to expand export volumes, while influences were increasing supplies on various markets. (See ODI 1988 for a succinct discussion of these and related developments. For fuller treatments see MacBean and Nguyen 1987; Maizels forthcoming; World Bank 1987.)

Figure 2-3. Real Non-Fuel Commodity Prices, 1980-92
(1980 = 100)

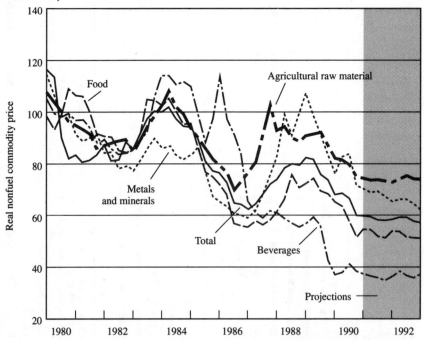

Note: Commodity prices calculated as the nominal prices deflated by the export price of manufactures of industrial countries. The total is based on world trade weights.
Source: IMF, (1991, chart 2).

These developments on world commodity markets illustrate the danger of thinking in terms of shocks, however, most economists now accept that real commodity prices tend to fall in the long term. By 1987 they had reached their lowest point since at least the 1870s. They revived temporarily in 1988, but even though the position varies greatly from commodity to commodity, recent studies have concluded that during the twentieth century real non-oil commodity prices, taken together, have declined at a trend rate of 0.6 percent per annum (see Ardeni and Wright 1990; Grilli and Yang 1988; Sapsford 1985; Spraos 1983).

Thus, many changes have clearly taken place on the trade side in recent years, generally in the direction of making life harder for non-oil developing countries. In addition, adverse changes have affected the capital account. Line 3 in table 2-5 records inflows of capital to small low-income developing countries and to Sub-Saharan Africa during the 1980s. Substantial falls occurred in 1982-85, in the case of Sub-Saharan Africa by nearly a half, although both country groups then saw a substantial revival. The decline was, of course, a result of the debt crisis that surfaced during 1982. Although severe, its impact of this on the SLICs was smaller than on the Latin American and other countries that had been borrowing heavily from commercial banks, which experienced a traumatic and more lasting decline in access to the world's savings.

An important factor contributing to the debt crisis was the very large increase in world real interest rates during the 1980s, as recorded in line 4 of table 2-5.[6] From having been negative or negligible in the early 1970s, real interest rates rose steeply during 1975-85 and remained high to the end of the 1980s. They also varied considerably year by year. This too was a shock, hitting hardest those countries that owed large accumulations of variable interest debt to commercial banks, and that unexpectedly found the real cost of their debt had

---

6. A real interest rate is one that has been adjusted for changes in the price level. Table 2-5 gives two alternative measures. In principle, deflating nominal interest rates by an index of the export prices of the borrowing countries would be preferable as a measure of the real cost of borrowing. The second entry under line 4 does this. However, this procedure gives highly variable results. The first entry deflates by a measure of inflation in industrial countries, which is less appropriate, but which gives results that are better behaved.

greatly increased. This was less the position of most African and other SLICs, few of whom had borrowed heavily on commercial terms, but it nevertheless had an impact upon them.

Table 2-5 also records some of the consequences of the developments just described. Line 5 shows the contrast in the terms of trade between the 1970s, when they were on an improving trend, and the 1980s, when they stagnated, with similar period averages for both groups of countries. Given the large falls in petroleum prices in the second half of the 1980s, it is remarkable that this did not improve their terms of trade, but declining commodity prices were more than enough to outweigh the favorable movement of oil prices. Note also the very large year to year variability in the terms of trade as shown by in column (11).

A further consequence of increased balance of payments difficulties in the 1980s was that many developing countries had to cut back on imports, often severely. This is reflected in line 6, second entry, which shows the severity of the cuts for Sub-Saharan Africa, with 1989 imports well below their 1981 levels, although the broader grouping of SLICs fared substantially better. With this item too the fluctuations around the trend were very large.

Another way to approach this matter is to add up the combined effects of all the adverse developments described above. This has been done for Sub-Saharan Africa, for the United Nations (1987, especially table 4) has estimated that the size of terms of trade losses, higher interest costs, and reduced credit and private investment flows in 1980-86 amounted to US$6.5 billion per annum, even after allowing for enlarged aid grants.[7] This was equivalent to nearly half of export earnings and about a third of total imports. By any standards, these are large magnitudes.

The extraordinary political developments in Eastern Europe and the former Soviet Union during 1989-91 could also be interpreted as a shock to which developing countries must adapt. From a SLIC point of view these developments present both dangers and opportunities. The dangers are that OECD interest in assisting Eastern European

---

7. In some respects the impact was even more severe on the heavily indebted countries (see Selowky and van der Tak 1986, who emphasise the long-term nature of any possible economic recovery by the heavily indebted countries).

countries' transition to political democracy and market economies will divert aid, private investment, technical assistance, and political attention away from the SLICs. It is also likely that these former Communist countries will intensify competitive pressures on various world markets, further constraining SLICs' export earnings. On the positive side, the opening up and eventual faster growth of these economies will generate additional trading opportunities and stimulate demand for many primary and other products exported by SLICs. Where the balance of costs and benefits will fall is impossible to predict at this stage. What is certain is that the developing world cannot ignore the enormous political and economic changes occurring in Europe. Once again, the advantage will go to those who are flexible, and who respond quickly and positively.

Troubles at Home

Quite apart from the influence of the world economy, economic policymakers must also cope with domestic difficulties that are largely outside their control (although they are sometimes worsened by human actions). **Climatic** difficulties are the chief of these, and these too can be divided into shocks and trends. Perhaps the most spectacular example of a country plagued by an unreliable climate is Bangladesh, which is chronically prone to floods and cyclones. During 1960-81 Bangladesh experienced no fewer than seventeen major floods and thirty-seven cyclones, leading to a recorded loss of life of nearly 800,000 people, probably far more if the full facts were known (World Resources Institute and International Institute for Environment and Development 1986, table 9.4), and culminating in especially devastating floods in 1988.[8]

The Sahelian zone of Africa where average rainfall is not only slight, but with an annual variability 30 to 40 percent around the mean, is another region deeply affected by an unreliable climate. This brings with it vulnerability to droughts, making farming something of a lottery. The famine that ravaged much of Africa in 1983-84 dramatized the unreliability of that continent's rainfall. Or perhaps it signi-

---

8. The following paragraphs are largely based on chapter 8 of World Resources Institute and International Institute for Environment and Development (1986) and on ODI (1987).

fied something more. A consensus is developing among scientists that a gradual warming up of the earth's atmosphere is under way, a concept known as global warming or the greenhouse effect. Resulting principally from accumulations of carbon dioxide in the earth's atmosphere, this may have dramatic effects on future rainfall patterns by changing flows of moisture bearing air, even though it may affect average temperatures by only a few degrees. Within the next fifty years the earth's average temperature may be caused to rise by about 1.5° centigrade.[9] A global warming of 1.5°C would be greater than that experienced during the last 10,000 years! Scientists do not yet fully understand the regional implications of this development, but believe that they will place the Sahelian zone, for example, particularly at risk.

Two other sources of domestic disturbance may be mentioned. One is **organized violence**, that is, civil and international wars, border incursions, and the forcible overthrow of governments. The world is full of such events and they feed through to economic performance in many ways. Wheeler (1984), in an econometric study of Sub-Saharan Africa, found a highly significant negative correlation between the incidence of violence and economic growth, with causality running from violence to slower growth. Clearly an invasion or a *coup d'état is* a shock, but since the government is itself a protagonist, it strains the language to talk of the need to adjust to such a shock, so we shall not consider it further here.

However, both organized violence and climatic events can result in major **migrations** of people, often across international boundaries, seeking peace and sustenance. Many countries have large populations of refugees. Africa has been described as the continent of refugees, with at least 2.5 million, and Pakistan and Thailand are among other large-scale recipients. The need to care for these large, sometimes

---

9. In a carefully considered and cautious report issued in May 1990, the science working group of the Intergovernmental Panel on Climate Change concluded that emissions of carbon dioxide and other manmade gases are enhancing the natural greenhouse effect that keeps the globe warmer than it would otherwise be. Assuming unchanged trends in coal, oil, and gas use, the panel predicted that the global mean temperature would rise about 0.3°C per decade, within an uncertainty range between 0.2° and 0.5°. On the same "business as usual" assumptions, it also expected the global mean sea level to rise about 6cm per decade (from *Policymakers Summary*, IPCC Working Group 1).

sudden, influxes amid indigenous populations who are often already
.poor can impose major economic strains, to say nothing of political
and security complications.

In addition, problems are created by sudden, large-scale return
movements of nationals who have emigrated in search of a better living, which can be triggered by a change in employment or immigra-
tion policies on the part of recipient countries, or a sudden flare-up of
ethnic or international tensions. A number of such episodes have occurred in West Africa and elsewhere. Perhaps the most dramatic example was in January 1983, when the Nigerian authorities suddenly
expelled an estimated 1.2 million Ghanaians (equivalent to nearly a
tenth of the population then living in Ghana), at a time when Ghana's
economy was already depressed.

The other side of this coin is a problem that has affected many of
the countries with which we are concerned: the **international brain
drain.** This loss of educated and highly trained personnel is less a
shock than a gradual depletion. It is often the result of economic
mismanagement at home, but in some countries it has reached a point
where the dearth of local high-level manpower seriously hampers the
implementation of improved policies and economic recovery.

Some have written of economic disruptions resulting from government *policies* as a domestic shock. Policy deficiencies can no
doubt aggravate problems or cause new ones, but thinking of these as
shocks seems artificial. How policy can be changed from being part of
the problem to part of the solution is the subject of most of the rest of
this volume.

The Special Importance of the Foreign Exchange Constraint

The external shocks and trends described above feed themselves
through to the SLICs' domestic economies principally through their
effects on the balance of payments. In addition, some of the climatic
and other domestic shocks are liable to have adverse balance of payments implications due, for example, to an increased need to import
food. As a result of developments of the type summarized in table 2-5,
shortages of foreign exchange became acute for many developing
countries during the 1980s, which is why they had to embark upon the
import compression already described.

Because they are so important, we will now consider how shortages of foreign exchange can constrain economic progress. We shall analyze this from two viewpoints. The first focuses on the connections between imports and economic performance. The SLIC's economies are likely to have rather strong structural links between imports and output (see Mirakhor and Montiel 1987 for a valuable discussion of this issue, from which the following paragraphs borrow heavily). Probably the strongest of these will be with respect to **capital goods**. Small low-income economies, where much of GDP is derived from primary production, are unlikely to have much capacity for producing modern capital goods, nor are they likely to be able to create such a capacity at production costs even remotely close to international prices. So a high proportion of investment will depend upon the availability of foreign exchange for the importation of such goods, as will much of the maintenance of the existing capital stock. To put it another way, there is little substitutability between imports of capital goods and local products.

The position with regard to **raw materials and other intermediate inputs** is likely to be more complex, and more amenable to policy. The industrial sector, in particular, is liable to depend upon imported inputs, although, in general, industries are more likely to be competitive internationally if they are based upon local supplies. However, past policies that fostered import substitution through indiscriminate protection from overseas competition and that maintained overvalued exchange rates commonly resulted in industrial sectors that depended almost entirely upon imported supplies (discussed more fully in chapter 7). Particularly in the short to medium term, severe technical constraints are likely on the extent to which SLICs can substitute locally produced intermediate goods for imported ones; and, as with many capital goods, producing some of industry's needs locally would not be economic. Thus, these considerations also point to a strong connection between the abilities to import and produce, particularly in the shorter term. Over a longer period there are greater possibilities of introducing locally produced alternatives.

Taking these two variables together, we might expect strong correlations between imports and economic growth. However, other factors mitigate this connection. For one thing, much depends on the sectoral source of the growth. Agriculture and many service activities are fairly economical in their requirements for imported producer goods. It is industry that is particularly vulnerable. Moreover, and as already hinted at, the relationship is not independent of policies. Exchange rate policy, for example, will make a key difference to the relative costs of imported and domestically produced supplies, as might trade and interest rate policies. Rising world prices will also encourage a search for domestic substitutes.

For the purposes of statistical testing, quantitative restrictions and fluctuations in inventory levels of imports may further weaken the relationship, as may the choice of period for study. As a result of such influences, econometric tests for a correlation between imports and growth, although finding the expected positive association, found that other variables also have important explanatory power, and that output growth alone could "explain" only a modest part of changes in imports (see Mirakhor and Montiel 1987, pp. 78-81; also see Helleiner 1986, who did not find any statistically significant relationship between GDP growth and changes in the share of imports to GDP in samples of low-income and African countries).

However, three other types of connection may also be mentioned. One relates to the **stability** of import volumes, as the evidence suggests that growth is adversely affected by import instability (Helleiner 1986). The reason why this might be so is not entirely clear, but presumably relates to the difficulties of planning production and of maintaining an even flow of outputs in the face of volatile supplies of imported inputs.

A further connection may exist in the form of a type of vicious circle in which **import scarcity interacts with export performance**. This is really a special case of the import-output connections just discussed. In this case, imports are required as inputs into export activities. In conditions of import compression even the export sectors may be unable to maintain supplies, and will hence be forced to reduce output. This in turn reduces foreign exchange earnings, leading to further import cuts, and so a vicious circle is under way. Khan and Knight (1988) tested a model along these lines for a sample of thirty-four developing countries and found a large and highly significant correlation between export volumes and the availability of imported inputs. The obvious implication here is that for governments to starve their exporters of needed imports is self-defeating, and that they should give high priority to keeping them supplied. A further lesson is that IMF-style stabilization programs that necessitate large reductions in imports are similarly liable to be self-defeating.

The final connection relates to imports of **consumer goods**. In certain circumstances the availability of such imports can have productive value by providing an incentive for effort and output. Where an acute scarcity of imports exists and these are rationed by quantitative restrictions, this may not only weaken the incentives of farmers and other workers to produce because there is "nothing to spend our money on"; it may in certain circumstances induce actual reductions in domestic output. Offered higher producer prices, farmers may reduce their output of cash crops because the fixed supply of desired imported consumer goods that are available can now be purchased from a smaller output (see Bevan and others 1986, 1987). The circumstances described are admittedly rather special, but the evidence suggests that such a process did occur in Tanzania, and similar behavior has occurred in other import-starved countries, such as Ghana.[10]

So-called two-gap models provide a more formal way of analyzing the nature of a foreign exchange constraint. A crucial issue here is the ease with which resources and demand can be switched between tradables and non-tradables. Imagine first a flexible economy in which demand shifts readily between domestically produced and imported goods, producers switch easily between the production of tradables and non-tradables, and the exchange rate moves freely in response to changes in supply and demand. Imagine also that companies, households and the government find switching between saving and consumption relatively easy. Such an economy is unlikely ever to experience more than a temporary foreign exchange constraint. If a payments problem begins to emerge, this will set in train income, monetary, and exchange rate movements that will reduce the demand for

---

10. Given the rather restricted circumstances in which we would expect imports to have a measurable incentive-goods effect, it is perhaps not surprising that Wheeler (1984) did not find general econometric evidence of this, although he did call for more refined testing of this hypothesis. One of the limitations of this model is that it does not sufficiently acknowledge the role of parallel (unofficial) markets in relieving shortages, so that supplies are not fixed, merely expensive.

imports and investment, and increase the incentives for producing exports and import substitutes and for saving. The balance of trade will be improved, the savings-investment gap will be narrowed, and before long the payments situation will be back in equilibrium.

Now take the case of an economy with more rigid production and demand structures, while retaining the assumption of an elastic supply of savings. If the balance of payments—and therefore the saving-investment gap—deteriorates, perhaps because of a sudden worsening in the terms of trade, raising savings will be feasible, but converting this into foreign exchange will not. It will be difficult and costly to switch resources from nontradables to tradables, and foreign protection or depressed world demand might also hamper export expansion, as might shortages of imported inputs. Import demand will be price inelastic in the short term because of domestic producers' inability to supply local substitutes. In such a situation the payments problem will persist, even though there may be excess savings capacity, and substantial costs will be incurred in bringing the foreign exchange balance in line with the domestic saving-investment balance.

It is this latter type of situation that is analyzed in two-gap models (see Bliss 1989 and Eaton 1989 for accounts and critical assessments of such models, together with the references they cite). These envisage either (ex ante) savings or the availability of foreign exchange to be the binding constraint on the economy's growth. In the situation just described foreign exchange holds back the economy. Such models depend on some rather restrictive assumptions, however, for example, about import requirements, the fixity of exchange rates, and the productivity of investment. Distinguishing between saving and foreign exchange constraints is difficult in practice and mistaking the former for the latter is easy. Thus, while it seems obvious on casual observation that shortages of foreign exchange are holding back many African economies, it is also the case that saving in such economies has generally fallen to very low levels (World Bank 1991, table 9 shows that the gross domestic savings of low-income countries other than China and India stood at only 18 percent in 1989, with a figure for Sub-Saharan Africa of 13 percent. It is for reasons such as these that IMF economists tend to trace balance of payments deficits to large budget deficits, that is, to dis-saving by governments.[11] Nevertheless, the two-gap model continues to offer useful insights into the problems and adjustment costs of the structurally rigid economies on which we are concentrating in this volume.

Thus, what emerges from the foregoing is that the structural imbalances, shocks, and adverse trends discussed earlier are likely to place particularly large burdens on a country's balance of payments, and that this in turn will hamper growth and development. When, therefore, in succeeding chapters, we consider policies to adapt the economy to changing conditions, measures directed at the balance of payments will receive much attention.

Three country illustrations

We now turn to the experiences of three countries to provide more concrete illustrations of the difficulties analyzed above. Box 2-1 illustrates the need for prudent policies in the face of favorable, as well as adverse, shocks.

External shocks for Malawi (see Kydd 1988 and works cited there). During the 1970s Malawi was regarded as an African success story. Per capita income grew rapidly, buoyed up by a good agricultural export performance. The balance of payments was strong, with modest current account deficits comfortably covered by capital inflows. The second oil shock of 1979-80 changed all that, however. Import prices rose by an average of 54 percent and the balance of payments deteriorated sharply, despite a two-thirds expansion in the quantity of exports in the three years to 1981 and a policy of maintaining a competitive exchange rate. By 1986 the country's terms of trade were 40 percent worse than in 1978. The increased need to finance payments deficits and rising world interest rates caused a rapid growth in the cost of ex-

---

11. Interest has recently been growing in the development of three-gap models, where the third constraint is a fiscal gap. This takes a positive view of the impact of government capital formation on development, partly by stimulating private investment, and posits structural rigidities in increasing tax revenues and in the scope for noninflationary government borrowing. These models focus on economic situations characteristic of some of the heavily indebted countries of Latin America, where the local currency cost of servicing the external public debt preempts a large proportion of total revenues. See Bacha (1990) for an exposition of this type of model.

ternal debt servicing, which doubled from under 13 percent of exports in 1973-78 to nearly 25 percent in 1979-84, and was as high as 40 percent in 1984.

Box 2-1. Surviving Favorable Shocks

Not all shocks are adverse. Good weather can bring bumper harvests. World interest rates can go down as well as up. Commodity prices can boom as well as slump. However, economies and policies need to react to these favorable changes no less than to the adverse ones, and failure to do so can turn the good news into an unwanted gift.

Take the example of an unexpected but temporary increase in the world price of a country's chief commodity export, such as a boom in coffee prices in the latter 1970s.* Such a development will commonly raise tax revenues, either directly, as in the case of export taxes, or indirectly, as a result of the higher level of economic activity that the commodity boom will generate. Faced with an unexpected bonus of larger revenues the government will be tempted to step up its own spending by raising civil service salaries, expanding various activities, or starting new capital projects. The larger export earnings will increase the liquidity of the banking system and enable it to expand its lending to domestic borrowers. There may also be greater willingness by foreign banks to provide new credits, raising external indebtedness.

Increased spending in both the public and private sectors will suck in additional imports, weakening the beneficial effects to the balance of payments of the higher exports prices and putting pressure on the price level, and these effects may be magnified by the diversion of resources out of other exports to goods for the home market in response to the higher commodity price.

When the boom ends and commodity prices go back down again, the government and the private sector will find it much harder to cut back than it was to expand. As the figure illustrates for Côte d'Ivoire and Kenya, any cut in government spending will probably lag well behind the declines in revenue, leaving an enlarged budget deficit that will threaten both inflation and the balance of payments. Moreover, experience suggests that the new projects that were quickly embarked upon during the boom will often not have been carefully considered and will do little for economic development. It is likely also that the monetary authorities will have difficulty in cutting back adequately on credit to private borrowers, thus further adding to excess demand in the economy. In the worst case—of which there are examples—the economy ends up in a weaker state than it was at the beginning of the boom. Without careful management "favorable" shocks can be bad news!

Box 2-1. (continued)

Government Revenues and Expenditures during Commodity Booms

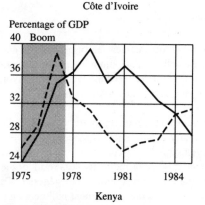

Côte d'Ivoire

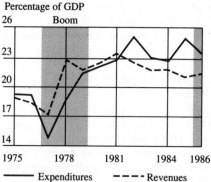

Kenya

——— Expenditures   ‒ ‒ ‒ Revenues

* For fuller discussions of this topic see Bevan, Collier, and Gunning (1990); Cuddington (1989); World Bank (1988a, pp. 71-74).
Note: Both revenues and expenditures exclude transfers, so their difference is not equal to an overall public sector balance. Figures for Kenya are for the central government only.
Source: World Bank (1988b, figure 3.6).

For a time a drought and subsequent crop failure compounded the problems, and the position was also made worse by South Africa's destabilization policies in the region. As a landlocked country Malawi had traditionally moved almost all its imports and exports by rail through Mozambique. After disruption of this rail link by the South African-backed Mozambique National Resistance Movement, Malawi was forced to divert traffic to other routes. The economic cost of this was estimated to have been at least US$50 million per annum, equivalent to about a fifth of the value of exports. There was also an influx of refugees from Mozambique, imposing further economic costs.

Associated with the deterioration in the balance of payments was a severe economic recession. Having grown at over 3 percent a year in 1965-80, per capita income fell back by nearly 1 percent a year in 1980-88. Both saving and investment ratios fell, and the government was forced to impose severe import cuts.

Bolivia: the perils of commodity concentration (see annual reports on Economic and Social Progress in Latin America by the Inter-American Development Bank, Washington). Bolivia was another country that experienced a boom in the 1970s, funded mainly by foreign borrowing, but rooted in favorable world markets for its exports. Tin made up over half of total exports in the early 1970s, but natural gas became important during the decade and surpassed tin as a source of export earnings in the early 1980s. By 1985 these two products made up 90 percent of all exports.

In the belief that past loans had not been wisely invested, international lenders became increasingly reluctant to extend new credits at the beginning of the 1980s, and at the same time world tin prices began to weaken. The value of Bolivia's tin exports fell by 46 percent in 1981-85, and although this decline was partly offset by the emergence of natural gas as a major export, the high cost and physical difficulties of piping this from a landlocked country to an Argentine port imposed limits.

Thus by 1985 the economy was already in decline, with a large debt servicing problem, major reductions in imports, four-digit inflation, rising unemployment, and severe reductions in average incomes. In 1986 a large further external shock made things even worse: a decline in realized tin prices from an index of 71 in 1985 (1980 = 100) to 34 in 1986, with only a slight recovery the following year. The price of natural gas also plummeted in 1985-87, by nearly two-fifths. Not surprisingly, this combination led to huge increases in the balance of payments deficit, with all the consequences that was bound to have for the domestic economy. By 1986 per capita income was down 25 percent compared to the 1981 level.

Without doubt domestic mismanagement compounded these problems, although important policy reforms were introduced in the latter part of the decade, but Bolivia's heavy dependence on exceptionally volatile world markets that became weak in the mid-1980s imposed a considerable additional cost.

Climatic and other shocks in the Sudan (culled from various sources, including Ati 1988). Although some have seen a potential for Sudan to become "the bread-basket of the Middle East," and agriculture dominates as a source of livelihood for four-fifths of its population and of over nine-tenths of export earnings, the country has experienced acute agricultural difficulties in recent years. The years 1981-85 saw a prolonged drought when famine affected half the population, and estimates suggest that 60 to 65 percent of the value of the country's livestock was lost. This resulted in large-scale unemployment, displacements, and mass movements of people in search of a livelihood.

The effects of this natural catastrophe were multiplied by civil war, forcing the national government to devote large resources it could ill afford to fight a secessionist movement in the south. In addition to large numbers of southern Sudanese fleeing the civil war, the government had to cope with the influx of an estimated 1.5 million refugees from wars and famines in neighboring countries, and to do so with an extremely weak system of transport and communications. A coup in 1985 added further to the disruption and uncertainties, although it replaced a government that had become notoriously unable to cope with the economic and social problems confronting it. Then, to cap it all, in 1988 abnormal rainfall caused extensive flooding, leaving many thousands homeless and causing much disease and death.

Conclusion

The conclusion suggested by the analysis of this chapter is that an economy with a flexible structure is likely to achieve more rapid development than one that responds only slowly and reluctantly to changing conditions. If this is accepted, the task becomes that of ensuring that economies are able to respond promptly and efficiently, and that policies assist this process, not get in its way. To obtain a clearer idea of how adaptability may be increased, and what governments should do to promote it, however, we need a clear idea of what the attributes of a flexible economy are. To clarify this is the task of the next chapter.

Summary

This chapter has considered reasons why the flexibility of an economy and of economic policies is an important attribute. It has shown that major structural change is intrinsic to long-run economic development. The pattern of this change is powerfully influenced by worldwide regularities in consumer preferences, by technological and other influences on the side of supply, and by the shifting composition of international trade. We have suggested that an economy with a flexible structure, which can more readily adjust to the changing needs of the time, is liable to achieve faster development. Conversely, an economy with a rigid structure, incapable of responding to changing conditions, can expect retarded development, with disjunctures between demand and supply creating bottlenecks and balance of payments strains, inflationary pressures, and other economic dislocations.

Furthermore, the chapter suggested that some kinds of structural change are of particular importance, enabling more rapid progress elsewhere in the economy. These include industrialization, financial deepening, and high levels of human and fixed capital formation. Thus, structural rigidity is bad for development; flexibility is a plus.

The chapter then turned to other reasons for valuing this attribute. These are often expressed in terms of external and domestic shocks, such as sudden changes in world commodity or capital market conditions and natural disasters. However, the existence of a variety of longer-lasting trends to which adjustment is also necessary, including long-term adverse trends in the markets for primary commodities, a possible secular slowing-down in the growth of the OECD economies, and the adverse consequences of the warming-up of the earth's atmosphere.

These considerations constitute further reasons for placing a premium on the flexibility of an economy and of the policies that influence it. Taken together, they create, at first glance, a powerful expectation that countries blessed with such adaptability will be better able to satisfy their citizens' material aspirations than those that are not.

A Note on Further Reading: The principal sources used for this chapter were writings relating to long-run structural transformation. Simon Kuznets undertook the pioneering work on this and many of his insights remain valid today. Kuznets (1966) provides probably the best overview of his work, but see also Kuznets (1965). Work in his tradition has since been carried forward by various writers, most notably Hollis Chenery and Moshe Syrquin. Chenery (1979) and Chenery, Robinson, and Syrquin (1986) are particularly recommended, while Syrquin (1988) offers an up-to-date account of the present state of this literature. Their work is complemented in the financial sector by the pioneering historical investigations of connections between financial development and long-run economic growth by Raymond Goldsmith (1969, 1983, 1985).

3

THE FLEXIBLE ECONOMY

Chapter 2 describes the manifold changes in the international and domestic environments to which economies have to adapt, and having concluded that flexible economies are likely to develop more rapidly and painlessly, the next step is to elucidate the determinants of flexibility. Unfortunately, this question has received limited attention in the economics literature, so our search for an answer must be rather tentative.

The Attributes of a Flexible Economy

Expressed in its broadest terms, a flexible economy is one in which ends and means are readily adjusted to changing constraints and opportunities. This includes flexibility in the institutional base of the socioeconomic system, as well as flexibility on the part of the government in adapting policies to changing conditions. It implies an economy in which movement of resources among alternative uses is relatively low friction, low cost, and rapid and leads to changing factor proportions, technologies, and composition of output. On the demand side, it implies responsiveness by purchasers to changing relative prices, and comparative ease of substitution in the disposition of income between consumption and saving. The response speed and the costs that must be incurred to achieve a given adjustment are the key indicators that differentiate flexible from rigid economies.

The extent to which an economy possesses flexibility of this type depends, in turn, on two sets of conditions. First, efficient informational and incentive systems must exist. Adequate data on changes in economic conditions to which the economy must adapt must be available, and a way of giving people incentives to bring about those changes that the data indicate to be desirable must also be present. Given the information and incentives, the second set of conditions relates to people's reactions to these stimuli, that is, their responsiveness to economic signals.

Information and Incentives

Even the least developed economy is complex, with many linkages between its various parts. A huge number of decisions has to be taken, for example, about how incomes should be used, what should be produced and in what quantities, and about investment and employment. In addition, these decisions must somehow be coordinated, so that the preferences of purchasers and sellers are made consistent, and human needs and economic aspirations can be satisfied. In theory, this coordination can be achieved through one of two alternatives: the market mechanism or planning.

Starting with the former, a market may be said to exist when there are buyers and sellers for some commodity or service who are in sufficiently close touch with each other to be aware of, and affected by, the actions of the rest. The market price will be the outcome of the interacting preferences of buyers and sellers, who will respond to the positive and negative incentives offered them by prices. Of particular interest for our purposes, however, is that markets may also be viewed as means of processing very large amounts of information about the preferences of buyers and sellers, disseminating this in the form of price signals.

Such a market should exist for every good and service. These markets will be influenced by each other, and will thus constitute an interdependent network called the "price system" or a "market economy." Its distinguishing features are a high degree of decentralization of decisionmaking through the workings of myriad markets in which enterprises and persons pursue their own interests by responding to the incentive signals of market prices, and in which the interactions between markets can be thought of as a coordination mechanism. In a pure market economy the state's role is restricted to providing the framework of law and order essential if markets are to work efficiently, and to intervening only to ensure that the system works as it ought.

A fully planned economy stands at the opposite end of the spectrum, for it is characterized by a high degree of centralization, with decisionmaking powers concentrated in the state's planning authorities. Planners receive and process information about the economy and take most important decisions. It is they who play the coordination role, which they achieve through the conscious exercise of forethought rather than through the "invisible hand" of the market. Individuals have a more restricted role, with their freedom of choice subordinated to planning decisions.

There is, of course, a long-standing controversy about the relative merits of market and planned economies, although in practice the choices are about the balance that should be struck between market and nonmarket mechanisms, not about pure forms. We cannot go into the relative merits of the alternative systems here. However, we can note the clear shift in professional opinion during the last two decades. Economists now tend to place greater emphasis on the efficiency of market mechanisms and stress the sometimes high costs of planning and other forms of state intervention (see Killick 1989 for a survey of the relevant literature).

Politicians and those they represent have moved in the same direction. This was most spectacularly demonstrated by the remarkable changes that occurred in most Eastern European countries and the former Soviet Union in 1989-91, moving them toward democratic political systems and market-oriented economies. Even where the modalities of planning are retained, there is a greater tendency to design these to work through, rather than in opposition to, market mechanisms, if only because market forces have a way of successfully asserting themselves against the planners' wishes. Within the already market-based economies of the OECD countries a related trend has also been apparent, resulting from the conservative revolution that was a feature of the 1980s, that reduced the scope of state interventions and placed greater reliance on markets.

In practice, most countries have mixed economies, in which most production is undertaken in the private sector and the basic allocative mechanism is a market system, modified to a greater or lesser degree by government interventions. In what follows we shall take the mixed economy case, but however the balance is struck between the market and the state, we should note the importance of adequate information flows. The flexible economy needs good intelligence: about changing conditions in world trade and finance; about developments within the domestic economy; about scientific matters, for example, as they bear upon technological progress or climatic changes; and about how these and other variables interact with each other.

This sounds so obvious that it can be taken for granted, but in many countries data are still sparse, unreliable, and out-of-date. In such circumstances neither private nor government decisionmakers can operate efficiently. Thus, more than a few governments have lurched into a debt problem simply because they did not know the rate at which debts were being accumulated; businesspeople have overinvested because they did not know about investments elsewhere; and countries have experienced famines because early warning information systems were not in place. There are, moreover, reasons why one cannot assume that market incentives will throw up the necessary information or make it available to all who need it. Indeed, an influential body of writings, particularly associated with the name of Joseph Stiglitz, sees imperfect information—and consequentially high transactions costs—as one of the key features that distinguish developing from developed economies, and as a serious type of market failure (see in particular Stiglitz' essay in Chenery and Srinivasan 1988 vol. 1, chapter 5, and the references cited there, and the September 1990 special issue of the World Bank Economic Review on imperfect information and rural credit markets).

Thus governments everywhere include information gathering as one of their tasks. There is little controversy about this, but in developing countries data flows often remain woefully inadequate. Flexibility is bound to be limited in the face of ignorance about changes in circumstance to which the economy must adapt (a point taken further in chapter 5).

Information is not enough, however. Once gathered it must be fed into decision systems and translated into rewards and penalties that will induce appropriate responses. It is here that markets generally excel. Their decentralized nature and their ability to translate information into price incentives and to coordinate a huge number of individual decisions through an interacting network of markets are usually well in advance of what central planners can hope to achieve. Quite apart from the huge volume of information that planners need to be able to receive and absorb, one problem is that controls often create incentives for misinformation: state enterprises exaggerate their output or efficiency to secure larger allocations of supplies; private firms exaggerate their costs to persuade the government to raise controlled prices; exporters understate the value of their sales to retain some of the foreign exchange they earn; borrowers misstate the uses for which they require a loan to get access to funds earmarked by government policy for other uses; and so on.

In short, a well-functioning market system is conducive to economic flexibility. By comparison, central planning creates rigidities, as illustrated in box 3-1. The key word, however, is well-functioning, as many factors exist that prevent markets from achieving maximum efficiency, particularly from a social viewpoint. It is the existence of such market failures that constitutes the case for state intervention in a mixed economy, always assuming that the costs of the interventions are smaller than the benefits produced. We return to this topic of market failure shortly.

Responsiveness

Turning now to consider the responsiveness of economic agents to information and incentives, it is useful to separate two related aspects: receptivity to change and demand and supply elasticities.

Receptivity to change. The influence of tradition on people's attitudes toward change provides a natural starting point, although it takes the economist into controversial territory. A market-based adaptive economy requires a population that is willing to take action to maximize whatever material benefits it may derive from changing conditions (or to minimize the costs). This implies an individualistic (or family-based), welfare-maximizing approach, and mobility in pursuit of this objective. These attributes may clash with traditional values, which often place more stress on collective well-being and erect a number of obstacles to mobility.

The pursuit of economic self-improvement, for example, requires some faith that advancement will be on the basis of personal ability and effort. Traditional mores may undermine such faith, with promotion decided on the basis of seniority or caste. An attribute of many traditional societies is that they deny equality of opportunity to

---

Box 3-1: Rigidities Among State-Owned Enterprises in China

Perhaps the fundamental feature of a centrally planned economy is the sovereignty of the planner, under which the informational and incentive system will reflect the planners' priorities. This, and its economic effects, is illustrated by China's contract responsibility system. Under this, a contract is negotiated between the responsible government department and the potential manager of a public enterprise stipulating various targets, beyond which managers are free to pursue their own interests. Contractual obligations may cover items such as product choice, quotas to be sold to the state at fixed prices (with above quota production freely disposable at market prices), taxation, investment, and pricing and employment policies.

A widely adopted variant of the system has been the enterprise operational responsibility system, under which the profit level of the previous year, or some other base figure, is taken, with profits up to this base figure (plus a negotiated growth rate) taxed at 55 percent, and any additional profits taxed at only 30 percent. Any net profit is then usually left at the disposal of the enterprise manager to award as bonuses, contributions to welfare funds, or to retain for future investment.

While these measures, adopted in the early 1980s to enhance management autonomy from state interference, have met with some success, a number of major problems persist. First, a system intended to strengthen the position of enterprise managers has actually legitimized further state interference in that all contracts—and the decision whether a particular enterprise is allowed to enter into a contract—have to be negotiated with a ministry. Given the breadth of potential obligations, in particular the strict stipulations preventing wage and job reductions, targets are an impediment to flexible management. For example, in the first six months of 1989 the Gold Lion Bicycle Group in Changzhou City suffered a substantial loss due to a decline in demand, increased input costs, and severe competition from higher quality brand-name bicycles, but because of contractual obligations and the inability to shed labor or reduce wages to cut costs, it was unable to regain competitiveness quickly.

Furthermore, in so far as past (or industrywide) performance is used as the basis for targets, the target-setting mechanism obstructs flexible responses to changing conditions. For example, the fixed obligation of Changzhou City to deliver a certain amount of tax revenue to the central government caused it to give revenue extraction a much higher priority than the health of enterprises in contract negotiations.

Source: Liqing (forthcoming).

women, discouraging the education and weakening the economic incentives of over half the population. Equality of opportunity is also often denied on ethnic grounds (although not just in traditional societies), where a dominant tribe or race holds down the progress of others and gives preferment to its own members.

Traditional values may also be opposed to the self-regarding pursuit of material well-being. Extended family obligations, for instance, can weaken incentives, when people believe trying to improve their lot is pointless because they will have to share the benefits with numerous relatives. Similar traditional influences may stand in the way of, or weaken the incentives for, public servants adopting the role orientation necessary to conduct their duties efficiently. In short, traditional values may be at odds with the modernization of outlook that is necessary for the adaptive economy, and hence may dull responsiveness.

For reasons such as these, the Economic Commission for Africa (1989, p.6) has written that:

> Among the internal factors in the current crisis (in Africa) is the persistence of social values, attitudes and practices that are not always conducive to development. Such values tend to nurture cultural cleavages that make nation-building difficult, provoke cultural conflicts, and promote multiple loyalties that render efficient management as well as administrative discipline difficult. The cultural milieu also exhibits lingering problems of lack of identity and dominant values for propelling development.

The extent and quality of education are of key importance. Educated people will understand more of their environment and how they can take advantage of it. They will be more knowledgeable about changing opportunities and more self-confident about being able to take advantage of them.[1] It is from the well-educated that an upwardly mobile middle class with capitalistic values is most likely to be created, and it is from this group that most modernization is likely to originate. This is the group that may then come to serve as exemplars to the rest of the population, issuing an implicit invitation for them also to shed the influence of tradition.

Religion is another potent force. Perhaps the key question here is what a religion teaches concerning mankind's relationship to the envi-

---

1. Highly pertinent in this context is Theodore Schultz's (1975) essay, in which he argues that one of the chief benefits of education is the way it enhances people's ability to deal successfully with economic disequilibria.

ronment. Some faiths see human fate as predetermined by God's will and acceptance of poverty in this world as a mere prelude to a better life in the next. Such a faith is not likely to encourage enterprising self-help in response to a changing environment. A more likely result is passive fatalism that dulls responsiveness to economic challenges. The Buddhist and Hindu religions are perhaps most often associated with such teachings. Conversely, the Christian and Jewish faiths emphasize individuals' responsibility for their actions and well-being, with the "Protestant ethic" sometimes particularly associated with capitalistic values. The Islamic faith falls somewhere in the middle.

Religions of all kinds are often seen as conservative, protectors of traditional values, resistant to modernization and materialism. Some religions have placed limited value on secular education; many have resisted scientific explanations of the world's workings when they appear to conflict with religious teachings. The validity and influence of such considerations remains highly controversial, of course, not least because of large differences within all the main religions, and the sensitivity of this topic becomes immediately obvious as soon as particular faiths are mentioned. Thus, the Iranian revolution is widely interpreted as an Islamic rejection of the modernizing model but box 3-2 points out that the position is not so straightforward.

Comments on earlier drafts of the above paragraphs have been uniformly critical, charging that they are ethnocentric or culturally biased. Apparently offering generalizations in this area is impossible without causing controversy, yet the influence of tradition on receptivity to change is too strong for us to ignore. On this we are one with the earlier quotation from the Economic Commission for Africa; observations about Africa written from an African standpoint. Note that the comments here should not be read as an attack on tradition or religion. The individualistic pursuit of self-welfare that lies at the heart of the capitalist economy does not represent man's most elevated moral state. Moreover, some reject the modernization model that is implicit in the above (although the evidence on income elasticities in chapter 2 does suggest that most consumers behave as if they favor modernization). Our task here is not to argue the advantages and disadvantages of these viewpoints, but the narrower one of elucidating the nature of a flexible economy.

Box 3-2: Religion, Culture, and Modernization: The Case of the Iranian Revolution

---

Islam is often characterized as emphasizing respect for, and obedience to, authority and hence as antagonistic to individualistic achievement-orientation and modernization. A widely cited case is that of the Iranian Revolution, which, in the name of Islam, has strongly condemned the perceived materialism and immorality of the West. However using this as evidence of a general Islamic anti-modernism is simplistic.

Iranian Shi'ism has been built up over the centuries on a base of pre-Islamic belief, particularly Iranian aesthetic and philosophic doctrines. Two of the major religious-cultural value sets that emerge from this are the contrasts between the "internal" and the "external," and between "hierarchy" and "equality." Under the former, Iranians view the external world as a corrupting influence, both on the spiritual and socioeconomic levels. This is reflected in the Sufi concerns with suppressing all passions and desires related to the external on the road to mystic enlightenment, and the fear of foreign domination fueled by Iran's historical subjugation by and influence of the Greeks, Arabs, Mongols, and, in more recent times, Russia, Great Britain, and the United States. This helps to explain the strong desire to preserve indigenous values. On the second complex of values, while Iranian society is very hierarchical, this is balanced by the obligation placed upon those in authority to assist those in inferior positions.

Iran experienced a heavy external influence after 1945 through foreign investment and a large expatriate population accorded important privileges by the monarchy. Furthermore, the new urban elites created by the top-heavy distribution of income and their espousal of international values further elevated the external relative to the internal. There was also a breach of the hierarchy-equality equilibrium, with policies engendering ever more centralization, and the beneficiaries of the rapid growth showing increasing disregard of the traditional sectors of Iranian society. Perhaps most important, the power of the religious establishment was threatened, with the clergy's legal and educational functions being taken away, and their landholdings being placed under government control. Furthermore, with the imposition of measures such as Western dress codes for men, the outlawing of the veil for women and harshly imposed price controls, the Shah lost legitimacy as a ruler.

Thus, the Iranian Revolution cannot be characterized as purely Islamic, but as the result of a development path that breached the religious-cultural value system unique to Iran. Indeed, the vibrancy of entrepreneurial activities in countries like Pakistan, Turkey, and parts of Islamic Africa has led many to conclude that the precepts of Islam have not seriously hindered the capitalist orientation taken by the Muslim world during the last 100 years.

Source: Beeman (1983); Rodinson (1974).

Similarly, the remarks on the influence of tradition should not be interpreted as suggesting that major societies are unresponsive to material incentives. The evidence provides few such examples, and indicates rather that "economic man" populates all countries. The negative influences mentioned are best viewed as dulling responses and reducing elasticities, not as giving rise to perverse responses. The economic life of some traditional societies can be very vigorous and highly resilient in the face of adversity; hence the persistence of parallel markets and informal sectors in many countries. All societies contain obstacles to responsiveness and no form of cultural determinism is intended. However, we do insist on the main point: tradition is more likely than not to reduce receptivity to change.

The supply of entrepreneurs is another important influence on responsiveness to change (see Elkan 1988 for a discussion of entrepreneurs in Africa). The most important characteristics of an entrepreneur in this context are the ability to think ahead, take an active interest in information about economic conditions, look for opportunities, move quickly to be a step ahead of competitors, try to anticipate future opportunities; and be willing to take risks, to innovate, and to embrace the unfamiliar. An economy with an ample supply of such dynamic characters should be a flexible one.

Unfortunately, enterprise of this kind is unevenly distributed within and across peoples. There is no assurance that an economy will have an adequate supply of this quality, with the possible result being a creative market failure, that is, a failure to invest and innovate on an adequate scale (Kaldor 1972 as discussed in Arndt 1988).

Even more unfortunately, we understand little about the determinants of the supply of entrepreneurs. This issue has strong links with the earlier discussion of the determinants of public attitudes toward change. Societies that value individuality and award status to the prosperous apparently provide an environment more conducive to the flowering of enterprise. Societies that are culturally rich are perhaps more likely to engender the self-confidence that the entrepreneur must possess, or perhaps entrepreneurship is rather a response of disadvantaged groups, those denied status by society at large, who cannot expect normal preferment to push them up the ladder (Hagen 1962). On the basis of this view we would expect entrepreneurial groups to emerge particularly from minorities of various kinds, including immigrants. The important role of the Indian and Lebanese communities in commerce and manufacturing in Africa and the South Pacific is an example, as are the Chinese in Southeast Asia.

An economy's maturity will be a further, negative, influence on its receptivity to change. There is an analogy here with human beings. As they grow older people tend to become more set in established habits, more resistant to change, less adaptable. Flexibility is an attribute of youth. We need to be wary of simple biological analogies in economics, but this one is logical.[2] The chief point here relates to the age structure of the stock of physical capital and the technologies embodied in it. As we saw earlier, a mature economy will be relatively capital intensive. The volume of new investment will be small relative to the existing capital stock, and that stock will therefore tend to be relatively old. By this reasoning, the German and Japanese economies eventually benefited from the destruction of much of their capital stock during World War II, giving them today a more modern infrastructure than most of their European and North American competitors.

Conversely, an economy at an early stage of development is likely to be adding to its capital at a faster rate and, at least in principle, will be in a better position to alter the disposition of capital across activities and to incorporate technological advances. There are, of course, major disadvantages to set against this, but it is as well to remind ourselves that low-income countries do possess some advantages (see Kuznets 1965, pp. 186-190).

Plunging yet further into the quicksands of amateur sociology, we come next to a variety of factors that influence receptivity to change and that relate to the nature and actions of governments. The influence of political systems is among the issues explored in chapter 9. We conclude there that political realities may easily act as barriers to adaptation. A government that has become insecure, corrupt, and repressive is unlikely to give much priority to economic flexibility, or to have the legitimacy necessary to carry through the policies needed to adjust the economy to changing circumstances. Existing policies,

---

2. For a far wider-ranging analysis of how aging societies lose their flexibility see Olson (1982) who develops the idea of a sclerotic economy.

however ill-chosen, often have large inertial force because those who benefit from them become powerful enough to block change.

Even so, change is not impossible. Chapter 9 suggests that a cost-benefit logic is at work, in which the economic deterioration that results from anti-adaptation policy stances throws up a countervailing public discontent that will either impel the government to act or overthrow it for a more reform minded one. When combined with strong leadership and government, public acceptance of the need for change can render politically feasible policy shifts that would formerly have been judged suicidal. Ultimately, economic flexibility has more friends than enemies.

A closely related issue concerns the appropriateness of the **institutional basis of economic activity** discussed briefly in chapter 2. Outdated laws, a reactionary or corrupted judiciary, or a hidebound public administration can be potent obstacles to responsiveness, frustrating entrepreneurs and others wishing to take advantage of new opportunities. But here too, there is no reason to exaggerate the stifling effect of such rigidities, for institutions do adapt, albeit in ways that we do not fully understand.

Under this heading we should also mention a delicate **balance to be struck between flexibility and continuity in government policies.** Modern macroeconomic theory has taught us the importance of the ways in which the public reacts to—and seeks to anticipate—government actions, and of the techniques that it develops for frustrating government intentions.[3] Corruption and parallel (or black) markets are examples of the latter. To have maximum effect policies must be credible; people must believe they will be implemented and will stick (see Lächler (1988) for an exploration of this theme applied to anti-inflation policies in Southern Cone Latin American countries). For example, if the government embarks on a currency devaluation, economic agents must take the new exchange rate as a reliable basis for decisions about the future. Signals have to be believed. This is why

---

3. This is based on rational expectations theory. Although the direct relevance of this theory in all its rigor and on all its necessary assumptions is limited, there is now wide acceptance of the importance of taking public reactions into account when devising macroeconomic policies.   See Shaw (1984) for a straightforward exposition of rational expectations theory and Corden (1987) for a discussion of its relevance to developing countries.

unstable or inconsistent governments have difficulty in improving the performance of the economy: citizens do not believe that their government means what it says or will enforce its decisions. This is a reason for valuing political stability, for who can plan on the reliability of some new policy signal if governments have only brief life expectancies?

Economic responsiveness will be much enhanced when these various conditions for receptivity to change are satisfied. To revert now to the language of economics, satisfaction of these conditions will result in large price elasticities, which brings us to the second aspect of responsiveness to information and incentives.

Supply elasticities. The above discussion of receptivity to change concerns a variety of pervasive influences within a socioeconomic system on its willingness to embrace change and to respond to altering opportunities. We now narrow the discussion to consider the factors that will influence peoples' responsiveness to changing incentives emanating from the market, for we have emphasized throughout the importance for the flexible economy of translating information into price signals and of securing vigorous responses to these changing signals. This latter requirement implies the desirability of large price elasticities of demand and supply. We therefore now turn to consider what determines the elasticities of response to changing price relativities, over and above those discussed in the preceding paragraphs. We shall concentrate on supply elasticities as the most important for our purposes.

Assuming that a price change is taken to be more than temporary, for the economy as a whole supply elasticities will be strongly influenced by the availability of factors of production and other inputs. Key factors will include the following:

- **The prior existence of unutilized capacity of both labor and capital.** Response to improved profit opportunities is likely to be rapid and substantial if these can be reaped simply by bringing into production underemployed plant or labor. Industrialized economies will be at an advantage in this respect, for it is in manufacturing and mining that excess capacity is most likely to occur that can fairly readily be brought into production, as against agriculture, where there are larger difficulties and longer time lags (see Schydlowsky 1982 for a discussion of economic management in the face of excess capacity).

- **Factor mobilities.** The mobility of labor and capital refers to the ease with which they can move between alternative employments. This, in turn, will be influenced by the efficiency of the factor markets, including the flexibility of wages and returns to capital, and the speed with which these markets clear. It will also be influenced by the degree of specificity of the factors, that is, the extent to which they are versatile or are trained or designed to perform a narrow range of tasks. This too works in favor of relatively industrialized economies, for factors tend to be particularly specific in the primary sectors of production: the skills and physical capital employed in a coffee plantation or a bauxite mine cannot readily be used in other activities. Related to factor specificity is the extent to which technologies are embodied in equipment and other fixed capital, or are available in the form of disembodied knowledge for a wide range of applications.

- **Credit for working capital** is a special case of factor mobility. New or increased output will create a need for additional working capital to finance the necessary additions to inventories and the time lags between production and receipt of sales proceeds. If producers cannot finance this from their existing resources, they will look to the banks for credit. Thus, their ability to expand will be sensitive to their access to such credit and the terms upon which it is available. This is important because during periods of structural adjustment a country will commonly be undertaking a stand-by program with the International Monetary Fund, which invariably incorporates restrictions on domestic bank credit. The IMF's pursuit of short-term balance of payments stabilization can thus come into conflict with the longer-term restructuring with which we are principally concerned here (an issue that is taken further in chapter 9).

- **The extent of competition.** Elasticities of supply are larger in competitive firms and tend to be so for competitive industries. Conversely, a firm that is a sole producer has no particular incentive to respond strongly to changes in market conditions, for its monopoly power can already earn it large profits. It can get away with unnecessarily high cost structures—what is known as

X-inefficiency (see Leibenstein 1966 and 1976)—and it can postpone the discomfort of change.

• **Availability of raw materials and other intermediate inputs.** There are a number of considerations here. Where an industry uses inputs from agriculture or elsewhere in the domestic economy, the issue becomes one of how large are their own elasticities of supply; a reason already mentioned in chapter 2 for not neglecting the primary sectors of production. Where an industry depends upon imported supplies for raw materials, spare parts, or capital equipment, the key question becomes that of the economy's import capacity, including its access to international liquidity and capital. This has often been a particularly serious issue in the conditions of import strangulation mentioned in chapter 2 and illustrated in box 3-3. The state of the economy's basic infrastructure is also relevant here. If this is inadequate, obtaining ample and secure additional supplies will be difficult. The state of the infrastructure also has a direct bearing on the mobility of labor and, more generally, on an economy's structural flexibility, for a well-developed infrastructure helps to integrate markets and raise their efficiency.

Although it is related only indirectly to the elasticity of supply, we should also mention the elasticity of substitution. If we confine ourselves to labor and capital, this measures the proportionate change in the capital:labor ratio in response to a given change in the relative prices of these two factors. The size of this elasticity tells us about the flexibility of the productive system in the face of changing conditions. In economies generally marked by underutilized labor forces and scarcities of capital, the extent to which labor can be substituted for capital, and hence reduce unemployment, is an issue of much importance, particularly when it comes to policies that reduce real wages and raise the real cost of capital.

There has been much controversy about the likely size of substitution elasticities in developing country conditions. Writers in the structuralist tradition have been pessimistic, emphasizing technical and other constraints on factor substitution, while neoclassicists have been more optimistic. Elasticities of substitution are difficult to measure reliably, and large differences are apparent across industries and coun-

---

Box 3-3: Import Strangulation and Industrial Performance in Zambia

---

Since the mid-1970s the Zambian economy has become increasingly dependent on imports of raw materials and other intermediate goods, with the ratio of imported goods to manufacturing output increasing from below 40 percent in 1973 to well over 50 percent through the 1980s. As the country suffered increasing shortages of foreign exchange as a result of decreasing earnings from copper, its dominant export, and transport dislocations resulting from instability in Southern Africa, so capacity utilization in its industrial sector suffered.

This is illustrated by the experiences of a battery producing enterprise set up to manufacture locally goods previously imported. This join Zambian-Finnish project, operational in 1978, rapidly faltered due to defective equipment, inadequate technical expertise, and, above all, shortages of foreign exchange to pay for its twenty different items of imported raw materials and spares. Capacity utilization between 1978 and 1983 averaged a mere 20 percent. This was principally due to interruptions in production, of which over 40 percent could be attributed to input shortages, and a further 40 percent to machine breakdowns themselves exacerbated by lack of spare parts.

The problems were compounded by the fact that the actual and prospective domestic demand for the enterprise's batteries is constrained by the country's ability to import battery-utilizing consumer goods. Thus, both from the supply and demand sides, an on-going balance of payments problem, embodied in almost exclusive dependence on a metal export with an uncertain world market and rapidly depleting domestic ore reserves, plus severe external debt servicing difficulties, places the economic viability of this enterprise in serious jeopardy.

Source: Rajeswaran (1986).

---

tries, but to the extent that it makes sense to generalize, the truth seems to be somewhere down the middle: there is often scope for substitution, but this is commonly subject to considerable limitations and complexities (see Bruton 1987 for an authoritative survey of the evidence).

In addition to stressing the importance of being able to switch resources from nontradable to tradable production in the face of a structural balance of payments problem, chapter 2 drew attention to the key importance of export performance, but also stressed the desirability of avoiding overproduction of exports and of diversifying away from an export market in the face of unfavorable trends in price or comparative advantage. In addition to the general influences on supply elasticities discussed above, **the ease of substitution between production for the home and foreign markets** will be another important variable. Once again, this is a consideration that works to the advantage of more advanced economies. There will often be a sizable domestic demand for manufactured goods that are also exported, making it easier to switch between production for domestic and foreign markets. Those concentrating on the exportation of primary products will not usually be in such a position because domestic demand for the commodities in question will normally be slight.

Time is another variable with a crucial influence on the size of supply elasticities. For supply to respond to altered price signals decisions have to be made: by businesspeople about whether to invest in additional capacity, by workers about whether to change jobs, perhaps to undertake re-training or move to a new locality; by financial institutions about whether to agree to credit requests. People need time to decide on their response to new opportunities and for those decisions to take effect. Sometimes long gestation lags occur between a decision and the resulting change in production, particularly when major new investments or the re-training of labor are necessary. Prices are not completely flexible, particularly those that are settled contractually for fixed periods of time, so that markets may be slow to clear. Labor markets are particularly likely to clear only slowly, if at all. For all these reasons, elasticities are larger in the long run than in the short.

This, however, points to a dilemma. Often countries faced with severe balance of payments or other disequilibria need quick results. Certainly, many of the adjustment programs with which the IMF, and to a lesser extent the World Bank, are associated are predicated on quick results. Responses are generally small in the short term, however, which points to the danger of placing too much reliance on market forces for rapid structural change. As Arndt (1988, p. 227) points out "Markets . . . work incrementally. All required changes - in price signals, in people's responses to incentives, in shifts in resources - take time. These lags account for the fact that elasticities of supply and demand are larger in the long than in the short run. Even in Western market economies, it has been recognized that very large changes that have had to be accomplished quickly . . . cannot be left to market forces. The likelihood of market failure therefore is a function of the degree of urgency - or impatience - attached to a particular change."

Other kinds of market failures may also reduce results. Dualism is common in the SLICs' economies. This refers to various asymmetries of production and organization that confront buyers and sellers with varying prices for the same good or service, preventing productivities from being maximized at the margin and obstructing the free movement of resources. For example, different lenders and borrowers often face large discrepancies in the rates of interest obtaining on different parts of the capital market, with the greatest variations being between the formal and informal segments of the market. There may similarly be large and nonequalizing differences in wages between urban (or formal) and rural (or informal) employment.

Industry is liable to be marked by relatively high concentrations of monopoly power in poor economies with small domestic markets, depending on government policies of protection, for the market will not be large enough to support more than one or a small number of firms. The banking sector may be marked by monopolistic or oligopolistic dominance by a few large banks. We have already mentioned the negative influence of labor market segmentation on the basis of sex or ethnic affiliation. Markets may also be less "complete" than in more developed economies, particularly in the rural economy, creating vacuums in such areas as food marketing and credit. There are likely to be few forward or futures markets, increasing risks and reducing the efficiency of investment.[4] It is because of the adverse consequences of these deficiencies that we earlier stressed the importance for economic flexibility of a well-functioning market system.

Adaptability, Openness, and Development

Before concluding our exploration of the characteristics of an adaptive economy, two additional questions deserve an airing. The first takes us back to the relationship between adaptability and devel-

---

4. A forward (or futures) market is one where a good or service is contracted to be delivered at some future date at a price agreed today. It is a device chiefly used to reduce risks, for example, when dealing in foreign currencies in the face of uncertainties about future exchange rates.

opment. Even though we were cautious about attributing causality from structural transformation to development, the thrust of chapter 2 was nonetheless to stress the beneficial effects of economic flexibility for long-term development. However, considering what is written above about the nature of an adaptive economy, it is equally clear that development aids flexibility.

Consider the reasons for this. First, the data base and flows of new information will be superior in a more developed economy, because it will be feasible to devote larger resources to this task, and also because a larger part of economic activity will take place within the organized sectors of the economy that are more amenable to measurement. Second, the hold of traditional values and modes is likely to be weaker, and modernizing attitudes more the norm. Third, the economy will be more industrialized. For reasons already mentioned, this will give greater potential for the rapid response of output to changing price relativities, and factors of production will be less specific than in the primary sectors. Partly because the domestic market will be larger, there will be more competition among domestic producers, increasing pressures upon them to be responsive. Markets will be better integrated and dualism reduced, for dualism is characteristic of SLICs. Markets will be more complete, and in other respects we would expect the market mechanism to work better.

The larger size of developed economies is an advantage in other ways. They will be less vulnerable to shocks transmitted from the rest of the world. They will have more diversified patterns of demand and production, facilitating the movement of resources between activities.[5] They will also be able to shift more easily between production for the home and export markets. Finally, we would expect there to be at least some tendency for government policy implementation capacities to be greater. The only disadvantage of more developed economies was the greater difficulty they may have in modernizing their capital stock.

---

5. Thus, the United Nations *World Economic Survey, 1985* (p.15) commented that the larger and more diversified economies with large production capacities were better able to adjust to external shocks, taking advantage of underutilized manufacturing capacity and an ability to switch from home to foreign markets in order to expand their exports.

An implication of this is that SLICs are liable to have inflexible economies. Thus, something of a vicious circle is at work: inflexibility retards development, but underdevelopment retards flexibility. Indeed, in many cases this understates the problem. A substantial proportion of the SLICs in Africa and elsewhere not only experience the rigidities just mentioned, but have suffered serious economic and social deteriorations: declining incomes and living standards, decaying transport systems, a worsening quality of health and education services, and a shrinking tax base leading to serious inflation and adding to already acute balance of payments problems. In at least some of these cases, the state's capabilities have decayed simultaneously, with economic life increasingly conducted through unregulated parallel markets, extensive corruption, a serious erosion of senior personnel and morale in the public services, and widespread alienation of the people from the actions of their governments.

Where such conditions prevail, the difficulties of successful adaptation are greatly increased, but one cannot justify going go so far as to describe this as a low-level trap. The link between flexibility and development is not so strong as to determine outcomes completely, and there are things that governments of even the poorest, most run-down countries can do to increase the adaptability of their economies. What is clear, however, is that they will face an uphill task and will require more time than more advanced economies. It is for such reasons that there have been calls for the international financial institutions to recognize these special needs in their policies toward African and other small low-income countries.

Since most low-income countries have small economies and small economies are almost always heavily dependent on international trade, the further question arises, is this openness good for economic flexibility? The answer is yes. One of the great advantages of trade is that it allows local manufacturers to escape the confines of domestic demand to sell on world markets. This permits them to specialize more and achieve more economies of scale, as is elaborated in chapter 4 (Kubo and others 1986, p.224, note this, and that in consequence, trade led to more rapid structural transformation than otherwise would have occurred in the countries they studied.) Openness also exposes local producers to more competition than could be sustained domestically, which as suggested earlier is likely to make them more responsive to changing conditions and opportunities.

The high levels of imports that mark the open economy also have the advantage of giving low-cost access to intermediate and capital goods that could be produced at home only inefficiently, and to the technological advances incorporated in them. More generally, a society that is thoroughly exposed to commerce with and investments from the rest of the world is more likely to be aware of actual and prospective trends, and more receptive to new ideas. Finally, chapter 4 argues that the economic policies that governments must adopt if they actively promote an outward-oriented development strategy will themselves probably lead to greater economic efficiency and flexibility.

Against these considerations, however, we must set the fact that open economies are more vulnerable to shocks from the outside, relative to the scale of domestic economic activity. The greater instability of world economic conditions that marked the 1970s and 1980s increased the risks and costs associated with integration into it. In short, openness both facilitates flexibility and necessitates it! What seems to be indicated, therefore, is a judicious blend of policies intended both to protect the economy from the worst of these risks and to open it up to the opportunities of trade and investment. These arguments are taken further in chapter 4.

The Place of Structural Adjustment

During the 1980s structural adjustment became one of the most commonly used expressions in discussions of development policies and of the international financial institutions: the IMF and the World Bank. The question arises, therefore, how our usage relates to the term as these institutions use it. One major difficulty here is that structural adjustment is an expression that has been used far more often than it has been defined. Moreover, various definitions have been offered, these have changed over time, and no consensus has emerged on a "proper" meaning.

Adjustment as Induced Adaptation

In the light of the discussion so far, how might we understand the term structural adjustment? We can usefully introduce here a distinction between change that occurs automatically through the market as the response of economic agents to changing demands and opportunities, and change that is induced by the manipulation of policy. Although we have emphasized the largely autonomous or external nature of many of the trends and shocks to which economies need to respond, one should not infer from this that the pattern of adjustment is beyond government influence. Much scope for choice exists, particularly in the longer term, and we have stressed the importance of having regard to the special characteristics of the home economy. Thus, the quality of a government's response to the available alternatives can make all the difference between a laggard and a thriving economy. The potency of its decisions are all the greater if past policies have actually been retarding the economy's responsiveness. Later chapters provide many illustrations of the ways in which policy mistakes can have such a consequence. A willingness to recognize past policy mistakes and introduce the necessary reforms may thus be central in attempts to increase the economy's flexibility.

What if a government declines to make such decisions and refuses to recognize the need for hard choices in these matters? The answer is not that the economy will cease to respond, but that its responses will be suboptimal and will impose heavy avoidable costs on its inhabitants. This is most easily explained when the balance of payments is the chief symptom of structural weakness. In this case, a shortage of foreign exchange imposes adjustment and the only real choice is whether adjustment will be planned or involuntary. In the latter case, that is, in the absence of effective policies, import supplies will dry up as international creditworthiness is eroded and the availability of foreign exchange to pay for imports diminishes. The economy will thus be forced to live with whatever reduced volume of imports it can afford, and adjustment will take the form of reduced output, income, employment, and living standards.

Adjustment can hence be thought of as induced or planned adaptation, in which case adjustment policies are the instruments deployed to achieve the desired adaptation and to enhance the economy's flexibility. Structural adjustment should logically be regarded as measures to adapt specifically structural variables, as discussed in chapter 2, particularly the productive system and the physical and institutional infrastructure. How does such an approach square with the usages within the international financial institutions?

IMF and Bank Approaches

The item structural adjustment entered into international parlance in 1980 when the World Bank introduced structural adjustment loans (SALs) as a new type of credit. There were two principal reasons for this innovation (for an account of the early history of SALs and an espousal of this type of lending by the Bank see Please 1984, chapters 3 and 4):

- A perception that the world environment had become markedly more hostile for most developing countries—remember this was the time of the second oil shock and an associated recession in the industrial world—and that these countries stood in urgent need of longer-term support for their efforts to cope with the resulting balance of payments dislocations than the IMF was designed to provide.
- A growing perception that policy mistakes in developing countries were in some cases preventing an adequate response to the worsened environment and, more generally, were retarding economic development as well as reducing returns on past Bank-financed projects.

SALs were thus to provide quick-disbursing loans to finance general imports over a period of years in support of an agreed set of measures intended to strengthen the balance of payments while maintaining a development momentum. During the course of the 1980s, however, the Bank's original emphasis on the balance of payments gradually faded, with a corresponding increase in the stress it placed upon "economy wide programs of reforms." More recently, the Bank has switched emphasis from SALs to sectoral adjustment loans, which have narrower policy objectives, although the general policy thrust is similar.

The position was further complicated when in 1986 the IMF set up a new Structural Adjustment Facility. This too was intended to provide medium-term balance of payments assistance to low-income countries facing protracted balance of payments difficulties for a program of policy measures to be worked out with IMF and Bank staff. It was augmented at the end of 1987 by an Enhanced Structural Adjustment Facility, with considerably greater resources than the original Structural Adjustment Facility. In some respects, the Extended Facility of the Fund set up in 1974 was a precursor of the Enhanced Structural Adjustment Facility, not least because, for the first time, it engaged the IMF in medium-term policy programs aimed at strengthening the productive structure (see de Vries 1987 for the Fund's official account of the Extended Facility of the Fund and Structural Adjustment Facility and Killick 1984, pp.247-50, for an evaluation of the Extended Facility of the Fund). Given the nature of the IMF, the chief objective in each of these facilities was to help a country achieve balance of payments viability. In most cases, the supply-side measures written into their programs were in addition to the IMF's traditional emphasis on short-term demand management, which involved credit restrictions, reduced budget deficits, and exchange rate depreciations.

The World Bank (1988a, p.11) has offered the following description of its usage of the terms as it had developed by the late 1980s, and the IMF subsequently provided a similar account (see IMF Annual Report, 1989, box 4):

> *Adjustment.* Policies to achieve changes in internal and external balances, changes in the structure of incentives and institutions, or both.
>
> *Structural adjustment.* Reforms of policies and institutions—microeconomic (such as taxes), macroeconomic (such as fiscal imbalance), and institutional (public sector inefficiencies). These changes improve resource allocation, increase economic efficiency, expand growth potential, and increase resilience to future shocks.

It is apparent from this that there are areas of overlap between these usages and our own definition offered earlier. Common to them all are the ideas that adjustment is a response to shocks and other changes in the economic environment; that it involves policy changes, that is, it is a planned process; that it is not a short-term task; and that it involves attention to an economy's basic structure. Important differences may be noted, however, concerning breadth and length.

As regards breadth, our own approach has stressed a wider range of influences to which economies must adapt than those to which, understandably, the international financial institutions confine themselves. We agree with them about the special importance of the foreign exchange constraint, but also bring in factors such as changing climatic conditions, technological progress, and long-term shifts in the pattern of demand. We have also introduced a wider range of factors that influence adjustment, including political, social, and environmental, and therefore place less emphasis on purely economic interpretations.

The point about length is more important. It has to do with the speed with which economies can respond to changing circumstances and to the period over which such responsiveness is necessary. A long-standing complaint about the IMF's policies toward developing countries is that its programs are too short-term to be able to cope with the often deep-seated nature of the countries' payments weaknesses. The Extended Facility of the Fund and Enhanced Structural Adjustment Facility were responses to this complaint. Even the Bank's longer-term programs have been criticized along similar lines, and its own evaluations of SALs have drawn the conclusion that structural change takes longer than originally envisaged. No less significant, both institutions, at least their governing bodies, want to phase down structural adjustment lending (a process that had already begun by 1990) so that each can return to its more traditional roles, whereas our own treatment has shown adaptation to change as a continuous necessity. The international financial institutions appear to view adjustment as "the economics of transition," a preliminary to resumption of the development effort, and to address themselves particularly to the management of shocks, while we have stressed that it is long-term, inseparable from development and not merely transitional.

In other words, we can think of the structural adjustment programs of the IMF and World Bank as an important subset of our own understanding of the term: more confined in time and coverage, but nevertheless addressed to some of the most pressing of economic adaptation problems. Difficulties are, however, created in reconciling these approaches by the differing time spans over which adjustment is viewed. There is difficulty, too, in reconciling policies for the control of aggregate demand with those for the restructuring of the productive system. We return to these matters in chapter 9.

Summary

The main purpose of this chapter was to explicate the attributes of a flexible economy. We have argued that one basic requirement is efficient informational and incentive systems, and that a well-functioning market system is conducive to flexibility. This is because it can handle large volumes of information in a decentralized way and convert this into appropriate incentive signals. However, we also stressed the important role of government in marshaling information, a task that markets cannot be relied upon to perform adequately.

The second basic requirement is that economic agents—in the public and private sectors alike—must be responsive to the information and incentives, and we broke this responsiveness into receptivity to change and elasticities. We suggested that receptivity will be strongly influenced by the balance in a society between traditional and modernizing values, with education a particularly important factor; by the size and quality of the entrepreneurial class; and by the maturity of an economy and its capital stock. We suggested finally that the government's ability to promote an adaptive economy will be affected by its perceived legitimacy and stability; and the credibility of its policies as enduring signals for decisions about the future.

We then considered the factors that promote the large supply elasticities that are an attribute of flexibility, emphasizing again the importance of market forces, but drawing attention to various market failures that may stand in the way of adequate supply responses. We further suggested that flexibility is a rising function of the level of development, and is thus not a natural quality of poor countries; and that integration into the world system of trade and payments increases both an economy's vulnerability to adverse external developments and its ability to adjust to these.

Finally, we defined structural adjustment as induced adaptation, and adjustment policies as the instruments governments employed to bring this about. This discussion served to provide a broader context within which to set the structural adjustment policies of the IMF and World Bank. We suggested that their approaches were more confined than ours in breadth of coverage and the treatment of time. Nevertheless, their programs do address crucially important aspects of the task of economic adaptation, particularly as it relates to adjustment to shocks and the foreign exchange constraint.

Having defined adjustment in this way, the next task is to consider the role of economic policy in the process. We have referred at a number of points to ways in which government policies may actually make things worse and to the task of ensuring that policies are part of the solution rather than part of the problem. The role of policy is the subject of chapters 4 to 8.

A Note on Further Reading: Unfortunately, the literature contains very little systematic discussion on the determinants of economic flexibility in low-income countries, although Olson (1982) is concerned with this type of question as it relates to mature industrial economies. No general recommendation can therefore be made for this chapter, but the interested reader is encouraged to follow up the references provided in the text.

4

THE STRATEGY OF ADJUSTMENT POLICY

Chapter 3 set out a number of the characteristics that make for a flexible economy, one that can adjust to changing circumstances and take advantage of opportunities. To nurture such characteristics can thus be described as one of the chief objectives of adjustment policies. However, we have also suggested that policies themselves can be a source of inflexibility or can hamper adaptation. The task of this chapter and the next four is to explore ways in which policy can contribute to the solution rather than being part of the problem: how mistakes can be rectified, how policies can promote flexibility. Chapter 5 surveys the policy instruments that are available to governments in the pursuit of adjustment, while chapters 6 to 8 take a more detailed look at specific policies and sectoral issues. Our task now is to take up some of the more basic, or strategic, policy issues that arise in the context of adjustment.

The Role of the State

There has in recent times been some ferment in economics about the role of the state in economic life (the literature on this and its relevance to the role of the state in developing country circumstances is explored in Killick 1989, on which the next few pages are based). Many now take a more skeptical view of what the state can—or should—do, and this change has in turn fed into the conservative revolution that during the 1980s had a profound influence on policies in many industrial countries, as well as in some developing countries. This subject remains highly controversial, however, and we will start our discussion of adjustment policies by briefly surveying the state of this argument.

Market Failures

Traditionally, the state's economic role has been defined in terms of a responsibility to correct for or eliminate various market failures.

There is an extensive literature on this subject, from which the following list of failures can be distilled (for discussion of these see Stiglitz 1986, upon which much of the following list is based; see also Arndt 1988, particularly on the subject of dynamic market failures).

- **Failures of competition.** Briefly, these can be said to occur whenever monopoly or monopsony power exists in a market. It has led governments to promote greater competition by various means or to safeguard against the abuse of monopoly power.

- **Externalities.** These are costs associated with an output that accrue to society at large and are not reflected in producers' costs of production, or benefits that are not reflected in their revenues. The damage caused to the environment by industrial effluents is a common example of an external cost. The value to local farmers of tracks created by timber haulers is an example of an external benefit.

- **Incomplete markets.** This condition exists when markets fail to produce items that people desire and for which they are willing to pay more than the costs of production. Widespread examples include the frequently incomplete coverage of credit and insurance markets in rural areas. Another is the paucity of futures markets, which would permit people to enter into contracts for the supply of a good or service at some future date at a price determined now. One consequence of this is to increase uncertainty, thereby discouraging investment or leading to investment mistakes.

- **Information failures.** Market forces result in an underproduction of information to which public access cannot easily be limited, and which, therefore, cannot be profitably sold. The role of government to remedy this defect has already been given some prominence in the discussion in chapter 3 of the importance of information for economic adaptation.

- **Public goods.** This is the name given to various desirable goods and services that would not be supplied (or not supplied efficiently) by private enterprise, including the maintenance of law and order, national defense, and public health. The type of co-operative actions needed to provide this type of service will not normally result from the competitive maximization by individuals of their own welfare, necessitating imposed provisions by the state.

- **Merit goods.** These relate to items that the state views individuals will not use in their own best interests. Most of the examples are negative: laws against the use of narcotics or the discriminatory taxation of alcohol. Compulsory education is a positive example.
- **Macroeconomic instability.** This refers to the tendency for unregulated market economies to experience cyclical or short-term instability: the periodic occurrence of recessions and inflationary booms. Keynes' chief contribution to the theory of economic policy was his analysis of this, and his assertion of the state's duty to rectify this failure.
- **Creative failures.** Most of the above relate to failures that reduce the efficiency with which resources are allocated at a given time. The idea of creative or dynamic failures relates to situations where the production frontier is not being expanded over time at an optimal rate. This may result from suboptimal levels of saving and investment, perhaps due to scale economies, or from inadequate supplies of entrepreneurial skills to exploit economic opportunities and propel the economy forward. Indivisibilities, high risks, or inefficient capital markets may similarly result in suboptimal rates of innovation. This type of failure is liable to have particularly serious consequences for the processes of economic adaptation.
- **Poverty and inequality.** The existence of such conditions may be regarded as a type of failure when market forces result in conditions that are inconsistent with what society regards as equitable or reasonable.

Although some of the above items are disputed, most economists agree that market failures—illustrated in box 4-1—are widespread and often serious. What is now a good deal more controversial is the traditional inference in the theory of policy that the existence of market failures constitutes an adequate case for state interventions to rectify or compensate for them. Economists and development practitioners no longer assume that government intervention will make things better. Experience has taught caution for a number of reasons (see Lal 1983 for a highly skeptical treatment of the state's efficacy in developing country circumstances).

Box 4-1: Market Failures

Segmented and Incomplete Markets: Dualism in Zambia's Agricultural Sector

Before 1980 Zambia's agricultural sector was split between about 700 large commercial farms and approximately 600,000 smallholder farmers, mostly cultivating less than 2 hectares each. Underlying this split was dualism in input and product markets. Financial dualism meant that commercial farmers had access to banks and other institutions, and could borrow at lower interest rates than smallholders, who were forced to turn to moneylenders or who had no access to credit. Differential access to finance in turn contributed to technological dualism. Smallholdings remained labor-intensive and dependent on simple hand tools: they were unable to purchase oxen or tractors, and their small unspecialized farms permitted no economies of scale. Meanwhile commercial farmers were able to invest (notably in irrigation), and modern technology became concentrated in the commercial sector. Other inputs, such as fertilizers, pesticides, and improved seed varieties, were largely confined to the commercial farmers. Their greater buying power and access to information and credit made them able to purchase at wholesale prices (while smallholders paid retail prices), to take advantage of changes in subsidies on fertilizer, and to direct agricultural research and extension services to their needs. They were also better able to compete for labor, while smallholder production was constrained by labor shortages.

Commercial farmers also had greater access to and control over product markets. They were located closer to major transport links and were able to organize their own road transport or storage of produce. This enabled them to overcome seasonal and regional price variations, to reduce losses due to crop spoilage, to avoid middlemen by selling directly to retailers, to cut the costs of transporting inputs, and to respond more quickly to changes in the prices of different crops.

Thus input and product markets were segmented or incomplete, with access to both of them easier for commercial farmers, resulting in dominance by overmechanized and import-intensive commercial farms.

Environmental Externalities: Estuarine and Marine Pollution in West Africa

Thousands of substances enter river estuaries and coastal marine waters due to industrial and agricultural production processes. Some, like DDT and artificial radioactive materials, are alien to the water; others, such as mercury and lead, are naturally present, but unregulated industrial waste disposal or agricultural pesticide use increases their concentration and combines them in ways that pollute marine and fresh waters, with negative effects on marine wildlife, fishing, and human health.

Box 4-1 (continued)

Pollution of West African coastal waters became increasingly severe in the 1960s and 1970s. Unregulated growth of industrial production in coastal urban areas led to a rapid rise in industrial waste. Outside urban areas, industries (for example, making timber products, processed foods, and textiles) released unprocessed effluents into waterways. Oil exploration and exploitation brought pollution through spills of crude oil and refined products during extraction, loading, and transport. Commercial farmers used more chemical fertilizers, herbicides, and pesticides, which led to discharges of wastes and residues into estuaries and coastal lagoons.

These were all examples of external diseconomies. Producers were able to keep down their internal costs by dumping their wastes instead of dealing with them within the production process, and it was society that paid. Thus, fishermen were hit in all coastal waters between Côte d'Ivoire and Gabon. Shrimp catches collapsed in the lagoon fisheries of Abidjan and several commercial seafood and fish species entirely disappeared from all waters between 1973 and 1980. Surface oil slicks killed tuna larvae in breeding grounds off Ghana, with adverse results for regional tuna stocks. Adverse effects on the health of the wider population probably occurred as well, with both human and economic consequences.

Source: Zambia: unpublished World Bank sources; West Africa: Based on Ruddle and Manshard (1981).

The Costs of Policy

One reason for caution relates to the complexity of an economy— even a low-income economy—and of the effects on it of a given policy change. For one thing, varying time lags are involved: between government perception of a need for action, a decision to introduce a policy corrective, the implementation of that decision, and its effects on the economy. In consequence, the economic situation may materially have changed by the time a policy shift works its way through the economy, making it less relevant, maybe even harmful. Moreover, the government's knowledge of how the economy works is inevitably imperfect, making some policies rather hit or miss, and sometimes unwittingly magnifying mistakes by individuals in the marketplace. Governments, furthermore, have only imperfect control over the ways in which their policies are actually implemented on the ground and, therefore, over the consequences of their actions. In addition, as discussed in chapter 3, public reactions can render government policies impotent. We shall return to this later.

Government actions have a habit of necessitating higher tax revenues, and a further reason for some turning away from the market failures approach, in industrial countries at least, was a seemingly inexorable rise in the share of national income taken in taxes. The beginnings of a tax revolt were evident as indicated by growing tax evasion and changes in voting patterns in favor of political parties promising to give priority to lowering taxes.[1] This was not just a matter of public preference. Economists began to place greater weight on the potential disincentive effects of high taxes and on the distortions such taxes can create. One aspect of this was a greater tendency to see a tradeoff between economic efficiency and measures to reduce poverty or income inequalities.

In short, economists are now more aware that state interventions involve costs as well as benefits, and that state failures are possible as well as market failures. Two illustrations are provided in box 4-2. Macroeconomic instability is one of the market failures listed earlier, but this provides a further illustration of state failure, for there is now wide acceptance that the state is itself a potent source of such instability, not least because of fiscal mismanagement. Economists also recognize that medium-term development planning has often failed to bring many of the benefits expected of it. At more microeconomic levels, they see government policies as a source of inefficiencies, for example, ad hoc and unsystematic decisions about industrial protection, policies biased in favor of the urban population, or controls over prices and wages.[2] The poor economic and financial performance of many state enterprises has similarly contributed to the new skepticism about the state's efficacy, and as we shall see later,

---

1. In the OECD countries taken together, current government receipts as a percentage of GDP rose from an average of 28 percent in 1960 to a peak of 36 percent in the early 1980s (see Killick 1989, p.16). Unfortunately, equivalent time series are not available for low-income developing countries.

2. See Balassa (1988) on policy-induced distortions in developing countries. He is particularly concerned with tracing how such distortions in product and factor markets interact with one another.

economists are less inclined to assume that the state's intentions are benign, with some writers seeing it instead as predatory.

Box 4-2: Government Failures

Kenyan Price Control

Long before independence in 1963, the Kenyan government regulated the prices of basic foodstuffs. To combat inflation and protect its own popularity, the government decided in the early 1970s to extend controls to nonfood consumer goods, construction materials, and agricultural inputs. Prices of a list of manufactured items and some services were frozen and could not be increased without ministerial approval.

The effect was to politicize price decisions, with ministers reluctant to be seen to be raising prices. They thus deferred decisions by insisting on complex supporting documentation and postponing face-to-face talks. Even then they delayed approval and implementation until the applicant gained the support of the Office of the President.

By the early 1980s this policy had become a drag on the industrial sector. Several enterprises forced to hold down prices became a burden on the credit system. Profitability was reduced, diminishing incentives for expansion and new investment. Industries, such as dry-cell batteries, which had invested ahead of domestic demand and exported the surplus, were discouraged by an artificially stimulated domestic demand from exporting. Price controls came to retard industrial development.

Indian Regulation of Industry

Until 1984, India's industrial policy was based on government controls designed to direct investment to priority industries and backward regions, and to conserve scarce resources by striking a balance between domestic supply and demand. The key regulatory mechanism was restriction on entry into various industries. The private sector was barred from setting up new capacity in certain subsectors, large industrial groups and foreign companies were barred from others, and their success with applications in other subsectors was under 25 percent. More than 800 items were reserved for production by small firms.

Control was exercised through industrial licenses, which were required for firms intending to establish new undertakings, to expand capacity substantially, or to manufacture certain new products. Furthermore, site selection for plants had to be approved by central, state, and local governments. Imported capital goods also required official clearance, as did technological or financial collaboration with foreign companies.

Box 4-2: (continued)

This system (including high rejection rates) helped create an industrial structure of high concentration and cost, and often of low technological adaptation and product quality. It was easily manipulated by large companies, which cornered high percentages of licensed capacity by submitting multiple preemptive applications through chains of associate companies. Having beaten off all competition, they then delayed actual creation of new capacity in order to create near monopolies that yielded excessive profits. Indeed, these activities illustrate well the concept of rent seeking referred to in the text. The licensing system also prevented technological and productivity improvements, notably in automobile manufacturing. Reservation of items for small firms often fostered uneconomic capacity and outdated technology and limited economies of scale. The necessity for multiple approvals made project delays and cost overruns inevitable. The negative effects of these controls were demonstrated by a surge of new investment and rapid rises in productivity when licensing was partially liberalized after 1984.

Source: Kenya: Gray (1991); India: Behara and Chandrasekhar (1988, pp. 142-47) and World Bank (1987, p.116).

This type of re-thinking about the state is, moreover, occurring across the political spectrum; it is not just a product of the "conservative revolution." Thus, writing from a socialist perspective Dearlove and White (1987, p.2) concluded that "The case for the market and against the state is now widely accepted, not the least among socialist economists."[3] Certainly it has been accepted by the peoples of Eastern Europe, who, in the countries that have held multi-party elections, appear to have opted for a rapid transition from a planned to a market economy. Underlying this was a large momentum for reforms to create a market-based system from within the Communist parties of these countries.

So, both markets and states can fail. The activities of each are associated with both costs and benefits. Ideological approaches—left or

---

3. See this and various other issues of the *IDS Bulletin* for documentation of the re-examination by socialist writers of the role of the state in developing countries.

right—to what ought to be the respective sizes of the public and private sectors are unlikely to be very sensitive to these complications, and hence are unlikely to strike the best balance. Indeed, ideology is apt to impose large burdens on society. Posing the question of the desirable role of the state in general terms is actually unhelpful. Rather, this is something that has to be worked out against the specific history, socioeconomic system, ethical values, and goals of the country in question.

Within such a context, the pragmatic solution is then a matter of determining the comparative advantages of the private and public sectors, and of balancing the costs against the benefits of any possible intervention. The strategy suggested here is one of neutrality, of a case-by-case consideration of the relative merits of any action or inaction. This approach is powerfully reinforced by modern economic theory, which stresses the difficulties of deriving general policy prescriptions in a second-best world, and the desirability of carefully balancing the merits of voluntary (chiefly market) and coercive (chiefly governmental) decision mechanisms.

Having thus declared our neutrality and advocated a comparative advantage or cost-benefit strategy in defining the state's role, a great deal is still left to be settled. For one thing, the boundary between the public and private sectors is often unclear. Some enterprises are jointly owned. The state may subsidize private products and the private sector may provide services normally associated with the public sector, for example, in education and health. Politicians, even public servants, may engage in business activities, and business people may depend on favors provided by the state. Similarly, disentangling market and state failures is often difficult, for the deficiencies of both sectors often work together and reinforce one another.

At a different level, the cost-benefit approach will rarely be capable of being effected literally, as if it were a project evaluation. There will be too many uncertainties, too many factors that cannot be quantified or expressed in monetary values. Rather, the approach is suggested as a logical framework for thinking about the issue. As such, much is left for questions of judgment, and for disagreements about goals and how best to achieve them. What is likely to emerge is that the nature of state interventions is likely to be more important than their extent, particularly whether policies work through and with market forces or against them. The comparative advantage line of approach suggested here is taken further in a more concrete context in chapter 7, which examines the respective roles of the state and of markets in agricultural and industrial adaptation.

Other Strategy Choices

In its approach toward economic adaptation a government is confronted with a number of further strategic choices. Three key choices are discussed here, but they are not of equal status. The first decision is about whether the government's approach to the tasks of adjustment is to be a positive, passive, or defensive one. A decision on this has a logical priority because it will influence second-order strategy decisions.

The next decision concerns the view the government takes about integration into the world system of trade and payments. This can be dramatized as a choice between open-economy or closed-economy policies. A decision on the open versus closed question will in turn strongly influence the third-order strategy choices discussed later about (a) the nature of supportive policy interventions, and (b) the role of macroeconomic management. However, the open versus closed choice will also feed back into the first-order choice between positive and other policy stances.

Positive, Passive, or Defensive?

The question whether the stance of policies toward adaptation should be positive, passive, or defensive appears to answer itself in favor of a positive approach, but we should first clarify what these options mean. A **positive** strategy is one where the state plays an active role in facilitating adjustment, seeking to anticipate problems and opportunities and to put in place policy measures that will induce or support the appropriate changes in economic and institutional structures. It is a stance that embraces change as positively desirable and that seeks to maximize benefits from it. It sounds like "A Good Thing," but it is apt to be uncomfortable and can imply a strong state willing to ride roughshod over tradition, noneconomic values, and opposition.

The **passive** alternative can be defined as an approach that still recognizes the desirability of adaptation, but is more content to allow this to happen automatically in response to economic pressures and incentives, and with a less active role for the state. It implies a more reactive, gradual pace of change, in which the country is unlikely to be among those taking advantage of the opportunities created by it.

Finally, the **defensive** sounds like an unattractive stance, but it characterizes the position of a large number of governments, in industrial and developing countries alike, which suggests that it too has its virtues. Perhaps the key characteristic of a defensive approach is that it seeks to reduce the social costs of change by slowing it down and/or by compensating the losers. Protecting industries that have lost their ability to compete is a typical example of a defensive policy. Faced with the threat of unemployment in these industries, the defensive response is to protect the jobs for as long as possible, as against a positive stance of labor retraining and relocation. Since structural adjustment can result in social costs, in particular it can threaten some of the poor, it is entirely appropriate that governments should try to minimize such risks, so the defensive stance is perhaps not such a bad thing after all.

The question posed here is how much weight the government wishes to accord to economic adaptation among its policy objectives, given the possible tradeoffs between this and other goals. Similar types of issue are raised with regard to the desire to safeguard the environment. The smaller the relative weight the government apportions to the adjustment objective, the more inclined it will be to adopt a defensive stance.

The great weakness of such a stance, however, is that it may prevent the economy from adapting to the extent, and at the speed, needed to prosper in the modern world. Thus, over time it may seriously undermine the economic base necessary for the state to be in a position to safeguard the living standards of the disadvantaged. The United Kingdom in the 1960s and 1970s provides a good example of an industrial country adopting an essentially defensive stance and losing economically as a result.

As this brief discussion shows, the respective merits of the positive, passive, and defensive stances are not as obvious as they may at first have seemed. Each has its strengths and weaknesses. As with so many policy choices, it is a matter of striking the right balance, in this case between the advantages and costs of change. A positive approach appears the most likely to facilitate successful adaptation, but this needs to be tempered by concern to minimize the economic and social costs that adaptation will cause. However, a government's choice between these stances will be intimately connected with the choice between an open-and a closed-economy approach.

Open- Versus Closed-Economy Strategies

For reasons that will become clear shortly, autarchy, or self-sufficiency, is not a serious option for SLICs, whether governments desire it or not, but open-economy policies can facilitate trade and capital flows, and closed-economy policies can discourage such integration into the world economy. What then is meant by open- or closed-economy strategies?

Meaning and significance. So far as trade is concerned, the meaning relates particularly to the profit incentives between producing for domestic or external markets created by policy decisions about exchange rates, protection, exchange controls, and the like. Closed-economy policies will tip incentives in the direction of producing for the home market, emphasizing import-substitution, food self-sufficiency, and perhaps nontradables, while open-economy policies will create greater profitability in producing for export. One can identify two versions of an open-economy strategy: (a) one that skews price incentives positively in favor of exports, for example, through export subsidies; and (b) one that aims for approximate price neutrality between production for domestic and production for external markets. Strictly speaking, the second, being neutral, ought not to be labeled open economy at all. The fact is, however, that most governments have policies that are skewed in favor of the domestic market, chiefly through protection, so the effect of adopting price-neutral policies is to move incentives in favor of greater openness. We shall call this price-neutral openness.

The essence of price-neutral openness is that it adopts international competitiveness as the key test of efficiency, which is close to saying that it allows comparative advantage to determine the composition of imports and exports. Import substitution may still be a policy objective, but only substitution by producers who need little protection or no more than that provided by the transport and other costs involved in importing from abroad. This is a clearly different policy stance from the protectionism normally associated with an import substitution approach.

An open-economy strategy thus has strong implications for tariff and other forms of protectionist policies. More positively, since it seeks to remove any profitability bias against production for export, such a strategy also has strong implications for exchange rate policies, requiring these to be maintained at levels that ensure export profitability. In principle, competitive exchange rates also promote import substitution, but in practice import substitution has commonly been associated with a reluctance to use the exchange rate as an active policy instrument, with the result being currency overvaluation. In addition, there are implications for domestic macroeconomic management, in that executing an open-economy strategy successfully is difficult in the face of rapid inflation and other major imbalances at home, particularly because inflation tends to erode the effects of exchange rate policies.

The openness discussed thus far has been related to imports and exports or to the current account of the balance of payments. However, one can argue that the full advantages of openness will be secured only by adopting a thorough-going approach extended to the capital account that involves the liberalization of payments, an absence of controls over capital movements in and out of the country, and policies to encourage foreign investment. That, however, is a separate set of choices, for combining an open trading policy with the maintenance of exchange controls and discrimination in favor of local investors is quite possible.

However the open-closed balance is struck, this is clearly a decision with important ramifications for many aspects of economic life. For one thing, it will make a major difference to the very process of structural change: to the distribution of production between tradables and nontradables, and among tradables between exports and imports; to the relative intensities of resource use, because exports, import substitutes, and nontradables each have their own production characteristics; and to the distribution of income through the effects on factor and product markets. In manufacturing it will greatly affect the pattern and pace of industrialization. In agriculture it will affect the allocation of land and other resources between foodstuffs and export crops. As already implied, it will also have a large influence on the type of economic policies that the government can successfully pursue and on the degree of freedom the government possesses in choosing its policies. Indeed, one of the continuing attractions to governments of a closed-economy strategy is that it gives them a greater degree of discretionary action.

The Advantages and Disadvantages. The decision about the open-closed balance is thus a major one, arguably "the big one." Perhaps because of this, the advantages and disadvantages of these alternatives remain the subject of fierce controversy. During the 1960s and beyond, governments tended to be more influenced by those advocating relatively closed-economy approaches, particularly import-substituting industrialization behind protective barriers. During the last decade or so, the balance of opinion, at least among development economists, has swung toward the virtues of an open economy. The arguments can be organized around the different types of effect the two approaches are expected to have.

The first effect of the strategy choice is on the **efficiency of resource use**. We have already seen that an open-economy standpoint uses international competitiveness as the key test of efficiency. Thus, the argument here is that bringing incentives for domestic resource use closer to international opportunity costs favors a more efficient, that is, more productive, use of resources. The greater degree of competition domestic producers face will increase the pressures on them to keep their costs down to an unavoidable minimum (what is known as X-efficiency) to maintain the quality of their products and to respond to changing technologies and user preferences. Negatively, a protective import-substitution stance is liable to result in fewer competitive pressures; greater industrial concentration; and probably a less responsive, more "frozen" productive structure (recall the earlier argument that competition promotes economic flexibility). Moreover, a protection-based, import-substitution strategy is likely to be accompanied by bribery and other directly unproductive profit seeking activities of the kind described in box 4-3, as domestic producers use their skills and other resources to lobby politicians and officials for tariffs, import restrictions, and monopoly power—resources that could otherwise be put to productive use—and this is likely to be particularly important if the strategy is accompanied by the use of exchange controls.[4] The static efficiency argument, then, is one that goes in favor of openness, although it is intrinsically difficult to measure these benefits and economists disagree about how large they are likely to be.

The arguments are better balanced when we turn to more dynamic considerations relating to **innovation and investment**. On the one hand, one can argue that full involvement in competitive international markets brings the benefits of learning-by-doing and acquaintance with up-to-date production techniques, which suggests that openness is associated with more rapid innovation and productivity growth. Counter arguments point to the beneficial effects of having a substantial locally-based capital goods sector meeting local needs (even if it needs protection), as against the negative effect on local know-how of dependence on imported capital goods and technologies, and to the experience of countries like Japan, which achieved its present day technological leadership on the basis of highly protective policies.

Efficiency, technologies, and innovation are all affected by one of the most important features of modern production: economies of large-scale production. This brings us to a crucial point, for we must bear in mind that this study is primarily concerned with small, low-income countries with economies in a poor position to take advantage of scale economies. The argument here is that the only way producers in a small economy can take advantage of scale economies is by selling on world markets, because their domestic markets are far too small for this purpose. This is even argued within the industrial coun-

---

4. On rent seeking and other directly unproductive profit seeking activities (DUPs) see Bhagwati 1982; Bhagwati and Srinivasan 1983; Kreuger 1974; Tullock 1980. Bhagwati and Srinivasan place DUPs into two categories: those triggered by policy actions and those seeking to influence policy. They may also be divided into legal (lobbying) and illegal (bribery) activities. DUPs may, however, occur wholly within the private sector and be unrelated to state policy interventions.

Box 4-3: Rent Seeking and Directly Unproductive Profit Seeking

Economic analysis has traditionally focused on productive activity, but economists are now taking a closer look at unproductive activity. The terms rent seeking and directly unproductive profit seeking (DUP) have become common parlance in economics. While unproductive activities arise in the private sector, economists have been particularly interested in those arising from policy interventions of various kinds.

Rent seeking embraces lobbying (and often corrupt) activities designed to capture the rents—that is, scarcity premiums—that are attached to licenses and quotas. Typical examples include the lobbies that aim to secure import licenses in trade and payment regimes that rely, in many developing countries, on exchange in import controls. Another example is lobbies seeking the lucrative premiums generally associated with industrial licenses. Such rent seeking is common in industrial countries too, for example, in the allocation of import quotas and in public purchasing.

The concept of directly unproductive profit seeking is more comprehensive. It includes all ways of making a profit by undertaking activities that are directly unproductive. That is, DUP activities yield income or profit, but do not produce goods or services directly or indirectly. They are economic activities that produce zero output while using up real resources.

Thus, DUP activities include rent seeking, but they also cover activities where resources are devoted to encouraging policy interventions that create rents, for example, lobbying efforts can be directed at creating or sustaining quota or tariff protection against imports. DUP also embraces activities designed to make money by evading policies, for instance, tariff evasion yields pecuniary income by exploiting the difference between legal (tariff-paying) imports and illegal (tariff-evading) imports.

In an analysis of the costs and benefits of policy intervention, these activities cannot be ignored. Economists have therefore begun to explore ways of estimating the costs of DUP. The conventional costs of protection are estimated by calculating the loss that arises from distorting the prices consumers and producers face. These so-called deadweight losses, however, are now supplemented by estimates of significantly larger losses from associated rent seeking and DUP.

One way rent-seeking costs have been estimated is by assuming that license premiums would lead to equivalent resource costs by lobbyists. For India, the resulting cost estimates for 1964 were roughly 7 percent of GNP; for Turkey, they were 15 percent of GNP in 1968. These estimates may be on the high side, because administered allocations may be routine, and thus reduce the real resources profitably diverted to seeking the licenses, but the full effects on economies with extensive interventions and associated DUP activities are likely to elude quantification. What is remarkable is that even the quantifiable part of the costs is so large.

Source: World Bank (1987, box 4.7).

tries of the European Community.[5] How much more true must it be of producers in SLICs. Consider the illustrative figures in table 4-1, which provides alternative measures of economic size for four country groupings.

This shows first how misleading measuring country size in terms of population is likely to be. By this measure the averages of the large low-income countries are huge compared to the other groupings, yet their average GDP is little more than a sixth of that of the average OECD economy. If we are concerned with total market size, GDP is a better indicator. If we are concerned with the market for consumer

Table 4-1: Indicators of Average Domestic Market Size, 1988

Country type	Population (millions) (1)	GDP (2)	Private consumption (3)	Private consumption of manufactures[a] (4)	Gross investment (5)
Small low-income countries[b]	14.1	3.3	2.5	0.6	0.6
Large low-income countries[b]	400.7	129.4	81.6	20.3	35.7
Middle-income countries	20.2	46.8	27.6	8.8	11.7
Industrial market economies	41.7	755.7	461.0	182.6	166.3

a. An approximate indicator only, calculated from the share of private consumption devoted to clothing and footwear, and other consumption as a rough proxy for expenditures on manufactures.

b. Small and large are defined as countries with populations of below and above 50 million. The large low-income country group consists of Bangladesh, China, India, Indonesia, Nigeria, and Pakistan.

Source: World Bank (1990b, tables 3, 9, 10, and 26).

---

5. The desire for European producers to be able to take greater advantage of scale economies was, for example, one of the reasons for the move to fuller integration of the European Community economies in 1992. Thus, the OECD (1983, p.63) writes of firms in medium-sized industrial economies being squeezed out because of their inability to achieve scale economies, and Pratten (1988) sees the 1992 integration as an important means of achieving greater scale economies through longer lines of production and increasing returns to R&D expenditures.

goods then the averages for total private consumption in column (3) are more useful. If we want to focus particularly on industrial consumer goods—for it is in manufacturing that scale economies are most important—then column (4) is the most useful. If, finally, we are concerned with the size of the domestic market for capital goods, viewing it as influencing the ability of domestic capital goods industries to achieve scale economies, then the column (5) averages are the most pertinent.

By all measures except population, the results are dramatic for the SLICs: their average GDPs, consumer good markets, and capital good markets are tiny by comparison with the other three groupings, but especially by comparison with an average industrial economy. No refinement of the figures would significantly alter this result. For industrial consumer goods and investment goods, their markets are around one-three-hundredth of the size of the average industrial economy, yet even in these latter economies there is concern that some producers are unable to take full advantage of scale economies!

Of course, scale economies vary in importance for different types of output. They do not matter much for quite a few agricultural products and services. Even within industry, their importance varies. They are relatively insignificant for a variety of consumer goods, such as clothing, food processing, and jewelry. They are far more important in the production of most consumer durables and capital goods: steel and other metals, motor vehicles, chemicals, and so on. Taking manufacturing as a whole, however, scale economies are large and it is therefore worth quoting the conclusion of a thorough survey of the importance of this for developing countries (Sutcliffe 1971, pp.226):

> There is a large number of industries . . . in which economies of scale can be obtained up to levels of output greatly in excess of those in most underdeveloped countries, and also greatly in excess of current consumption of those commodities in the same countries.

As noted in chapter 2 it is because of such factors that country size has a strong influence on the importance of international trade relative to domestic economic activity (see Perkins and Syrquin 1989). What this suggests is that the costs to a small low-income economy of adopting a closed-economy strategy are liable to be large. These include effectively foreclosing the possibility of sustained industrialization. Thus, the scale economy argument is strongly in favor of openness.

However, there is an ambiguity for policy about this conclusion. If the local market is as minuscule as table 4-1 indicates, the question that arises is how can local manufacturers ever get started and grow to a size that would enable them to compete with the giants of the industrial world? As we shall see in chapter 7, the importance of scale economies can be used as an argument in favor of protecting local industry until it has moved far enough down its cost curve that it no longer needs protection. This runs against the general thrust of open-economy policies.

Its impact on the **balance of payments** is another dimension of openness to which much weight should be attached given the importance of the foreign exchange constraint. Generalizing about whether an open or closed approach will be best for the balance of payments is difficult. In principle, policies that emphasize self-sufficiency and import substitution can, by reducing import needs, leave the balance of payments in a satisfactory condition, but in practice they tend not to. This is chiefly because closed-economy approaches are commonly (but needlessly) associated with overvalued exchange rates and price biases in favor of the production of nontradables. Many countries have also found that "import-substituting" industries save little or no foreign exchange, as they are often heavily dependent on imported production inputs, investment, and skills.

If openness is indeed associated with maintaining more competitive and flexible exchange rates, there must be a general presumption that it will produce better balance of payments results by giving greater encouragement to exporters and placing more importance on international competitiveness. It may also do better by providing a more favorable environment for inflows of foreign capital, although here too the contrary argument could also be made: that protecting local industry will encourage foreign investors anxious to maintain a foothold in the local market. While on balance the balance of payments consideration points in favor of openness, the validity of this conclusion depends on the conditions that are assumed to exist in the rest of the world.

One should be able to settle disagreements about the advantages and disadvantages of open and closed approaches by reference to the evidence. The balance of the arguments presented favors openness, and from this we could hypothesize that developing countries that have pursued open-economy policies have achieved superior economic performance. Considerable effort has been devoted to testing the relationship between export performance and economic growth, with results that mostly conclude that export performance does indeed have an important bearing on growth. Thus, Ram (1987) found positive associations between export performance and growth using both cross-country and individual-country tests. Moreover, he found that the influence of exports on growth has been increasing over time, and in more recent years has been of particular importance to low-income countries. A study of determinants of long-term growth in fifty-five countries during 1970-85 by Otani and Villanueva (1990) similarly found export performance to be the single most important explanatory variable. Moschos (1989) also found a positive association between exports and growth that was particularly strong among less advanced developing countries, and a test confined to African countries (Fosu 1990) found the same positive correlation, although his test was confined to 1960-80. The evidence also indicates that countries pursuing export-led strategies have enjoyed more rapid structural transformation and faster productivity growth (see the literature reviewed by de Melo and Robinson, 1990, Part II).

However, the results of the empirical work have not been completely conclusive, much of it dependent on how the problem is defined and tested. Researchers have also undertaken in-depth studies of the experiences of specific countries, but these too are inconclusive (see, in particular, Bhagwati 1978; Krueger 1987; Taylor 1988b). Nevertheless, the results of most empirical studies are clearly in favor of openness.

Interpretation of the evidence is complicated by the large amount of attention that has been paid to a small number of success stories of openness, particularly the "Four Little Tigers" of Southeast Asia: Hong Kong, Singapore, the Republic of Korea, and Taiwan. These and a limited number of other newly industrializing countries in Asia and Latin America have achieved major success is expanding their exports of manufactures, chiefly to industrial country markets, and have undergone remarkable economic transformations as a result of this success. Even here, however, economists can not agree about the interpretation that should be placed on their records and the inferences that might be drawn for other developing countries: are they exemplars or special cases?

For one thing, most of the success stories do not provide pure examples of an open-economy approach, as (with the exception of Hong Kong) the have also pursued protectionist, import substitution policies. They also benefited from relative ease of access to U.S. markets and from being the first developing countries to achieve major success with industrial exports. Those who would emulate them face a harder task. Notwithstanding these qualifications, however, each of these countries has pursued relatively open strategies, with governments supportive of private enterprise and willing to allow the composition of exports and imports to be broadly determined by comparative advantage. Each has benefited enormously as a result, so the onus of proof is now upon those who argue that the Little Tigers should not serve as exemplars for the rest of the developing world (for a brief discussion of these cases see Campbell's 1988 review of three recent books on these countries and chapter 6, box 6-3).

Conclusions. What conclusions should we draw on this crucial question of openness? Here the decision to focus this study on SLICs is crucial, for it is the economies of scale argument, dramatized in table 4-1, that is decisive. Leaving aside all the other advantages and disadvantages, governments of such countries seem to have little choice but to adopt an open-economy stance, especially if they are to develop the industrial base that we have identified as one of the key enabling determinants of flexibility. Among writers on this subject, Lance Taylor (1988a, p.67, emphasis added) is one of the most skeptical about the virtues of openness, but even he has concluded that: "In a smaller nation, more openness becomes inevitable. The constraint may bind at a population of (say) 20 million - *surely no less.*"

As suggested earlier, expressing economic size in terms of population is not ideal, but if we bear in mind that the average population of the countries we are concentrating on here is about 14 million (table

4-1) and that they have below average per capita incomes compared
with the developing countries as a whole, the implication of Taylor's
conclusion supports our own: that for the SLIC the costs of a closed-
economy approach will be prohibitive.[6] The case is further strengthened if one agrees that such an approach is also likely to worsen balance of payments performance, and hence the foreign exchange constraint; and reduce competitive pressures for efficiency. It was for reasons such as these that we concluded that openness was favorable to
economic flexibility. Moreover, the balance of the evidence supports
the view that openness has a favorable effect on GDP growth.

If we conclude in favor of an open-economy strategy, however, do
we mean price-neutral openness or one in which prices are positively
skewed in favor of producing exports? There is one theoretical and
various pragmatic reasons for preferring price neutrality. The theoretical argument takes us back to efficiency considerations. Price incentives skewed in favor of exports are no less distortions—departures
from the perfectly competitive case—than incentives skewed in favor
of the home market. The logic of static efficiency arguments points
generally in favor of price neutrality, although the recent literature on
trade policy contains some sophisticated arguments in favor of export
subsidies, and we suggest shortly the desirability of policies that favor
nontraditional exports.

The pragmatic considerations have mainly to do with the risks and
potential costs of overexposure to a sometimes hostile and unstable
world economy. Indeed, as suggested earlier, decisions about openness
must also be influenced by expectations about the global economic
environment. How fast and how smoothly will the world economy and
trade be growing? What is the likely trend in the world prices of the
country's exports and in its terms of trade? What is the probability that
exports, particularly of manufactures, will hit against protective barriers, in other words, how good will the SLICs' market access be? How
realistic is the expectation that greater openness will increase access to
world capital markets and private investment, and on what terms is any

---

6. It seems likely that Taylor primarily had Latin American economies in mind in
this comment. In 1988 they had a per capita GNP of US$1,840. A country at this level
with a population of 20 million would thus have had a GNP of around US$37.0
billion, compared to the average for SLICs shown in table 4-1 of US$3.3 billion.

capital likely to be made available? The gains to be had from openness will largely depend on the answers to these questions. The risk that world conditions will be unfavorable argues against going too far in promoting openness.

A further precautionary consideration, is food security. Although exaggeration is easy, there is a case for policies that give some preference to producers of strategic foodstuffs. Unfavorable weather can easily lead to a sudden harvest failure, perhaps for a succession of years, and depending wholly on international markets to make good the shortfall is risky. World prices may be too high at that time, or imported supplies slow or unreliable. What is needed is a judicious blend of policies that protect the economy from the worst risks of exposure to world economic conditions and those that open the economy up to trade and investment opportunities.

Thus, we can conclude in favor of a pragmatic, price-neutral, open-economy strategy as the one most conducive to economic adaptability, and, therefore, to long-run development. However, what do we now say about the choice between the positive, passive, and defensive postures with which we began this discussion of strategies? In part, this choice relates to the view we take of comparative advantage. In trade theory this is a static concept, that refers to countries' relative efficiencies in producing tradable goods. This type of static efficiency view implicitly favors a passive stance: in the absence of major distortions price signals will automatically lead countries to export those goods to which they are best suited.

Comparative advantages change over time, however, and in recent decades have done so particularly rapidly. In this situation those countries that succeed in anticipating changes in demand and production conditions so as to "get there first" in world markets stand to make large gains. Such a dynamic view of comparative advantage points more toward a positive policy stance, with governments (among others) taking a conscious view about how their countries' competitive advantages are likely to change in future. One of the lessons that can be learned from the Asian Tigers is the importance of taking a positive view of dynamic comparative advantage: encouraging resource shifts in favor of industries facing dynamic world markets that generate technological and other externalities at home, and not being too protective of those industries that face decline.

For the SLICs, these considerations draw special attention to the desirability of governments' reviewing their future dependence on traditional primary product exports. We can do no better here than to quote the conclusions of two recent studies, first, an IMF study of export diversification, although the authors do follow this passage with some qualifications (Bond and Milne 1987, p.120):

> Recent empirical evidence shows that export diversification into manufactured goods can raise the trend path of export earnings since: (1) the net barter terms of trade for primary products, as a group, compared with manufactures has deteriorated over the long term; (2) the income elasticity of demand is higher for manufactured goods than for primary goods, in aggregate - implying that, for a given increase in trading partners' income, the increase in demand for manufactured imports will be greater than for primary products; (3) the demand for imports of primary products is less price elastic than that for manufactures - so that an increase in the total volume of primary exports will lead to a greater reduction in export price than would an equivalent increase in that of manufactured exports; (4) in the short run, supply elasticity for primary products is less than that of manufactured goods; and (5) export diversification may help circumvent barriers to trade.

The second quote is the conclusion of a study of the development experiences of commodity-exporting countries (Lewis 1989, p. 1596):

> While the evidence is clear that is possible to achieve high levels of economic development and diversification while remaining well above `normal' in dependence on primary exports, it is also clear that successful countries actively promoted the diversification of their economies, in both the primary and manufacturing sectors. Furthermore, there are no cases of relatively high income countries that have reached that stage by continued emphasis on only one primary export.

Here too caution is needed, however. To urge diversification is not the same as advocating neglect of traditional commodity export industries. In the short and medium terms, it may well be to the benefit of countries with an established comparative advantage in certain primary products to continue to invest in them, if only because they have few immediate alternatives. This is particularly likely to be beneficial when the country's output of the commodities in question is small relative to total world supplies, so that it can expand output without much risk of depressing export prices. For the longer term, however, it must also be looking for the types of diversification described above.

Thus, the strategy suggested here is a positive one of diversification away from traditional primary products. Openness is imposed by smallness. The task is to treat this as an opportunity, not an encumbrance; to get the most out of openness.

The Policy Environment

We concluded our earlier discussion of the state's role in fostering the adaptive economy by urging a cost-benefit approach, allowing the respective roles of the public and private sectors to be determined by their comparative efficiencies in undertaking various tasks. In the light of this and the above discussion of alternative strategies, we might now pose the further strategic question, how active should the state be in fostering the positive, open-economy strategy as against leaving it to market forces?

On the one hand, the state could confine itself to a rather limited set of interventions, encouraging structural adaptation by providing information, advice, and infrastructure, and a legal and financial framework that will foster the desired pattern of change; and seeking to reduce or manage the conflicts of interest that arise and to ameliorate the costs of adjustment. It could, however, go well beyond such a minimalist role by adopting specific changes in economic structure as objectives of policy; actively manipulating price and other incentives in favor of such changes; and directly participating in the change as regulator, employer, and investor. Returning to the Little Tigers of Southeast Asia, Hong Kong could be cited as a successful example of the minimalist position and Korea as an example of a state that has pursued very active strategies. Japan should be added as an earlier Asian example of successful state activism.

Lurking beneath these questions is whether we follow the neoclassical tradition of faith in the workings of the market or adopt the more skeptical view of the structuralists. However, one of the effects of present-day interest in structural adjustment has been to erode the previously rather sharp division between the neoclassical and structuralist schools. As Hirschman (1982, pp. 181-82)) has wryly noted, there is a real sense in which we are all structuralists now:

> Whereas the Latin American economists who had first advanced the structuralist thesis were in general identified with the Left, it now appears that

structuralist theorizing is a game at which all kinds of believers in the need for 'fundamental' reform can and do play.

A more positive way of putting this is to suggest that the literature generally agrees that adjustment is likely to be particularly costly in output, employment, and welfare foregone unless appropriate policy responses are put in place. Large disagreements remain about what "appropriate policies" should consist of, but even here the literature agrees that a blend of market- and nonmarket-oriented policies is required, with the disagreements being about where the balance should be struck. Disagreements remain on the extent to which developing economies differ from the industrial countries in the degree of market failure and the state's efficacy as an economic agent, but saying that markets are a prime mechanism of adjustment and structural change is not very controversial, any more than arguing for the importance of an active policy response. In that case, how should decisionmakers determine where to strike this balance?

In support of an activist state one can argue that market forces work only gradually and incrementally—shifting resources at the margin—whereas structural transformation involves more radical, more discontinuous change that, therefore, will require the state's guiding hand. The argument has particular force under current conditions, when governments are under much pressure to achieve rapid adjustment in the face of pressing foreign exchange and savings constraints. Short-run price elasticities are often small, initially producing only limited responses to changed price signals. In addition, market imperfections are liable to be substantial in SLICs, and this adds to the reasons for the state playing a substantial role in promoting economic adaptation.

This set of arguments should not be overdone, however. While markets do work incrementally, the same is often also true of governments faced with many uncertainties, inertia, and the larger risks of radical change (for a description and espousal of incremental government decisionmaking see Braybrooke and Lindblom 1963). Moreover, a succession of market-induced incremental changes can surprisingly quickly add up to a major structural shift. After all, the patterns of transformation experienced earlier in their histories by the now industrialized countries were, in a rough and ready way, brought about by market forces, although admittedly at often high social costs.

We suggested earlier that the choice between open- and closed-economy strategies would itself have a strong bearing on the state's policy stance. Krueger (1978, p.284) has put the point forcefully:

> An export-promotion strategy appears to place certain kinds of constraints upon economic policy and its implementation; those constraints, in turn, limit the magnitude and duration of policy mistakes and also tend to force policies to work through pricing, rather than quantitative, interventions ... a growth strategy oriented toward exports entails the development of policies that make markets and incentives function better.

The crucial decision is to allow resources and the pattern of production to be shaped largely by international norms of competitive efficiency, for that is very close to a decision to permit resources to be allocated through market signals, as against controls and planning. While in such countries as Korea the state has been active and interventionist, the interventions have generally worked through markets, influencing prices and incentives. Finding a country that has successfully pursued an open-economy strategy on the basis of central planning and extensive nonmarket controls would be hard. It is also the case that few governments could be relied upon to match Korea's toughness in dealing with the pleadings of industrialists and other special interest groups.[7]

In particular, an open strategy demands that the real exchange rate should always be such as to keep the country's exports and import substitutes highly competitive. More generally, the constraints imposed by international competition may be thought of as imposing relative consistency of policy upon governments: they have fewer degrees of freedom and the costs of policy mistakes bite harder and more quickly. Such consistency is likely to give policies the credibility they need if they are to offer reliable bases for decisions about the future.

---

7. Roemer (1988, pp. 9-10) sees the Korean state as "hard" in the sense of being the opposite of the "soft" states that characterize many low-income countries. It exerted strong controls over subsidized credit, promoted large firms at the expense of small, and then pressured the large to meet export targets. In doing so it was willing to see nonperformers go into bankruptcy, with resulting job losses, and was strong enough politically to get away with it.

The case for policies that work with and through market forces can be augmented by returning to another consideration: the importance for economic adaptation of the supply of entrepreneurship. If we extend a little further the lessons that might be learned from the more activist of the Asian Tigers, it is the relationships between the state and private enterprise that are supportive rather than confrontational. While economists understand little about what determines the supply of entrepreneurship, the belief that the policy environment can do much to stimulate or repress potential entrepreneurs is reasonable: taxation and other policies affecting profits, the extent of regulation of business, access to finance (affected by the extent of the government's own deficit financing), the provision of public infrastructure and training in support of private investments, and so on.

The policy environment matters in other ways too. The government's ability to maintain reasonable macroeconomic stability—the avoidance of rapid inflation, large-scale deflationary unemployment, and large balance of payments deficits—is of crucial importance. It provides the steadiness and predictability of incentives that encourage the long-term investment and price responsiveness that are so important to the adaptive economy. Rapid inflation is particularly destructive in this context, overshadowing price signals and increasing the riskiness of investment and innovation.

We thus conclude in favor of an activist state that prefers to work with and through market forces rather than against them, that establishes supportive relationships with the private sector, and that places a large weight on avoiding major macroeconomic disturbances. In common with our earlier conclusion in favor of a broadly price-neutral open-economy strategy, this conclusion is very general. How might it be translated into specific policy changes? To begin an answer to this we turn in Chapter 5 to consider the policy instruments that are available to government in its pursuit of the adaptive economy, while Chapter 7 takes the theme further in connection with industrial policy.

Summary

This chapter has been taken up with some of the more basic, or strategic, policy issues that arise in the context of adjustment. It started by considering the large issue of the desirable role of the state in the pursuit of flexibility in relation to market mechanisms. We pointed out the existence of a well-established body of theory on ways in which markets fail, but that economists have recently been paying more attention to state failures or to the costs of policy interventions. We suggested a neutral, pragmatic solution of allowing the comparative advantages of the private and public sectors to determine the balance, setting the costs against the benefits of any potential policy intervention. Application of this comparative advantage rule would leave much scope for judgment and disagreement, but we suggested that its application would show that the nature of state interventions was likely to be more important than their extent.

We then turned to consider other fundamental strategy choices that decisionmakers must consider when approaching the design of adjustment policies. The first was between positive, passive or defensive approaches, where we suggested that the choice was less wholly in favor of a positive stance than might have been presumed, that it was a matter of striking a reasonable balance between the advantages and costs of change, but that a relatively positive approach was the most likely to facilitate successful adaptation.

However, we suggested that the "big" choice was between relatively open- or closed-economy policies; a choice that would have many ramifications for the economy's structure. Our conclusion in favor of price-neutral openness was strongly influenced by the small size of the SLIC economies, but we took balance of payments and efficiency considerations into account as well as the evidence on the effects of openness of economic performance. However, we qualified this conclusion in important ways, particularly by urging the need for those dependent on primary products to diversify their exports into goods and services facing markets with higher income elasticities of demand.

A final strategic question concerned whether or not the state should take on an activist role in regard to markets in pursuit of the adaptive economy. We noted that the prior choice between open- or closed-economy approaches to policy had a strong bearing on this, and concluded for an activist state that works with and through market forces rather than against them, that establishes supportive relationships with the private sector, and that places a large weight on avoiding major macroeconomic disturbances.

A Note on Further Reading: see the end of chapter 5.

5

CHOOSING POLICIES

So far we have written of policies in a rather abstract way. The task of this chapter is to describe more specifically the policies available to governments seeking to promote flexibility. It then sets out principles that policymakers can use when designing policy packages, before concluding with some cautionary words.

Policy Instruments

We begin by surveying the range of policy instruments that can be brought to bear on the adjustment task and the various ways in which these are likely to impinge upon an economy, before providing a more specific illustration of a typical adjustment policy package.

A Policy Matrix

For the time being we shall focus our discussion on the policy matrix presented in table 5-1. The column heads are the various target variables or policy objectives identified in chapter 3 as being of particular importance for economic flexibility, with the addition in column (10) of the objective of minimizing the social (poverty-worsening) costs of structural change. The row heads are categories of government policies that might contribute to achieving these objectives, or in other ways impinge upon them. The matrix itself indicates when the policy is likely to have a positive (P) or negative (N) effect on the various target variables. Absence of an entry implies that the policy is not expected to make much difference one way or the other.

The target variables have already been explained. We saw in chapter 3 how efficient factor and product markets assisted flexibility by increasing resource mobilities, price elasticities, and economic responsiveness generally. Similarly with the others listed in the table, we have shown that each of these contribute in varying ways and degrees to an economy's capacity to adjust. The policy instruments listed in the left-

Table 5-1: Illustrations of Target Variables and Policy Instruments for Economic Flexibility

Policy Instrument	Example of use	Factor market efficiency (1)	Efficiency of product markets (2)	Enterprise and innovation (3)	Saving (4)	Private investment (5)	Financial deepening (6)	Industrialization (7)	Domestic macro-stability (8)	Balance of payments (9)	Social cost minimization (10)
Fiscal Policies											
Taxation	a. Investment incentives	N	—	P	—	P	—	P	—	—	—
	b. Tariff protection	—	N	P	—	—	—	P	—	—	—
	c. Taxation of fuel	—	P	—	—	—	—	N	N	P	N
Expenditures	d. Food subsidies	—	N	—	—	—	—	—	—	N	P
	e. Economic services	—	P	—	—	P	—	—	N	P	—
	f. Social services	P	—	—	—	—	—	—	—	—	P
	g. Infrastructure (maintenance & investment)	P	P	—	—	P	—	P	—	—	—
'Fiscal stance'	h. Increased taxes (spending cuts)	—	—	N	P	—	P	—	P	P	N
	i. Domestic borrowing (non bank)	N	—	—	—	—	N	—	P	P	—
	j. External borrowing	—	—	—	—	P	—	—	P	P/N	—
Financial-monetary											
Interest rates	k. Decontrol	P	—	—	—	—	P	—	—	—	—
Domestic credit control	l. Manipulation of bank reserve ratios	—	—	—	—	N	N	—	P	P	—
Exchange rate	m. Devaluation	P	P	—	—	—	—	—	P/N	P	N
Administrative controls											
Exchange controls	n. Restriction on capital outflows	—	—	—	N	P	—	—	—	P	—

Table 5-1 (continued)

Policy Instrument	Example of use	Factor market efficiency (1)	Efficiency of product markets (2)	Enterprise and innovation (3)	Saving (4)	Private investment (5)	Financial deepening (6)	Industrialization (7)	Domestic macro-stability (8)	Balance of payments (9)	Social cost minimization (10)
Price and wage controls	o. Minimum wage laws	N	—	—	N	N	—	N	—	—	P
	p. Increased agricultural producer prices	—	P	—	—	—	—	—	—	P	P/N
Legislative & institutional											
Relating to firms	q. Company law; anti-monopoly law; patent law	—	P	P/N	—	—	—	P	—	—	—
Relating to land tenure	r. Break-up of large estates	—	P/N	P	—	—	—	—	—	—	P
Public enterprises	s. Development banks	P/N	—	P	—	P	P	P	P	P	—
Information services	t. Economic indicators	P	P	P	—	P	—	—	P	P	P

P = Positive effect
N = Negative effect
— = No effect

hand column are rather broad types of actions that governments may take, with more specific illustrations provided in the next column. These too are intended to be self-explanatory, but note that by fiscal stance we mean the extent to which the overall balance of government revenues and expenditures has a stimulating or dampening effect on economic activity.

To illustrate the use of the table, see line c., the taxation of fuel. This subject arose as a controversial policy issue for many developing countries following the very large increases in petroleum prices in 1973-74 and 1979-80: should governments also raise their taxation of this product? Assuming the country to be an oil importer, the effect of an increase in such taxation would be to dampen demand for the product, which indicates a positive effect on the balance of payments. More controversially, we have also marked it as having a favorable effect on the efficiency of product markets because the tax increase would result in a final price for fuel that more accurately reflected its scarcity value, and because it could improve incentives for developing locally produced alternatives to imported oil. However, we have suggested that this measure would tend to discourage industrialization, because fuel and other energy costs are particularly important inputs to the manufacturing sector. In addition it would impose social costs, as higher fuel prices would affect the costs to poor people of transport, cooking, and lighting (kerosene).

To pick out another illustration, line i. suggests that domestic government borrowing from outside the banking system would have positive effects on macroeconomic stability and the balance of payments situation by providing a source of deficit financing that is not expansionary, and is thus unlikely to generate inflationary or payments pressures. It further assists the future condition of the balance of payments by providing an alternative to borrowing abroad and accumulating hard currency debt servicing obligations. At the same time, it may impair financial deepening by absorbing credit that could otherwise strengthen financial institutions dealing with the private sector and, for related reasons, may reduce the efficiency of the market for capital. The table raises a few other points worthy of discussion.

Comments on the Table

Note first how rare it is for a policy action to be an unmixed blessing. Both the examples just provided were expected to have some negative effects, which is typical of almost all the policy instruments listed in table 5-1. In some cases a policy instrument may have both positive and negative effects on the same target variable. Thus, in cell m.8 a currency devaluation may both improve macroeconomic stability by absorbing excess domestic demand and worsen it by raising prices. Similarly, in cell p.10 increased agricultural producer prices may reduce the welfare of the urban poor by raising food prices while raising the welfare of the rural poor by increasing their incomes.

This mixture of effects underscores the complexity of economic policymaking. With few exceptions, policy choices entail carefully weighing their potential positive and negative effects; a task made more difficult by the large uncertainties that generally surround policymaking. Rarely do all the indicators point to the same conclusion or can one even be confident about what the precise effects of a policy change will be. Beware the peddler of simplistic, single-policy solutions!

Table 5-1 does provide some exceptions, however. The provision of economic and informational services (lines e. and t.) is recorded as having only positive effects, as is the maintenance and creation of the basic infrastructure: roads, communications, power, and so on. These are expected to improve the efficiency of factor and product markets, incentives for private investment, industrialization, and the balance of payments, among others. However, this points to one of the weaknesses of the matrix format, it does not address the efficiency with which these services are provided or their quality. Often inefficiency rules: extension services that do not reach farmers with practical advice; roads built for political reasons with little consideration of economic costs and benefits; statistics that are tardy and unreliable. In such cases, measures to improve the quality of public sector services are themselves to be considered part of the adjustment effort, given the large benefits expected to arise from the proper provision of these services.

A further point is the tendency for tensions between the pursuit of improved flexibility and the minimization of social costs. Food subsidies are an obvious example. On the one hand, they are likely to reduce the efficiency of product markets by distorting relative prices, and to threaten domestic macroeconomic stability and the balance of payments through the large strains they place upon the government's budget. On the other hand, they will benefit those families that are net consumers of the subsidized foods. Their removal can scarcely fail to hurt some disadvantaged groups, even though blanket subsidies are a notoriously inefficient way of aiding poverty groups. Similar tensions exist with the enforcement of statutory minimum wages: they reduce the labor market's efficiency and discourage corporate saving and investment and industrialization, but they protect the living standards of some unskilled workers and their dependants who would otherwise be at risk.

Another limitation of the policy matrix format is that all target variables and policy instruments appear to be given equal importance, which is far from the reality. The difficulty is that relative importance can be determined only in the context of a concrete country situation. All are potentially very important.

In addition, the examples of use presented in the second column provide only a small sample of the total number of specific policy instruments available to governments, and some of the examples provided are aggregations. Thus increased taxes (line h.) leaves unsettled crucial questions about what kinds of taxes might be raised and what rate structures they might be given. The entry for tariff protection similarly fails to draw attention to the crucial question of the structure of protection, which can have a major influence on the pattern of industrialization, and which typically discriminates against domestic production of producer goods. If the table were to list all the specific policy instruments that the government might use in its adjustment effort, and all the decisions that present themselves concerning how these policies should be designed and executed, it would be a long list indeed.

Finally, many of the instrument-target relationships postulated in the table rely heavily on this writer's understanding of how economies and policies work and could be disputed. More to the point, the relationships will vary from one national economy to another. The matrix is intended to be illustrative, not to lay down universal truths. To give but one more example, line r. is rather positive about the effects of land reforms that break up large estates. Some country experiences support that view, others do not. A country's socioeconomic structures, its factor proportions, and the literacy of its peasantry would all have a crucial bearing upon the outcome, as would the precise design of the land reform and the way it was implemented. This reminds us once again of the complexity of policy choices and of the importance of designing policies to match an economy's specific characteristics .

A Comprehensive Adjustment Program

Merely being reminded of the complexities inherent in making policy choices does not necessarily help the decisionmaker understand the specifics of adjustment policies. Thus, this section presents in more concrete terms what a comprehensive adjustment program might look like. First, let us imagine a country that has hitherto been pursuing an inward-looking strategy and has been run along command lines, with extensive controls on prices, wages, interest rates, imports, and capital movements; widespread recourse to parallel markets; and extensive state participation in the productive system. We assume further that the country has serious balance of payments and inflationary difficulties and an overvalued exchange rate. Per capita incomes have been static or declining for some time and savings and investment have fallen to low levels. Taken together, these circumstances are perhaps rather extreme, but many countries have confronted such difficulties. What package of policies might be brought to bear to improve this economy's performance and flexibility?

In such a situation many of the required actions would be the negative ones of loosening existing controls to free up markets, reintegrate the parallel economy with the formal one, and improve incentives. Thus, the government would consider abolishing or modifying many of its controls, although it would have to tread carefully in doing so, particularly when liberalizing imports in the face of balance of payments difficulties. Also in the interests of greater competition and more efficient markets, it would need to reduce the general level of protection and anomalous discrepancies in the extent of protection enjoyed by different producers. It might also consider introducing legislation aimed at preventing the misuse of monopoly power.

These actions would go some way to improve price incentives for economic flexibility, but the government might wish to go further. In the face of an overvalued currency, it might engineer a devaluation; one that stuck, in the sense of not being undone by inflation. Devaluation would increase the incentive to produce tradable goods rather than nontradables. Where the government controlled the domestic prices received by exporters, or taxed these heavily, it might review its policies to ensure improved producer incentives, an action that would be made easier to reconcile with avoiding large budget deficits by the devaluation.

Bearing in mind the importance of the overall macroeconomic environment, the government would also wish to ensure against large budget deficits, for they would add more inflationary fuel, weaken the balance of payments, and frustrate the private sector's need for credit by preempting much of it for government. As macroeconomic stabilization would also involve keeping the total expansion of credit under careful control, this gives added importance to avoiding large public sector borrowing requirements.

To reduce budget deficits, the government would therefore need to look hard at both its tax revenues and its expenditures. It would want to consider new taxes that would not adversely affect incentives and ways to improve the collection of existing taxes. In the face of overall budgetary stringency, it would also need to look hard at its spending pattern to reorient it toward those economic and social services likely to promote economic recovery; at ways to improve the quality of these services; and at ways to increase the productivity of its investment decisions, for example, through improved project evaluation procedures. Given the wastefulness of rent-seeking activities and of corruption, it could consider ways to reduce the discretionary powers of tax and regulatory bodies, for it is by exercising such discretion that public servants assert bureaucratic control over private activities, creating delays and eliciting bribes. The government would also want to take a critical look at the economic and financial performance of its public enterprises, rehabilitating, privatizing, or closing down the poor performers. Among other institutional initiatives, it might consider promoting the creation of new financial institutions and instituting land reform.

The above description contains an element of caricature, not least for the simplifying assumptions that underlie it. We have, for example, ignored constraints on the government's ability to formulate and implement such a wide range of policies in a short period, although in practice such constraints would probably stand in the way of a comprehensive program. We have left aside the objective of minimizing the social costs of the adjustment, as well as more overtly political constraints on action: the likely reaction of powerful interest groups to some of the changes and the effects of these on support for the government. We have said little about the desirable sequencing of the program, or about likely interactions between its components. The package described is also ultra-orthodox. However, caricatures can also illuminate, and the purpose of these paragraphs has been to provide more of a flavor of what specific policies may be involved in an adjustment program.

Principles of Policy

In the face of the real world's complexities, policymakers need guiding principles to aid them in their work. Our next task, therefore, is to examine what might be learnt from writings on the theory of economic policy and past experience that will throw further light on the design of policies for economic adaptation.

Targets and Instruments

We can start by looking a little more closely at the notions of target variables and instrument variables. Beginning with target variables, table 5-1 has already made explicit an important feature of the policy problem: governments pursue multiple objectives. They wish to improve market efficiency, stimulate saving and investment, industrialize, and so on. However, these are only subsidiary, or instrumental, objectives selected because they will contribute to economic adaptation. Adaptation, in turn, will not be the government's only economic objective: the growth, and perhaps redistribution, of income are likely to be among the others. Nor will the government's objectives be confined to the economic sphere. This then brings us to the concept of multiple and hierarchical objectives.

Turning to policy instruments, these can be defined as means controlled by the government of changing the economy's behavior. For some purposes distinguishing among policies according to whether their effects are direct or indirect is useful. The provision of a road or the administration of rent controls are examples of instruments that operate directly on economic life. Policy instruments that operate indirectly include attempts to discourage the consumption of luxuries by imposing heavy taxes on them or to encourage job creation by holding down wages. Indirect measures, by and large, work through markets and have their effects by altering pecuniary incentives; direct measures often work independently of market forces. Thus, one of the features of the type of adjustment program described earlier is that it represented a shift from direct to indirect measures. To introduce a further type of distinction, differentiating between instruments that have an impact on a wide range of economic variables—the interest rate is an example—and those which are much narrower in their incidence—an import duty or an export license, for example—can also sometimes be useful.

The language of targets and instruments is at the center of much of the theory of economic policy that is particularly associated with Tinbergen (1955, 1967). He developed a mathematical model of policy formation that concluded that a government must use at least as many policy instruments as the number of its target variables. Of course, this result reflected the nature of the model he used, and the need for exact equality between the number of instruments and targets falls away on alternative formulations. The Tinbergen rule nonetheless serves as a warning against trying to use just one or a few policy measures to achieve a multiplicity of objectives. Since adjustment programs normally possess a number of target variables, they also need to employ a range of policies. Once again, we are warned against single-instrument solutions. To put the matter another way, if political or administrative constraints prevent a government from implementing more than a small number of policy changes, then it can only expect to achieve a limited number of objectives.

Tradeoffs and Adjustment Costs

The pursuit of multiple objectives brings with it the potential for conflicts among them. This brings in the idea of tradeoffs, when progress toward one objective can be achieved only at the cost of a retreat from another objective. This is the classic guns versus butter choice: restricting bank credit may ease inflationary pressures, but at the cost of reduced investment; protecting those who depend for their livelihood on some declining industry is liable to preserve existing production and employment structures, retarding necessary structural adaptation; protecting the poor with state welfare programs may generate destabilizing fiscal deficits (see box 5-1). The rate at which one objective must be sacrificed in order to promote another is the rate of tradeoff between them. Tradeoffs are pervasive and further complicate the policy problem.

In principle, governments can resolve choices between conflicting objectives according to their place in the hierarchy, or according to the weight that the government places upon each of them. Unfortunately, though, governments are rarely precise or consistent about their objectives, which leaves the resolution of tradeoffs a hit or miss affair. Political scientists are inclined to say that in such situations political logic dominates economic logic.

Although table 5-1 indicates a potentially large number of possible tradeoffs, we focused on the tension between the pursuit of adjustment and the minimization of its costs. The idea of tradeoffs in adjustment policies is intimately connected with the concept of adjustment costs, which are discussed later.

Choosing among Instruments

Given the multiplicity of policy instruments available and the tradeoffs between them, the further question arises of how governments should choose among them so as to select those that combine efficiency and equity at minimum cost. This too is a neglected topic, but we can suggest a number of criteria. At least the following questions need to be asked about an instrument in evaluating its likely cost-effectiveness:

Box 5-1. Policy Tradeoffs in Sri Lanka

After independence Sri Lanka pursued vigorous welfare policies, such as free education and health and the subsidization of foodstuffs, but at a growing cost to public finances. In 1977 the incoming government faced a situation of excess demand in the economy, with a potentially large budget deficit and the threat of unprecedented levels of inflation. The situation was exacerbated by the impact of the political cycle on fiscal commitments, and by heavy dependence on imports of the key staple, rice, creating shortages of import capacity for other sectors of the economy. The government saw itself faced with a choice between cutting the budget deficit and reallocating expenditures in favor of investment (a course supported by the international agencies and other aid donors) or maintaining the hitherto unquestioned social programs.

The government opted for cuts in welfare expenditure that it hoped would be made politically more palatable by the expected gain in employment and long-term growth to raise welfare standards. In January 1978, the food ration program was restricted to poor households and in September 1979 a targeted food stamp program was introduced. Government outlay on food subsidies consequently fell from the very onerous level of 5.0 percent of GDP in 1978 to 1.3 percent in 1984. There were also cuts in state funding of education and health, which went down from 3.5 percent of GDP in 1978 to 3.0 percent in 1984.

Some of the worst fears and best hopes from these changes were fulfilled. Investment increased, based largely on the externally-financed public investment program. Imports grew rapidly, with a change in composition toward intermediate goods, and agricultural production expanded in response to the decontrol of prices. The rate of growth of GDP doubled, averaging 6 percent between 1978-84, and the unemployment rate declined from 14.7 percent in 1978-79 to 11.7 percent in 1981-82.

At the same time, the switch to targeted welfare programs was only partially successful (see box 9-5). Nutritional standards of the poorest 40 percent declined as the real value of the subsidy was eroded by inflation and income disparities increased. Given a sudden increase in school enrollments in 1977-78, per student real expenditures fell significantly, while restricted recurrent expenditure in the health sector created difficulties in maintaining buildings, equipment, and personnel standards. The quality of service in both sectors deteriorated.

Sources: Cornia, Jolly, and Stewart (1988, UNICEF essay); Jayawardena, Maasland, and Radakrishnan (1987).

- How large will the response of the target variables be to a given change in the instrument variable?
- How probable is it that the expected results will actually be achieved, and how quickly will they occur?
- Does the policy act upon the causes of the problem at which it is directed?
- What are the resource costs of the policy?
- Is the policy selective in its application and flexible over time?
- What indirect economic effects will the instrument have and will they be positive or negative?
- In what ways is the public likely to react to the policy?
- What will be the sociopolitical effects?

In the case of the magnitude of response, the general rule is to choose the more powerful instrument. This is partly because SLICs typically face large adjustment problems, and therefore need powerful instruments if they are to be able to cope. In addition, public acceptability of a policy change is liable to depend upon the extent to which it represents a break with the past, with incremental changes usually tolerated better than large discontinuous shifts. To achieve a given change in a target variable, a powerful instrument needs a smaller change than a weak instrument, thus raising its acceptability.

Regarding the probability and speed of results, the advice to choose the faster acting policies (other things being equal) needs no elaboration, but the probability dimension needs a little more explanation. An important influence on the probability that a measure will achieve the desired results will be the ease with which it can be implemented. This is something to be considered at the planning stage, for the more difficult the execution the smaller the probability of success. A second, more obvious, influence has to do with the state of knowledge: we may have only a hazy idea what the effects of a policy change will be, but greater ignorance may surround some instruments than others. On the whole, this consideration also favors an incremental approach, for we are likely to have a better idea of the consequences of modifying an existing instrument—raising the income tax rate, for example—than of introducing a new one.

Most policy measures are responses to perceived problems. Hence, we can ask whether a particular measure acts on the causes of the problem, or whether it merely suppress its symptoms or compensates for them. The general rule is to choose policies that act upon causes. That may not always be practical, however, as in the case of problems emanating from the world economy. A government faced with a rise in import prices can do little about the causes and has to respond indirectly by measures that will boost foreign exchange earnings and reduce the demand for imports. Similarly, acting upon causes will not always be desirable. For example, a firm may possess monopoly power stemming from its superior ability to reap economies of scale. In this case, the government will be wise not to discourage large-scale production, but should instead erect safeguards against abuse of the resulting market power. Nevertheless, the rule of thumb is to choose measures that act on causes. It is a rule that derives more from common sense than economic theory, but there is a close affinity between it and the so-called assignment rule developed in the theory of trade policy (see box 5-2).

The next of our efficiency criteria concerns the resource costs that the instrument's deployment will necessitate, with the general principle being to adopt the least-cost alternative. Almost all policies involve some use of government revenues, but some much more than others: a targeted food subsidy is likely to be far more cost-effective than a general subsidy, for example. Policies may impose resource costs on the private sector too, which may be minor and overt, as in the costs to employers of administering a pay-as-you-earn income tax system, or large and covert. Examples of the latter might include the running of a large budget deficit that is financed by borrowing from the banks and that crowds out the credit needs of private producers.

The notion of rent seeking can also be relevant here in that some types of policies, particularly those that involve licensing and regulating, create scarcity rents that can bring large profits to those who can take advantage of them. Import licenses are an obvious example. Because the potential profits are large, aspirants to these rents will use skills and other resources (often including bribes) to take advantage of these opportunities. These efforts will thus absorb economic resources in a way that is unproductive in that it does not add to total output, which will impose an opportunity cost on the economy. In this sense, one may think of a shift, say, from exchange controls to an active ex-

---

Box 5-2. Attending to Causes: The Assignment Rule

Many policy interventions are directed at remedying the effects of some type of market failure or distortion in the economy. The assignment rule states that the best results will be achieved from that policy intervention that most directly addresses the original source of failure. This is because policy measures tend to introduce distortions of their own, and the further removed they are from acting on the original cause of the failure the more likely they are to introduce new distortions. Although this is a general proposition, it has mainly been taken up in the trade policy literature because so many arguments for protection do not address failures resulting from the characteristics of international trade as such, but are intended to compensate for other types of distortion.

Take the well-known infant industry argument for protection. This argues that, where a newly created firm's costs are above internationally competitive levels because it has yet to take advantage of learning-by-doing, it should be protected because after a while its costs will fall and it will then be able to compete. To be strictly valid, however, this argument has to show why this learning period cannot be anticipated and privately financed. To do so, it is likely to be necessary to invoke some imperfection in the capital market. If indeed some such imperfection does exist, application of the assignment rule would result in adoption of policies that would directly address the capital market imperfection. A protective tariff is likely to be a suboptimal policy choice, since it can only compensate for the capital market deficiency at the cost of introducing new distortions: creating protection for established firms in the same industry that cannot justify it, affecting relative prices and the distribution of resources between them, adversely affecting incentives to export through its influence on domestic cost levels and the exchange rate, and so on.

For a lucid exposition of the assignment rule, see Corden (1974, pp.28-31).

---

change rate policy as a shift in the direction of greater cost-effectiveness in that it is likely to reduce rent seeking, replacing licensing by price rationing. Policy interventions may also impose costs by creating distortions in the economy, reducing the efficiency of resource use. Strictly, this is not a resource cost, but its effect is the same: to reduce output.

Our next efficiency criterion is an instrument's selectivity and flexibility. By selectivity we mean the extent to which its effects are confined to furthering whatever objective the government is using it for. By and large, selectivity is to be preferred because it reduces the risk of unintended effects and improves the predictability of the outcome. In the case of flexibility, this refers to the ease with which an instrument can be varied or discontinued over time. Some instruments are less flexible than others: altering tax rates in either direction is fairly easy; minimum wage regulations are flexible in only one direction; reforming institutions is notoriously slow work and frequent changes are likely to be undesirable. Thus other things being equal, the general rules are to choose instruments that hit their targets in a selective manner and to prefer those that are flexible.

This brings us to the indirect economic effects. The discussion of table 5-1 stressed the complexity of the ways in which policies interact with the economy. Even the most selective policies are liable to have effects on variables additional to the intended ones. An advantage of quantified modeling approaches to policy formation is that they increase our ability to predict these indirect effects. A positive effect is one that promotes some policy objective in addition to the one that was the chief motive for introducing the measure; a negative indirect effect is one that conflicts with other objectives. The general rule is obvious: choose the instrument that maximizes the excess (or minimizes the shortfall) of favorable over unfavorable indirect effects.

The importance of how the public reacts to a policy measure was already raised in chapter 3 when discussing the delicate balance that governments must strike between flexibility and continuity in their policies. How the public reacts can render policies impotent as people learn to anticipate them and to protect themselves from their effects. One example is the ways in which parallel markets spring up when governments try to control prices at below market levels, sometimes entirely evading the government's intentions. If reactions to a policy are to be supportive rather than subversive, that policy must be credible: people must believe it can work and that the government will enforce it and persist with it. For example, Edwards (1987. p.27) in discussing import liberalization, stresses the importance of credibility. He points out that this, in turn, will be influenced by the internal consistency of the government's policies, for if they are inconsistent people will see that the contradictions cannot be sustained. He cites Argentina as an example. Thus, the rule is that policymakers should take an explicit view of the ways in which people are likely to react to alternative instruments, choose those least likely to spark a hostile or countervailing response, and be concerned with the credibility of those instruments.

Finally, let us consider sociopolitical effects. Many policies are chosen—or rejected—on noneconomic grounds, often reasonably so as ministers have more to worry about than just economic problems. In any case, any sharp distinction between economic and noneconomic effects is rather arbitrary and often breaks down in practice, although it is convenient for our present purposes. Expressed generally, the rule is to choose those instruments that will bring the maximum sociopolitical benefits or the minimum sociopolitical costs, all judged in terms of the society's values and the government's objectives.

Circumstances will decide what type of consideration should be brought in under this heading. Among the most pervasive we can include (a) the expected popularity, or otherwise, of the measure (closely related to the previous question of public response); (b) its effect, if any, on the country's relationships with the rest of the world (might an export subsidy provoke retaliation, for example?); and (c) its effects on personal liberty (sometimes used as an argument against direct controls).

Dealing with Uncertainty

How should policymakers deal with the uncertainty that, to varying degrees, accompanies virtually all policy decisions? Information about the nature of the problem, the policy options available, and the ways in which they will affect the economy is always incomplete, often seriously so. Should those responsible for policy adopt a wait and see stance in the hope that better information will be available in the future? Or should they disregard the uncertainties on the grounds that decisions have to be made in any case?

For example, chapter 2 mentioned the future need for national economies to adapt to global warming. However, little is known about the speed, incidence, and effects of global warming, so how should analysts go about the task of providing advice on how policies should respond to the greenhouse effect? A further set of rules can be suggested for decisionmaking (for some elaboration of these and an application to the case of national rural development policy response to global warming see Killick 1991a) under conditions of major uncertainty, namely that policymakers should:

- **Anticipate adaptive inadequacies.** As suggested in the previous chapter, a good deal of adaptation occurs naturally or automatically. One task, then, is to seek to anticipate areas in which automatic adaptation will fall short of what is necessary. To a substantial extent this will boil down to trying to forecast what market failures are likely to occur, for adaptation will not occur if markets do not generate the price signals that would induce it.

- **Seek to reduce uncertainty.** Since the risk of policy mistakes and wasted resources is large when decisions have to be made in conditions of ignorance, investing resources in information gathering, research, and dissemination promises to yield high economic returns.

- **Create incentives and aid responsiveness.** The acquisition of information needs to be translated into incentives for people to adapt their behavior in desired directions and into measures that will maximize the extent to which they respond to these incentives.

- **Avoid planning on extreme outcomes, the adoption of inflexible policies, and premature high-cost commitments.** We have already discussed inflexibility, and the desirability of avoiding high-cost commitments for as long as possible when new information may enforce a change of direction. Avoiding planning on extreme outcomes steers policymakers toward getting as far as they can with assigning probabilities to the range of possibilities and choosing measures that will provide satisfactory outcomes for the most probable range of possibilities. It generally steers them away from planning on the basis of worst-possible cases and from do-nothing responses.

- **Search for multiple or versatile responses.** When highly uncertain about what the future holds and what form a problem might take, policymakers should not put all their eggs in one basket. They need to bring a variety of measures into play, especially ones that are not highly specific to narrowly defined circumstances, in the hope that at least some of them will eventually prove effective.

Policies as a System

While the various criteria and rules presented in the last two sections and the earlier discussion of targets and instruments can provide useful guidance to policymakers, there is also the danger that while each policy decision may be carefully considered, this individual consideration may divert attention from the overall design and coherence of policies when taken together.

This would be unfortunate for a number of reasons. For one thing, our earlier discussion of policy strategy implied that an overall view should be taken because a strategy is an internally coherent package of measures applied consistently over time. Another reason relates to the complexity of the ways in which a policy change will work its way through the economic system. An implication of this is that a given policy change may necessitate changes in other policies as the economy responds. Thus, an increase in administered interest rates designed to encourage the financialization of private saving (and thus to contribute to higher investment levels) may at the same time discourage investment in sectors to which the government attaches priority— say export industries—indicating a need to re-examine the taxation of profits or to introduce other policy changes that could counter the unwanted reduction in investment.

A further reason for taking an overall view has to do with the incoherence that can easily result from a succession of ad hoc decisions, even though each decision may in itself have been carefully considered. Thus, analyses of countries' patterns of industrial protection commonly find very large variations in the levels of protection given to different industries; variations that cannot be rationalized in terms of economic priorities. The most common reason for this incoherence is that governments often take decisions about protection in response to individual requests for relief. Unless an unusually strong and clearly defined set of guidelines governing such matters exists, the end result is a series of decisions that do not add up to a consistent whole. If they are to have maximum effect, policies need to be mutually reinforcing. Thus, a currency devaluation may make little lasting difference to the balance of payments unless other policies back it up. Other examples include the need for close coordination of fiscal and monetary policies so that, for example, a tightening of fiscal policies is not undone by expansionary credit policies. At a more microeconomic level is the desirability of coordinating agricultural pricing policies with the provision of extension and marketing services. Figure 5-1 provides one view of key interconnections based on the World Bank's experiences.

Another closely related reason for looking at economic policies as a system is the importance of the sequence in which policies are introduced, even though economics does not yet have very much to say on this subject. The issue of sequencing has arisen, for example, in controversies about the timing of trade liberalization (see box 5-3). Even though liberalization can be seen as part of an effort to strengthen a country's trading position, its premature introduction can undermine the process by sparking an import-led payments crisis. This is but one of a number of policy areas in which introducing measures in the right order is important, even though in practice governments often have only imperfect control over the order in which things get done.

So although each policy decision must be carefully considered, part of this consideration must be to see how it fits into the overall design of the government's economic policies: is it consistent with, and helpful to, other policies? Does its effectiveness depend upon making additional supportive policy changes? Is it likely to set up reactions in the economy that necessitate further policy decisions? Is this the right point in the sequence for the policy to be introduced?

Implementation and Sustainability

To our efficiency criteria for the selection of policies we could have added another: is the policy likely to be implemented successfully and sustained over time? A decision to adopt some policy is often the easy part of the process. It then has to be executed in ways that preserve the policymakers' intentions. Its success is also likely to depend on whether the government will persist with it over time, after opposition to it has had the chance to emerge and to organize.

Although we treat them separately, strong connections exist between implementation and sustainability. Thus, a weak government is likely neither to implement well nor to persist in the face of opposi-

Figure 5.1: The Interaction of Adjustment Policies

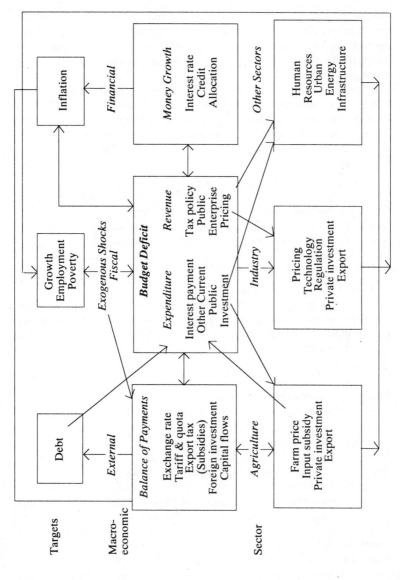

Source: World Bank (1988a, p.34).

Box 5-3. Sequencing Trade Liberalization

Authors do not agree on the sequencing of trade liberalization, although all agree that the best solution depends upon country situations and that the approach should be flexible. There is, nevertheless, substantial support for the view that liberalization should follow a four-stage timetable:

• *Stage 1: Stabilization*

This is likely to include a large nominal devaluation, with complementary tight fiscal and monetary policies to counter inflation, intended to increase the profitability of exporting and discourage imports. These policies will need to be maintained during subsequent phases, though for countries with low inflation and realistic exchange rates only minor subsequent currency depreciations should be needed.

• *Stage 2: Liberalization of domestic factor markets*

The principal elements of this phase may include lifting wage controls to liberalize the labor market; financial sector reforms to strengthen the credit market, to ensure adequate investment and working capital for export expansion, to prevent import-competing firms that become "unprotected" from excessive domestic borrowing if this would jeopardize the financial system; removal of investment controls; and reduction of price controls.

• *Stage 3: Import liberalization*

This may take two steps. The first could consist of removing quantitative import restrictions and replacing them with a rationalized tariff system that reduced the extremes in tariff rates. The second step could involve reducing tariffs by cutting the highest tariffs first and others later.

• *Stage 4: Relaxation of controls over capital movements*

This type of sequencing is not without its disadvantages, including political ones. Waiting until the first two stages have been completed may give lobbies opposed to import liberalization time to organize, although the time involved in the sequence may also provide opportunities for countervailing exporting lobbies to emerge and become organized. In any case, the economic consequences of neglecting the order in which changes should be introduced—or of getting it wrong—can be large. Thus import liberalization without first going through stages 1 and 2 will risk creating a balance of payments crisis, for an overvalued currency and domestic price level will make imports cheap, and the potential for exporting and import-substitution created by devaluation will not be fully realized if factor markets remain highly imperfect.

Similarly, relaxation of capital controls must await the other measures. If not, high domestic interest rates and the need for investment by exporters may suck in foreign capital, push up the real exchange rate, and create a recession in tradable goods industries. Premature liberalization of exchange controls may also accelerate capital flight. Both will undermine trade liberalization.

Sources: Edwards (1987); Mussa (1987); Wolf (1986).

tion. The prospects for both will also be influenced by the circumstances in which the policy was decided on in the first place. If, for instance, it is an action taken reluctantly in crisis conditions or is forced on an unwilling government as a condition for an international credit, the odds against sustained execution are poor. Nonetheless, it seems preferable to treat them separately. Implementation is conventionally (although dangerously) regarded as being more of a bureaucratic, administrative matter—the domain of the civil service—that may prevent a decision being given practical effect, distort the intended results, or entirely negate it. Sustainability is seen as belonging more in the political domain, relating to the possibility that a measure will be abandoned or reversed.

Dealing first with implementation, difficulties of two types can arise: those charged with executing a policy may be simply unable to cope with the informational and administrative demands that it creates; or those responsible for, or influential in, the administration of a measure may deliberately set out to thwart the policymakers' intentions because they see their interests as threatened by it or for other reasons do not agree with it. Both are illustrated in box 5-4, which describes attempts at land reform in the Philippines.

In the first category, there are many examples: expenditure taxes too complicated to enforce properly; comprehensive price controls that require vast amounts of information and much scarce manpower to administer and enforce; industrial safety laws that require an unrealistically large inspectorate. There are also many examples in the second category: import liberalization that threatens to reduce the income that customs officials can collect through bribery; agricultural services intended to benefit poor, smallholder farmers that are captured by the well-to-do elites; credit institutions intended to encourage small-scale business that channel much of their funds to big business. It is often at the implementation phase that groups or individuals can influence who gains or loses by a measure, so the administrative process can become an arena in which people pursue special interests, with an obvious risk to the policymakers' intentions.

How does one guard against these pitfalls? The most important advice is to avoid a process in which implementation is seen as some-

Box 5-4. The Failure of Land Reform in the Philippines

There have been two attempts at land reform in the Philippines in recent decades in response to widespread rural poverty, large inequalities in land ownership, and militant peasant agitation for agrarian reform. The first was by President Marcos in 1972. The hope was that an effective land reform could be implemented at that time without the constraint of a landlord dominated Congress because the country was under martial law. In the event, even the limited reform that was attempted failed. Landlords took evasive action. Land was divided between relatives. Tenants were evicted or forced to hide their tenant status, frustrating attempts to survey the land and ascertain the number and size of holdings and tenants. The onerous legislation proved beyond the country's administrative capacities. Many of those who eventually received land were forced to sell it because they defaulted on payments, partly due to high prices for landlord monopolized agricultural inputs. Thus, landed interests—well-represented in politics, the police and military, and in the bureaucracy—succeeded in subverting the reform. By 1986 only about 1.5 percent of the intended total area of land had actually been redistributed, and only a little over 3.0 percent of intended beneficiaries had received titles to land.

The efforts of the Aquino government in the late-1980s, although occurring within a democratic constitution, were no less problematic. Despite the large popular support enjoyed by Mrs. Aquino and the commitment of her party to land reform, landed interests repeatedly succeeded in delaying any such measures. It was only after a massacre of protesting peasants marching on the presidential palace that a hastily drafted proposal was introduced. Even this was watered down in the period between the massacre and final draft, postponing the politically difficult issue of private landholdings for a three-year period and allowing landlords time to take evasive action. Despite offers of generous compensation, landlords and their political allies mobilized in opposition. Landlords on the island of Negros formed an armed independence movement. The financial community declared itself concerned and froze all agricultural loans, ostensibly due to uncertainty surrounding the reform legislation. Foreign investors, multinational agribusinesses, and some technocrats also aligned themselves with the anti-reform movement. In consequence, executive order 229 eventually further diluted the program, creating loopholes that look set to render the reform ineffective.

Sources: Canlas, Miranda, and Putzel (1988); Thiesenhusen (1989).

thing separate from, and subsequent to, policy formation and to recognize that the prospects for implementation are intimately connected with the nature of the policy decision itself. In other words, implementation aspects should be explicitly included in deliberations leading to choices between policy alternatives. To leave them as something to be worked out afterwards is to court a choice of policies that will not be successfully executed. However, one can go beyond this general principle to suggest some further rules of thumb, which can be thought of as augmenting the cost-efficiency criteria set out earlier. A policy instrument is most likely to be effective if it meets the following conditions:

- The **objective** it is intended to further should be clearly and precisely specified. The notion of implementation presupposes an agreed yardstick against which we can measure actual results.
- The chosen instrument should be **simple**. By this we mean minimizing the number of agencies, offices, and individuals involved in implementation and the levels of skill needed. The larger the number of people and agencies and the greater the required sophistication, the bigger the risk of delay and distortion. Coordinating the activities of a number of agencies is especially difficult, so the use of multiple agencies should be kept to the unavoidable minimum.
- Administering the policy within an already existing **institutional and bureaucratic framework** and adapting this for the new tasks through training and other provisions is preferable. When this is unfeasible, explicit provision should be made to create whatever special administrative capability the measure calls for.
- Decisionmakers should clearly specify where the **responsibility** lies for putting the policy into effect. It is all too easy to take this for granted and not identify clearly which agency is to carry out the policy.
- Decisionmakers should be aware of the **interests and motives** of those who will be involved in implementation. A measure that cuts against the interests of those who are to carry it out may be doomed unless special care is taken.

This last point may be of particular relevance to adjustment policies because these are likely to include the substitution of market measures for administrative controls and discretionary power. At the least, civil servants are liable to see such changes as reductions of their power and influence. They may well also see them as diminishing their ability to augment their incomes through corruption. In other words, specific difficulties may stand in the way of successfully implementing liberalizing measures. However, once in effect such measures—and the shift from administrative to market measures—will place fewer demands on the public administration: compare the bureaucratic needs of wide-ranging credit controls with those of an active interest rate policy.

Next, what will determine the sustainability of a measure? Probably the most decisive influences will be how the policy affects the public's interests, how the gains and losses are spread across society, and the government's strength compared with other centers of power in society. If the bulk of the population regards itself as having been harmed by the measure, or if the losses are concentrated within powerful groups in society, it will need a determined and resourceful government to persist. This is one of the difficulties of measures heavily indebted countries adopt to avoid debt default: their citizens perceive their own interests as being sacrificed to those of foreign creditors, even though the government may be convinced that avoiding default is in the national interest.

Political institutions and traditions will also affect sustainability. Some observers have suggested that adaptation of the economy requires strong, authoritarian governments. However, the power of a government to implement and gain acceptance of its policies will be strongly influenced by what political scientists call its legitimacy: an acceptance by the general public that it has a proper claim to exercise authority derived from some constitutional or other principle. Authoritarian, often military, governments tend to be short on legitimacy. The evidence on the relationship between regime type and ability to implement major policy reform programs is indecisive. Indeed, whether the type of regime is a key determinant is not clear. (For a survey of the relevant literature see Nelson et al. forthcoming, chapter 1; see also Findlay 1988; Remmer 1986; Sheahan 1980. Unfortunately, much of the literature is confined to Latin American cases). Some dictatorships are weak, some democratic governments are strong, but a government that is in constant fear of being overthrown, governing within a system that does not have deep roots in the public's loyalties, whether or not it is democratically elected is unlikely to win prizes for persisting with unpopular policies.

The circumstances under which a policy is adopted are also likely to be influential. Although this is admittedly more of an untested hypothesis, a reasonable assumption is that policy reforms that have gestated gradually, have been discussed with interested parties and developed within existing institutions, and have been subjected to careful weighing of the advantages and disadvantages stand a better chance of being successfully implemented and sustained than measures hastily put together in response to a crisis. Unfortunately, political realities are such that it often takes a crisis to elicit tough decisions.

A closely related point concerns the government's sense of ownership of the measures in question. In the 1980s many of the adjustment programs adopted by developing countries were initiated by the IMF and World Bank, with governments not uncommonly regarding the measures as having been forced upon them as conditions that had to be satisfied to secure urgently needed loans. In such circumstances, governments are likely to have little sense of ownership, and it is not surprising if they quietly drop (or negate) such measures as soon as they get the chance.[1] Similarly, a government may lose popular support if the public perceives it following policies forced upon it from outside, thereby reducing its legitimacy and the likelihood of sustained implementation. More positively, home-grown reforms stand a better chance of determined execution by the government and may be better tolerated by the public.

Conclusion

The last few pages presented rules of thumb by which to assess the comparative efficiency of alternative policy interventions and safeguard the successful implementation of the measures selected. In view of the complexity of instrument-target interrelationships and the interconnectedness of different policies, we have urged the adoption of a systems approach, with policies viewed as a consistent, mutually supporting package. In doing so, however, we have opened ourselves to the charge of naïveté. Arguably, policymaking processes can never

---

1. The World Bank's 1988 review of its experiences with structural adjustment lending found that program implementation was strongly correlated with the extent to which governments had played a leading role in designing the program, and identified this sense of ownership as a prerequisite for future such lending.

meet this ideal because of the many interest groups that will have an influence on decisions, ministers' needs to balance these and to maintain their own legitimacy, and the uncertainties and instability of political life; in short, because "politics isn't like that". Contrast our model with the following account of actual policymaking in an un-named African country (quoted by Lamb 1987, p.18):

> A consistent and timely response to the deepening crisis was impeded by the fragmentation of information and decision-making. All major decisions . . . are visibly concentrated in the person of the Head of State, but many other decisions are taken in a dispersed, haphazard way throughout the administration . . . What planning has taken place has largely been in a formal bureaucratic sense and rarely linked to what has actually to be done to make what is planned materialize . . . economic priority is granted to short-term political considerations, often in a disconcertingly erratic manner.

Certainly, policymaking in practice tends to be crisis induced, ad hoc, and highly political. Nevertheless, policies will not be fully effective unless they are well designed, and in the end politicians' popularity and security will be strongly influenced by the effectiveness of their economic policies. Thus, economists who advise or influence governments should urge them to look at policies systematically, although economists also need to tailor their advice to political and bureaucratic realities.

Cautionary Words

Lest it be thought that a naively optimistic view of the task is being offered here, some cautions should be entered about both the willingness and ability of the state to employ the available policy instruments so that the economy can achieve the necessary adaptations.

The Nature of the State

The last few paragraphs hinted at tension between how economists have viewed the state as an economic agent and how governments actually behave. Our somewhat naïve view conformed to what has been called the rational actor model of policy formation (the phrase is from Allison's classic 1971 study of the Cuban missile crisis). This sees governments as motivated by a collective desire to optimize social welfare through the careful analysis and anticipation of problems, and the choice of technically optimal policy solutions. Of course, as a citizen the economist knows that the reasons why governments adopt policies and the ways they get chosen are less simple than that, and that there are many constraints acting upon them. Nevertheless, the basic premise of most writings about economic policy is that governments see themselves as promoting the general good of the public by promoting growth and development, trying to ensure that resources are used efficiently, preventing excessive inequalities in the distribution of income, and so on.

Against this basically optimistic view, others have presented less encouraging accounts of the state (see Grindle and Thomas 1989 for a brief account of alternative methods of policy choice). Some view the state as analytically separable from society and as having its own interests: maintaining its own power within society, maximizing its independent freedom of action, and promoting the economic interests of the elites that control or dominate it. Within this orientation there is an influential body of writings on African political systems that describes the state as "patrimonial" (see especially Sandbrook 1985, 1986; Beckman 1988; Jackson and Rosberg 1984). This means a system of personal rule based on communal or ethnic ties. In this view the state becomes penetrated by personalized relations operating to satisfy individual and communal aspirations at the expense of those functions of the state that would more widely be accepted as legitimate. Profits accrue to those who can manipulate the instruments of the state rather than through production, but this creates a self-reinforcing spiral of political and economic decay. Development, and the economic adaptation on which it depends, are frustrated.

From models such as these it is a short step to the positions of those who see the state as downright predatory on the general public and the economy (see Lal 1984; Wellisz and Findlay 1988). In formal terms, this sees the state as using its legal monopoly over the use of violence to maximize the government's revenues or "profits" in the interests of those who control the machinery of state. Or in the starker language of a political analyst (Sandbrook 1985, p.41): "At the nadir of this spiral lies chaos. A fictitious state of armed men detaches itself from society and preys upon a dying economy."

Nor is this view so distant from the Marxist view of politics as a manifestation of class conflict, in which the state's primary function is to perpetuate the economic and political dominance of the capitalist class.

All the views just outlined have in common a denial that governments are principally motivated by a desire to pursue the public interest, or even that they will see it as in their interests to pursue it. To the extent that this denial is valid, it must condition our espousal of the use of public policy to promote adaptation and other economic objectives. Indeed, many of those who belong to the skeptical schools just summarized urge a minimal role for the state, leading to a paradoxical advocacy of the use of the state to change policy in a less statist direction (Kahler 1990).

One can hardly deny that the skeptics have a point. We can all think of countries that one or other of these descriptions fits well. Some readers will no doubt be living in countries where many see the state as an instrument of oppression and economic exploitation, and where people have little confidence that adjustment policies will not be perverted to protect or favor the interests of a minority. At the same time, we should not plunge too deeply into gloom. For one thing, countries do differ a great deal; no single model can cover them all. In some it is difficult to see a way forward other than by revolution. In most the position is less desperate, and in some there is wide support for the government's economic policies. Moreover, many economies do make progress, and the evidence does not support those who argue that its benefits are invariably concentrated on a small elite to the exclusion of the majority (see Bigsten 1983, chapter 5, for a survey of the evidence).

Rather than trying to fit governmental behavior into a single "pure" model of political behavior, it is reasonable to think of policies as an outcome of conflicting motivations, pressures, and interests. Bad governments that run down the economy are apt to be removed and the worst policies and practices do eventually generate counteracting forces. In many countries, the scope for using the state's instrumentalities to promote adjustment is available. What we must learn from the skeptics, however, is that we should not expect too much of governments, and that where a decision whether or not to adopt a policy intervention is fairly evenly balanced their warnings may predispose us to avoid the intervention. By generally shifting decisions away from state planners and toward market mechanisms, the types of policy advocated in this book reflect a degree of skepticism about the state.

Big Problems but Weak Instruments

Continuing in a cautionary mood, we should also be careful about the natural tendency to believe that where a problem exists a solution also exists. The adjustment problems of many SLICs are very severe, while the policies available to their governments are often weak. For reasons outlined in chapter 3, the least developed countries have the least flexible economies. They may also be apt to have governments unwilling or unable to execute rigorous economic policies. A narrow tax base constrains the use of fiscal policies. A shallow financial system inhibits the successful use of monetary policies. The changes in price incentives required in the face of small short-term elasticities may be too large to be politically acceptable. The government and its civil servants may be unable to implement the laws and regulations intended to promote flexibility.

Countries whose economies have already deteriorated—where production is stagnant, living standards declining, savings low, the black market rate is only a fraction of the official exchange rate, other price relativities are also severely distorted, and local industry is propped up by high levels of protection—are likely to face a particular problem of transition. That major changes are needed is obvious and there may be a fairly clear idea of what the desirable end situation should be, but how to get from here to there? Economics is largely silent on this issue, being concerned mainly with marginal changes, not large discontinuities. The problem is partly technical, the design of optimal transition paths, and partly political, the management of the opposition and tensions that the transition is bound to create. The problem is aggravated by the crisis conditions in which policies often have to be devised in such countries, reducing governments' degrees of freedom, making the application of the orderly rules for policy cost-effectiveness and sequencing propounded above far more difficult, and rendering optimization little more than a distant ideal.

In the face of these difficulties governments, however well-intentioned, may simply be unable to cope. The uncertainties and the magnitude of the problems they confront may be disproportionate to the instruments available to them, external financial support may be inadequate, and the quality of their leadership may not be up to sustaining adequate policies through the transition. In the end sheer desperation will throw up radical policy changes, but in some countries things have to get worse before they get better, with all the human suffering that entails.

Summary

This chapter has examined the instruments available to the state when approaching the task of adjustment, and the principles that policymakers can apply when selecting among them. We started by considering the instruments available to governments in pursuing adjustment, how these relate to policy objectives, and how a policy package might be chosen. A target-instrument matrix was presented that illustrated the range of policies that governments might employ and how they might influence the various target variables, and that demonstrated the inherent complexity of designing policies. The existence of multiple objectives also introduced the notion of tradeoffs.

Given the availability of many potential policy instruments, governments need criteria for selecting among them, and we suggested a number of cost-effectiveness rules. Other things being equal, we suggested choosing those policies that:
- Have the most powerful impact on the target variables;
- Are the most likely to succeed and to bring the quickest results;
- Act upon the causes of the problem, whenever appropriate;
- Are selective and flexible;
- Maximize favorable rather than unfavorable indirect economic and sociopolitical effects;
- Are most likely to evoke supportive public responses.

We went on to consider supplementary principles intended (a) to guide decisions that have to be taken in the presence of large uncertainties, (b) to enhance the probability that the chosen policies would be successfully implemented, and stressed the importance of taking an overall view: seeing policies as a whole. We pointed out, however, that a rational actor view of the policymaking process was implicit in our recommendations and contrasted this with more pessimistic views of the state as an economic agent. To the resulting caution that we should not expect too much of the state we added the further caution that in many SLICs the magnitude of the adjustment problems they face is great relative to their technical and political ability to solve them.

A Note on Further Reading for Chapter Four and Five: For text-book treatments of the theory of economic policy see Stiglitz (1986) and Spulber and Horowitz (1976), although neither is written with developing countries in mind. Killick (1981) was an attempt to fill this gap, but is now out of print. Killick (1989) covers some of this ground and develops some of the arguments summarized above, but not in textbook form. Tinbergen (1955, 1967) sets out the theory upon which most later work has been based. Arrow (1987) strongly influenced our approach to policymaking under uncertainty. On implementation see Grindle and Thomas (1989) and Lamb (1987) on the institutional aspects of this topic. The relative sparsity of the literature on principles of policy fortunately does not extend to that dealing with open versus closed economy choices. See Bhagwati (1987) and Krueger (1978) for statements of the open economy case and Taylor (1988a) for a view more favorable to a closed economy approach.

6

USING THE EXCHANGE RATE

It was suggested earlier that the exchange rate is one of the key policy instruments available for promoting structural adaptation. It is time now to explore the uses and limitations of this instrument in more detail.

Exchange Rates and Structural Adaptation: A First Statement

The exchange rate places a value on a unit of a country's currency in terms of the amount of a foreign currency it will buy. It is therefore a price. Like other prices it conveys information and incentives to guide decisions about what to produce and consume. In particular, it determines the relative prices of tradable and nontradable goods.[1] As such, it will likely have a potent influence on the composition of aggregate demand and supply, and hence on the process of structural adaptation. Among policy instruments available to governments, the exchange rate is one of those that has the greatest potential to effect long-term structural change. This helps to explain why exchange rate policies are normally at the center of structural adjustment programs supported by the IMF and World Bank. So too does the severity of the foreign exchange constraint in many developing countries.

Considered as a price, however, the exchange rate has special properties. As it affects many other prices and touches everyone's interests, one could argue that it is the single most important price in the econ-

---

1. Chapter 2 made the point that there are few, if any, pure nontradable goods or services and described tradability as a quality possessed in greater or lesser degree by most products. While it is convenient here to follow the usual course of referring to tradables and nontradables as if they were distinct types of products, bear in mind that the exchange rate has the effect of regulating the relative prices of products that are freely tradable and those that have less of the quality of tradability. Thus, an exchange rate depreciation will favor the former category relative to the latter, but since there is a spectrum of tradability, a depreciation will clearly affect the prices of almost everything in varying degrees, and can thus be expected to have rather complex effects on the productive structure.

omy. Furthermore, it links the general level of prices in the economy with prices in other countries. Given these qualities, its use as a policy instrument is bound to excite controversy, not least because almost all exchange rate adjustments by developing countries are in the downward direction, thereby depreciating the national currency and reducing the amount of foreign exchange it will buy. Even its advocates agree that it is not a straightforward instrument, and its critics argue that it often cannot be made to stick, that it will damage the economy, or that responses to it will often be inadequate.

There is, perhaps, wider agreement that an overvalued exchange rate is likely to have a variety of adverse effects on an economy, namely:

- It will discourage exports by reducing the profitability of producing for world markets.[2] This is a crucial consideration given our earlier conclusion in favor of an open-economy strategy. Export performance is probably the single most important determinant of the progress of small open economies.

- It will discourage national production of importables because the local currency cost of imports will be kept artificially low. This bias is likely to have serious consequences both for agriculture (as a producer of foodstuffs as well as cash crops) and manufacturing (the chief import substitution sector). These biases may be eased by protection, but by restricting competition this is likely to breed inefficiency and low-productivity resource uses. In a small economy, sustained industrialization is incompatible with overvaluation. Moreover, encouraging imports (like discouraging exports) will hasten the emergence of a foreign exchange constraint.

---

2. Some people argue that the exchange rate will not affect the performance of primary product exports because the prices of these goods are denominated in dollars or other foreign currencies and determined by world supply and demand conditions, and will thus not be influenced by the domestic exchange rates of small suppliers. This is a fallacy based on confusion between foreign currency and local currency effects. While the dollar price of a country's exports will probably be largely unaffected by its exchange rate, that rate will determine how many units of local currency the dollar price will buy. A devaluation will increase the local currency value of a unit of exports, raising profitability and encouraging greater output. By the same token, an overvalued exchange rate will hold down the local currency proceeds of exports, which will discourage production, particularly if inflation raises production costs.

- It will skew the distribution of income away from producers of tradables and in favor of services and other nontraded activities. This will frequently show up as a bias in favor of urban dwellers, discriminating against the rural economy where most of the poor usually live. And where shortages of foreign exchange necessitate the imposition of import controls, large excess profits are likely to accrue to those well connected enough to secure import licenses.

- It is liable to destabilize capital movements and to be associated with an external debt problem. This will occur partly through the weakening in the balance of payments already mentioned: the larger the current deficit to be financed, the greater the need to borrow abroad. This may be aggravated by capital flight: when a currency is clearly overvalued, those who can do so have the maximum incentive to move their capital out of the country while it will still buy relatively large amounts of foreign exchange. By the same token, incentives will be reduced for foreigners to invest in the domestic economy so long as they think that a large devaluation may occur at any time.

- It will contribute to an unstable macroeconomic environment that is detrimental to enterprises, investment, and price responsiveness over and above the more specific depressing effects already listed.

One can thus view overvaluation as detrimental to structural adaptation, biasing production and demand in ways that aggravate foreign exchange shortages and hampering the economy's ability to respond to them. By the same token, establishment of a competitive exchange rate ought, in principle, to be conducive to adaptation, providing an incentive to produce tradable goods and a disincentive to buy imports. Whether exchange rate policy can produce such a desirable outcome is the subject of most of the following discussion. First, however, we must be clear about the concepts we are using.

Which Exchange Rate?

We have thus far referred loosely to "the" exchange rate as if there were only one. We should now introduce greater precision. First, any one country has as many exchange rates as other currencies into which the national currency can be changed. Thus, a unit of the home currency will buy x U.S. dollars, y yen, z deutschmarks, and so on. These are known as bilateral rates, in contrast to effective rates.

In most usages, an effective exchange rate is an average expressed as an index series. It is usually a weighted average of the most important bilateral rates, with the weights determined by each foreign currency's share in the country's foreign trade. The advantage of using an effective rate is that it smooths out most of the movements caused by fluctuations in the value of whatever foreign currency enters into a bilateral rate. Thus, if a country pegs its own currency to some fixed rate against the U.S. dollar at a time when the dollar is rising in value relative to other major currencies, then effectively the home country's currency is also appreciating, weakening its competitive position in nondollar trade.

Because of the pitfalls of using a single bilateral rate, an increasing number of countries now define their official exchange rate in terms of a basket of currencies. This can be seen in table 6-1, which summarizes exchange rate arrangements in force as of March 1991. This shows a long list of countries that have pegged their currency to a composite, or basket, of currencies. The countries in the preceding column are in a similar position because although they are pegged to the SDR, the value of this is a weighted average of movements of a basket of seven of the world's major currencies. However, the table also shows that many countries still peg to the U.S. dollar, the French franc, or some other single currency.

Note that the concept of an effective exchange rate is sometimes used in a different way to refer to the number of units of local currency actually paid or received for an international transaction. Actual rates will often differ from official rates, chiefly because of import and export taxes. Most important, many devaluations are accompanied by changes in taxes on trade in directions that muffle the impact of the devaluation. As a result, a study of twenty-four devaluations estimated the following average increases in exchange rates (Cooper 1971):

Nominal		34%
Effective	- exports	26%
	- imports	28%

As one can only expect people to respond to changes in the prices they actually receive or pay, this second meaning of the term effective is important. However, for the sake of simplicity we shall conform to the general parlance of using effective to mean a weighted average of bilateral rates.

This brings us to an even more central distinction: between nominal and real exchange rates (see Dornbusch and Helmers 1988, chapters 2 and 5, for a more detailed discussion of the concept of the real exchange rate). Take a country that pegs its currency to that of another country, say the U.S. dollar. If it decides to devalue against the dollar, the effect will be to raise the local currency prices of tradable goods relative to the costs of producing them and to raise the local currency prices of imports relative to locally made goods. Now imagine instead that the country wishes to avoid a devaluation and tries to achieve the same results by means of anti-inflationary policies. Suppose it manages to get its inflation rate well below that in the United States and for other goods traded in U.S. dollars. After a while the effect will be that domestic producers of tradables will find their local currency costs diminishing relative to the prevailing level of world prices, and domestic consumers will find the local currency prices of imports rising relative to the prices of locally made substitutes. The effect of the anti-inflationary strategy, in other words, is much the same as a devaluation, encouraging local production of tradables and discouraging imports. The strategy has achieved a "real" devaluation even though the nominal rate has not been changed. See box 6-1 for definitions of different kinds of exchange rates.

Unfortunately, the opposite is the more common case, with inflation in the developing countries exceeding inflation in the rest of the world, which, when combined with inflexible nominal exchange rates, results in real appreciation of their currencies, eroding competitive advantages and weakening the balance of payments. It is because of this tendency that the concept of the real exchange rate (RXR) has become an important one in policy analysis.

As already suggested, we can think of the RXR as determining the relative prices of tradable and nontradable goods and services. This draws attention to its important influence on the allocation of

Table 6-1 Exchange Rate Arrangements as of March 31, 1991

Currency pegged to					Flexibility limited in terms of a single currency or group of currencies		Adjusted according to a set of indicators[d]	More flexible	
U.S. Dollar	French franc	Other currency	SDR	Other composite[a]	Single currency[b]	Cooperative arrangements[c]		Other managed floating	Independently floating
Afghanistan	Benin	Bhutan (Indian rupee)	Burundi	Algeria	Bahrain	Belgium	Chile	China	Australia
Angola	Burkina Faso		Iran, I.R. of	Austria	Qatar	Denmark	Colombia	Costa Rica	Bolivia
Antigua & Barbuda	Cameroon	Kiribati (Australian dollar)	Libya	Bangladesh	Saudi Arabia	France	Madagascar	Ecuador	Brazil
Argentina	C. African Rep.		Myanmar	Botswana	United Arab Emirates	Germany	Mozambique	Egypt	Bulgaria
Bahamas	Chad	Lesotho (rand)	Rwanda	Cape Verde		Ireland	Zambia	Greece	Canada
Barbados	Comoros		Seychelles	Cyprus		Italy		Guinea	Dominican Rep.
Belize	Congo	Swaziland (rand)		Czechoslovakia		Luxembourg		Guinea-Bissau	El Salvador
Djibouti	Côte d'Ivoire			Fiji		Netherlands		Honduras	Gambia, The
Dominica	Equatorial Guinea	Yugoslavia (deutschemark)		Finland		Spain		India	Ghana
Ethiopia	Gabon			Hungary		United Kingdom		Indonesia	Guatemala
Grenada	Mali			Iceland				Korea	Guyana
Haiti	Niger			Israel				Lao P.D. Rep.	Jamaica
Iraq	Senegal			Jordan				Mauritania	Japan
Liberia	Togo			Kenya				Mexico	Lebanon
Mongolia				Kuwait				Pakistan	Maldives
Nicaragua				Malawi				Portugal	Namibia
Oman				Malaysia				Singapore	New Zealand
Panama				Malta				Somalia	Nigeria
Poland				Mauritius				Sri Lanka	Paraguay
				Morocco				Tunisia	Peru

Table 6-1 (continued)

	Currency pegged to					Flexibility limited in terms of a single currency or group of currencies			More flexible	
U.S. Dollar	French franc	Other currency	SDR	Other composite[a]		Single currency[b]	Cooperative arrangements[c]	Adjusted according to a set of indicators[d]	Other managed floating	Independently floating
St. Kitts & Nevis				Nepal					Turkey	Philippines
St. Lucia				Norway					Vietnam	Sierra Leone
St. Vincent & the				Papua New Guinea						South Africa
Grenadines				Romania						United States
Sudan				Sao Tome &						Uruguay
Suriname				Principe						Venezuela
Syrian Arab Rep.				Solomon Islands						Zaire
Trinidad &				Sweden						
Tobago				Tanzania						
Yemen, Republic of				Thailand						
				Tonga						
				Uganda						
				Vanuatu						
				Western Samoa						
				Zimbabwe						

Note: The table excludes the currency of Democratic Kampuchea, for which no current information is available. For members with dual or multiple exchange markets, the arrangement shown is that in the major market.
a. Comprises currencies pegged to various baskets of currencies of the members' own choice as distinct from the SDR basket.
b. Exchange rates of all currencies have shown limited flexibility in terms of U.S. dollar.
c. Refers to the cooperative arrangement maintained under the European monetary system.
d. Includes exchange arrangements under which the exchange rate is adjusted at relatively frequent intervals on the basis of indicators determined by the respective member countries.
Source: IMF International Financial Statistics (June 1991).

resources within an economy. Thus, an appreciation of the RXR means that the relative price of nontradables has risen so that capital, labor, and other resources will tend to be attracted out of tradables in favor of nontradables (the direction of change would be reversed in the case of an RXR depreciation). The real exchange rate thus has a potentially large influence on the structure of output, and can be used to adapt it to changing world and domestic circumstances.

Unfortunately, as we saw in chapter 2, the distinction between tradables and nontradables is difficult to operationalize, for tradability is a quality that almost all types of output possess, but in widely varying degrees. Hence, if we want to measure changes in the RXR we are unable to calculate it as a ratio of price indices of these two types of output, although crude proxies are sometimes employed. For these and other reasons, the practical solution most commonly employed—and which is equivalent in principle—measures the RXR as the nominal exchange rate (NXR) times an index of domestic prices divided by an index of world trade prices:

$$RXR = \frac{NXRPd}{Pw}$$

where Pd = the domestic price level (often proxied by a consumer price index or the deflator) and Pw = an index of world prices. Thus, if the NXR remains unchanged in a period when world prices rise by 5 percent and domestic prices by 15 percent, then the RXR in period 2 (with period 1 = 100) is:

$$\frac{100 \times 1.15}{1.05} = 109.5$$

that is, the domestic currency has appreciated by 9.5 percent in real terms, while the NXR has remained constant.

The concepts introduced in the glossary in box 6-1 can be illustrated using the example of francophone African countries that are members of the *Communauté Financière Africaine* (CFA) zone described in box 6-2. This arrangement has maintained a fixed NXR of 50 CFA francs to one French franc since 1948. We can ask two questions about this. As this is a bilateral rate, what has happened to the effective rate, taking into account the trade of the CFA members that is not denominated in French francs? Figure 6-1 provides the answer

---

Box 6-1. Glossary

Bilateral exchange rate: The rate of exchange between two national currencies, e.g., 49 Nepalese rupees = 1 U.S. dollar.

Effective exchange rate: Average of a basket of bilateral rates, usually weighted by each foreign currency's share in the trade of the home country and expressed as an index series.

Real exchange rate: The rates defined above are nominal rates. A real exchange rate expresses the relative prices of tradables and nontradables in an economy and may be calculated as the nominal rate adjusted for any differential in the inflation rates of the home country and its trading partners. See formula provided in the main text.

---

for a sample of three CFA countries and shows the existence of an appreciating trend in recent years. However, it is also apparent that each country has had a somewhat different experience despite a common bilateral rate with the French franc that reflects the differing commodity and geographical compositions of their trade.

The second, more important, question is what has been happening to the real effective exchange rates (REXR) of these countries? This is illustrated in figure 6-2, to which France's REXR has been added. Comparison of figures 6-1 and 6-2 reveals substantial differences for the CFA countries between their NEXRs and REXRs, underscoring the importance of the distinction between the two. Figure 6-2 also shows (a) a real depreciation for all countries except Cameroon in the early and late 1980s; (b) considerable divergences in trends in-between; and (c) large divergences between the REXRs of France and the CFA countries despite a pegged nominal rate. The CFA zone arrangements have failed to achieve similarity of experience among the CFA countries and to keep the CFA countries in line with the country to whose currency they are pegged. As described in box 6-2 these divergences are beginning to strain the CFA zone arrangements. For present purposes, however, the important point is that a stable nominal rate does not necessarily mean a stable real rate.

Box 6-2. Adjustment and Exchange Rates in the Franc Zone

The *Communauté Financière Africaine* (CFA) zone is made up of monetary unions for Central and West Africa. Thirteen francophone countries are members. These arrangements
- Create a fixed nominal exchange rate pegged to the French franc;
- Create monetary integration among members through the common currency and the pooling of international reserves;
- Provide a French guarantee of the convertibility of the CFA franc.

The objectives of these arrangements include maintaining a stable macroeconomic environment and encouraging foreign investment. There is little doubt that member countries have benefited from them: the CFA countries achieved higher growth rates in the 1960s and 1970s than other African countries and avoided the severe economic crises that some of these other countries suffered. However, by the early 1990s the scheme was coming increasingly into question.

Part of the reason is illustrated in figure 6-2, namely, the arrangements' failure to result in stable and uniform real effective exchange rates (REXRs). This partly reflects differences in the commodity and country composition of member countries' trade (for example, while most are oil importers, Gabon and Cameroon are oil exporters) and, therefore, in their terms of trade experiences, but it also results from some differences in domestic inflation rates. While the CFA arrangements include provisions limiting the freedom of action of members' fiscal and monetary authorities, for example, by limiting the amount of credit they may receive from their regional central bank, there are loopholes. In particular, the arrangements have not prevented the expansion of domestic credit, particularly to parastatal agencies, which is inconsistent with the viability of a fixed rate system. They have similarly not exerted effective restraints over capital flows, so that several CFA countries have experienced large external debt servicing problems, aggravated by capital outflows and a serious shortage of international liquidity. Another symptom of stress was that for the first time the two central banks simultaneously went into deficit in the mid-1980s, creating an unprecedented demand for credits from the operations account (*compte d'opérations*) at the French Treasury, which guarantees the convertibility of the CFA franc.

What is clear from figure 6-2 is that the currency union has not stabilized REXRs. Indeed, they have been less stable than a comparator group of other African countries, and the evidence suggests that the financial transfers implicit in French willingness to replenish the operations account of the scheme have contributed to this destabilization. Equally serious, a number of

Box 6-2. (continued)

CFA countries experienced an appreciation of their REXR during the 1980s at a time when they were already in payments difficulties, and several of them are now regarded as having seriously overvalued currencies. With a fixed NXR this leaves fiscal and monetary retrenchment as the main means for depreciating the REXR, but whether member governments are willing or able to impose the necessary degree of austerity, with all the socioeconomic costs it would impose, is doubtful. Attempts to do so in the Côte d'Ivoire in 1990, for example, by cutting civil service salaries, quickly led to political unrest, forcing the government to relent.

English-language readers wishing to pursue this topic in greater depth should refer to Bhatia (1985); de Macedo (1986); Devarajan and de Melo (1987); Honohan (1990); Lane and Page (1991); ODI (1990).

Figure 6-1: Nominal Effective Exchange Rates, Selected CFA Countries, 1981-89
(1980 = 100)

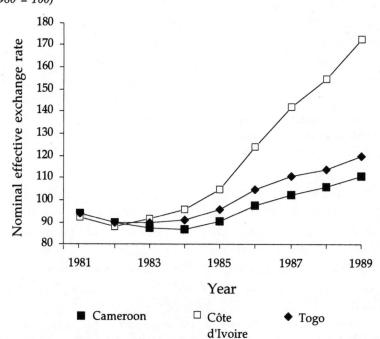

Source: IMF *International Financial Statistics.*

Figure 6-2: Real Effective Exchange Rates, Selected CFA Countries and France, 1981-89
(1980 = 100)

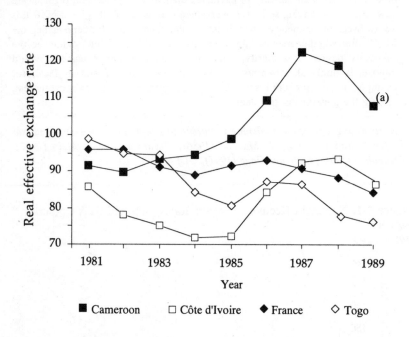

a. Entry based on September-November 1989 average.
Source: IMF *International Financial Statistics.*

For structural adaptation, the real rate is the most important. As structural change is a long-term process, necessitating innovation and investment, the price signals that can induce such changes must themselves be persistent to provide a basis for decisions about the future. Leaving aside the possibility of short-term "money illusion"[3] we must expect people to respond to real changes because they quickly

---

3. A money illusion may be said to exist when people respond to a change in nominal magnitudes as if they were real changes. Such behavior may be of importance in the short run, when, say, a devaluation is not fully anticipated, but illusions are unlikely to persist for long, as when inflation cancels out the incentives created by the devaluation.

learn how inflation can erode a nominal change. Indeed, we shall see shortly that one of the issues concerning the use of the exchange rate as a policy instrument concerns the extent to which nominal devaluations can be translated into real changes. Many countries have seen the incentive effects of a nominal devaluation quickly eroded by rapid domestic inflation.

In the early 1980s, based on a belief in the central importance of the REXR, much concern was expressed about trends in sub-Saharan Africa for reasons illustrated in figure 6-3. The figure shows a substantial real appreciation for Africa as a whole during the early

Figure 6-3. Developing Countries: Real Effective Exchange Rates, 1980-90 *(1980 = 100)*

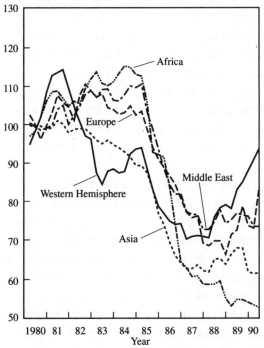

Note: Composites for regional groups are weighted averages, where countries' weights are dollar values of their respective GDPs during 1982-87. Because of the lack of appropriate domestic price date, the countries included for the Middle East and Africa cover only about 50 percent and 85 percent, respectively, of their regional GDPs. Coverage for the Western Hemisphere, Europe, and Asia is complete.
Source: IMF (1990, chart 15).

1980s (continuing the trend of the 1970s), contrasting strongly with real depreciations for the Asian and Western Hemisphere countries. However, we also see a particularly rapid real depreciation for Africa from the middle of the decade, although the trend is strongly influenced by the depreciation of the Nigerian naira, which carries a substantial weight in the African average (this illustrates the point that dramatically different regional averages can be produced by changing the countries included in the sample, the weights attached to them, the period selected, or other factors).

The Problem of the Moving Target

If indeed the exchange rate is of such importance in adjustment policies, the further questions arise of how a government can judge when action is necessary and how it should determine the optimal rate to aim for. The first of these questions is the easiest. Various symptoms will show up when a currency becomes misaligned. If we take the case of a currency that has become overvalued, a likely result is the emergence of a black market that offers more local currency per unit of foreign currency than the official rate. Where a long-standing black market exists, the overvaluation will show up as a widening of the spread between the official and black rates. At the same time international reserves are likely to decline as the (recorded) balance of payments deteriorates.

An excess demand for imports is another likely sign as imports become cheaper relative to local products, which leads either to an import boom or to the imposition (or tightening) of import restrictions. Controls will lead to scarcity premiums on imported goods, resulting in widening profit margins for traders and rising prices. Where the government responds by imposing price controls this is likely to spawn black markets for imported goods at above controlled prices. The same forces creating an excess demand for imports will also be at work eroding the profitability of the country's exports. This is likely to show up first in the form of complaints by exporters, possibly followed by reduced production. Where the government taxes exports, it will come under pressure to reduce this in order to sustain export profitability.

Misalignment can be gauged in more formal ways (see Johnson and others 1985). One is to calculate a time series for the country's REXR of the type illustrated in figure 6-2. If the year chosen as the base is one in which the REXR was regarded as satisfactory, misalignment can be judged as the degree of deviation from the base REXR. As the REXR is a measure of the relative prices of tradable and nontradable goods and services, another possibility is to compare the price indices of these categories of goods. Where a downward trend in the relative price of tradables is shown, again starting from a base period in which the price relationship was considered satisfactory, this too can be taken as evidence of overvaluation. Detailed studies of exporting or import substituting industries are another possibility, again with the intention of examining trends in profitability and international competitiveness.

Through these various indicators, overvaluations of any magnitude are likely to make themselves felt soon enough. They will raise the question of a devaluation of the currency, but the more difficult issue is how to determine the rate to which the currency should be depreciated.

Economists like to define this in terms of an equilibrium rate, although this terminology is only of limited practical use. The equilibrium exchange rate can be formally defined as that rate that is consistent with the simultaneous achievement of external and domestic balance. That is to say, it is that rate that will confine any deficit on the current account of the balance of payments to a level that can be financed by inflows of foreign capital on terms regarded as consistent with the recipient country's expected debt servicing capacity and without necessitating unwanted restrictions on trade and payments or on domestic economic activity. One can consider domestic balance to be achieved when the desired excess of expenditures over income—or of investment over saving—is the same as the expected capital inflow or the balance of payments current account with the opposite sign.

Evidently, determination of an equilibrium exchange rate is a complex exercise. For one thing, it is dependent upon world economic conditions; it can only be specified given world prices, interest rates, and capital movements. It is also contingent upon a wide range of government policies in other areas: the stance of fiscal policy and the extent of deficit financing, domestic credit policies, the structure of taxes on imports and exports, and restrictions on trade and payments. To put the matter another way, fiscal, monetary, and regulatory policies have to be consistent with exchange rate policies. The worst case of all is where the government pursues expansionary fiscal-monetary policies while trying to maintain a fixed NEXR. In the absence of large excess capacity in the economy, an appreciation of the REXR is almost guaranteed. Many governments have run into difficulties via this route, for commitment to a fixed rate presumes a particularly strong discipline in fiscal and monetary policies (as illustrated in box 6-2 on the CFA zone).

Note an important implication of the above: an exchange rate misalignment does not necessarily imply a policy failure; it can occur as a result of forces beyond the government's control. Thus if a satisfactory REXR is established and the government succeeds in keeping domestic inflation within the limits set by world price increases for tradables, the currency can still become overvalued if a persistent deterioration occurs in the country's terms of trade or in world capital market conditions. Indeed, the adverse terms of trade effects of the second oil shock at the beginning of the 1980s set in motion the explosion of structural adjustment programs that was such a landmark of that decade. Countries faced with long-term declines in their terms of trade need to compensate by depreciating their REXR.

A further complication is that the equilibrium exchange rate, besides being difficult to determine, will change over time as conditions in the world and domestic economies alter. Governments will find themselves aiming at a moving target. Thus, a persistent deterioration in the country's terms of trade will point in the direction of a depreciation, improved access to world capital markets or lower world interest rates will point the other way, and so on. As a practical matter, governments may find it difficult to go much beyond the earlier suggestion of fixing on a year when the REXR was regarded as satisfactory, in terms of external and domestic balance, and treating maintenance (or restoration) of this rate as the target, subject to adjustments for changes in the terms of trade and other basic determinants. The policy would then be to manipulate the NEXR and other policies to produce this result.

Starting from a position of overvaluation, the government will know the direction in which the exchange rate must be moved, but still has to decide by how much to devalue. Some of the indicators of overvaluation already mentioned will convey an idea of this. Thus, if the objective is to restore the REXR to some former level, the government should be able to estimate the nominal devaluation necessary to produce that result, given information about world and domestic prices (and including an allowance for the price-raising effects of the devaluation itself). Studies of the profitability of producing tradables should yield an idea of the size of nominal change necessary to restore international competitiveness. This might be especially useful where one or two products dominate a country's exports.[4] The size of the discrepancy between the official and black market rate will also give an indication, although as it is the product of a residual and illegal market, the black rate will tend to overstate the size of the needed depreciation or will mark the upper end of the range of needed change.

The use of price elasticities provides a further technique. Given the type of economy with which this book is concerned, making a "small country assumption" will generally be appropriate, that is, assuming that the country's exports are small in relation to total world supplies of those commodities and that the country's demand for imports is an insignificant proportion of total world demand. The effect of this assumption is to treat the country as a price taker: unable to influence the world price of its exports by altering supply or to influence the world price of its imports by manipulating its demand. On a small country assumption, the price elasticities that matter are the domestic price elasticity of demand for imports and the domestic price elasticity of supply of exports and other tradables.[5] Given some desired im-

---

4. However, governments should beware of determining exchange rates simply in terms of the competitiveness of their traditional exports in situations where a diversification of exports is desirable. The government would then have to ensure that the new rate is such as to provide incentives for the production of nontraditional exports.

5. Under what is known as the Marshall-Lerner condition, a devaluation will result in a net improvement in the balance of trade if the combined value of the elasticities of demand for imports and exports is greater than one. Although this result is quite influential in the literature, it is actually not very helpful for present purposes because it assumes (a) that the value of imports and exports are initially equal (which assumes

provement in the balance of payments, in principle it is possible to use the relevant elasticities to calculate the size of devaluation necessary to achieve the desired reduction in imports and expansion of exports.

Apart from the now familiar warning to concentrate on real, as against nominal, changes there are other cautions about using the elasticities approach. One is that it is likely to work better for modest, incremental changes than for situations of gross overvaluation. The elasticities approach is derived from neoclassical microeconomics and is less well suited to the analysis of large disequilibria, the solution of which requires discontinuous change. A second caution is against too unthinking a use of the small country assumption. A small country can produce a large proportion of the one or two export commodities in which it specializes. Thus, Zanzibar, a tiny, semi-autonomous island that is part of Tanzania, appears to be a totally insignificant member of the world trading community, but actually produces about a third of total world exports of cloves. Were Tanzanian exchange rate policies to lead to a large expansion of its clove exports, the world price would probably fall and the small country assumption would be invalid. Note also that the elasticities approach (and some of the other indicators mentioned above) relates only to the trading or current account of the balance of payments, whereas the exchange rate can also have an important influence on capital movements that is, however, difficult to predict in advance.

Third, while the analysis has so far been in terms of the exchange rate's effects on the balance of payments current account, we should observe that the increasing scale of world capital movements—and the importance to SLICS of investment inflows—means that the government must also consider the capital account when determining exchange rate policy. Given the international mobility of capital (and the general ineffectiveness of capital controls), it is increasingly imperative that investors, domestic as well as foreign, should have confidence in governments' exchange rate (and other macroeconomic) policies.

---

away a lot of the problem), and (b) that supply elasticities are infinite. While (b) is appropriate for the supply of imports to a small country, it is not appropriate for the export supply part of the story.

This necessity will considerably narrow governments' freedom of choice.

Finally, a solution is available that absolves the government from forming a view of the necessary size of devaluation: to leave the currency free to float to whatever level is determined by supply and demand. We will return to the advantages and disadvantages of this device later.

To sum up, the REXR is the key variable for purposes of structural adaptation. Unfortunately, the REXR is not strictly a policy instrument as its determination depends on a wide variety of external and domestic economic conditions in addition to policy actions. The REXR can be manipulated, however, by a combination of adjustments to the NEXR and supporting domestic economic policies. We have discussed the symptoms that will show up a misalignment, the causes of misalignments, and ways to judge the desirable scale of change, but do exchange rate changes actually produce the benefits the textbooks say they will? Does devaluation work?

Does Devaluation Work?

In this discussion of devaluation, the term devaluation is used loosely to refer to any substantial and deliberately engineered nominal depreciation of the currency. Those who are skeptical about devaluation suggest (a) that devaluation tends to have stagflationary effects; (b) that responses to the changed price incentives will be small; and (c) that it tends to place excessive demands on governments' abilities to manage their economies.

Stagflation

This is a condition in which an economy simultaneously experiences accelerated inflation and depressed levels of output and employment (see, for example, Krugman and Taylor 1978; Taylor 1988b). Take first the inflationary component, bearing in mind that we are writing of small open economies. Imports will be large relative to economic activity in such economies, providing necessary raw material and other productive inputs, capital equipment, and finished consumer goods. A devaluation can normally be expected to raise the domestic prices of these items by raising the local currency cost of imports.[6] Indeed, it will often be important that it should do so to accomplish the desired shift in relative prices. This initial price-raising effect may then set off defensive reactions by groups within society seeking to protect their living standards, for example, where organized labor is strong and is able to secure wage increases to compensate for the effects of the devaluation, or where producers follow cost-plus pricing rules. In short, a devaluation may trigger an acceleration of inflation, depending on the nature and strength of the transmission mechanisms within the socioeconomic structure (Montiel 1988 suggests, for example, that large exchange rate depreciations triggered inflationary episodes in Argentina and Brazil, both countries where there are strong transmission mechanisms). Where this happens, the real effects of a devaluation of the NEXR will quickly be eroded and the REXR may soon be left no lower. This criticism, then, is that governments are commonly unable to translate NEXR actions into sustained changes in the REXR.

This brings us to the alleged recessionary effect of a devaluation. The effect of its initial price-raising effects will be to absorb purchasing power while lifting domestic cost structures. The pre-existing volume of monetary demand will now be able to sustain a smaller volume of production. Of course, to the extent that workers and others are able to protect their living standards—the transmission mechanism—this effect will be reduced. There will be a tradeoff between inflationary and recessionary effects, but the end result may be a mixture of more inflation and lower real economic activity. The demand-absorbing effects of a devaluation may, however, be increased if it results in a transfer of real incomes from producers of nontradables with low marginal propensities to save to producers of tradables with higher saving propensities.

When a devaluation is substantial, it is also quite common for domestic producers and traders reliant on imported supplies to suffer a squeeze on their working capital, for they now have to pay larger amounts of local currency to permit an unchanged volume of business

---

6. When devaluation is preceded by a situation where imports are held down by quota restrictions, final prices may not rise by the full extent of the devaluation because previously existing scarcity premiums will tend to be eroded, so that part of the effect will take the form of reduced profit margins rather than higher prices.

in advance of their ability to pass their increased costs on to final consumers. This effect will be magnified if the local businesses have debt obligations denominated in foreign currencies, as the local currency cost of servicing these will increase by the proportion of the devaluation. Such a liquidity squeeze is quite common and can add substantially to the deflationary effects already described, especially when credit restrictions prevent the banking system from meeting businesses' enlarged working capital needs.

These potentially recessionary effects may be used as an argument against the use of the exchange rate in two ways. First, the recession might lead to reduced investment because of smaller demand and weaker confidence, and this may retard the structural changes necessary for a successful reallocation of resources in favor of tradables. Second, one can argue that the cost of using this instrument is too high if it leads to large losses of production, employment, and income. The task then would be to find alternative, lower-cost policies that would permit adjustment to be achieved at higher levels of output.

Against these possibilities, however, we should set other considerations. First, devaluations often occur in situations where an excess of demand already exists that it is desirable to absorb if the balance of payments is to be strengthened and inflationary dangers avoided. In this case, a devaluation may be twice blessed: encouraging the production of tradables and mopping up excess demand. However, the devaluation is extremely unlikely to mop up exactly the required amount of demand, and the danger of overkill remains. The other consideration has already been mentioned: that devaluation also has a stimulating effect on output and incomes in the tradable goods sector. If the size of the positive response among tradables is larger than the contraction among nontradables, there will be a net injection into the economy, tending to offset the demand-absorbing effects already discussed, although this may take time to emerge.

Thus, there is nothing inevitably recessionary about a devaluation. The outcome will depend upon the initial situation, and the respective magnitudes and time profiles of the demand-depressing and output-stimulating effects. This, in turn, will depend on the relative sizes of the tradable and nontradable sectors, their responsiveness to changed price relativities, the elasticities of demand for imports and local substitutes, and various other factors. It is not a matter that can be decided without due reflection. As one recent theoretical study has concluded (Lizondo and Montiel 1989, p.44): "There can be no presumption as to the nature of the impact effect of a previously unanticipated devaluation on domestic macroeconomic activity."

Elasticity Pessimism

For a devaluation to improve the balance of trade the relevant price elasticities must be above some minimum size. If we make the small country assumption, the crucial elasticities are the domestic price elasticities of demand for imports and supply of exports. The argument then concerns whether these elasticities are likely to be large enough in developing country conditions to produce the desired balance of payments improvements.

To some extent, this controversy is part of a much wider argument about price responsiveness in developing countries; an argument that has gone against the pessimists. However, we should also recall from chapter 3 the reasons why small, low-income developing countries are less flexible—and have lower elasticities—than more developed economies. More specifically, in the type of economy dealt with here elasticities of demand for imports and supply of exports will be dampened by a limited degree of substitutability between imports and locally produced goods; dependence on exports of agricultural or mineral products subject to substantial gestation lags and with little, if any, domestic demand; immobility of factors between sectors; poor information flows; other types of market failure; and an underdeveloped infrastructure. Local producers of tradables may also rely on imported inputs, which will dampen the incentive effects of a change in relative prices. In other words, the characteristics of the SLIC economy are among the least favorable for strong responses to devaluation-induced incentives (see Branson 1983 for an interesting exploration along these lines of the relationship between economic structure and the choice of trade policy). One can therefore argue that measures targeted directly at the structural weaknesses that retard elasticities could be more effective than the broad-brush approach of devaluation. We should also bear in mind the earlier warning against too ready an adoption of the small country assumption.

Managerial Capabilities

A devaluation must be accompanied by supporting measures, and implementing such a package successfully is difficult, particularly in light of the potentially large effects of a devaluation on the government's budget. Fiscal, monetary, and regulatory policies have to be consistent with exchange rate policies. In some degree they may be substitutes, with rigorous fiscal-monetary discipline permitting a stable exchange rate, or with a flexible exchange rate accommodating a more expansionary fiscal and monetary stance. The need to coordinate macroeconomic policy is also implicit in the foregoing discussion of the potentially stagflationary effects of a devaluation: the government must manage aggregate demand so as to avoid accommodating an inflationary process that would eliminate the real effects of the devaluation, while also avoiding the opposite danger of excessive demand absorption and depressed investment. Easier said than done! In addition, devaluations often will not bring their full benefits unless accompanied by supporting measures of a more microeconomic, supply-side nature (see box 6-3) to strengthen the infrastructure, provide extension and marketing services, and so on.

The range and difficulty of these tasks is large enough, but the complexities will be compounded by the effects of the devaluation on the government's own revenues and expenditures (for discussions of the budgetary effects of the exchange rate changes see Reisen and van Trotsenburg 1988; Tanzi 1988). Here again, conflicting tendencies will be at work. First, a devaluation is likely to increase government revenues. This is most obviously the case with taxes on international trade, for the local currency unit value of imports and exports will be increased. Given the probability of only a modest price elasticity of demand for imports, a positive net effect on receipts from import duties is likely unless the duties are expressed in fixed (*ad valorem*) terms or the government partly compensates for the devaluation by reducing tariffs.

To the extent that imports are also subject to excise duties and locally made excisable goods are based on imported inputs, revenue from excise taxation is also likely to go up. If the devaluation

Box 6-3: Sudan: Devaluation in a Rigid Economy

In 1978-79 the Sudanese government devalued the Sudanese pound in moves seen as central to a program of stabilization measures agreed on with the IMF. The appropriateness of this approach in Sudanese conditions was subsequently criticized, however.

It was argued, first, that the structural rigidity of the economy meant that export supply elasticities were inevitably small, while import demand elasticities were likely to approach zero. An estimate of the supply elasticity for the chief export, cotton, yielded a figure of 0.38, while the elasticity for total exports was estimated as 0.49. Secondly, it was suggested that domestic export production costs were sensitive to the exchange rate, with substantial imported inputs, and with wages and other local costs also being strongly affected. The long-run elasticity of wages to the exchange rate was estimated as 0.68, and of all domestic resource costs as 0.75. In other words, there was a tendency for the NEXR devaluation to be eroded, leaving a much smaller change in the all-important REXR. Indeed, an estimate of Sudan's REXR for 1981 shows it only 5 percent below the 1978 level despite a 30 percent nominal depreciation.

Third, critics suggested that the small country assumption was inappropriate for Sudan because increases in its export supplies depressed the world prices of the commodities in question (in 1970-80 Sudan accounted for 80 to 90 percent of world exports of gum arabic, 45 to 60 percent of long staple cotton, 30 to 55 percent of sesame, and 14 to 20 percent of groundnuts). For exports as a whole this offset some 9 to 46 percent of the local currency revenue-raising results of the devaluation. Thus, the balance of payments outcome of a devaluation from this combination of structural characteristics was uncertain, and it had left the profitability of traditional exports unchanged overall. Devaluation in this situation was described as a second-best solution by comparison with measures designed to tackle specific structural weaknesses, such as shortages of labor, fertilizers, fuel and spare parts; frequent power failures; and rehabilitation of the Gezira and other irrigation schemes.

All the writers used as sources for this box agreed about the importance of such supply-side measures in Sudan. It was not obvious, however, that these were competitive with action on the exchange rate. Indeed, devaluation and the consequential ability to pay higher wages could help to alleviate labor shortages experienced by the cash crop industries. It could also encourage the development of nontraditional exports and it stimulated a larger inflow of foreign aid that could assist with supply-side measures.

Source: This box is based primarily on Hussain and Thirlwall (1984); supplemented by Nashashibi (1980); and an interchange between these writers in the *Oxford Bulletin of Economics and Statistics* 48(1) in February 1986.

succeeds in increasing the production of tradables greater than the reduced output of nontradables, a net gain in receipts from corporate and personal income taxes is also likely. There will also be increased local currency receipts from aid grants from other governments. Thus, in general, a devaluation is likely to widen the tax base and raise budget revenues.

But what of the expenditure side? Three crucial variables are involved here: (a) the extent to which the government is itself a purchaser of imports; (b) the extent to which the government needs to raise public sector salaries as a result of the devaluation; and (c) the size of the external public debt. The first two of these are self-explanatory. The third merits further discussion given the important of the debt overhang in many developing countries.

For countries with a large external public debt, one of the disadvantages of the exchange rate weapon is that it raises the local currency cost of servicing that debt by the same proportion as the currency depreciation. Since revenues net of increases in other types of expenditure may well not rise to the same extent, the result can easily be a deterioration in the overall budgetary position.[7] Moreover, heavily indebted countries have frequently found that large devaluations can place private businesses that have borrowed abroad in great financial difficulties, and that governments have felt obliged to "nationalize" these debts, taking over the servicing obligations as an alternative to bankruptcies and unemployment. Naturally, such a situation further increases the probability that the net budgetary effect will be negative, increasing the government's deficit and the danger of its inflationary monetization. Possible conclusions from this discussion, then, are that in all countries the budgetary effects are likely to be substantial, but hard to forecast with accuracy, thereby increasing the difficulties of putting adequate supporting fiscal-monetary policies in place, and that heavily indebted countries run a considerable risk that the net bud-

---

7. To be more precise, this argument should be expressed in terms of net public financial resource flows into and out of the country, *i.e.*, the net balance of inflows of credits to, or guaranteed by, the government and outflows of amortization and interest payments in respect of past credits to the state. In some of the most heavily indebted countries, the net balance is heavily to their disadvantage, *i.e.*, there has been a net financial resource flow from them, giving rise to the types of fiscal difficulty described in the text.

getary effect will be negative, undermining the government's ability to restrain aggregate demand and raise savings. The extent of indebtedness thus emerges as a variable of particular importance.

The Evidence

Ultimately, the question, does devaluation work, is an empirical one. So what does the evidence show? One difficulty here is that most of the available cross-country evidence does not differentiate between different types of developing countries. This is unfortunate if it was correct earlier to suggest that use of the exchange rate is likely to bring fewer results in SLICs than in larger and/or more wealthy countries. The results summarized below may thus have an optimistic bias.

One obvious question we can ask is whether devaluations actually succeed in converting a depreciation of the NEXR into a depreciation of the REXR and in raising the prices of tradables by more than the general price level. If the answer to this is negative, then devaluation cannot be expected to assist structural adaptation or the balance of payments. The answer to this question will give us an important clue to the strength of the managerial problem just discussed: if governments are unable to prevent inflation from canceling out the effects of an NEXR devaluation, that would suggest an inability to cope with the management problems created.

Most devaluations have a price-raising effect.[8] The crucial question is whether this initial effect will be truly inflationary in the sense of setting off a cumulative process. The answer to this depends upon particular country conditions, and the evidence is therefore mixed. Table 6-2 (which unfortunately contains few SLICs) analyses twenty-eight devaluations in 1962-79 by measuring the extent to which a

---

8. Indeed, the price effects of exchange rate changes are regarded in some industrial countries (for example, the United Kingdom) as so important that they have sometimes sought a nominal revaluation as an instrument of anti-inflationary policy. Whether using the exchange rate in that way is wise is questionable, however. In any case, there are two features of such economies that differentiate their positions sharply from those of most SLICs, namely, that international capital movements bulk large in their balance of payments relative to trade transactions and that there are highly developed transmission mechanisms feeding price impulses emanating from the exchange rate through to further rounds of wage and price increases. For a survey of the evidence on the price effects of devaluations see Bird (1984, pp. 103, 109-10).

Table 6-2. Index of the Effectiveness of Nominal Devaluation

Country	Year	Quarter of devaluation	One quarter after	Four quarters after	Eight quarters after	Twelve quarters after
Bolivia	1972	0.68	0.66	0.36	0.09	0.03
	1979	0.51	<0	<0	<0	*
Colombia	1962	0.94	0.48	<0	<0	<0
	1965	1.00	0.88	0.50	0.57*	0.66*
Costa Rica	1974	0.82	1.04	0.75	0.75	0.83
Cyprus	1967	1.00	0.19	0.27	0.31	0.32
Ecuador	1961	1.05	1.06	0.93	0.51	0.03
	1970	0.88	0.74	0.73	0.59	0.66
Egypt	1962	1.03	1.03	0.98	0.85	0.32
	1979	0.99	1.05	0.98	0.93	0.76
Guyana	1967	1.03	0.96	1.10	1.31	1.42
India	1966	0.92	0.81	0.56	0.56	0.62
Indonesia	1978	1.00	0.98	0.73	0.64	0.61
Israel	1962	0.94	0.87	0.74	0.63	0.53
	1967	0.95	0.93	0.99	1.05	0.57
	1971	0.98	0.64	0.53	0.23	<0
Jamaica	1967	0.96	0.99	0.83	0.57	0.37
	1978	0.46	0.43	0.31	0.26	0.20
Malta	1967	0.93	0.88	0.99	1.12	0.99
Nicaragua	1979	0.17	<0	<0	<0	<0
Pakistan	1972	1.00	0.99	0.78	0.61	0.45
Peru	1967	0.89	0.65	0.40	0.41	0.36
Philippines	1962	0.97	0.89	0.87	0.73	0.69
	1970	0.72	0.65	0.49	0.47	0.55
Sri Lanka	1967	0.82	0.71	0.54	0.70	0.69
Trinidad	1967	0.82	0.71	0.54	0.70	0.69
Venezuela	1964	0.98	0.95	0.96	1.00	1.02
Yugoslavia	1965	0.67	0.46	0.42	0.29	0.26

Note: This index is the percentage change in the real exchange rate between one quarter before the devaluation and the quarter given, divided by the percentage change in the nominal exchange rate during the same period. An asterisk indicates that a new devaluation took place.
Source: Edwards (1989a, table 1.6).

nominal devaluation was reflected in an REXR depreciation at various times after the devaluation. To illustrate, take Bolivia's 1972 devaluation. Three months later the depreciation of the REXR was 66 percent of the nominal change, a year afterwards it was only 36 percent, and two years later rising prices had virtually canceled out the effect.

As expected, table 6-2 provides a mixed overall picture. There is a clear tendency for the REXR depreciation to be eroded over time, with coefficients in the last column generally well below those of the earlier periods. In a few cases rapid inflation quickly left the REXR higher than before devaluation (see the entries marked <0, for Bolivia, Colombia, Israel, and Nicaragua). By contrast, nineteen of the twenty-eight devaluations had coefficients of 0.5 or more after a year, and for over half of them (fifteen) this was true even after three years. These results are consistent with the findings of earlier researchers (Bird 1984, p.103). No grounds are provided for blanket pessimism, therefore. Edwards found that trends in the budget, wages, and, in particular, domestic credit creation were the chief variables explaining the results in table 6-2.

Where countries could avoid large budget deficits, did not index wages so that they rose to compensate for the devaluation, and limits on the expansion of bank credit were enforced, much of the devaluation would be reflected in the REXR and this effect would persist over time. Note, however, that the table includes almost no SLICs, and that it refers only to the 1960s and 1970s, leaving open the possibility that results were weaker in the less favorable decade of the 1980s.

If, indeed, devaluations do succeed in raising the relative prices of tradable goods and services, a further question is whether the price elasticities of supply are large enough to induce a significant response in terms of greater output of exports and import substitutes. The most substantial evidence relates to supply elasticities of primary product exports, that is, that category of tradable goods for which we would expect elasticities to be smallest. Bond (1987) surveyed a large volume of evidence contained in other studies, made her own estimations, and concluded that, taking all countries together, there were positive and significant elasticities of supply for agricultural products in response to changes in export prices in both the short and long runs, with the elasticity estimates summarized in table 6-3.

Table 6-3. Supply Elasticity Estimates

Product	Other studies		Bond's
	Short-run	*Long-run*	*own*
Food	0.43	0.80	0.70
Beverages and tobacco	0.27	0.46	0.66
Agricultural raw materials	0.33	0.51	0.43
Minerals	0.00	0.27	0.24

Source: Bond (1987).

Here again the data relate mainly to the 1960s and 1970s. Short-run elasticities for minerals are typically zero, but in the long run are positive and significant. Once more no grounds for blanket pessimism are provided, even though few of these averages approach 1.0. Bond's evidence also suggested that supply responses in Africa were weaker, sometimes apparently negative, but this seems likely to have been due to failures to pass export price increases on in the form of higher producer prices.

No equivalent survey is available for manufactured exports and import substitutes, but there is a good deal of impressionistic evidence that nontraditional exports are more responsive than traditional ones (see Donovan 1981 for supporting evidence and Bird (1984, pp. 103-5) for a general survey of the evidence on export supply elasticities). If so, we would expect devaluation to be an important stimulus for the diversification of exports advocated in the previous chapter. In this connection, Bond and Milne (1987, p.119) report that the REXR strongly influenced export diversification in the countries they studied, as did the general absence of major macroeconomic disequilibria.

There is also a dearth of recent cross-country evidence on import demand price elasticities. In a sample of fifteen developing countries, Khan (1974) found elasticities of close to or greater than 1.0, but this evidence is now out of date. Given the characteristics of the type of economy dealt with in this book, with little industry and limited substitutability between imports and local goods, the general expectation must be that import price elasticities will be small. Indeed, evidence suggests that import volumes initially tend to rise following a devaluation, due not to perverse price responses, but to the income effects of improved export earnings and a relaxation of import controls that may accompany the devaluation (see Moran 1990; also Bhagwhat and Onitsuka 1974; Donovan 1981). If the balance of payments is to benefit, we would therefore expect this to come chiefly from improved export performance (and perhaps a strengthening of the capital account) rather than from a reduced import bill.

To sum up our overall conclusion, we can borrow the politicians' cliché about being cautiously optimistic. The evidence does not support any across-the-board pessimism about governments' abilities to manage devaluation successfully nor about price elasticities. In particular, we emphasize the potential importance of the exchange rate for providing the incentives for diversifying exports away from traditional primary products. However, small low-income economies have characteristics unfavorable to strong results from devaluations and we need more systematic and recent evidence before arriving at decisive assessment.

Modalities

At this point we should give further consideration to the modalities of exchange rate policy. If we return to table 6-1, we see that it is arranged roughly according to the degree of flexibility of the exchange rate. At one end of the spectrum are the pegged currencies. For these a fixed exchange rate is maintained, sometimes for long periods. The CFA zone provides an extreme example, with a fixed nominal exchange rate between the French and CFA francs unchanged since 1948. However, a pegged currency is not necessarily inflexible as the government can change the peg as often as it chooses. Thus, although Tanzania pegs its shilling to a basket of other currencies, this has not prevented it from devaluing on a number of occasions in recent years. The case of an unchanging rate is called a fixed peg, one that is subject to infrequent changes an adjustable peg, and a frequently changed rate a crawling peg.

The independently floating currencies in the final column of the table are at the other end of the flexibility spectrum. In principle, these currencies float freely in response to changes in market conditions, either on the basis of a foreign exchange auction or an interbank market. A floating currency might be regarded as completely flexible, but in practice the countries' monetary authorities intervene on the market from time to time, if only to smooth out short-term fluctuations, so-called dirty floating. A number of developing countries have adopted auctions in recent years, but these have proved open to rigging and other disadvantages. Thus, the current tendency is toward interbank markets.

Also of interest is the group classified in table 6-1 as having currencies adjusted according to a set of indicators. Included here are a number of countries that explicitly attempt to maintain a target REXR. In such cases the indicator used is an index of local prices relative to the foreign prices of tradables, or Pd/Pw from the formula on page 146, with the authorities adjusting the NEXR in the light of changes in Pd/Pw.

The information under table 6-1 reveals some further wrinkles. The note, for example, refers to dual exchange markets. This refers to the simultaneous maintenance of two exchange rates, with one (usually giving a higher value for the domestic currency against foreign currencies) typically reserved for certain official transactions and essential imports, and a second (often more freely adjusted) for all other foreign exchange transactions. Such systems give rise to difficulties, however, particularly if a large gap opens up between the two rates. Sometimes countries maintain an elaborate system of multiple rates, but these tend to be even more problematic. Finally, note that governments can manipulate the REXR without touching the NEXR, chiefly by fiscal means. The effect on the final prices of imports of an across-the-board increase in tariffs, for example, is similar to that of a devaluation. The subsidization—or reduced taxation—of exports is another example. Some governments have simulated a devaluation by imposing a special tax on foreign exchange transactions. Such fiscal measures bring only some of the advantages of an overt devaluation, however, and generally create problems of their own (see Laker 1981 for a discussion of this topic; and Bird 1984, pp. 114-15, for a brief review of the literature).

How should governments choose between the alternative styles of exchange rate management? It is beyond the scope of this chapter to treat this question in any depth, but as the discussion shows, we favor flexibility of the NEXR in order to achieve and maintain the desired REX. (For surveys of this subject see Joshi 1990; Wickham 1985; Roberts 1989 on African experience. Quirk and others 1987 provide a valuable study of the use of floating rates in developing countries.) The case for flexibility and against a fixed or infrequently changed peg is that small, frequent changes are easier to adjust to, less likely to have adverse political repercussions, provide fewer incentives for destabilizing speculation, permit easier adjustment to unwanted movements in the foreign currencies to which the domestic currency is denominated, and require smaller international reserves.[9]

But if the case for flexibility is accepted, should it take the form of a crawling peg system or a float? There is no general answer to this. It will depend on a country's circumstances. Circumstances favorable to floating include the prior existence of a substantial cushion of international reserves, sufficient inflows of foreign capital and other foreign exchange receipts to put on to the market in order to avoid a precipitous overshooting depreciation, a substantially developed financial system, liberalized exchange and trade systems, and a reasonable level of public confidence in the adequacy of government policies and in the economy's future prospects. By and large, these are conditions more likely to be satisfied in relatively advanced developing countries and/or in countries whose exchange rate is not much over-valued.

One of the advantages of floating, however, is that it depoliticizes exchange rate decisions, whereas all the pegging arrangements keep such decisions within the sphere of discretionary action by the gov-

---

9. There is an important and increasingly influential argument against flexibility, however, to the effect that this will result in more inflation than would otherwise be the case. We have already seen that devaluations lead to price increases, but the additional point is that with flexibility, the NEXR can be readily depreciated to accommodate expansionary fiscal and monetary policies, thus further undermining the goal of avoiding inflation. Those who place top priority on this goal therefore argue in favor of maintaining a fixed NXR to act as an anti-inflationary anchor, imposing financial discipline and demonstrating to the public that the government is serious about restraining inflation. This, however, presumes that it is both technically and politically feasible to manage the REXR through domestic fiscal and monetary means. The brief discussion in box 6-2 of the predicament of some Franc zone countries in the early 1990s suggests that presumption may often not be valid in the circumstances of the SLICS, whatever may be the case of advanced industrial countries.

ernment. The crawling peg is less likely to generate great political attention than the adjustable peg, with frequent small—and therefore not very noticeable—changes being made according to some more or less objective formula. The crawling peg thus has considerable attractions provided the government is determined to allow it to work without interference. The temptation is always for it to intervene to defend some particular value of the NXR, which then becomes a riskless target for speculative capital flight. A further danger of the crawling peg (and of floating) is that it may be seen as an alternative to fiscal and monetary discipline, as a form of indexation to accommodate whatever inflation may be generated by deficit financing and monetary expansion. Whatever mechanism a government chooses for the exchange rate, none can substitute for the advantages of a stable macroeconomic policy environment.

The Efficiency of the Exchange Rate Mechanism

This discussion began with a statement of the theoretical case for regarding the exchange rate as a primary instrument in the pursuit of adjustment, and of the ways in which an overvalued rate is liable to damage an economy. In the light of the complications and evidence introduced, what should we conclude now? We can try to sum up by going through the most relevant of the various criteria for gauging the efficiency of a policy instrument set out in the preceding chapter, namely:
- How large will the response of the target variables be to a given change in the instrument variable?
- How probable is it that the expected results will actually be achieved, and how quickly will they occur?
- Does the policy act upon the causes of the problem it is directed at?
- What are the policy's resource costs?
- Is the policy selective in its application and flexible over time?
- What indirect economic effects will the instrument have and will they be positive or negative?
- In what ways is the public likely to react to the policy?
- What will the sociopolitical effects be?

- Is it likely that the policy will be implemented successfully and sustained over time?

How well does action on the exchange rate pass these tests? (The following is summarized from Killick 1981, pp. 209-20, which provides a fuller discussion of the comparative advantages of use of the exchange rate and exchange controls.) As regards the magnitude of response, much will depend on the sizes of the relevant price elasticities. We have suggested that there are no grounds for generalized elasticity pessimism, particularly on the export side. Much will depend, however, on the extent to which changes in the NEXR are translated into changes in the REXR, and the benefits passed through to exporters as higher prices; on the extent to which complementary policies are enforced domestically; and the particular circumstances of the country in question. Some of the same considerations will apply to effects on capital movements. Devaluation is likely to move the current and capital accounts in the desired directions, but the magnitude will vary according to circumstances.

What about the speed and probability of results? These are not tests by which devaluation scores well. The results may well be slow, because price elasticities are smaller in the short run. Indeed, devaluation is probably better thought of as a medium-term measure, as producers and consumers need time to adjust their decisions to changed price relativities. Moreover, the size of the outcome of a devaluation is likely to be quite speculative, particularly for large changes. The sizes of elasticities are unlikely to be known with any accuracy, the effects on the capital account will be even harder to predict, and government economists are unlikely to have a sufficiently good econometric model of the economy to be able to trace through the indirect effects in a more than approximate way.

The next test—whether the policy acts upon the causes of the problem—is much more favorable. If we take the case of a country facing payments difficulties because of import demand growing faster than export earnings, devaluation acts directly upon incentives to reduce import consumption and to increase export and import substitute production. In this sense, it acts upon the causes, by comparison with controls on imports and capital movements, which merely suppress the symptoms.

Is use of the exchange rate selective in its application and flexible over time? Selectivity is not one of its qualities. It is a broad-brush instrument that changes relative prices economywide and relies for its effects on the workings of market forces. This will often be what is called for, but this quality does imply that it is liable to be a mistake to use the exchange rate to resolve sectoral bottlenecks or other specific structural weaknesses. This was one of the issues in box 6-3 on Sudan, and other examples exist.[10] It is this lack of selectivity that has led to the introduction of multiple exchange rates mentioned earlier, although these are usually an inefficient response if maintained for long. As regards flexibility, a market-determined exchange rate is fully flexible and a crawling peg only a little less so.

This brings us to the indirect economic effects of exchange rate policy. We discussed the most important of these earlier under the heading of stagflation, and concluded that a devaluation will have an initial price-raising effect and could trigger an inflationary episode, but that the strength of the transition mechanism, including the power of organized labor, would determine the extent to which the initial price rise led to a sustained acceleration of inflation. We further saw that a devaluation contains both recessionary and expansionary impulses and concluded that there was no advance way of telling which influence would be dominant. The outcome is thus indeterminate. A devaluation is indeed likely to have significant indirect effects, but saying much about their general direction or magnitude is difficult.

We must take further considerations in account, however. A devaluation is likely to have a substantial effect on the distribution of income. Income will be redistributed away from those whose incomes are derived from the production of nontradables in favor of those engaged in tradables, and in favor of net earners of foreign exchange to the disadvantage of net users. The government itself, as a major producer of nontradables and net user of foreign exchange, is likely to be a loser, and therefore those employed by it, but whether the pattern of

---

10. The situation of agricultural marketing in Tanzania, cited in the next chapter, illustrates this point. There, inefficiency in the marketing boards led to drastic declines in the share of the world price being passed on to farmers. Unless specific measures were put into place to tackle the marketing inefficiencies, the effects of any devaluation were likely to be quickly eroded as the boards absorbed yet more revenue.

changes just described will be in favor of the poor is impossible to generalize. This will depend upon the factor proportions employed, the ownership pattern of those factors, and other considerations, although it may often produce a shift in favor of the rural population. What can be said more firmly is that if import controls are the alternative to an active exchange rate policy, these are liable to have severely inegalitarian effects on income distribution, generating large unearned scarcity rents for those with the contacts to get licenses. Another consideration is that exchange rate flexibility is likely to improve the allocation and productivity of resources by making greater use of the gains from international trade and by shifting resources into internationally competitive industries.

Next, what may be the sociopolitical effects of exchange rate policy? One of the problems here is that citizens are prone to identify the exchange rate with national prestige. Another is that it affects everyone's interests, with the losers from the shifts in the distribution of income liable to be politically powerful. The exchange rate can thus be a political hot potato. However, much hinges on the type of exchange rate regime. There is empirical evidence, admittedly old, that devaluations are politically risky, which helps to explain why some governments try to cling to patently overvalued rates. Cooper (1971) found that in seven out of twenty-four cases he examined the government fell from power within a year of devaluing; about twice as many as would otherwise have been predicted. Finance ministers were even more at risk, with fourteen out of twenty-four losing their jobs within a year; about three times as many as would have been predicted. It is significant, however, that Cooper's study was of substantial devaluations of the type that occur under an adjustable peg system. One of the hypothesized advantages of a crawling peg, or of floating, is that they take some of the political heat out of exchange rate decisions, weakening the identification of the government—and the minister—with depreciation.

Finally, is it likely that the policy will be successfully implemented? One of the features of this instrument is that it meets most of the implementation criteria set out in chapter 5. It is relatively simple to administer, it can be executed within existing institutions, and it is clear who is responsible for implementation. It may, however, act against the interests of some of those who are responsible when a devaluation is used to liberalize imports, as officials may have been benefiting from the power that comes with administering import licensing. Overall, however, and depending on the technique chosen, it is among the easiest instruments to use.

We should also relate discussion of this point to the earlier treatment of governments' abilities to manage devaluation in the sense of successfully carrying out a necessary package of supporting measures. Whatever technique the government uses, fiscal-monetary and exchange rate policies need to be made consistent with one another. This task is complicated by the strong influence of the exchange rate on government revenues and expenditures, especially in heavily indebted countries. Supporting supply-side, microeconomic measures are also likely to be needed, as in the Sudanese example. It is in this task of policy coordination that the true difficulty of devaluation lies, but it is the damage that an overvalued currency can do that makes it such a necessary task.

A Note on Further Reading: Edwards' (1989a) article is an excellent brief introduction to the subject of this chapter; see also his 1989b book. Also recommended are Dornbusch and Helmers (1988); Frankel and Mussa (1985); and Hallwood and MacDonald (1986). Pfefferman's (1985) article provides a trenchant statement of the disadvantages of currency overvaluation, outlined at the beginning of this chapter. Joshi (1990) provides a valuable survey of the considerations bearing upon developing countries' choice of exchange rate regime.

7

MARKETS AND GOVERNMENTS IN AGRICULTURAL AND INDUSTRIAL ADJUSTMENT

What is the appropriate balance between the "invisible hand" of the market and what has unkindly been called the "invisible foot" of state policy interventions in pursuit of the adaptive economy? This question has been a recurring one in this volume. We take it up again here in the context of two crucially important sectors: agriculture and manufacturing. In the case of agriculture the discussion centers around the uses and limitations of price incentives as instruments of adjustment policy. For manufacturing it is raised more fundamentally by way of questions about whether the state has more than a passive role in the pursuit of industrialization.

Before taking up these large issues, however, we should be clear about the problems we are addressing. No attempt is made to cover the full range of policy issues relating to these sectors. Thus, in agriculture no substantial coverage is offered of such key issues as research and extension policies, marketing arrangements, the special problems of women farmers or pastoralists, and so on. Similarly with industry, the rehabilitation or privatization of public enterprises, policies toward multinational corporations, and the special problems of informal or small-scale manufacturing are among the topics omitted.[1] The approach is consciously selective in order to focus on what is probably the most central issue. Also, because obtaining aggregated sectoral data to cover all small low-income countries is difficult, the emphasis is on Sub-Saharan Africa (SSA).

---

1. For present purposes we will use the terms industry and manufacturing interchangeably, even though mining, construction, and utilities are also included in international classifications of industrial activities. In most countries these other industrial activities are also important, and in some cases contribute more to GDP than manufacturing. Thus, one should bear in mind that manufacturing and industry are not strictly synonymous.

A Statement of the Problems

As in most countries agriculture and industry are the two most important sources of output, their performance is clearly crucial to the economy's ability to cope successfully with changing economic circumstances. Chapter 2 argued the special importance of manufacturing in terms of its influence on the balance of payments; its larger short-run supply elasticities; and its superior ability to generate technological advances, take advantage of scale economies, and stimulate production more widely through its linkages to other parts of the economy. It thus described industrialization as one of the enabling elements of structural adaptation.

At the same time, chapter 2 cautioned against neglecting the primary sectors and drew attention to the strong dependence of manufacturing on agriculture as a source of final demand, as a supplier of raw materials, as a source of labor and capital, and probably as a source of the foreign exchange necessary for the earlier stages of industrialization. Substandard performance by agriculture and industry is thus among the commonest sources of economies' inability to adjust successfully.

Agriculture

In the long run the agricultural problem in structural adaptation is how to manage its decline, given the strong tendency for agriculture to contribute diminishing shares of output and employment relative to industry and services. This is a problem many industrialized countries have confronted, and most have responded defensively by protecting agriculture, often to an absurd extent. It is a problem that is also beginning to surface in some of the newly industrializing countries such as the Republic of Korea.

In the small, low-income countries, however, the characteristic present-day problem is the opposite one of how to reverse agricultural decline. In their cases agricultural decline results more from poor performance than from long-term processes of structural transformation.

Concentrating on SSA for the time being, table 7-1 provides a number of comparative indicators of the sector's weaknesses. Note first that agricultural growth in SSA has consistently been far slower than for the developing countries taken together, and that even the faster growth in 1980-88 was still well below the rate of population growth (about 3.2 percent per year) and only about half the rate of all the developing countries taken together. If we confine ourselves to food production, item 2 of the table shows a decline during the 1980s for SSA against a 9 percent increase for all the developing countries. Partly in consequence, SSA's dependence on food imports (item 3) has increased a great deal and at a rate twice as fast as in other countries in 1974-87/88. Even with these imports, however, nutritional standards, as measured by the admittedly partial indicator of calorie intake (item 4), have remained static, while they have increased appreciably in other countries; a result all the more serious because of the poor diets that characterized SSA even in the 1960s.

Increased imports spell trouble for the balance of payments as does the export performance displayed in item 5. Indeed, this is arguably the most serious indicator of poor performance in the table, for SSA is heavily dependent on its earnings from primary product exports, but has seen its share of these world markets decline over time. The table shows that in agricultural commodity markets, Africa's share halved during the period, accounting for almost all the reduction in the share of all the developing countries taken together. While adverse terms of trade and other external developments also contributed to this decline, this poor export performance was a major source of the foreign exchange constraint that became so acute in the 1980s, aggravated in some cases by substantial food imports.

Items 6 and 7 provide productivity indicators and point to a serious technological backwardness in African agriculture. The figures on fertilizer consumption, for example, show far lower application rates in SSA than for the developing countries generally in both periods, and although SSA's use of fertilizer has increased from 1970/71-1987/88, the gap has widened. Item 7 compares yields for a number of major crops, and shows that (a) in every case yields are lower in SSA than in other countries; and (b) while the trend was upwards in other countries, it was static or deteriorating in SSA (see Jamal 1988, table 1 for further, but not directly comparable, evidence of technological backwardness in SSA agriculture by comparison with other developing regions).

Table 7-1. Indicators of Weakness in the Agricultural Sector, Sub-Saharan Africa

Indication	Date	SSA	All developing countries
A. Output, trade and consumption			
1. Growth of agricultural output (percent per year, real)	1965-80	1.3	2.8
	1980-88	1.8	3.7
2. Food production per capita (1979-81 = 100)	1986-88	94	109
3. Cereal imports and food aid (1974 = 100)	1987/88	235	167
4. Daily calorie supply per capita	1965	2,092	2,116
	1986	2,096	2,507
5. Share in world agricultural primary product exports (percent)	1967/68	8.3[a]	33.6
	1986/87	4.2[a]	28.5
B. Productivity indicators			
6. Fertilizer consumption (hundreds of grams of plant nutrient per hectare of arable land)	1970/71	33	238
	1987/88	85	680
7. Average annual yields (tons per hectare)			
(a) Coffee	1969-71	0.40	0.47
	1978-80	0.33	0.49
(b) Rice	1969-71	1.35	2.28
	1978-80	1.34	2.63
(c) Maize	1969-71	1.02	1.62
	1978-80	0.93	1.85
(d) Sorghum	1969-71	0.68	0.85
	1978-80	0.69	1.06
(e) Groundnuts	1969-71	0.77	0.88
	1978-80	0.76	0.91

a. Includes North Africa.

Sources: Item 5: UNCTAD *Commodity Yearbooks* (1988, 1989).
Item 7: Singh (1983, table 4).
All other items: World Bank, (1990b, tables 2, 4, and 28).

Thus, poor agricultural performance, and the inferior cultivation techniques which underlie this, is a serious problem. It is an obstacle to raising living standards in the rural economy, to improving nutritional standards, and to strengthening the balance of payments. Given the importance of the agricultural sector in most SSA economies, it also exerts a major drag on overall economic expansion, including industrialization.

Some would argue that this is overstated. To begin with, major problems exist with the data, notwithstanding the confidence with which we have commented on table 7-1. Indeed, one writer has gone so far as to assert that: "The quality of agricultural production and price data for Africa is so poor that nothing reliable can be said about the nature and direction of agricultural production trends" (Fones-Sundell 1987, p.18). Fones-Sundell provides examples from Tanzania of inconsistent and widely varying production estimates that could be matched in many other countries. However, to sustain the argument that the type of comparisons set out in table 7-1 are meaningless it is not sufficient to show that the data are subject to large error margins. It is also necessary to show that they are systematically biased relative to other developing countries, and that position is harder to sustain.

Indeed, some biases may be present. For one thing, part of the apparent stagnation may be the result of shifts of marketed output from official marketing channels (where the enumerators can operate) to traditional ones, which are likely to slip through the statistical net. Similarly, actual production trends may be more favorable than those counted because of a shift from marketed to subsistence (or barter) production. One difficulty about this line of argument, however, is that the same biases are liable to be present in the statistics of other developing countries, although perhaps to a lesser degree. A further difficulty is that a retreat from formal sector marketing into subsistence production is itself likely to be a symptom of agricultural distress, and thus cannot reassure us that African agricultural production is not suffering from problems.

A second type of objection is that we have been overgeneralizing, which is basically true. There have been large differences in agricultural performance among African countries and between different agro-climatic zones within them.[2] Here again, however, it is difficult to see how this fact could vitiate the type of comparison offered in table 7-1, although it does caution us to be careful about how we interpret the results.

Other objections have been offered, chiefly by Jamal (1988), as follows: that criticisms of Africa's agricultural performance overlook the damaging effects of adverse terms of trade movements and of the foreign exchange constraint; that rising food imports are partly a result of urbanization and changing tastes and, in any case, still form only a modest part of total imports; and that production was particularly hard hit by the severe drought of 1983-85, which was exceptional and wholly outside government control. Again, however, the first two of these points appear no less valid for many non-African developing countries and do not, therefore, explain the contrasts in the table. The final point, about the influence of the drought, is valid but is weakened by generally better than average rainfall in the following years. We must therefore reiterate that SSA suffers from a real problem of lagging agricultural performance and that has been creating major economic difficulties.

Industrial Weaknesses

As industrialization is an important enabling component of structural transformation, which in any case features prominently among the goals of most developing country governments, one way of gauging the industrial sector's performance is to examine its growth performance. Confining ourselves to SSA, the region for which data are readily available, what emerges is that the fairly rapid industrialization that occurred in the 1960s has been running out of steam. Table 7-2 shows steadily declining rates of manufacturing growth for SSA as a whole, so that by the 1980s it was barely faster than the growth of population. Industrialization means that manufacturing leads the growth of the economy, but as the table shows, this process almost halted in the 1970s. While the relative growth of manufacturing

---

2. The conclusions of a major study of African agriculture (Lele forthcoming) emphasize the diversity of country experiences in terms of variations of agricultural growth performance between and within countries.

showed some rise in the 1980s, this was due entirely to a slowdown in GDP growth, not to any revival of industry.

Perhaps even more revealing evidence of substandard performance is provided by statistics on Africa's record as an exporter of manufactures, which give an indicator of overall efficiency levels. In the absence of subsidies a firm must be efficient to compete successfully on world markets, and there is a presumption that many firms that rely wholly on the domestic market do so because their costs are too high for them to succeed on world markets. By this test the figures in table 7-3 reveal that African industry is indeed inefficient, with a truly appalling export record. Thus, while developing countries as a group were greatly expanding the value of their manufactured exports and their penetration of world markets, the nominal value of African industrial exports was static, and their share in world markets and in developing country exports plunged to minuscule levels. This was surely related to the appreciation of SSA real exchange rates that occurred over this period. In consequence, African manufacturing had become almost wholly dependent on selling to the domestic market.

Table 7-2. The Growth Performance of Manufacturing in Sub-Saharan Africa, 1960-89
(percent per year in constant prices)

Period	Manufacturing growth	Ratio of manufacturing growth to GDP growth
1960-65	7.3	1.7
1965-70	9.3	2.1
1970-75	5.3	1.0
1975-80	4.4	1.2
1980-89	3.4	1.6

Source: Meier and Steel (1989, table 3.1.1.) updated from World Bank (1991, table 2).

Table 7-3. African Manufactured Export Performance, Sub-Saharan Africa, 1960-85

Category	1960	1965	1970	1975	1980	1985
Total world manufactured exports (US$ billions)	58.00	90.00	167.80	438.90	943.20	983.60
Total developing country manufactured exports (US$ billions)	2.20	3.70	8.40	28.00	90.50	135.80
Sub-Saharan Africa manufactured exports (US$ billions)	0.21	0.38	0.56	0.76	1.46	0.54
Ratio of developing country to total manufactured exports (%)	3.80	4.10	5.00	6.40	9.60	13.80
Ratio of Sub-Saharan African manufactured to total manufactured exports (%)	0.36	0.43	0.33	0.17	0.15	0.05
Ratio of Sub-Saharan African manufactured to total developing country manufactured exports (%)	9.30	10.40	6.60	2.70	1.60	0.40

Source: Riddell and others (1990, table 2.A3).

Underlying and compounding this evidence of inefficiency and stagnation are a number of structural weaknesses. These include the following:

- A heavy dependence on imported raw materials, equipment, and skills. This severely limits linkages with the rest of the economy and the potential contribution of manufacturing to the balance of payments.

- Levels of capacity in excess of the economy's ability to utilize it, in terms both of the size of the domestic market and of the availability of necessary imported inputs.

- A bias toward final-stage processing of consumer goods (symbolized by—invariably inefficient—assembly plants for vehicles and electronic goods), relative to the processing of local raw materials and the production of intermediate and capital goods.

- A dualistic structure, with large numbers of informal and small-scale enterprises coexisting with small numbers of relatively large-scale modern plants, and with few transactions between them.
- A still very small base of industrial skills and supporting services; an absence, therefore, of `agglomeration economies'; and much inappropriate, low-productivity technology.
- A heavy investment in state-owned enterprises that often—but not always—incorporate the worst of the above characteristics, and also depend on large government subsidies that add to already acute budgetary difficulties.[3]

As a result of these various deficiencies industrialization in most African economies has failed to raise the countries' adaptive capacities along the lines predicted. The structural transformation has gone only skin deep, and few of the expected externalities have been realized. Box 7-1 on Nepal, which provides a thumbnail sketch of a typical industrial situation in a SLIC, suggests that many of the deficiencies described above are by no means peculiar to SSA.

We should, however, qualify our bleak account of the African situation. First, we have been overgeneralizing. The position differs among countries even within SSA, to say nothing of the small low-income countries in other parts of the world. There have been bright spots. Many countries have a thriving informal manufacturing sector that often meets local needs at low prices and provides a cockpit from which genuine entrepreneurs graduate to running larger-scale businesses. Even within modern industries, generally characterized as inefficient, enterprises vary enormously, with some managing to achieve high productivity and low costs. Some progress has been made in terms of building up a labor force with industrial skills, developing local sources of supply, and moving up the learning curve. Nevertheless, the success stories are overshadowed by the many inefficient

---

3. The subject of public enterprise performance is largely outside the scope of this chapter. Readers wishing to pursue this topic further should refer to Killick (1983); Meier and Steel (1983, chapter 10); Millward (1988). See also Grosh (1990) for an interesting study of the Kenyan case that disputes the generalization that state manufacturing enterprises are particularly inefficient. Jones (1975) reaches favorable conclusions about the efficiency of state enterprises in the Republic of South Korea.

Box 7-1. Portrait of the Manufacturing Sector in Nepal

With a per capita income in 1987 of just US $160, Nepal rates as one of the world's poorest nations, and with a population of around 18 million the economy offers a small market for manufactures. It remains chiefly agricultural, and manufacturing makes up only 4 percent of GDP, a share that has changed little since the mid-1970s. Typically, the manufacturing sector is bimodal, with a third of its output coming from cottage industries (much of it the processing of food for family consumption). Even many of the modern enterprises are very small. Nine-tenths of the output of modern manufacturing is of consumer goods, with food processing easily the most important branch. A high proportion of manufacturing output is sold on the domestic market (for example, only about 6 percent of the output of the dominant food processing sector was exported in 1983/84) and dependence on imports of many manufactured goods remains heavy. Nevertheless, some industries are successful exporters and—untypically for such a poor country—manufactured goods make up over half of the country's total exports: 59 percent in 1985/86. The chief manufactured exports are jute products, hand-knotted woolen carpets, and garments, from one may judge that Nepal's revealed comparative advantage is based on local raw materials.

Another characteristic that Nepal's manufacturing sector has in common with other countries is the wide variations in efficiency when measured in terms of the amount of domestic resources used to earn or save a unit of foreign exchange. Industrial domestic resource cost calculations vary from well under 1.0 (including jute goods and carpets) to a maximum of 21.2 for footwear. The most inefficient, like footwear, survive by a structure of protection that—also characteristically—contains large variations, with effective protection rates at the sectoral level varying between -4 percent for jute processing (for example, an implicit tax) to +10,989 percent for furniture. It seems the Nepalese pay dearly for having a furniture industry. Nevertheless, the average protection rate for manufacturing as a whole is relatively modest. There is much underutilization of capacity, with eight of the most important industries showing an average utilization rate in 1985/86 of 49 percent.

Both private foreign subsidiaries and public enterprises are important within modern manufacturing. Information on the former is sparse, while the latter have well below average, and declining, gross profit rates, and seem to depend upon budgetary subsidies or government guaranteed loans to meet their capital needs.

Growth of manufacturing productivity has been slight in recent years. The sector's performance has been influenced by the overall condition of the economy, with per capita incomes growing at only 0.5 percent per year in 1965-87, and with serious problems in agriculture. Manufacturing is particularly hard hit by high transport costs arising from an underdeveloped infrastructure, with under 3,000 kilometers of paved roads and just 52 kilometers of railways in an often severe terrain.

Source: UNIDO (1988).

enterprises that have come to comprise part of the adjustment problem rather than part of its solution.

Finally, having drawn attention to deficiencies in both agriculture and industry, it is hardly necessary to point out that these interact upon each other. Past agricultural stagnation has limited the market for local manufactures, has made it difficult for industry to rely upon local raw materials, and has contributed to a scarcity of foreign exchange that during the 1980s starved factories of the imports upon which they relied. In turn, inefficient factories weakened agricultural incentives by offering inadequate supplies of consumer goods at high prices and of poor quality; by raising the costs of farmers depending on locally made implements, fertilizers, and so on; and by absorbing resources that otherwise could have been devoted to agriculture.

The Role of Price Policies in Agriculture

A number of fundamentals constrain agricultural output and productivity: ecological conditions, including the climate and the inherent fertility of the soil; the availability of labor and capital; and the technologies employed. In the long run the sector's performance and adaptability will depend on such factors as these. The chief focus of the next several pages, however, is on the role of pricing policies in agricultural adjustment. This is because the intention of this chapter is to explore the relative roles of the state and markets rather than to offer comprehensive treatments of the massive subjects of agricultural and industrial policy, and also because the uses and limitations of agricultural pricing policies have become one of the liveliest areas of controversy in the literature on adjustment policies.

The Taxation of Agriculture

Given this focus, the first question that arises is whether we can explain the laggard performance of African agriculture, described earlier, in pricing terms. That inadequate price incentives are indeed likely to be part of the story is suggested by the long-term downward global trend in the real prices of the agricultural and other primary product exports on which SSA, in particular, depends. The signal conveyed by this trend is for countries to reduce their reliance on such goods and to shift resources in favor of exports with more dynamic

markets. In some cases, however, the unintended effects of state interventions have magnified the effects of such adverse trends.

The most notorious example of this in the past has been the taxation of export crops many governments engaged in the 1960s and
1970s, either directly or through transfers from state marketing board
monopolies. A World Bank report (1981, box D, p.56) studied the
extent to which African governments taxed or subsidized export crops
in 1976-80. All but four of twenty-nine separate estimates were negative, that is, showed net taxation, and the estimates showed an overall
average tax rate of 35 percent. Table 7-4 shows a similar result, with
export crop producers receiving an average of only two-thirds of
world price values, and with all but three of twenty-eight observations
showing ratios of less than 1.0. For reasons given shortly, the position
for cereals was less unfavorable, but even for these crops farmers were
receiving an average of 15 percent less than the border price.
Moreover, such figures take no account of the widespread existence at
that time of overvalued currencies.

Table 7-4. Ratio of Farmgate to Border Prices for Selected Commodities in
Eleven SSA Countries, Late 1970s / Early 1980s

Ratio	Cereals[a]	Export crops[b]
>1.25	2	0
1.00 - 1.24	2	3
0.75 - 0.99	2	5
0.50 - 0.74	3	12
<0.5	1	7
Average ratio	0.85	0.66

The eleven countries are Burkina Faso, Cameroon, Côte d'Ivoire, Ghana, Malawi,
Mali, Senegal, Sudan, Tanzania, and Zambia. Border prices converted at official exchange rate.

a. Wheat, rice, groundnuts, maize, and sugar.

b. Tea, coffee, cocoa, tobacco, cotton, groundnuts, and sugar.

Source: Beynon (1989, table 1).

To some extent the taxation of agricultural exports is understandable. It has commonly represented the only effective way of taxing a major source of income accruing to relatively prosperous farmers in countries with narrow tax bases and fragile tax administrations. Had it been combined with positive inducements to develop alternative products, it could have been seen as encouraging a desirable diversification of exports and safeguarding against excessive investment in traditional products facing weak long-term market prospects. However, it often went too far, imposing an excessive burden of taxation in an environment that also discouraged the development of nontraditional alternatives. Moreover, much of the resulting tax revenue was poorly spent.

The taxation of exports is, however, by no means an exclusively African tendency, as table 7-5 illustrates. The column showing the direct protection of agricultural exports shows negative protection, that is, net taxation, in all but three of the entries, with an average net rate of tax of 11 percent. (Note, however, that the authors of the study from which table 7-5 is derived calculated their results from a notional free market price, with the numerical results depending on the assumptions used in calculating this notional basis.) Comparison of these figures with those for the direct protection of cereal foodstuffs shows that the net taxation of agricultural products was confined mainly to exports, with most of the governments listed providing positive protection for local producers, at an average level of 21 percent. Within SSA and excluding some cereals, most foodstuffs fall outside the net of taxation, not least because of the infeasibility of bringing them within it, although there are cases in which governments attempt to regulate food prices in favor of urban consumers and to the disadvantage of farmers by means of marketing monopolies or other devices.[4] Usually, however, as table 7-4 shows, net taxation is far less for food producers than for export producers. If governments seek to enforce severely submarket prices the effect will simply be to push food supplies onto parallel markets, an option not so readily (or cheaply) available to the cultivator of export crops. Thus: "It sounds terrible that official maize procurement in Tanzania has been at 'only a quar-

---

4. Prices may also be shifted to the disadvantage of local farmers if overvalued exchange rates or subsidies result in large-scale competing imports, depressing domestic prices to the advantage of urban and other consumers.

ter of the border price,' but of course farmers act so as to evade such extraction. Thus in 1982-5 about 85% of Tanzanian maize output was consumed by the grower or traded locally; 10% was traded more widely, but in unofficial 'parallel' markets; and only about 5% of production was procured at the very low official price" (Lipton 1987, p.204).

Table 7-5. Direct and Indirect Protection of Agriculture, 1980-84
(percentage deviation from the price that would have prevailed in a well-functioning market at free trade)

Country	Export products			Food products (cereals)		
	Product	*Direct*	*Indirect*	*Product*	*Direct*	*Indirect*
Argentina	Wheat	-13	-37	-	-	-
Brazil	Soybean	-19	-14	Wheat	-7	-14
Chile	Grapes	0	-7	Wheat	+9	-7
Colombia	Coffee	-5	-34	Wheat	+9	-34
Côte d'Ivoire	Cocoa	-21	-26	Rice	+16	-26
Dominican Rep.	Coffee	-32	-19	Rice	+26	-19
Egypt	Cotton	-22	-14	Wheat	-21	-14
Ghana	Cocoa	+34	-89	Rice	+118	-89
Korea, Rep. of	-	-	-	Rice	+86	-12
Malaysia	Rubber	-18	-10	Rice	+68	-10
Morocco	-	-	-	Wheat	0	-8
Pakistan	Cotton	-7	-35	Wheat	-21	-35
Philippines	Copra	-26	-28	Corn	+26	-28
Portugal	Tomatoes	+17	-13	Wheat	+26	-13
Sri Lanka	Rubber	-31	-31	Rice	+11	-31
Thailand	Rice	-15	-19	-	-	-
Turkey	Tobacco	-28	-35	Wheat	-3	-35
Zambia	Tobacco	+7	-57	Corn	-9	-57
Unweighted means		-11	-29		+21	-27

Source: Krueger, Schiff, and Valdes (1988, tables 1 and 2).

The direct effects of taxation and protection are, however, only part of the story. One of the themes emerging from the preceding chapters is the pervasive influence of the general policy environment. We saw this in chapter 3's discussion of influences on the supply of entrepreneurship, in chapter 5's warning of the importance of designing policies as a system, and in chapter 6's stress on the importance of supporting policies for translating nominal devaluations into real ones. The columns in table 7-5 showing the indirect protection of agriculture attempt to capture some of the consequences of the broader policy environment, specifically the effects of policies on the exchange rate and on industrial protection.

Every entry in the two indirect protection columns is negative, indicating that the effects of these two aspects of policy have been to the disadvantage of agriculture. This arises partly from exchange rate overvaluation, (we saw in chapter 6 how overvaluation discourages exports and the domestic production of importables). Industrial protection has a negative effect because it is a kind of transfer tax, shifting welfare in favor of manufacturers at the expense of their customers. Industrial protection works against farmers by making them pay more for their locally manufactured inputs and consumption purchases. Moreover, these two policy biases interact, with protection encouraging currency overvaluation and overvaluation appearing to justify more protection. The combined effect is strongly negative for agricultural exports and for foodstuffs facing competition from imported substitutes, as the table shows. Indeed, the size of the indirect effects is larger than the direct effects for both categories of crop and, in the case of foodstuffs, is large enough to dominate the nominal protection provided. (Bear in mind, however, that many locally grown foodstuffs do not face much international competition, so the position of the whole foodstuffs sector is not as adverse as that shown in the right-hand part of table 7-5 Green [1989, p.40] suggests that in Africa well under 10 percent of all food output is directly affected by prices set by the government). In the case of export crops, the average combined effect of the two types of influence is to impose implicit taxation of 40 percent.

The concept of the internal or domestic terms of trade also illustrates the type of anti-agriculture bias just described. This measures movements in the prices received relative to the prices paid by farmers (or some other group in society) for their purchased producer and consumer goods. By way of illustration, figuré 7-1 shows long-term trends in the agricultural terms of trade in Kenya, revealing an apparent long-term downward trend periodically arrested by short periods of improvement (chiefly resulting from movements in world coffee and tea prices).

Figure 7-1. Agricultural Terms of Trade, Kenya, 1964-88
(1964 = 100)

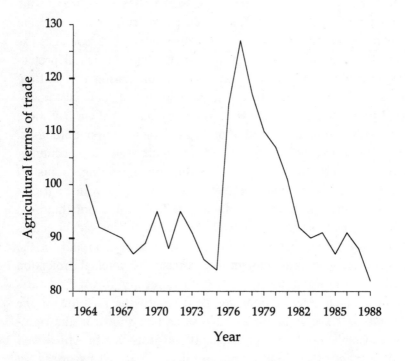

Source: 1964-77: Sharpley (1981, table 1); 1977-88: Government of Kenya *Economic Survey* (various issues).

Although few hard statistics are available, an adverse trend is regarded as common. The results in table 7-5 help to explain why, showing that the net effect of government interventions is often to reduce the prices farmers receive for some of their crops and increase the prices they must pay for industrial goods. A particularly useful feature of the domestic terms of trade concept is that it provides an indicator of the price incentives for agriculture as a whole, as distinct from incentives for particular crops. An adverse trend in the agricultural terms of trade can be expected to result in a relative, and possibly absolute, migration of capital and labor out of the sector to more favored parts of the economy, thereby reducing agriculture's productive capacity.

We thus have grounds for believing that inadequate price incentives, often government induced, have contributed to agricultural stagnation, and nowadays few economists would dispute this. There is much less agreement, however, on how much weight should be given to these pricing considerations. For one thing, not all the policy-induced price distortions work to the disadvantage of farmers, for example, explicit or implicit subsidies on fertilizers, insecticides, farm equipment, and other inputs. Again, Beynon (1989) has pointed out that the evidence suggests that the degree of taxation of SSA agriculture has been gradually decreasing over time, so that it cannot easily explain deteriorating performance. Finally, we shall show later that the output of the agricultural sector as a whole (as distinct from production of particular crops) is not very sensitive to relative price movements of the type measured by the domestic terms of trade.

Influences on Farm Profitability

To achieve a proper perspective, we can approach the issue of influences on farm productivity by attempting a systematic consideration of the factors that are likely to affect farmers' production and marketing decisions.[5] We start from the premise that, other things being equal, agricultural production—or that part of it that is marketed

---

5. In the case of smallholders, the family is the key production and decision unit. Production decisions will thus also be influenced by the distribution of the costs and benefits of agricultural work within the family, particularly how it is shared between husband and wife.

(as distinct from subsistence self-consumption)—will be a function of the profitability of output. We can then consider the influences on costs and on revenues that will determine profitability.

On the side of costs, the price and availability of material inputs, labor and capital (including credit) will be crucial variables, as will the state of knowledge and technology. State price interventions of the type already discussed are liable to affect the prices farmers pay for imported and domestically manufactured inputs, such as fertilizers, insecticides, and tools. The relative protection of industry (and other urban-based activities) is also liable to attract labor and capital out of agriculture, thus tending to raise their prices, and countries apparently faced with large-scale underemployment of labor in the towns nonetheless commonly experience acute seasonal shortages of agricultural workers.

Input and factor availabilities will, however, also be affected by nonprice influences, such as population growth, the borrowing requirements of the public sector, imperfections in the markets for these goods and services, the efficiency of the distributive system, and the influence of the balance of payments on import capacity. This latter consideration has been a heavy burden on many developing countries in recent years, with foreign exchange constraints starving productive sectors of essential inputs. The determinants of the state of knowledge and cultivation techniques also take us well beyond pricing considerations, into such questions as the quality and coverage of education, the adequacy of agricultural extension and research services, the influence of traditional *mores*, and so on.

Turning to the revenue side of the profitability equation, we can relate this (a) to the situation in the final markets for the commodities in question, and (b) to the various influences that drive wedges between the final prices and those received at the farm gate. As regards the final markets, we have already reminded ourselves of the fundamental weakness of the world demand for many primary products (a weakness related to universal regularities in income elasticities of demand). Engel's Law, which predicts a relative decline in demand for food as *per capita* income rises, is one of the most firmly established generalizations about economic behavior. This does not necessarily result in declining relative food prices, depending on what happens to supply, but it does caution against expecting final prices to be very buoyant.

In some measure, then, weak agricultural revenues may result from fundamental forces of demand and it is desirable for that price signal to be passed on to producers. However, as already discussed, they may also result from the taxation, protection, and pricing policies of governments. Further wedges will be created by the costs of storage, marketing, and transportation, with the scale of these depending upon location, the adequacy of the rural infrastructure, and the efficiency of the distributive system. This latter factor is, in turn, likely to be influenced by the extent of competition in marketing and transport, whether it be undertaken in the private or public sector. Some state marketing monopolies have generated notoriously exorbitant cost levels, absorbing large proportions of the final price and lowering the prices paid to farmers, as happened to the cocoa farmers of Ghana, to the producers of various cash crops in Nigeria, and in Tanzania. Rwegasira (1984) points out that inefficiency in Tanzania's agricultural marketing boards led to drastic declines in the share of world prices being passed on to farmers during 1969-80, including the following examples:

	1969	*1980*
Cashew nuts	70%	35%
Coffee	81%	45%
Cotton	70%	45%
Tobacco	61%	48%

Besides these influences on costs and revenues, other factors will affect farmers' production and investment decisions. One will be the overall macroeconomic environment, with rapid inflation, acute balance of payments difficulties, past economic stagnation, and ineffective government policies all tending to discourage investment and expanded output. Chapter 2 has already mentioned the role of imported and other manufactured consumer items as incentive goods, and of country examples where shortages of such goods (at any price) had acted as disincentives to greater agricultural output.

Closely related to the economic environment are the predictability and stability of the prices producers receive. Farmers are typically risk averse in the sense of placing a premium on the stability of their cash incomes, preferring to trade higher but less stable prices for lower but more dependable ones. Another important factor is the amount of food that they set aside for the subsistence requirements of their families. Although this, and the resulting surplus for sale on markets, will be affected by prices, it will also be influenced by risk aversion and the search for food security. It will be further influenced by family size and, therefore, by the use of family planning methods. Land tenure arrangements are yet another influence. Where sharecropping is common, for example, responses to price incentives may be dampened by the fact that sharecroppers will enjoy only part of any increase in revenue, but are likely to have to shoulder most or all of any increase in costs.

This review of the many influences on profitability and production demonstrates that important though they are, prices are only part of a rather complex story. Moreover, the influence of governments on prices is limited, with pricing policy considerably more important for exports than for food. So, while there is no serious dispute that prices matter and that excessive taxation of the sector has contributed to poor performance, price is by no means the only consideration.

Principles of Pricing Policy

Nevertheless, as price is important, so is the question of how prices should be determined. One issue that arises here is whether what is needed is for prices to be freer, to find their own levels according to supply and demand, or whether government-determined prices should simply be "better" and offer improved incentives. We shall return to this question shortly but, in either event, the general principle many economists urge is that producer prices should be equated with the prices at which the country could buy or sell the same products on world markets, subject to certain adjustments. This is known as the border-pricing principle, and may be thought of as reproducing the outcome that would result if prices were determined in a free and efficient market system without taxes or subsidies.

The idea underlying this principle is that border prices, expressed in local currency terms, represent the opportunity costs to the country of (a) forgoing a marginal increase in the output of an export crop, or of (b) a marginal increase in imports to fill a gap between domestic demand and production. Using this principle, adjustments then have to be made to determine the prices that "ought" to be offered to producers. Domestic marketing and distribution costs are the most obvious ones, with such costs being subtracted from the prices offered to export producers. Nonmarket adjustments may also be made, principally to accommodate taxes or subsidies. The government may wish, for example, to avoid penalizing remote regions subject to high distribution costs either by overt subsidies or by means of "national" prices, in which low-cost regions effectively subsidize high-cost regions. It may wish to promote export price stabilization by creaming off windfall gains during temporary booms on world markets and using the accumulated reserves to maintain better-than-world prices during temporary slumps (see box 2-1). It may wish to protect all or part of agriculture from foreign competition by means of export subsidies and/or import restrictions. Except perhaps in the case of price stabilization, such uses of fiscal weapons are liable, however, to incur an efficiency cost.

One feature of the border-pricing principle is that it draws attention to the crucial importance of the exchange rate, which determines the local currency equivalent of a given world price. Governments that maintain overvalued exchange rates have difficulty in maintaining attractive production incentives. Budgetary costs are unlikely to permit them to enter into extensive subsidies, but the world price multiplied by an overvalued currency (that is, a rate that results in a smaller number of local currency units per unit of foreign exchange) may not provide a sufficient margin over production costs to be attractive to farmers. To put it another way, a depreciated currency results in higher local currency border prices, and can thus improve farmer incentives. With overvaluation border pricing, even in the absence of taxation, provides no assurance of adequate producer incentives, particularly when world prices are weak. Indeed, a further possibility is that currency depreciations can help compensate for declining world prices (although governments need to be careful about policies that encourage production of commodities facing weak demand).

Even with appropriate exchange rates, the border-pricing principle is by no means without critics. A common objection is that market imperfections distort many international prices, an example being the high levels of protection most industrial countries offer to farmers, and hence international prices do not serve to guide resources into their globally most efficient uses. The standard response to that argument is that it is irrelevant. Whatever the admitted imperfections in these markets, there is nothing that a single, small, developing country can do about them, and world prices therefore still represent the opportunity cost of exports or import substitutes forgone. If agricultural protectionism by the European Community has the effect of depressing the world prices of, say, sugar or wheat, that is a factor that developing countries must take into account when making decisions about their own production of these goods, and is an opportunity that consuming nations can take advantage of.

This line of argument is valid, however, only if the factors making world markets imperfect can be depended upon over time. If that condition is not satisfied, then today's (distorted) prices will not provide a sensible basis for future production decisions. To continue with our earlier example, the protectionist policies of the European Community are, at the time of writing, the subject of intense negotiations as part of the Uruguay Round of trade liberalization negotiations under the General Agreement on Tariffs and Trade (GATT). They are also the subject of much controversy within the Community itself. It is thus possible that these policies could be significantly modified at any time. Whether current prices provide a sensible guide for the future is therefore essentially a matter of judgment about the likelihood of policy changes in the Community and elsewhere.

Quite apart from such considerations, as already mentioned, world commodity prices are notoriously unstable, with modest changes in conditions of supply or demand resulting in large price movements. To take another example, in May 1989 the world price for robusta coffee beans was $2.013 per kilogram, but two months later it had fallen to $1.438. What were the governments and farmers of Brazil, Kenya, and other coffee exporting countries to make of these signals? Maybe one or other of these prices provided a reasonable basis for decisions about production and investment, but certainly not both of them within such a short space of time. Production on the basis of either (and quite possibly both) could well turn out to be "wrong" in the light of subsequent market developments. Moreover, the fact of price instability (combined with incomplete or imperfect provisions of credit and insurance services) is itself likely to cause farmers to decide on a socially suboptimal level of investment.

Thus, even on efficiency grounds departures from the border-pricing principle to smooth out short-term fluctuations are desirable, a conclusion reinforced by our earlier observation that farmers are risk averse, placing a premium on the dependability of income and being unlikely to respond favorably to sharp, short-run price shifts (see Timmer 1989 for a statement of the case for governments to intervene to stabilize prices in the face of short-term fluctuations, and for a discussion of the practicalities of doing so). While we have stressed the taxation element in government price interventions, we should also note that price interventions have sometimes had beneficial effects in reducing price instability.[6] We should furthermore recall that there is a food security case for providing some protection to producers to reduce the risk inherent in dependence on international commerce in a volatile world economy.

Distributional or social issues may also argue in favor of protecting agriculture. It is on such grounds that the industrial countries rationalize their own often massive protectionism, although whether their policies could be justified in terms of any welfare calculation is very doubtful[7] (see World Bank 1986, chapter 6, for an excellent discussion of these issues). In reality the magnitude and persistence of their agricultural supports has far more to do with the farmers' political clout. In any case, we should note that despite their preachings to developing countries, most industrial countries in practice reject the border-pricing principle.

Where do these various considerations leave the border-pricing principle? They certainly suggest it is not sacrosanct. We have shown

---

6. Thus, the Krueger, Schiff, and Valdes (1988) study cited earlier also found that the effects of direct interventions were price stabilizing, reducing price variability for export crops by an average of 27 percent and by 31 percent for cereal crops facing import competition.

7. It is estimated that in 1980-82 average agricultural producer prices in Japan were 2.4 times higher than world prices, with ratios for the European Community and United States of 1.5 and 1.2, respectively. Ratios for individual crops were, of course, far higher.

that legitimate reasons for departing from it may exist, and that, in any case, it will be desirable, when feasible, to smooth out short-term movements in world prices. However, a country that allows its agricultural prices to diverge persistently by wide margins from border prices is likely to incur a substantial efficiency cost for the luxury of so doing, and this is not a luxury that low-income developing countries are likely to be able to afford. Trend (or moving average) values of border prices provide a useful norm for determining domestic prices.

What might we infer from this for the roles of the state and of markets in agricultural price determination? We stated earlier that the border-pricing result is the one that would be generated by a freely working and efficient market mechanism in the absence of taxes and subsidies. This suggests that our qualified conclusion in favor of border pricing points in the direction of leaving markets to determine prices, perhaps through the intermediation of a government stabilization fund, but are rural markets efficient, free of major imperfections, so that they would generate such an outcome in practice? There is no general answer to this, but we suggest later that often they are not. In situations where rural markets are seriously incomplete or uncompetitive large divergences may result between border prices and what farmers actually receive, with all the associated efficiency costs, as well as widening income inequalities.

These dangers thus have to be set against the risk of repeating the inefficiencies with which government interventions have been associated in the past. Governments, too, have armed themselves against farmers with monopsony powers, often by means of marketing boards that use their powers as legal monopolies to pay farmers far less than the border price, sometimes seriously delay payments, and sometimes fail to honor their obligations to accept all that is offered at the official price. Governments have also often got prices "wrong," although for reasons different from those resulting from market imperfections.

In short, we have no grounds for any across-the-board preference for market- or state-determined producer prices. It will depend on the circumstances of the case, on judgments about the strengths and weaknesses of alternative modalities. Often, we suspect, the best solution will be a combination of private markets and public interventions, with governments acting to improve the efficiency of rural markets and working through them to raise agricultural efficiency and pursue other social goals.

Farmers' Responses

In suggesting earlier that the direct and indirect taxation of the sector had contributed to the poor performance of African agriculture, and also in the discussion of the principles of pricing, we were taking for granted that farmers are responsive to price incentives. An overwhelming volume of evidence now indicates that this is indeed the case, but if farmers are responsive, just how large a result can we expect from a given price increase? How large is the elasticity of supply?

As we saw in the discussion of the determinants of supply elasticities in chapter 3, they are particularly influenced by the existence of excess capacity in the sector; the mobility of the factors of production; the availability of material inputs; the extent of competition in the relevant markets; and time, with elasticities larger in the long run than in the short. We shall return to a number of these determinants shortly, but here let us consider the effect of excess capacity. It is often said that a characteristic of agriculture, in contrast to manufacturing, is that excess capacity is relatively small. However, we should not accept this too readily. While for land to go completely uncultivated may be rare, the intensity of cultivation can vary substantially. Thus, the responses of the overtaxed cocoa farmers of West Africa included cutting back on the labor they devoted to weeding their farms and to harvesting the crop and the money and time they spent on spraying their trees against diseases. Cocoa production could then expand rather quickly and substantially when prices improved as previous levels of husbandry were restored.

Bear in mind also that farmers in low-income countries devote much of their land and labor to meeting their families' needs for food staples, even though only a small proportion are subsistence farmers in the sense of not normally producing any marketed surplus at all. In principle, the extent of this subsistence production is not insensitive to price. If farmers can obtain a good price for marketed output and feel reasonably secure economically, they can respond by switching resources to cash crops and by marketing more of their output, using the resulting increased cash income to buy more of their families' food requirements. The continuing importance of subsistence production can thus act as a reservoir of excess capacity that can increase short-term responsiveness to improving prices. Often, however, the price responsiveness of farmers operating near the margins of subsistence will be severely dampened by adverse climatic conditions; poor and possibly deteriorating soils; pre-modern cultivation techniques; and shortages of labor, draught power, and other inputs. The reservoir may be a difficult one to tap. This is another example of the general proposition that the less developed an economy, the less responsive it will be.

Bearing all factors in mind, how large a response to a given price change is it reasonable to expect? Here we introduce a further distinction: between the output response from a change in the price of one crop relative to that of another, and the response of the whole sector to an across-the-board increase in agricultural prices relative to nonagricultural prices, that is, to an improvement in its terms of trade. The importance of this is clear if we think back to factor mobility as a determinant of supply elasticities. If the price of a specific crop is raised, farmers can redirect their labor, land, and other resources away from other crops to grow more of the favored item. There will hence be a ready mobility of factors, a condition favorable to a good price response. Most measurements of agricultural supply elasticities relate to single crops, responding to a shift in relative prices within agriculture, and the evidence suggests that the response will be positive.

We have already presented some such evidence in chapter 6, but relating to export products only. This reproduced Bond's (1987) survey of other studies and the results of her own estimates, showing short-run elasticities of 0.27 to 0.43 for major product groupings and long-run figures of 0.46 to 0.80. The estimates in table 7-6 provide averages from other surveys for specific crops. The lower end of each entry represents an average short-term response and the upper end gives the long-run average. Here again we see that all the results are positive, and that some of the long-run elasticities are quite large (note, however, that the results of elasticity estimates are highly sensitive to the period chosen and the model specification, so that no great reliance should be placed upon the specific values reported in the table).

Table 7-6. Summary of Agricultural Supply Elasticities

Crop	Africa	Other developing countries
Wheat	0.31 - 0.65	0.10 - 1.00
Maize	0.23 - 2.43	0.10 - 0.30
Sorghum	0.10 - 0.70	0.10 - 0.36
Groundnuts	0.24 - 1.62	0.10 - 4.05
Cotton	0.23 - 0.67	0.10 - 1.62
Tobacco	0.48 - 0.82	0.05 - 1.00
Cocoa	0.15 - 1.80	0.12 - 0.95
Coffee	0.14 - 1.55	0.08 - 1.00
Rubber	0.14 - 0.94	0.04 - 0.40
Palm oil	0.20 - 0.81	—

— = Not available
Source: World Bank (1986, table 4.4).

When we turn to consider the responsiveness of agriculture as a whole the position is different, as the option of increasing output by switching resources between crops is largely ruled out. Greater applications of fertilizers, insecticides, and the like can produce some increases in total output, but if we consider the output of a sector as fundamentally determined by factor inputs and technologies, then agriculture can increase output in response to an improvement in its terms of trade chiefly by attracting factors from other sectors and/or by improving cultivation techniques. In the short run both techniques and factor supplies will be relatively fixed (except in countries still possessing an abundance of good uncultivated land); it is only after a considerable period—perhaps several years—that much can be done about these things. In brief, we must expect the sector's supply elasticity to be small in the short run and to be quite limited even over the longer term.

Aggregate elasticity estimates bear out these predictions. Chhibber (1989) estimates long-run elasticities in the range of 0.7-0.9 in land-abundant countries, but of only 0.3-0.5 in low-income developing countries. Even this range of values looks large by comparison with other estimates, and table 7-7 reproduces the results of Binswanger's (1989) survey of estimates by a variety of authors, and shows particularly low values for African countries. All the estimates are positive, however. Agriculture's terms of trade do matter, but expecting dramatic results from policies that enhance them would be a mistake.

Since the focus of this chapter is the respective roles of markets and the state, it is interesting at this point to compare the price elasticities just reviewed with output responsiveness to nonprice, or structural, variables, although only limited evidence is available. One result is drawn from work on India by Chhibber (1989, pp. 65-66), who compares aggregate short- and long-run elasticities with respect to changes

Table 7-7. Some Econometric Estimates of Agricultural Sector Price Response

Country or region	Short-run estimate	Long-run estimate	Period
Argentina	0.21-0.35	0.42-0.78	1950-1974
Argentina	0.07	—	—
India	0.20-0.30	0.30	1952/53-1974/75
India	0.28-0.29	—	1954/55-1977/78
India	0.24	—	1955/56-1976/77
Semi-arid tropical India	0.09	—	1955/56-1973/74
India	0.13	—	1961/62-1981/82
Burkina Faso	0.22	0.24	1963-1981
Côte d'Ivoire	0.13	0.13	1963-1981
Ghana	0.20	0.34	1963-1981
Kenya	0.10	0.16	1963-1981
Liberia	0.10	0.11	1963-1981
Madagascar	0.10	0.14	1963-1981
Senegal	0.54	0.54	1963-1981
Tanzania	0.15	0.15	1963-1981
Uganda	0.05	0.07	1963-1981
SSA average	0.18	0.21	1963-1981
Cross-country	0.06	—	1969-1978

— = Not available
Source: Binswanger (1990, table 2).

in agricultural terms of trade and access to irrigation facilities, the proxy for structural variables. He found some tendency for response to irrigation to be larger in the short run, but obtained a much stronger result from long-run elasticities: "In India in the period 1954-5 to 1977-8 the elasticity of aggregate output with respect to non-price factors, was approximately three times the elasticity with respect to inter-sectoral prices."

This result is consistent with others relating both to India and to a sample of other countries Binswanger surveyed (1989, pp. 13-16). He concludes that it is easier to show that structural variables have a positive impact on aggregate output than it is to show price effects. Access to irrigation again emerges as a highly influential force, as do educational and health indicators and measures of the quality and density of the rural roads network. Public research and extension services can have a powerful influence on the output of particular crops, but much less on total agricultural output. Diakosavvas (1989) provides further support in a rather different type of test. He investigates, for thirty-five developing countries in 1974-84, the impact on output of changing levels of government expenditures on agricultural services and infrastructure, and concludes that on average, a 10 percent increase in government spending will induce an approximately 3 percent increase in output.[8] The more common case of declining government expenditures was associated with reducing agricultural output, which also reacted adversely to instability in the provision of government services. Responsiveness to government services and elasticities with respect to price and structural variables are not independent of each other, however. One way of interpreting Diakosavvas' results is to suggest that poor infrastructure and other supporting services are a reason for low price elasticities, thus, improvements in supporting services would raise farmers' abilities to respond to changing price incentives.

Balance and Sequencing in Agricultural Policy

A strong implication of the above, and a theme that also emerges from the earlier discussion of influences on farm profitability, is that a

---

8. Statistically the result was highly significant; the response was recorded as simultaneous (or very short-run), but lagged variables were not tried. Diakosavvas cites Elias (1985) as having reached similar conclusions.

mix of price and structural measures is needed to maximize the output response of agriculture. Streeten (1987, chapter 7) has put the point memorably by referring to the "six ins" of agricultural policy:

- **IN**centives in the form of sustained adequate prices;
- **IN**puts and delivery systems, especially seeds and new planting stock, fertilizers and insecticides;
- **IN**novation: crop research and adaptation of existing knowledge to local circumstances;
- **IN**formation: education, extension, training, and other support services;
- **IN**frastructure: roads, particularly feeder farm-to-market roads and other links to markets; storage facilities; irrigation; water, power, and communications; and education and health services;
- **IN**stitutions, including for rural credit, marketing, and land reform.

In addition, most of these require a seventh "in": **IN**vestment.

The appropriate balance between these items is a matter that can only be settled case by case. Few generalizations can be made except to reiterate that neither price nor structural measures are likely by themselves to call forth an optimal response. Some combination of both is likely to be desirable in most cases, a conclusion illustrated by box 7-2 on the Tanzanian case. This suggests that what will usually be desirable is the simultaneous implementation of a package of price and structural measures.

Not all would agree with this, however. Those optimistic about the efficacy of market forces argue for a sequencing that gives priority to measures to improve price incentives. Their case is not merely that public, structural interventions will be wasted without such incentives, but that if strong incentives are provided, and sustained so that farmers come to believe that they can plan on the basis of a continuation of these in future years, this will raise private investments in rural infrastructure and improved technologies. It will also create a demand—and profit opportunities—for improved private transport and marketing services and for rural credit. Where the physical infrastructure is inadequate, these developments will, in turn, create more powerful political

---

Box 7-2. Complementarity of Price and Structural Measures in Tanzania

---

Tanzania's independent structural adjustment program (SAP) of 1982-85 and its IMF-sponsored economic recovery program (ERP) of 1986-68 provide examples, respectively, of nonprice response constrained by low prices, followed by gradual response to price and nonprice measures; and of price response constrained by inadequate nonprice measures.

The SAP relied largely on nonprice measures: increasing inputs and incentive consumer goods; improving farmer payment, crop marketing and collection procedures, and extension services; and raising budget expenditure on agriculture from 13 percent in fiscal year 1982/83 to 28 percent in fiscal year 1984/85. However, these measures were not successful: despite higher expenditure, there was no marked improvement in incentives. Inputs were given priority in foreign exchange allocations, but transport problems reduced their availability. Imports of consumer goods were cut until 1984 due to foreign exchange shortage. Producers had no additional nonprice incentive to sell to parastatal marketing organizations.

Producer prices were merely maintained for food crops at the depressed real levels that existed at the beginning of the SAP, with marginal rises for export crops. Rising parastatal marketing costs and appreciation of the real exchange rate reduced the share of f.o.b export prices going to producers, even though export duties were gradually removed.

Officially marketed production of most export crops fell each year during 1981-84. Where production grew (for example, sugar in 1983/84) it was due to excellent weather and targeted import support aid. Elsewhere drought, lack of incentive consumer goods and inputs, and the small price rises lowered responses. However, the parallel market offered incentives for food production: higher prices, immediate payment, and consumer goods and inputs. It handled 60 to 80 percent of maize traded by 1985 and, together with food insecurity due to drought and poor incentives for export crops, induced farmers to switch to maize production. Maize output grew each year in 1983-86, and production of all food crops rose sharply in 1985-86.

In 1984 agricultural buying was transferred to cooperatives, to increase marketing and input supply efficiency, but they faced the same transport and foreign exchange problems as had the parastatals and, although more efficient, could not boost supply. However, in 1984-85 real producer price rises, more consumer goods imports, and aid for inputs (helped by good rains) boosted maize production. In 1985-86, the same combination of price and nonprice measures (and advance notice of price rises for 1986-87) increased output of all food crops, and began to increase the marketed output of export crops, notably coffee, cotton, and cloves.

Thereafter, the ERP relied much more on producer price rises. Prices for export crops were raised by 30 to 80 percent in 1986/87, 15 to 30 percent in 1987/88, and 10 to 35 percent in 1988/89. Prices for food crops rose 20 percent in 1986-87, 25 to 50 percent in 1987-88, and 15 to 20 percent in 1988-89. The effects on production were mixed: food output reached record levels in 1986-87,

---

Box 7-2. (continued)

but in 1987-88 and 1988-89 maize and rice production fell by 10 percent per year. Price incentives were outweighed in both years by drought in some regions.

Export crops responded more where inputs were made available and payment and crop collection were improved. For example, 1987-88 saw record cotton production. In contrast, coffee production fell by 10 percent in 1986-87, due to disease, lack of fertilizer, and slow crop collection. Though prices rose less in 1987-88 and 1988-89, production increases matched 1986-87: higher availability of incentive goods and inputs was responsible. Price incentives elicited substantial supply responses only in individual crops, not an aggregate response throughout the sector, and only in specific seasons, not as a consistent trend.

While the ERP did not initially emphasize investment in fertilizer, seeds, technology, irrigation, replanting, and extension, by 1988 aid donors had realized the importance of nonprice measures: aid was being channeled to boosting fertilizer production, a World Bank loan to agricultural research aimed to improve seed and technology use, and subsector loans were stimulating replanting. However, by 1987-88 80 to 90 percent of fertilizer was still imported, less than 4 percent of land was irrigated, and there had been no overhaul of extension. All these factors were constraining response to price and other incentives.

Source: UNCTAD (1989, part II, section 2); see also World Bank (1986, pp. 74-75).

---

pressures for action by the state, whereas if the state comes in prematurely with a plethora of structural interventions this could undermine the development of local markets.

A weakness in this case, however, is that it rests tacitly on a presumption that the forces of competition are strong enough in rural areas to produce efficiently operating markets. In the circumstances of many low-income countries this presumption is open to question. Thus, according to Timmer (1988, p.326).[9]

---

9. This view is echoed by Lele (1988) examining the African situation. She writes of the absence of capital markets as a major constraint on production growth, and of inaccessibility of markets and poor and costly communications (p.199). She refers to unintegrated food markets (giving rise to large differences in the prices for the same products in markets of the same locality) and observes that, "Even where the private sector is allowed to operate freely in marketing and agro-processing as, for instance, in Nigeria, trade by licensed buying agents for cotton and rubber is often said to be far less than competitive" (p.202).

The strategic dilemma is how to cope with segmented rural capital and labour markets, poorly functioning land markets, the welfare consequences of sharp instability of prices in commodity markets, the pervasive lack of information about current and future events in most rural economies, and the sheer absence of many important markets, especially for future contingencies involving yield or price risks.

Where the conditions for competitive markets are not well satisfied the temptation is to suggest instead a "structures first" strategy, in which the institutional and infrastructural reforms are put in place prior to action upon price incentives, a line of action supported by the research findings discussed above showing elasticities of aggregate output to be greater with respect to structural than to price variables. Political considerations may also reinforce this sequencing, namely, that because raising producer prices is likely to involve the government in political costs, first ensuring that the conditions are in place that will maximize the production stimulus derived from improved prices makes sense (Lipton 1987, pp. 205-6).

A further implication of the evidence adduced above is that programs that seek to stimulate output through improved prices, but which simultaneously cut back on government services and investments in the rural economy, probably as part of wider attempts to reduce budget deficits, are liable to be self-defeating. This is a serious point because many of the adjustment programs currently in place in developing countries are required to conform to the IMF's policy conditionality, which often requires overall reductions in government spending. An apparent tradeoff is thus signaled between the requirements of macroeconomic management and the revival of agriculture as part of the process of structural adaptation.

However, this conclusion relates primarily to sectorwide policies to stimulate output, for we have shown that price elasticities are substantially larger for individual crops in response to changes in relative agricultural prices. The other side of that coin draws attention to the pitfalls of looking at these matters crop by crop. The danger of such a piecemeal approach to agricultural policy is that price measures to induce a desired increase in the output of one crop may simply be at the (undesired) expense of reducing the production of other crops. For example, Hugon (1988) has argued that in Madagascar a rise in the official price of cotton (which was a condition for an IMF credit) increased cotton output, but led to a sharp fall in peanut production. Similarly, improved rice prices led to greater output, but only by switching resources from the production of coffee, an important export crop. This type of consideration may be of particular importance for achieving a desired balance in the production of export crops and foodstuffs.

Concluding Cautions

However the balance is struck and whatever the sequencing chosen, the thrust of the foregoing is to urge the need for a mutually reinforcing combination of market-oriented price incentives and of nonprice, structural interventions by the state. Timmer (1988, p.328) again:

> The factors needed for inducing agricultural transformation, to 'get agriculture moving,' involve a complex mix of appropriate new technology, flexible rural institutions, and a market orientation that offers farmers material rewards for the physical effort they expend in their fields and households and for the risks they face from both nature and markets.

If this conclusion seems bland, even obvious, it is not without attendant dangers. One of these is the danger of using too broad a brush where greater refinement is called for. We have stressed the difficulties of generalizing across countries and within them. The level of development of the rural economy, how it meshes into the national economy, its infrastructure and markets, the ecological conditions in which crops must be cultivated, the mixture of crops grown, and the seriousness of initial problems are all liable to vary greatly within countries. No single policy decision or package can be uniformly appropriate in such circumstances. Rather the need is for flexibility, experimentation, and decentralization in policy. The devotion of additional resources to crop-and locality-specific research is also necessary so that local situations can be better understood and appropriate policy responses designed. Our conclusion may be bland, but it is certainly not easy or cheap.

A further way in which it may be difficult arises from the politics of agricultural reform. The taxation of agriculture described earlier did not occur as a result of carelessness. It was no accident. Rather it reflected a distribution of political power that favored the urban economy and those who depend on it.[10] By comparison with urban groups—and with the highly mobilized farming communities of Western Europe—farmers in low-income countries tend to be poorly organized, leaving them with less political clout than their numbers and their importance as producers should merit. One of the difficulties of urging more remunerative prices for farmers, especially for growers of foodstuffs, is that these are almost certain to result in higher food prices in the towns or in insupportably large subsidies financed from the exchequer.

Not that the reform of agricultural policy is politically impossible. Too great an urban bias and the overtaxation of agriculture tend in the end to break down as a political strategy, as failing supplies of food and industrial raw materials will eventually threaten the government's stability and create a powerful incentive for policy change. Thus, policymakers must give careful thought to the tactics of agricultural policy reform. This may strengthen the structures first school, which would first improve state-provided services and infrastructure before acting on price incentives, to maximize the output response to the price improvements. The greater the response the less the potentially adverse impact on the urban economy. There may similarly be a case for timing price improvements to coincide with a year of good harvests, although once embarked upon it will be essential for credibility that the government persists with the price reforms.

Finally, we should caution against the danger of "attention bias." The focus of our treatment here—on the respective contributions of market incentives and state interventions—reflects a present-day preoccupation in policy debates. But we should not let the influence of fashion on governments, aid agencies, and academics divert attention from the fundamental determinants of agricultural performance: the availability of land and other factors, the techniques employed, population pressures, and climatic and other ecological conditions. Exaggerating the extent and speed with which improvements in either government services or market incentives can influence these funda-

---

10. See Lipton (1977) for an early and influential statement of the urban bias argument, and Bates (1981) for a classical analysis of the politics of the taxation of agriculture.

mental is easy, but in the end it is the impact upon these that will determine the long-term strength of agriculture.

What Can Governments Do for Industry?

Earlier in this chapter we drew attention to the weakness of industrial performance in SSA. We pointed out that industrialization had virtually ceased in the 1980s, that an appalling export record pointed to inefficiency by international standards, and that various structural shortcomings are preventing African industry from performing its enabling role in economic adaptation. Before turning to consider possible policy responses to this situation, we should examine some of the causes of substandard industrial performance.

Diagnosing the problems

A convenient way to classify the causes of substandard industrial performance is to designate them as either exogenous, outside the industrial sector and the reach of industrial policy, or endogenous.

Exogenous factors. The heavy reliance of African manufacturing on the domestic market leaves it very vulnerable to fluctuations in the levels of activity at home, and most African economies were stagnant, even declining, during the 1980s.[11] Much of the industrial deceleration shown in table 7-2 is attributable to this general slowdown and the manifold causes that underlie it. Box 7-1 describes a similar situation for Nepal. One of these causes, of course, is the balance of payments constraint discussed earlier, but the resulting shortages of foreign ex-

---

11. Various authors have decomposed SSA's post-independence industrialization as stemming from (a) the satisfaction of an expanding domestic market for manufactured goods; (b) import substitution, in the statistical sense of reducing shares of imports in total consumption of particular goods; and (c) exportation. Both (a) and (b) represent sales to the domestic market, and both represent import substitution in the sense that the goods would have to be imported to meet demand if they were not produced at home. There is thus no rigid distinction between them, but there is a difference in that (a) results from increases in the total size of a domestic demand, while (b) is a result of the replacement of imports in the satisfaction of a given market. It is (a)-type industrialization that is particularly vulnerable to changes in the condition of the domestic economy. Riddell and others' (1990, p.32) seven country studies showed that between 54 and 72 percent of industrial expansion could be accounted for in terms of (a); similarly, Gulhari and Sekhar in Meir and Steel (1989, p.56) show domestic demand to account respectively for 70 percent, 96 percent, and 44 percent of the industrial growth of Kenya, Tanzania, and Zambia.

change have also contributed more directly to industrial stagnation because of industry's dependence on imported supplies. Here again many forces have been at work, prominent among them being adverse movements in African countries' commodity terms of trade and declines in their shares in traditional export markets. In some measure, industry's own export failings and import reliance have contributed to the foreign exchange constraint, and to that extent the problem cannot be considered exogenous to the sector, but manufacturing's own failings can explain only part of SSA's payments problems.

Weaknesses in other parts of the domestic economy have added further to industry's woes. We have already described the consequences of poor agricultural performance. High transportation costs have been another problem, illustrated in box 7-1 on Nepal. Another factor that deserves special mention is the inadequate support provided by financial institutions and capital markets, which has sometimes kept manufacturers short of risk capital and of credit to finance working capital needs.

So long as these exogenous factors remain in place, specifically industrial-sector policies can have only limited effect. We are reminded once again of the cardinal importance of the quality of overall economic management, but we should not shift the entire burden of policy responsibility in this direction.

Endogenous factors. Most of the sources of weakness internal to the sector can be summarized as inadequate concern with efficiency. The ideology of nationalist independence movements and the dominant opinions in development economics into, and beyond, the 1960s both stressed on the desirability of industrialization, and distrusted considerations of comparative advantage and international efficiency. Thus Obuagu (1989, p.16) refers to:

> . . . the indiscriminate establishment of various industries by Nigeria's policy makers. This was in their bid to achieve rapid economic development and self-sufficiency rather than give priority to manufacturing activities in which it had the highest 'comparative advantage' that could possibly have led to a more realistic economic development and the sustenance of that development over time. Put simply, it was a case of setting up industries at all costs and of every kind without careful consideration of other alternatives or competing industrial options given the local environment and capabilities.

One critical consequence of this was that it led to the development of high-cost and many a time high fixed costs and inefficient industries.

One consequence was the fostering of industry by an often undiscriminating but, ad hoc, provision of protection against competition by imposing tariffs or quantitative restrictions on competing imports, or sometimes by complete prohibitions. Another quite common action was to set up state-owned concerns to promote further the objective of industrialization on the basis of investment criteria that similarly placed little weight on considerations of international competitiveness.

In consequence, industries were able to achieve profitability without efficiency because they were selling to a more or less captive market, sheltered from foreign competition, favored by the state, and often with little domestic competition. One result of this was a bias against exports in favor of selling on the domestic market, meeting demands that otherwise would be met mainly by imports. This goes far to explain the export failure shown in table 7-3; exporting was simply not the motivation for establishing much local industry and there were incentive biases against it. It also helps to explain why industrialization has run out of steam, for it is the experience even of developing countries with much larger domestic markets that import substituting industrialization does not provide a basis for sustained industrialization (see Little, Scitovsky, and Scott 1970 for a classical critique of inward-looking industrialization based on six country studies). Such was inevitably the result for economies offering the minuscule markets for industrial goods shown earlier in table 4-1, even though there some scope for further import substitution remains.

Finally, the lack of concern with efficiency led to the creation of import substituting enterprises that turned out to be a net drain on countries' foreign exchange because of the enterprises' dependence on imported materials, equipment, skills, and capital, and because of the large inputs of domestic resources they required to save a unit of foreign exchange. Such enterprises thus added to balance of payments difficulties while contributing little or nothing to the transformation of the domestic economy.

Of course, we are painting with a broad brush here. The deficiencies just described are far more serious in some countries than others (for an example of an African country that generally avoided such mistakes see the study dealing with Botswana in Riddell and others 1990), and particular countries and industries encounter other more specific sources of difficulty. Nevertheless, writers from all parts of the theoretical spectrum agree on the essentially self-defeating waste of resources resulting from the inward-looking industrialization of the 1960s and into the 1970s.

A Consensual Minimum Role for the State

Many policy instruments are available to governments wishing to influence the pace and pattern of industrial development. Table 7-8 summarizes these instruments and is an augmented version of the results of a survey of industrial policy measures in use in developing countries. These could be reclassified in other ways, one of which would be to distinguish between positive and negative instruments. Into the latter class would come measures intended to regulate or control industry, including industrial licensing, labor legislation, price controls, and restrictions on foreign ownership. Examples of positive instruments would be the provision of tax incentives, favorable credit rules, protection, provision of supporting infrastructure, and the various forms of export subsidy listed in the table. As already mentioned, policy measures intended to have economywide effects (not included in the table) can also have a large impact on industry, the most obvious being the exchange rate. How, then, should governments deploy this formidable arsenal?

Although disagreement about the design of industrial policy abounds, by no means all of it is controversial. Most economists would agree that any country's industrial policies should, as a minimum, include measures providing a combination of supporting services, promotional measures, and public interest safeguards.

The category of supporting services would include the provision and periodic updating of an appropriate legal framework within which firms can operate, particularly in the laws relating to companies and to patents. It would also include the provision by the state of a supporting physical infrastructure—a transport network, modern communications, adequate and reliable power and water supplies—to which might be added measures to ensure an adequate supply of land for industrial

Table 7-8. Industrial Policy Measures in Developing Countries

Area of intervention	Examples of policy measures used
Production and marketing	Industrial licensing; regulation of restrictive business practices; tax incentives to particular industries; provision of land; creation of industrial estates; provision of power, water, roadways, communications, and other infrastructure; price controls; national planning; development and regulation of public enterprises and joint ventures; environmental regulations
Employment and other factor markets	Minimum wage legislation, labor training schemes, restrictions on use of foreign labor, interest rate and credit controls, capital subsidies, tax benefits for business income
Foreign investment	Prohibition of private foreign investment, requirement for domestic majority ownership, constraints on profit remittances abroad and capital repatriation, exclusion of foreign investment from key industries, direct subsidies and tax incentives for foreign investment
Technology	Patent laws, research and development support, regulation of transnational corporations and technology agreements
Imports	Import licensing, quotas and prohibitions, import tariffs, multiple exchange rates
Exports	Export licensing, taxes and customs duties on exports, income tax and customs duty concessions for export earnings, export credit, foreign exchange earnings retention schemes, favorable exchange rates, export processing zones, marketing assistance schemes

Source: Donges (1976); augmented by additional entries.

development and the provision of industrial estates for small and medium-sized firms. Most economists would also agree on the state's responsibility of the state to contribute a "human infrastructure" in the form of an effective national educational system, participation in industrial training programs, and support for industrial research and development (where the presence of externalities would otherwise lead to underinvestment by the private sector). Where comparable market failures occur in capital markets, the state should ensure the existence of an institutional and regulatory framework that meets the legitimate capital needs of industry. It should also provide specialist supporting services, for example, for marketing and insuring exports, when it has reason to expect that these will not be adequately provided by the private sector. There would nowadays also be wide support for avoiding overvaluation and maintaining competitive exchange rates to provide incentives for would-be exporters and producers of import substitutes.

Moving to more positive promotional measures, there is, despite often fierce arguments, support for the provision of moderate infant industry protection against competing imports, subject to certain public interest safeguards. Whether the state should enact special investment codes and other measures aimed at encouraging private foreign investment has in the past been highly controversial, but is becoming less so, if only because the plight of developing countries has become such that they need capital from wherever they can get it. A high proportion of developing countries have now enacted such provisions. Finally, we might mention the particular desirability for small countries of regional cooperation arrangements to minimize the disadvantages of small domestic markets and to foster trade among them. Most economists would agree that governments should seek to negotiate some form of regional trading arrangements, even though their realization is, of course, beyond the power of any one government, and the record to date has been discouraging.

Among the public interest measures for which one would expect wide support is legislation to safeguard against the abuse of unequal bargaining strength in labor markets in such areas as employment of children, excessive hours of work, safety, and so on, and while support for encouraging foreign investment is more prevalent than before, safeguards are needed there too on such matters as the training of local workers, technology transfers, and accurate financial reporting. The public interest also includes industrywide environmental safeguards, for example, against the destruction of nonrenewable resources and the discharge of poisons into the air, seas, and rivers.[12] Most economists would probably also concur with the need to safeguard the public against the misuse of monopoly power, given the prevalence of high degrees of industrial concentration in many small developing countries. In principle, they would also accept that governments should safeguard the public interest in their protection policies by carefully quantifying the costs and benefits to be gained from protection and by keeping protection to the minimum consistent with the achievement of the benefits.

Beyond the Consensus: The Swing Issues

On no reading does the above consensual program add up to a policy of *laissez faire*. Governments have much to do. Nevertheless, it is a program that relies heavily on the efficacy of creating an appropriate framework to encourage efficient, private industrial investment. It is, in that sense, a relatively passive, or enabling, program. The real controversies start when we consider whether governments should go further than this.

There are a number of swing issues around which opinions divide. One is whether the best way forward is to continue to promote industry or to concentrate on improving the efficiency of those industries already in place. Closely related to this is the question of what to do with the chronically inefficient industries: provide long-term support or allow them to go bankrupt? It is probably fair to say that the World Bank, for example, belongs more to the reform camp and is more apt to take a hard line on the chronically inefficient than many of the governments with which it deals.

Another swing issue concerns how to take key decisions about new industrial investments: should these be taken wholly by private investors acting upon present market signals, or does government planning have a role to play, seeking to "pick winners" in anticipation of future market developments? This is a well-trodden battleground. So too is protection policy. Our earlier claim of support for a moderate degree of protection of "infants," subject to public interest safe-

---

12. Significantly, Donges did not report finding any such safeguards in his 1976 survey, reminding us how recently it is that such "green" concerns have moved onto the policy agenda.

guards, leaves much to argue about: how much protection, for how long, and of what type? Another "how much" issue takes us back to the role of planning: how much control should be exerted over industrial development? This is likely to revolve around the use of industrial licensing: should industry be licensed at all and, if so, with what objectives, and how restrictive should it be? (For a valuable essay on the neglected topic of industrial licensing see Cody, Hughes, and Wall, 1980, chapter 6). We cannot cover all these controversies here as we wish instead to concentrate on the key issue of trade policy, but we can at least summarize the advantages and disadvantages of the larger debate before turning to trade questions.

An Outline of the Arguments

To a large extent, the swing issues turn on the alleged failings of markets and governments. Those who argue for confining the role of government broadly to the minimum role described above draw attention to the negative results secured from past attempts at industrial planning and control. We have already suggested that much of the poor record of industry in SSA can be attributed to the industrialization policies pursued in earlier decades, and some would go further to suggest that there are few grounds for expecting much better of governments in the future. This has to do partly with objectives. Ministers are not just concerned with promoting long-run development. They are also concerned with staying in power, with rewarding supporters, and, sometimes, with party or personal gains. Their officials also sometimes have mixed motives and, in any case, too few able officials are available to give disinterested advice and to administer industrial policies as intended.

The result, the argument continues, is that the realities of planning and control are far removed from the textbook advantages. Thus, for all the lip service that may be paid to confining protection to the quantified and temporary needs of genuine infant industries, real-life protection continues to be arbitrary, excessive, and permanent. The realities of licensing and controls are similarly alleged to be strongly at variance with the theoretical benefits. Thus, experiences with industrial licensing show that it adds to uncertainties, is inflexible, slows down investment decisions, favors the large firms that can afford to devote resources to lobbying the licensing authorities, and invites inefficiency and malpractice through its lack of transparency. Price controls are another example of a policy instrument whose results are often perverse. In Zimbabwe, for example, an official commission of inquiry (Republic of Zimbabwe 1986, p.195) reported that price controls were being asked simultaneously to pursue a number of potentially conflicting objectives, were unable to reduce the underlying rate of inflation significantly, were associated with long delays and the politicization of pricing decisions, and were administered by too few staff and thus could not be used systematically to control the abuse of monopoly power. In consequence, the controls were having an adverse effect on industrial investment, output, and profitability. Similar conclusions have been reached elsewhere (see Killick 1973).

The end result of these government failures, the critics argue, is to create precisely the types of weakness diagnosed in our earlier discussion of the performance of industry in SSA, to divert large resources into unproductive rent seeking, to discourage investment, and to make industrial profitability more a function of an enterprise's relations with the machinery of state than with its international competitiveness. More positively in favor of the market, many have pointed to the excellent industrial progress achieved by various Southeast Asian countries, although discussion of these cases in box 7-3 points to more ambiguous conclusions.

Against these considerations, those who favor a more active state role (whom we shall call the planners) point to evidence that a liberal economic regime is by no means necessary for industrial efficiency. This is a feature of some of the Asian cases discussed in box 7-3. An African example is Zimbabwe, which built up a substantial and relatively efficient industrial sector behind protective barriers and with energetic government promotion during the pre-independence years, when many other countries had imposed sanctions on trade with what was then Rhodesia. They also point to the wide range of efficiencies commonly found within individual branches of industry, which suggest that micro-level influences, including the quality of management and choice of technology, are no less important than the sector-and economywide policy environment, and that efficiency may best be

Box 7-3. Lessons from Southeast Asia

The success of a number of southeast Asian countries in rapidly expanding their exports of manufactures has generated a great deal of interest, and controversy abounds about what general lessons other countries might draw from their experiences. Some hold them out as illustrating the superiority of market-based approaches, but others have disagreed with such an interpretation, pointing to the pervasive government intervention in all these cases except Hong Kong. Spurred by small domestic markets and technological backwardness, the governments of Taiwan and the Republic of Korea (and Japan before them) have provided protection to promote import substitution. Japan and Korea created public enterprises that were crucial to industrialization.

Some governments similarly took an active position on the desirable future structure of industry. The governments of both Singapore and Korea judged that their countries' initial advantages in labor-intensive manufacturing would not last and engineered shifts toward more capital- and skill-intensive industries. Similarly, the government of Taiwan deliberately fostered the development of small-scale enterprises. Industrial licensing was one of the tools used to achieve the desired results and (in Korea) a system of export targeting. There was also a good deal of unofficial "guidance" from officials to business people. Governments were also interventionist in the provision of certain supporting services, most notably by using controls over financial markets to ensure that industry's credit needs were met, and also with support for export marketing.

Besides questioning a proliberalization reading of the record of these countries, critics are also skeptical about whether they provide a model that could be replicated in the small developing countries of Africa and elsewhere. They point out that several of the most successful of these countries already had an import-substituting industrial base before World War II upon which they could build their export drive; that they started with larger economies than those of SSA (in 1960 Korea's GDP was about U.S. $11.5 billion in 1987 prices, against an average for the countries reported in table 4-1 of U.S. $3.3 billion); that they had a better foundation of infrastructure, skills, and technological capabilities upon which to build; and that they started with a distribution of political power that favored industry, and with substantial educated and trained professional bureaucracies.

While the presence of much interventionism is beyond doubt, it is also central to an understanding of these cases that their governments sought to work through, not in opposition to, market forces. Excessive protection of industry was rare, it was selective and time-bound, and the average was moderate; the net effect of the incentives offered was broadly neutral between import substitution and exporting; the input and output prices exporters faced were maintained at around world levels; and an aggressive exchange rate policy has been pursued to give strong incentives to the industrial sector. Moreover, state interventions were not infallible, as with Korea's promotion of heavy and chemical industries after the mid-1970s.

Box 7-3. (continued)

The lessons that appear to emerge from these success stories are the importance of:
- Having relationships between the state and private industry that are supportive and nonantagonistic;
- Maintaining a balance within the overall economy, both in terms of macroeconomic management and in not neglecting agriculture;
- Securing the political and administrative conditions that allowed their governments to intervene successfully without many of the costs and abuses that have occurred elsewhere.

Source: Sachs (1987); Weiss (1988, chapters 7 and 8).

---

raised by micro interventions to bring the less efficient up to the standard of the best (Riddell 1990 uses this argument).

The planners can also point to continuing and pervasive market failures as constituting a case for intervention. One such failure is a tendency to concentrations of monopoly power in the industrial sectors of small economies, and the disproportionate power these "big fish in small ponds" can exert. Conversely, there may sometimes be a tendency for too many firms to be created, leading to industries made up of firms too small to reap important economies of scale, and thus doomed to high cost structures, in which situation the case can be argued for using industrial licensing to permit only one or a few firms to manufacture a given type of product. The market may also fail because of external economies. We suggested earlier that industrialization has a special, enabling, value in progress toward an adaptive economy. The implication is that it is likely to bring benefits over and above the financial rates of return enjoyed by individual investors. From society's point of view, there may thus be underinvestment in industry. This tendency may be reinforced by exaggeration on the part of individual investors of the risks and uncertainties surrounding their decisions, for they will not have available to them a full range of information on future economic prospects and on investments others are contemplating.

Finally, the planners can urge the necessity for governments consciously to "take a view" on the products in which the country is likely to have a comparative advantage in the future. Indeed, we have already supported such a position in chapter 4, when urging the need to diversify out of primary product exports in favor of manufactured and other items facing more dynamic world markets. Here too, one can cite the example of the success of some of the Asian countries discussed in box 7-3 in taking a long-run view of comparative advantage, deliberately engineering a restructuring of industry in line with that view.

Before we try to draw any conclusions about these controversies, however, let us look in greater depth at what is arguably the key policy influence on industrial development: protection.

The Key Importance of Trade Policy

When we explored the attributes of a flexible economy, we emphasized the importance of competition and of well-functioning markets if economic agents are to respond flexibly to changing conditions. In this chapter we have drawn attention to evidence of pervasive inefficiency in African industry. Since the inefficient cannot survive in a competitive environment, this too points to the desirability of fostering greater competition in manufacturing.

However, we have also drawn attention to the minuscule size of domestic markets for industrial goods in SLICs and to the importance of scale economies in modern industry. Here, then, is a dilemma. Competition requires a large number of sellers in the market; scale economies in small markets will permit only one or a few efficient-sized firms. As a result the pursuit of multifirm competition within domestic industry may well not be in the public interest in many cases. For example, evidence from Africa suggests that large-scale manufacturing firms have greater success in exporting than small ones. (See Jebuni, Love, and Forsyth 1988 and Lall, Khanna, and Alikhani 1987, both of whom find export success to be positively associated with scale. The latter, however, also find export success to be negatively correlated with the degree of industrial concentration, which further points up the difficulty of striking the right balance between these two factors.) There is also a possibility that industrial concentration—the dominance of a given industry by one or a few firms—may in some cases be associated with greater efficiency, although the benefits of this are more likely to be retained as profits than to be passed on to consumers (see Lee's essay on industrial concentration in Kirkpatrick, Lee, and Nixson 1984, chapter 3, p.83).

How then can countries reconcile the desire to promote efficiency by more competition with the desire to promote efficiency through scale economies? The answer lies with trade policy, not least because manufactures are the tradable goods *par excellence*. A judicious trade policy will ensure that domestic industrialists are kept under pressure to minimize costs through competition from imports, while allowing them to reap scale economies by producing a large share of total domestic output of the good in question. To summarize it: monopoly at home but competition from abroad. A judicious trade policy will also allow local manufacturers to escape the confines of the domestic market by allowing them to compete successfully on world markets.

A judicious trade policy does not mean free trade, however, so the key question emerges, how much protection ought to be given, in what conditions, and by what means?

The Case for Protection

In reviewing the advantages and disadvantages of protection, we might start by pointing out that governments need to consider policy in this area in conjunction with exchange rate policy. The previous chapter points out that an overvalued exchange rate discourages both exports and import substitution. It has been a contradiction in the policies of many countries in the past that they have simultaneously clung to overvalued exchange rates and espoused protectionism. The thrust of chapter 6 was to recommend that countries maintain competitive real exchange rates. A move to such a position by countries with previously overvalued currencies would itself be a major shift in favor of local producers of tradable goods. To put the matter another way, currency overvaluation is one reason why many developing countries have judged the provision of protective barriers necessary.

As countries move to more competitive rates they reduce the need for protection.

A second preliminary comment is to point out that all local industry enjoys a degree of natural protection, which biases the pattern of development somewhat in the direction of production for the home market. The chief element here is the transport and related transactions costs that importers have to pay to bring competing goods into the country. For small, high-value products such natural protection is modest, but it can be large for items with the opposite attributes. In addition, the local producer has, or ought to have, the advantage of an intimate knowledge of the domestic market and of local *mores* and institutions. There may also be a local prejudice in favor of buying locally made over imported goods, although that can work the other way, with people preferring imports because they regard them as more prestigious or of better quality.

There are liable to be powerful offsets to these natural advantages, however. These include the generally greater financial strength of foreign competitors, their probable long experience in producing and selling the goods in question, and their ability to reap economies of scale. Such considerations have given rise to perhaps the best known and most appropriate argument for industrial protection in developing countries, the so-called infant industry argument. This is premised on the existence of significant start-up costs for a new industry and of a learning curve up which it must travel if it is to succeed. The expectation is that as they move up the learning curve—becoming established in the market, increasing their scale of production, and increasing their know-how—new firms' unit costs start at internationally high levels, but then fall until at some point they become able to compete with foreign producers. The argument, then, is for temporary protection until the firms reach this stage.

The infant-industry argument relates to the position of newly created firms, but its logic has been extended into an infant sector argument for the general protection of manufacturing in countries at an early stage of industrialization. In this form, the argument is that at the early stages of industrialization, the cost structures of industry as a whole are likely to be high, owing—in addition to the factors just mentioned—to shortages of skilled workers, undeveloped sources of raw material supplies, reliance on foreign technologies and other inputs, inadequate local infrastructure and supporting services, and inability to reap scale economies. The argument is that in the early stages local manufacturing cannot be expected to compete internationally and will need to be sheltered from competition from foreign producers.

Moreover, if we were right earlier in suggesting that manufacturing generates externalities that are not reflected in firms' revenues and profits, this too can be a public interest argument for general protection, to avoid what otherwise might be a socially suboptimal level of industrial investment. This is an argument that, for example, can be applied to industries expected to generate technological spillovers. Such general arguments are often buttressed by appeals to historical precedent, pointing out that many of the now high-income countries, including most of the southeast Asian countries discussed in box 7-3, achieved their own initial industrialization behind protective barriers.

We shall return to these arguments shortly, but let us first consider the modalities of protection. If the case for general protection is accepted, it is often suggested that this would be best secured by imposing a uniform proportionate tariff on all industrial goods. So far as import substitutors are concerned, the effect of this would be akin to a devaluation: it would affect the local price of manufactures relative to other goods and services, but would not change relativities within industry, and would thus still allow price signals to determine in which branches of industry investment should be undertaken.[13] More specifically, it would eliminate the near-universal bias in structures of protection that favor consumer goods (particularly those regarded as nonessentials) and that provide low, sometimes negative, rates of protection for the production of capital and intermediate goods.

Elimination of this latter bias is likely to be desirable, as also is minimization of the distortions created by the system of protection, but the logic of the protectionist case unfortunately does not point to uniformity. Take the scale economies argument, for example. The

---

13. This argument is closely related to the literature on the effective rate of protection, which measures the extent of protection of local value added, and where uniform nominal tariffs reduce (but do not eliminate) the distortions arising from widely varying effective protection rates.

importance of these economies varies greatly across different types of product, so that some industries would need more protection than others. Similarly with externalities. These will not be generated in equal degree by different branches of industry. Technological externalities are, for instance, likely to be particularly concentrated in the engineering and machine tool industries. By contrast, "finishing-touch" and some other consumer goods industries are unlikely to generate many externalities at all. These considerations point to selective discrimination in favor of producer-good industries, quite the opposite of the usual structure of protection.

Probably the best compromise between these competing considerations is to aim for a moderate, uniform level of protection that is, however, varied in either direction according to the special characteristics of the industries in question. Remember also that all the above arguments are for temporary protection, although there is much scope for argument about how long it should last. The practical point is that provisions of protection should be time-bound, phased out gradually according to a predetermined timetable.

Finally the question arises: if there is to be protection, by what means should it be provided? Although it is possible to do it in a variety of ways, the chief contenders are subsidies, tariffs, and quotas. Subsidies are the theorist's favorite on the grounds that they leave relative prices unaffected, and thus minimize any new distortions that might be created (although the taxes necessary to pay for the subsidies are themselves likely to introduce distortions), but they are usually ruled out in practice on the grounds that the exchequer could not afford them. As concerns that choice between tariffs and quotas, the arguments go strongly in favor of tariffs. For one thing, tariffs will bring in some revenue to the government, while quotas will confer scarcity premiums on local producers that are unrelated to their own productive efforts, resulting in adverse rent seeking and income distribution effects. Second, the degree of protection accorded by a given level of import restriction is difficult to judge and less transparent than the equivalent tariff. Quotas are thus more difficult to use in a discriminating and calculated manner. They may also be open to greater abuse. Finally, and partly in consequence of the above, the outcome of the use of quotas tends to be less competitive than that of the use of tariffs. Protective quotas are nevertheless common, not least because forecasting the consequence of a tariff on the quantities of demand for imported and local substitutes is difficult.

Is Protection Cost-Effective?

Let us now consider the arguments against a protectionist approach. One way of responding is to argue in terms of maximizing world economic welfare, for most protectionist arguments are about winning advantages for the home country at the expense of the rest of the world. Governments, however, have the pursuit of the national interest as their prime responsibility, so we shall not adopt an internationalist standpoint, and will rather ask whether the type of protectionism advocated in the previous section is likely to be in the national interest?

When discussing agriculture we noted that the protection of industry has an adverse effect on agriculture. Protection affects relative prices, so it imposes costs as well as conferring benefits. Favoring one sector of production will make others worse off. In the case of protection against imports of manufactured consumer goods, the consumer will bear many of the costs in higher final prices, but that is not the end of the matter. As we have pointed out, protection permits a country to maintain a higher exchange rate than would otherwise be viable, and the effect of this works against exporters and producers of other types of import substitutes, and encourages the production of nontradables. In the case of the protection of producer-goods industries, the same exchange rate influence is at work, but in addition, other productive sectors, including agriculture, have to bear additional costs in the form of higher prices for the inputs in question (again placing exporters at a disadvantage). In principle, providing subsidies could offset this anti-export bias, but in practice export subsidy schemes rarely provide full compensation, and shortages of government revenue militate against the widespread use of this technique.

Nor is this bias a minor one. Table 7-9 reproduces estimates of the so-called shift parameter, which measures the extent to which import protection becomes an implicit tax on exports. The lowest value in the table is the Côte d'Ivoire's 0.43, which tells us that a 10 percent level of protection against imports would have the effect of imposing a 4 percent tax on exports. In the highest case, Colombia, the ratio is almost one-to-one. An alternative way to calculate the bias is to compare effective protection rates for imports and exports. Here too the results are almost invariably to the detriment of exports, sometimes massively so (see, for example, the estimates for six countries in Weiss 1988, table 5.3, p.191.)

The obvious question to ask is whether countries facing acute foreign exchange shortages can afford to maintain this kind of bias, which again points up the importance of exchange rate policies. In addition, a more general question arises about the effects of protection on the efficiency with which resources are employed and on the pattern of investment. In principle, countries should aim at creating incentives that will steer investment and other resources into industries where they have a long-term comparative advantage, but this result is singularly difficult to achieve in practice. However good the intentions might be, studies of actual systems of protection almost invariably show an extremely wide dispersion of protection levels that, being

Table 7-9. The Protection Tax on Exports, Selected Countries and Periods

Country	Period	Shift parameter
Côte d'Ivoire	1970-84	0.43
Uruguay	1959-80	0.53
Chile	1959-80	0.55
Argentina	1935-79	0.57
Mauritius	1976-82	0.59
El Salvador	1962-77	0.70
Brazil	1950-78	0.70
Côte d'Ivoire	1960-84	0.82
Mauritius	1976-82	0.85
Colombia	1970-78	0.95

Note: The lower estimates for Mauritius and Côte d'Ivoire refer to nontraditional exportables; the higher estimates to traditional exportables.
Source: World Bank (1987, p.80).

usually the outcome of a series of *ad hoc* decisions, are difficult to rationalize by comparative advantage or any other efficiency criteria. Take, for example, the summary of effective rates of protection in Bangladesh shown in table 7-10.

The measurements in question are of effective protection, which can be positive or negative, the latter occurring when local producers pay more in duties on their imported input requirements than the value of the tariffs on imports that compete with their final products. The entries in the category of negative value added arise where the value at world prices of the imported inputs needed to produce a certain good exceeds the world price value of the final product. In this case, the firms are actually subtracting value from the country's domestic product and rely wholly on large-scale protection for their continued existence. Three features emerge from the Bangladesh case that are typical: (a) the spread of effective protection rates is extremely wide; (b) some manufacturers enjoy extremely high levels of protection, including some who contribute negative value added; and (c) the pattern of protection appears arbitrary and difficult to rationalize in economic terms.

In other words, protection in practice is apt to bear rather little relation to its theoretical justifications. A further way in which this gap

Table 7-10. Effective Rates of Protection in Bangladesh, 1985-86

Range	Products
> -100%	Textile machinery, machine tools
-1% to -99%	Nylon socks (domestic), cotton undershirts (domestic), paints and varnishes, diesel engines, power tillers (-1%), bulbs (-2%)
+1% to +100%	Nylon socks (exports), cotton undershirts (exports), trousers (exports), shipmaking, bicycles
Over +100%	Sugar manufacturing, cotton yarn, gray cotton, shirting (handloom and powerloom), gray polyester shirting and suiting (handloom and powerloom), sulphuric acid, transformers, assembled TVs
NVA (negative valued added)	Bleaching powder, caustic soda, dry-cell batteries, mild steel billets, plate (heavy)

Source: UNIDO (1989a, table 2.14, p.38).

manifests itself is in the tendency for firms' initial needs for temporary protection to become permanent, leading to what a disillusioned minister in Ghana called "infants with big teeth." One of the problems with infant protection is that it weakens the pressure upon infant industries to move up the learning curve and reduce their costs to an internationally competitive level. Another is that once established, protected firms acquire political clout, not least because of the jobs they have apparently created (the job creation their protection has frustrated in export and other industries is, of course, invisible), thereby increasing their ability to depend upon continued assistance in the future.

The theory-reality gap has made many economists who are sympathetic to the principle of infant sector protection wary of advocating it as a practical policy. As Helleiner (1990, p.888) has put it:

> Protection in support of import substitution may be usefully thought of as a temporary, and obviously costly, device to assist in the restructuring and development of an infant economy. Its costs are unfortunately . . . more certain than its ultimate benefits.

Given the realities of Africa's industrial record to date, we may wonder whether continuation of an approach based on the protection of industries producing for the domestic market in practice offers a workable way forward. An additional ground for doubting this concerns the scope for further import substitution. While there are undoubtedly specific products in particular countries where scope remains for local production to replace imports, much substitution has already occurred.[14] The figures in table 7-11 suggest that many of the easiest possibilities have already been taken up, with a sharp decline in the share of consumer goods in the end-use composition of African imports.

These statistics suggest that the greatest scope for import substitution now exists in the production of producer goods, and the desirability of moving in this direction is reinforced by the earlier identifi-

---

14. Riddell (1990, table 2.5) provides figures for selected products showing for SSA as a whole a number of cases where African production is only a small proportion of total purchases of the goods in question, although it is notable that most of the products for which the figures indicate much scope for further import substitution are producer goods.

Table 7-11. The Changing Pattern of African Imports
(percentage of total)

Import type	1960s[a]	1972	1978-82
Consumer goods	42	32	20
Intermediate goods	34	39	49
Capital goods	24	29	32

Note: The figures are the unweighted means of data for seven African countries.
a. The figures in this column relate to various years in the 1960s.
Source: Calculated from Steel and Evans (1984, table 12).

cation of engineering and other capital-good industries as those particularly likely to generate technological and training externalities. Unfortunately, this type of industry tends to be the most demanding in terms of capital, technological, and skill requirements, and most subject to economies of scale. In other words, it is generally not the type of industry in which SSA is likely to have a comparative advantage for a long time, even though specific exceptions to this generalization are likely.

Even in industries where trade theorists recognize the existence of a case for providing support, they tend to dispute that protection as such is the appropriate policy response. This takes us back to the assignment rule discussed briefly in box 5-2. This rule states that the best results will be obtained from policy interventions that most directly address the sources of the market failure in question. It is a rule used to question the appropriateness of using tariffs or quotas as an appropriate response to the failures giving rise to the need to support an industry. Take the infant industry argument, for example. This argument for transitional assistance during a growing-up period implies that consumers and others are being asked to finance transitional costs that the infant ought to be able to finance by borrowing. If it foresees an initial period of unprofitability prior to full competitiveness, why should the costs of that not be included in the investment's initial financing needs? The answer might be given in terms of the inadequacies of capital markets, that it is simply not possible to borrow on the appropriate scale or for long enough to finance the transition. If so, the argument concludes, the government can more appropriately help the industry by ensuring that credit is made available, either directly or through an agency like a development bank. This would have the great merit of being self-liquidating over time and of minimizing the risks of permanence. Of course, the need may arise because of externalities, but in this case the theorists point to the superiority of subsidies over tariffs.

A final argument that might be made against generalized industrial protection in SSA is that it may, in any case, be ineffective in stimulating additional investment, further reducing the chances that the benefits will exceed the costs. At the outset of this chapter we saw how strongly the economic health of the manufacturing sector is influenced by the economy's overall condition, particularly its growth and its access to foreign exchange. Industrialists are no less aware of this than economists. They will place little value on protection if they do not think they will be able to import essential supplies or repatriate their profits (in the case of foreign-owned firms), or if they see the domestic market as stagnant or shrinking. Indeed, if they recognize that the effects of protectionism actually contribute to the economy's wider problems, they may see it as a reason for not investing. In other words, governments that can relieve the foreign exchange constraint and revitalize the economy are likely to have greater success in stimulating industrial investment than those that rely upon the offer of special favors.

Managing the Transition

The balance of the arguments surveyed above suggests proceeding cautiously with protection, looking for alternative ways to promote industrialization, avoiding extreme protective barriers, and paying heed to political-economy questions about how protection is likely to work in practice. Movement to such a policy stance would often imply reduced levels of protection for many industries, allowing those that are unable to raise their efficiency adequately to decline in favor of developing efficient lines of manufacturing. At the same time, we earlier identified the problem of what to do with the chronically inefficient as one of the swing issues, separating the planners from the promarketeers.

This is a real dilemma. If SSA is to achieve any radical restructuring—and the performance data suggest it is needed—this implies the dying off of those firms that owe their existence to protection and that can never achieve efficiency in international terms. However, they represent sunk investment and they employ workers. In some cases firms may be the chief source of income for whole communities. The closure of factories will thus impose social costs, as well as being politically unpopular, and as we argue in chapter 9, actions to alleviate social costs are necessary.

Judging what proportion of SSA's manufacturing would eventually require closure is impossible. The strong words used earlier about its export record suggest a sizable proportion, but one expert takes a more optimistic view. Lall (1987, p.117) places modern SSA manufacturing into three categories:

1. A small group of firms already efficient in the sense of being successful exporters or with the capability of becoming so.
2. A large group of firms that are at present inefficient, but are not structurally unviable and could achieve efficiency with policy and other changes.
3. A group of white elephants, small in number although quite large in terms of resources used, embodying investments that were fundamentally mistaken and that should be written off.

For the firms in groups 1 and 3, what seems to be indicated is a gradual scaling down of protection according to a pre-announced schedule, accompanied by state provision of advisory and other back-up services, and measures to alleviate the unemployment and other social costs created by the restructuring. Such a strategy should allow those firms that are capable of it to adjust to this shift in policy by raising productivity, lowering costs, and perhaps diversifying output, at the same time allowing governments to put measures in place that would reduce the employment and other social costs of the restructuring (see Lopez-Claros 1988, pp. 18-19, for a description of a Spanish "industrial reconversion" program undertaken along these lines in the 1980s). The idea that restructuring can be painless is wishful thinking. For example, some argue that even the white elephants should be kept going so long as their short-term marginal costs are not uncompetitive, because past investments in them are sunk costs.

That proposition can readily be accepted, so long as one recognizes it as just a different way of saying the firm should wither away, for a firm that is selling at a price equal to short-term marginal cost will not be recouping its capital costs, and thus will not be in a position to renew its plant as it wears out. What should also be stressed is that the undoubted costs of restructuring should be seen in the context of its benefits. New investments will be made, new jobs created, new goods produced.

Overcoming the Anti-Export Bias

If we were correct in suggesting earlier that the scope for further industrialization on the basis of import substitution is limited and that past policies have created an anti-export bias, and in view of the need to diversify out of primary product exports, the question arises as to what the SLICs might do to achieve the kind of industrial exporting success some other developing countries have achieved. Africa's poor record to date suggests the need for fairly drastic action, and that merely diminishing the bias by reducing protection is unlikely to go far enough.

One absolute necessity, without which most other actions will prove fruitless, is to maintain a highly competitive real exchange rate along the lines of the southeast Asian countries discussed in box 7-3.[15] Once that is in place, however, governments can do a variety of other things to help exporters (see Lieberman 1990 and the essay by Donald Keesing in Meier and Steel 1989, chapter 5.4). A possible pro-active package of measures might include the following:

- Duty free access to imports and favorable treatment on other indirect taxes and on profits taxes;
- Foreign exchange retention schemes that allow firms to keep a proportion of their foreign exchange earnings that they can apply to meeting their import requirements;

---

15. This prerequisite points to a difficult problem for the member countries of the franc zone (see box 6-2), for we suggested there that this arrangement, for all its benefits, has tended to result in an overvalued CFA franc, and that it would be difficult for member countries to rectify this without some change in the nominal exchange rate between the CFA and French francs. Modification of this scheme will be necessary for any sustained resumption of industrialization and any major progress on the export side.

- Measures to ensure that exporters' credit needs are fully met;
- Provision of marketing, advisory, and export insurance services;
- Provision of industrial land and improved supply of utilities and other infrastructure;
- Provision of information services giving economic statistics, trade data, and market information;
- Assistance for research and development, including financial assistance and establishment of quality control facilities and standards;
- Programs for human resource development, namely, education, vocational training, and management development schemes;
- Exemption from certain labor market restrictions, for example, on dismissal of workers;
- Payment of export subsidies on infant industry or infant sector grounds.

Such a comprehensive package would probably go further than our espousal of price-neutral openness justifies. Arguably, not all the measures would be necessary if the exchange rate were competitive. The list does, nonetheless, give a good idea of the instruments available. Another possibility, which incorporates many of the features of the above package, is the creation of export processing zones (EPZs).

An EPZ has been defined as a clearly delineated industrial estate that constitutes a free trade enclave in the customs and trade regime of a country, where foreign manufacturing firms producing mainly for export benefit from a certain number of fiscal and financial incentives. Box 7-4 sets out a brief case study of a successful EPZ in Mauritius, which illustrates the wide range of incentives provided in that case. Export success and employment creation are the objectives. In pursuit of these firms are allowed to import freely and duty free, and are exempted from various restrictions on the use of foreign exchange, employment conditions, industrial licensing, and the like.

Devised initially in Ireland in 1959, such schemes have expanded rapidly in recent years. By 1986 some 1.3 million workers were employed in EPZs in forty-six developing countries (compared with only 70,000 workers in 1970), with many plans for new ones in the pipeline. By no means all of them have been runaway successes, how-

Box 7-4. Export Processing in Mauritius

During the 1960s the position of Mauritius typified that of many SLICs. It was heavily dependent on a single primary product, sugar, which made up over three-quarters of export earnings, but faced a weak world market and an exceptionally volatile price. There was a small and rather static industrial sector based upon import substitution, with effective protection rates varying from -24 to +824 percent, slow economic growth, high unemployment, and substantial balance of payments difficulties.

In 1970 the government set up an EPZ that provided unrestricted repatriation of dividends and capital, duty free entry of inputs, a ten-year holiday from company taxation, a five-year exemption from the taxation of dividends, and export financing on preferential terms. Restrictions on the dismissal of Mauritian workers and the employment of specialist expatriates were eased (although other laws protecting workers were retained). Land and factory space were developed. Later an export credit guarantee scheme was introduced.

No less important, the government pursued macroeconomic policies that have relative stability to the economy and an aggressive exchange rate policy. There were devaluations of 30 and 20 percent in 1979 and 1981 respectively, and thereafter a policy of exchange rate flexibility that resulted in average real depreciations of 2.5 percent per year.

When combined with a plentiful supply of entrepreneurial skills and a highly literate labor force, the results of these incentives were dramatic. The structure of exports was transformed, so that by 1988 EPZ manufactures—mainly knitwear and other clothing—made up nearly 60 percent of exports, from virtually zero in 1970, giving the country an overall export growth rate approaching 25 percent per year in the 1980s. The share of manufacturing in GDP rose, from 12 percent in 1970 to 22 percent in 1988, with industrial growth particularly strong in the 1980s and contributing much to a more general revival of the economy. By the end of 1989 about 89,000 workers were employed in some 600 EPZ companies, making up a third of total recorded employment and nine-tenths of employment in manufacturing. Much new investment had been attracted, a high proportion of it from Hong Kong.

So successful have Mauritian exporters been that they have begun to run into one of the biggest obstacles to successful developing country adjustment in the 1980s: protectionism in industrial countries. Even though its exports remain minuscule by world standards, its successful penetration of the markets of the United Kingdom, France, and the United States called forth defensive reactions by them to restrict Mauritian exports by way of voluntary or imposed sales quotas. Not all of these have been sustained, however, and, as in other countries, these measures have not prevented continued expansion of the country's manufactured exports. Perhaps of more fundamental concern were signs that rising labor absenteeism and pressures for higher wages were threatening the long-term international competitiveness of EPZ exporters, and there was a markedly slower growth in this sector in 1989-90.

Source: Meier and Steel (1989, chapter 6.4).

ever, and some may actually have involved net costs, so examining their record with care is important.

While most EPZs have resulted in the development of new industrial exports, much of this has been on the basis of imported raw materials and other inputs, so it is the net export record that is relevant. By this test the result is varied. The large net export success of Mauritius has not, for example, been replicated by any mainland SSA country. The employment record is rather ambiguous too, although for different reasons (see ODI 1989 in addition to the reading recommended at the end of the chapter). EPZs have proved effective means of employment promotion, as the figures suggest, but at a price. This has to do with the nature of the labor force and the conditions in which they are employed. By comparison with industrial employment outside, EPZ labor forces consist disproportionately of young single women employed because they are cheap and easier to discipline and dismiss. The physical working conditions and safety provisions are sometimes unsatisfactory. Women workers are sometimes required to work at night, contrary to international standards, and trade union rights are sometimes circumscribed. Attempts to apply more demanding labor standards to EPZs tend to be self-defeating because it is precisely the relative freedom from restrictions that is one of their attractions to investors. However, although there has rightly been much concern about the social consequences of EPZs, there is no clear evidence that the worst fears have been justified.

An acknowledged limitation of EPZs is that they tend to lead to an enclave development. The nature of the incentives encourages this, leading to domination by foreign-owned firms and by one or two industries (typically electronics or clothing) based upon imported materials and selling almost exclusively on world markets. There is little inducement, therefore, for the creation of backward and forward linkages with the rest of the economy. As a result the number of secondary jobs created as a result of EPZs may be quite small, perhaps only about one for every five primary jobs created. There may similarly be few technological or training spin-offs. In short, EPZs are not an ideal model for creating the type of external benefits that we have stressed in our advocacy of industrialization. At the same time, the costs incurred by the government in establishing an EPZ may be substantial, in infrastructural investments, and, perhaps, in tax revenues forgone.

However, governments can create inducements to stimulate linkages, for example, by favoring local suppliers of intermediate goods, and in some of the more successful cases the EPZ concept has been gradually widened to include all or much of the domestic economy (as in Singapore and Macau). One must also not simply judge the advantages and disadvantages of EPZs in static terms. One of their attractions is that they can provide a transitional device, from an initial situation where most manufacturers are relatively high-cost producers confined largely to the domestic market to a situation where a sizable part of manufacturing is export-oriented. For individual firms they may be a short cut into exporting without the normal initial phase of import substitution, and an escape from the constraints imposed by the congenital shortages of foreign exchange that mark so many of the economies we are concerned with. One of the advantages of this deliberately created dualism is that governments can simultaneously promote industrial exports while allowing existing, internationally uncompetitive firms time to adjust to a less protected environment.

Moreover, the enclave nature of this form of development is likely to be reduced over time, with increasing integration into the domestic economy, less domination by just one or two industries and by foreign capital, and reduced dependence on cheap labor. Successful EPZs evolve dynamically, typically in the directions portrayed in figure 7-2, which is based on a study of the actual evolution of some of the longer-established EPZs. Perhaps the most significant elements in this growth path are the increasing shares of sales on the domestic market, the rising curve of net exports, and the increasing diversification of output represented by the diminishing share of the dominant industry.

EPZs, then, are a valuable way of promoting industrialization in the context of an open-economy stance, with the potential of making a major contribution to structural transformation. In addition, special opportunities may arise during the 1990s created by the uncertainties Hong Kong's entrepreneurs are suffering prior to their integration into China in 1997. Many of them will inevitably move some of their capital to establish factories in other countries, just as they have in

Figure 7-2. The Typical Life Cycle of an EPZ

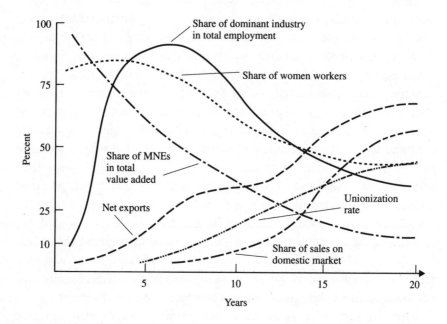

MNE = multinational enterprise
Source: ILO-UNCTC (1988, figure 8, p.151).

Mauritius, so that well-conceived EPZ schemes could prove more ef
fective in inducing investment than would be true in more normal
times.

Note that the model of evolution described in figure 7-2 describes
the development of a successful EPZ, and that success is not guaranteed. Apart from the specific conditions and inducements the government offers, and whatever natural geographical or other advantages
the country may possess, the key to success lies probably in the general economic environment, particularly the exchange rate (Warr 1989
stresses the importance of the general economic environment as a determinant of the gains to be achieved from EPZs). A government that
is not willing and able to maintain a highly competitive exchange rate

and reasonable macroeconomic stability need not waste its time with EPZs.

Still in cautionary vein, we should avoid giving the impression that success in the export of manufactures is likely to come easily. That some developing economies—the newly industrializing countries (NICs)—have already achieved success in this area may make it more difficult for late-comers.[16] Moreover, the NICs enjoy advantages not generally shared by the SLICs. Arguably the most important of these is what Lall (forthcoming) calls industrial capabilities: physical investment; human capital (including a good supply of entrepreneur and trained manpower); and what he calls technological effort, which includes research and development capacities. The NICs also have much larger economies as a base for industrial expansion. The protectionism of the OECD countries is another factor. If this has been unable to prevent continuing rapid expansion of NIC exports of industrial goods, it has certainly left this slower than would otherwise have been the case, and we saw in box 7-4 how even an insignificant exporter like Mauritius soon ran into obstacles when it began to penetrate the markets of OECD countries.

Nevertheless, world markets for manufactures have proved extraordinarily dynamic and new opportunities are being created all the time that protectionism has proved unable to suppress. It is in these markets that the future must lie for the expansion of SLIC exports, and general pessimism about the possibilities is not warranted so long as they are whole-hearted in pursuit of this goal.

Conclusion

In concluding on industrial policy, for the moment let us leave aside political-economy considerations to judge what seem to be the best solutions from a technocratic viewpoint.

First, countries clearly need to break with past patterns, which have led to the failings reported earlier. The protection and other devices governments often have employed to insulate domestic industry from

---

16. One possibility is that increased competition in these markets will lead to self-defeating reductions in world prices for the manufactures exported by developing countries and to a satiation of world demand, although it is easy to exaggerate this danger (see Faini, Clavijo, and Senhadji-Semlali 1989).

the rest of the world have reduced the capacity of manufacturing to compete effectively and increased the general rigidity of the home economies. Combined with the import substitution that has already occurred, the very small domestic market does not offer a base for sustained industrialization. Continued reliance upon it promises only stagnation. Moreover, countries need to diversify the export base away from reliance on primary products.

These considerations all point clearly toward a more open-economy, export-oriented approach, even though it involves entering the most fiercely competitive markets. This, of course, is consistent with the price-neutral openness advocated in chapter 4. It is also consistent with our earlier emphasis on the importance of competition in increasing an economy's flexibility. If the desirability of this strategy is accepted, what might be the government's role in pursuing it? Earlier we claimed that most people would support a substantial minimum set of interventions that included the provision of a variety of supporting infrastructural and other services; the pursuit of regional trading arrangements; and a variety of public interest measures to safeguard the position of workers, prevent environmental degradation, and protect consumers against abuse of monopoly power (including excessive protection). However, there is a case for going beyond this minimum and for the government to take a more active stance to influence the future structure of the industrial sector.

In the context of a generally open-economy stance, the active role would be for the government to take a dynamic view of comparative advantage, to identify the types of industry in which the country is likely to have an advantage in the future, and to manipulate price signals and other inducements to bring about the structural changes needed if the countries are to seize opportunities (on the Korean model). We have suggested that in many cases the advantage will lie with industries based on the processing of local raw materials, a consideration reinforced by the diminishing opportunities to base international competitiveness on cheap labor.[17]

---

17. See Roemer (1979) for a careful, skeptical evaluation of the potential of resource-based industrialization, which brings out the difficulties of generalizing in this area. He is rather skeptical about the benefits of any general strategy based on this type of manufacturing, but note that he is writing only about the processing of

Adoption of a comparative advantage yardstick, albeit future comparative advantage, implies the importance of achieving international competitiveness. Competitiveness will not come without competition, but at the same time there is the problem of the small domestic market in the face of major economies of scale. We have suggested that this points to a strategy of monopoly at home but competition from abroad. There is a case for using industrial licensing or other means to encourage one or a few firms to dominate local industry in products where scale economies are large, but then to safeguard against the losses of efficiency or welfare that would otherwise arise by ensuring that protection is never too great to remove the spur of competition from foreign producers. While we have supported the maintenance of a moderate and temporary infant sector protection, we have suggested that for many industries this will imply reduced protection. We have argued the desirability of a gradual transition to allow firms time to adjust to the changing policy and competitive environment and to minimize employment losses. We have suggested that EPZs can be a useful transition device, reconciling gradual adjustment with aggressive export promotion and job creation.

We have also stressed the desirability of removing some of the biases that commonly result from existing systems of protection and other industrial policy measures, namely, biases against exports and against the local production of capital and intermediate goods. This points to the desirability both of reducing the general level and of producing a more uniform and rational structure of protection. We have also pointed out that protection is not necessarily the most efficient way of encouraging industry, with assistance in meeting industry's credit needs a potentially effective alternative in some cases. We have gone further to point to a range of instruments that governments might use to promote manufactured exports, with EPZs again warranting serious consideration. Finally, our conclusion on EPZs can be writ

---

minerals and timber and excludes agro-processing. Drucker (1988) spells out the difficulties of industrialization on the basis of low-wage labor, and points out the falling significance of labor in total manufacturing cost structures and the correspondingly greater importance of managerial and technological determinants of industrial competitiveness.

large for the restructuring of industry as a whole: forget it unless a competitive real exchange rate is maintained.

This technocratic solution involves substantial interventions by the state and thus poses the question, why do we think such involvement in the 1990s will be more effective and less counterproductive, than in the 1960s and 1970s? We must not ignore the political dimension. In some ways the suggested positive approach will be welcome news to governments, who commonly attach considerable weight to industrialization as a policy goal, and many of whom have shown strong resistance to outside pressures for a more passive, hands-off approach. Nonetheless, our thrust is also in the direction of liberalization and restructuring, and is bound to meet strong resistance from vested interests.

The problem of the transition is likely to be particularly sensitive. Will governments be willing and able to allow chronically inefficient industries to close down? Will they be steadfast in implementing a phased reduction and rationalization of protection in the face of the industrial lobby? Will they be willing to resist nationalistic complaints about any increased influence of foreign investors and reliance on foreign management and other skills? Maybe not. This, perhaps, is the weakness of appealing to the example of the more interventionist of the southeast Asian examples discussed in box 7-3. As the box pointed out, the success of industrial policies in countries like Japan and Korea was a product of political conditions and administrative capabilities that often do not exist elsewhere. To put it another way, one can view past industrial policies in SSA as an expression of the distribution of political power, which implies that little policy reform can be expected if the power structures remain in place, not least because existing industrial structures have created vested interests that can be relied upon to defend their privileges.

It is for such reasons that modern trade policy theorists are wary of advocating protectionism. They acknowledge the theoretical case, but question the magnitude of the benefits it might bring and emphasize the dangers of political misuse. As Krugman (1987, p.143) has put it: "To abandon the free trade principle in pursuit of the gains from sophisticated intervention could . . . open the door to adverse political consequences that would outweigh the potential gains." In chapter 4 we discussed the nature of the state as an economic agent. While warning against overgeneralization and excessive disillusionment, we suggested that one should not expect too much of the state and that there should be some predisposition toward reducing state interventions.

Thus, in the end much of industrial policy comes down to whether we trust governments to "do the right thing." The only sensible way of settling that issue is to look at specific cases, and it is on that cautious note that we must conclude.

Summary and Conclusion

The purpose of this chapter has been to explore the appropriate balance between market incentives and state interventions in agriculture and industry rather than to attempt systematic treatments of policies toward those sectors. We started from the premise that substandard performance by agriculture and manufacturing is among the commonest sources of SLICs' inability to adapt successfully to changing conditions, and we illustrated this with reference to conditions in Africa.

We saw that agricultural performance had been particularly poor in terms of output, food supplies, and exports, and that productivity comparisons were also highly adverse. Although such broad generalizations, which are often based on suspect data, have to be qualified, we nonetheless concluded that Africa faces a real problem of lagging agricultural performance. Similar qualifications are necessary to generalizations about manufacturing performance in Africa, but here too we saw that the overall record has been poor in terms of declining growth and difficulties of sustaining the rate of industrialization, but particularly in terms of international competitiveness as indicated by an extremely weak export performance. We also suggested that the deficiencies of the two sectors interact upon each other, adding to the difficulties.

We next focused on the role of pricing policies in agriculture. We presented evidence suggesting that weak performance has been caused partly by overtaxation of agriculture, where taxation is used broadly to refer to the various state interventions that have driven wedges between the prices farmers receive for their crops and the international worth of these products. Such taxation takes direct and indirect forms, and we argued that the indirect effects of currency overvaluations and of industrial protection were particularly potent. Inadequate price incentives are, however, more of a problem for export crops. Governments' have less influence over food prices, not least because of their inability to prevent parallel markets.

To assess the weight one should attach to price disincentives as an explanation of poor performance, we then studied the various determinants of profitability and other influences on farmers' production and investment decisions. We found that a large number of factors were involved, and that prices are only part of a complex story. Nevertheless prices are important, so we then discussed the principles upon which prices should be determined, organized around the principle of border pricing, according to which local producer prices are set at world export or import price levels. We suggested that a number of legitimate reasons exist for departing from the border-pricing principle, but that persistent large deviations from it were likely to give rise to substantial costs. This left open the question of whether producer prices should be left free to be set by market forces or whether the government should set them, and concluded that the efficiency of rural markets in the country in question would be the key determinant of this.

We next turned to consider supply elasticities: what will determine the extent to which farmers will respond with extra output to improved real prices? The crucial distinction was made between the elasticity with respect to individual crops—for which there is abundant evidence of significant elasticities—and with respect to agriculture as a whole. The latter is more problematical because supply responses from the sector are more affected by the basic constraints on productivity and by the extent of intersectoral factor mobilities. We nevertheless found evidence of positive, if modest, sectorwide elasticities. Larger elasticities were, however, reported in response to structural reforms, such as improved access to education and health, rural roads, and irrigation.

This carried the strong implication that a mix of price and structural measures is needed to maximize agricultural output response: improvements in incentives, availability of inputs, innovations, infrastructure, and institutions. Ideally a government should introduce a mutually reinforcing package of price and nonprice measures simultaneously to maximize their impact, but that may not always be feasible and, in any case, must depend upon the precise circumstances of the case in question, including the efficiency of rural markets. Political considerations lent some support to those who argue for a structures first strategy.

We then turned to consider what governments can do for manufacturing. Since diagnosis must come before prescription, we began by inquiring into the sources of the manufacturing sector's weakness. We attributed this to a combination of factors exogenous to the sector—including the general stagnation of African economies, the failings of other sectors, and the effects of the balance of payments constraints—and to sources of weakness within industry itself, particularly past disregard of international norms of efficiency.

Turning to the part that the state might play in improving the situation, we noted a consensus on at least a minimum role, including the provision of a variety of infrastructural and supporting services, pursuit of regional trading arrangements, and a variety of measures to protect consumers and workers against monopoly power and environmental degradation. Beyond that the consensus tends to break down. The swing issues include what to do about existing inefficient industries, the extent to which the state should have a hand in industrial investment decisions through various forms of planning, and how much protection industry should be given.

We argued that the protection issue was the crucial one, with manufactures being tradable goods *par excellence*. We surveyed the arguments for and against protection and, because of the importance of scale economies in modern manufacturing and the small size of the domestic economy, suggested a profile of monopoly at home, but competition from abroad. The advantages of a more open-economy, export-oriented approach were urged, with industrial policy being based upon principles of comparative advantage, but with a period of gradual transition to allow existing enterprises to improve their efficiency and competitiveness. We suggested that export processing zones could be a useful transitional device, reconciling gradual adjustment with aggressive export promotion, although African countries have so far had little success with EPZs. We also urged the removal of existing biases against exports and the local production of intermediate and capital goods. This points both to the desirability of reducing the general level of protection and of adopting a more uniform and considered structure of protection than often exists.

The above technocratic solutions, involving substantial interventions by the state, were then confronted with political-economy considerations, and we discussed the powerful forces that can pervert the purposes of policy reforms, particularly during a period of transition to a more open-economy stance. We concluded that ultimately what is most appropriate for industrial (and no doubt much other) policy comes down to whether we trust the government to "do the right thing," a question it is sensible to try to answer only in concrete country situations.

As this summary underscores, we have taken a rather more positive view of the state's role in agriculture than in manufacturing. Why should that be? The answer lies in the different balance that typically exists between the extent of market and state failures in the two sectors. Both sectors have good reasons for expecting markets to be far from perfect, examples of past policy mistakes abound, and political forces tend to pull policy away from the technocratic intentions of economic advisers. However, for reasons given, we would expect markets to be particularly weak in the rural economies of low-income countries and have a smaller potential for private enterprise to provide services that would otherwise be supplied by the public sector (of which research and extension are examples). Similarly, we see greater risk of political lobbying and other factors distorting the intentions of industrial rather than agricultural policy, if only because the government ultimately has a lively interest in ensuring adequate food production. Nevertheless, the difference is one of degree only. The main point is that such questions should be resolved by comparing the likely costs and benefits of using market forces or state interventions.

A Note on Further Reading: Much controversy remains in the literature on where the balance should be struck between price incentives and structural factors in improving the performance of agriculture. The World Bank (1981, 1986) provides good statements of the case for emphasizing prices. A more structuralist view, related to SSA, is well presented by Beynon (1989), while Streeten (1987) and Timmer (1988, 1989) offer admirably balanced views.

On industrial policy, Weiss (1988) provides a valuable survey of the issues covered above (and of much else besides). Shapiro and Taylor (1990) provide a useful analytical treatment of the history of the debate between the neoclassical and structuralist approaches to industrial policy. Riddell (1990) provides a major discussion of the performance and problems of manufacturing in SSA and of the policy issues that arise, while Meier and Steel (1989) treat the subject of industrial adjustment in Africa. The ILO-UNCTC (1988) report on EPZs is excellent. See also Warr's (1989) analysis of the experiences of four Asian countries, which is helpful in isolating the key determinants of the costs and benefits of EPZs.

8

FINANCIAL POLICIES

with Matthew Martin

Why should a book about the promotion of economic adaptability merit a separate chapter on policies toward the financial system? Chapter 2 has already answered this question. We there noted evidence that at the earlier stages of development the financial system grows substantially faster than both GDP and wealth, and we reproduced Goldsmith's calculations of rising ratios of financial assets to the total stock of wealth during the earlier stages of development of economies as disparate as India, Japan, and the United States.

While the causality is by no means all one way, and financial sector development is partly a response to growing demands for its services by the rest of the economy, we went on to suggest that this financial deepening promotes the flexibility and growth of the economy in a number of ways. First, by reducing risks and losses of liquidity, and by offering a financial reward, it tends to increase total saving. By the same means it discourages capital flight (outflows of savings to the rest of the world) and encourages a return of past flight capital. It is also likely to attract a growing proportion of total saving out of real assets, such as jewelry or cattle, into the financial system, through which it is more likely to be devoted to productive investment. Any such effects in raising the availability of domestic savings are particularly important given the trend that has emerged during the last decade for developing countries to have less access to world savings, thereby requiring them to become more self-reliant in mobilizing resources for investment, although financial sector development can also help to attract inflows of savings from the rest of the world.

In these ways financial sector development also promotes capital formation by increasing the supply of investable resources. It also promotes both the quantity and productivity of new investment in other ways. Savings are transferred to investors with different needs, degrees of risk, and prospective rates of return, thereby permitting more diversified and efficient investment. Through diversification of financial instruments and access to better information than individual savers and investors can easily obtain, financial institutions reduce, bear, or transfer risks. Through maturity transformation, they allow savers to hold liquid assets while investors borrow long-term. They match savers and investors with congruent preferences for risk and return, and they "bulk-up" the small-scale savings of households for investment, sometimes in large projects, thereby increasing the volume of investment and enabling more risky investments with higher yields.

Capital markets further exert pressure on investors to use resources for the maximum return to be able to repay loans and qualify for new financing. Finally, they provide a safer, more efficient payments system that enables quick settlement of obligations, reducing both risk and the cost of financial transactions. In all these ways a well-functioning financial sector promotes more investment, with the highest available rates of return, and with minimum transactions costs.

Because of its beneficial effects on the volume and productivity of saving and investment, chapter 2 cited the relative expansion of the financial sector as one of the enabling ingredients of structural transformation, permitting and encouraging a pace of economic development that otherwise would be frustrated. Moreover, the shift that has been occurring in many countries to reduce the state's direct role in the production of goods and services and to look more to the private sector to provide the main dynamic of economic growth increases the importance of financial sector development. Unlike the government, the private sector cannot raise resources from taxation or from money creation. It must either save or borrow, and will need the financial system to facilitate these tasks.

A well-developed financial system can promote economic flexibility in another way: by raising the potential for effective monetary policy, and hence for creating the stable, balanced macroeconomic environment whose value this volume has emphasized. Financial development increases the potential for monetary policy by increasing the proportion of transactions that occur through banks and other intermediaries and, therefore, the responsiveness of the economy to monetary variables. Financial development increases the possibilities of manipulating the demand for money through interest rate policies and other means. It also improves the institutional basis for control over the supply of money, for example, by permitting the monetary authorities to manipulate banking liquidity through sales and purchases on securities markets, so-called open market operations.

Thus, the general aim of financial policy is to encourage the development and efficient functioning of the financial sector so that it can make the greatest possible contribution to the economy's growth and adaptability. How much one can realistically expect of this sector will, however, be influenced by the nature of the wider economy, for we have already noted the importance of the feedback from it to the financial sector. The key stimuli to financial development are higher capital intensity; more diversified and greater output; macroeconomic stability and factors that affect the savings ratio, such as per capita income; the need for security through hoarding; demographic dependence; and the propensity to save in growth sectors of the economy. As a result, the low level of development in SLICs will constrain the scope for financial deepening.

We should also caution that there is much that economists do not yet know about these matters, particularly as they relate to the circumstances of low-income countries. Data on such variables as saving are notoriously poor. Much of the available research relates to more advanced developing countries in Asia and Latin America, and we need to be cautious about extrapolating results from these countries.

In what follows we shall first examine the nature of the problems to be addressed by financial sector policies. The second part of the chapter will then be devoted to a discussion of the policies that might be adopted to remedy these failings.

The Nature of the Problems

What then are the problems that financial sector policies typically have to address? In answering this we will follow the now familiar procedure of examining the failings of both markets and governments.

Market Failures

One could be easily misled by the emphasis in the modern litera-ture on the ill-effects of state-induced financial repression and lose sight of the facts that market failures are common in the financial sectors of low-income countries, and that to some extent, "repressive" policies are a response to these imperfections in financial markets. (Unfortunately, the repression itself tends to spawn further imperfec-tions, however.) Five types of financial market failure are common: segmented, incomplete, or shallow markets; oligopoly; limited infor-mation; artificial excess demand for credit; and financial distress.

Segmented, incomplete, or shallow markets. Most financial mar-kets in SLICs are segmented. This can be on the basis of geography, with different types and qualities of provision for rural and urban credit. It can be by type of investor—small or large, newly-established or long-standing, locally- or foreign-based—or based on ethnic or re-ligious ties. Perhaps most common of all, formal and informal finan-cial institutions are likely to exist side by side in a dualistic, poorly in-tegrated manner. Even within the formal system the degree of integra-tion often leaves much to be desired, with poor flows of information and little competition between different types of institution.

Incomplete or shallow markets take two forms: where markets for particular financial services simply do not exist at all, or where they are inadequately specialized. In most SLICs formal rural credit facili-ties are underdeveloped. We already noted earlier the unavailability of capital market institutions as a constraint on both agricultural and in-dustrial production, pushing investors to less appropriate informal in-stitutions or discouraging investment altogether (see Von Pischke, Adams, and Donald 1983 on the economic role of rural financial market institutions and policies towards them). The absence of insur-ance facilities and forward markets prevents producers and savers from hedging to reduce risk, and the absence of markets in short-term financial instruments prevents them from saving at low risk, thus dis-couraging saving or pushing it into real assets—in which case it is un-likely to be devoted to productive use—or encouraging capital to flow to markets overseas.

Most SLICs have shallow financial markets characterized by low levels of specialization. Historically, financial deepening has involved a transition from savings mobilization by the informal sector, to formal intermediation by commercial banks and monetized economic activity, then to more specialized financial institutions (insurance companies, building societies, pension funds, savings banks, and so on), and finally to direct savings mobilization through government bonds, lotteries, equities, and other capital market instruments. We characterized this in chapter 2 as an example of the product diversification that occurs as economic development proceeds. The paucity of specialized institutions in most low-income countries is an important aspect of the incompleteness of their financial markets. Such specialization as does occur is often a result of government decrees and prohibitions rather than a competitive division of labor, as in the following description of the situation in the Philippines:

> When it was observed that commercial banks made little effort to penetrate the countryside and to supply financial services to its residents, a system of rural banks was set up (1952). When a rising demand for medium- and long-term development finance was felt in the early years after World War II, development institutions such as the Development Bank of the Philippines (1947) and a number of private development banks (1959) were created or encouraged. Recognition of unfulfilled credit needs of small-scale industries led to the creation of the National Cottage Industries Bank (1963). The perceived shortage of financial services in the Muslim provinces of Mindanao prompted the establishment of the Amanah Bank (1963). More often than not new financial institutions were 'tailor made' in the sense that the legal framework within which they operated reflected fairly rigidly the need - as perceived by the legislators - for additional financial services by particular types of potential customers (from a World Bank document cited by Fry 1988, pp. 312-313).

Such involuntary specialization may promote inefficient compartmentalization, raising intermediation costs rather than efficiency. This was the case in the Philippines, where there was little competition among the institutions, costs were high, and credit allocation was inefficient.

Oligopoly. Segmentation, incompleteness, and shallowness are likely to encourage oligopoly within specialized areas. Many formal financial markets in SLICs are marked by oligopoly or monopoly, especially in banking, security brokerage and the provision of insurance services. They may also be honeycombed with common ownerships in a holding company structure (Balbis 1986). Under pressure from the political power of existing institutions, the government may establish exclusive or oligopolistic franchises and barriers to the entry of foreign or domestic competitors. Sometimes, to the contrary, it may set up state-owned banks and other institutions intended to counter the monopoly powers of the private institutions, but all too commonly these public enterprises end up "joining the club" and becoming part of a cooperating oligopoly.

Box 8.1 illustrates a rather extreme example of the dangers with a case history of Chile, where oligopoly contributed powerfully to a near collapse of the entire financial system. Even in less severe cases, oligopoly raises intermediation costs and often enables institutions to widen the spread between borrowing and lending rates. Insofar as this depresses deposit rates, it discourages financial savings. As in Chile, it can divert credit to associated companies. Oligopoly readily leads on to collusion to limit competition and can create interest groups powerful enough to influence government policies in favor of perpetuating their monopoly privileges. Another possibility is that one or two firms will dominate, leading to virtual monopoly. Thus in anglophone Africa, where there is little tradition of competitive banking, the commercial banking sector is commonly dominated by two or three banks that cooperate to limit competition.

Limited information. Limited information applies to savers, investors, and financial institutions. Ignorance deters savers and investors by increasing uncertainty and risk with no compensating extra return. When the costs of information about the comparative riskiness of different borrowers are large the banking system will impose credit rationing, in what is known as adverse risk selection, so that even unregulated interest rates will not achieve an optimal allocation of investable funds.

Artificial excess demand for credit. All these market characteristics lead to malfunctioning financial institutions, which in turn cause two further imperfections. Banks engage in nonprice rationing of credit, allocating according to quality of collateral, political pressure, com-

Box 8-1. Financial Oligopoly in Chile, 1977-

During 1977-81, the Chilean government liberalized economic and financial policy. By 1979, inflation and unemployment had fallen and economic growth was at historically high levels. Yet by 1981 the financial sector was plagued by nonperforming loans, borrowers faced real interest rates of 40 percent, inflation and unemployment were rising, and production was declining.

One major cause of this reversal was the oligopolization of the financial system. A handful of economic conglomerates, known as grupos, gained control of most major financial institutions and used them to make speculative capital gains and to allocate credit in favor of associated companies. This ultimately undermined the quality of financial sector assets, provoking a major financial crisis when the economy began to slow down in 1982-83.

The grupos appeared to be relatively profitable during 1977-81, but in reality the underlying rate of return on their operations was poor. They offset this in two ways, both made possible by their ownership of major banks and financial institutions. They made capital gains by speculative purchases of shares in related industrial and commercial enterprises. Although they had inadequate supporting liquidity or other assets, their own banks and others lent them large amounts at high interest rates based on the capital gains they were making. These loans allowed them to consolidate shareholdings and borrow more.

The grupos also used their control over banks and their overseas contacts to obtain low-interest dollar loans, which they on-lent to other companies at high domestic interest rates to make large profits. The search for short-term profit led to a dramatic rise in demand for loans, which in turn sharply reduced their average maturity and pushed interest rates up. When combined with exchange rate overvaluation and a downturn in exports in 1981-83, falsely high interest rates slashed underlying operating grupo earnings. In addition, other domestic companies became unable to repay the high-interest loans and share prices fell. Both these developments undermined grupo profitability and made them a burden on the banks. As bad loans proliferated, banks capitalized interest and rolled it over by extending new loans, especially to companies in the same group. This "greenfielding" created more false demand for credit, pushing real interest rates to unprecedented levels, and exacerbated the mounting financial crisis. Banks nonperforming assets rose from 11 percent of capital and reserves in 1980 to 150 percent in 1983. From mid-1981, the government had to intervene to prevent collapse of the financial system. Initially it propped up financial institutions by expanding credit to the private sector (thereby undermining tight monetary policy) but during 1981-83 it had to nationalize most major institutions (so that the state came to hold 87 percent of financial system assets) to protect depositors and foreign creditors.

Source: Cho and Khatkhate (1989); Diaz-Alejandro (1985); Galvez and Tybout (1985).

pany reputation, or loan size. Lending decisions may also be determined by corrupt rent-seeking bank loan officers. Such decision processes discriminate inefficiently among loan opportunities, excluding less privileged borrowers, and creating an excess demand for credit.

Financial distress. Poor standards of bank management, described in box 8-2, are a more straightforward aspect of market failure that stem from organizational slack created by the possession of monopoly power, excess demand for credit, inadequate central bank supervision, and distortions resulting from economic mismanagement by the state. These factors can cause banks to become overextended and to make loans to borrowers of dubious creditworthiness. If these borrowers become insolvent and are unable to meet their debt servicing commitments, this in turn pushes the lending institutions toward insolvency, with bad loans beginning to exceed their capital bases. This creates a situation of financial distress, in which many borrowers and banks are close to collapse, as in the Chilean case. This is often hidden in bank or company accounts until state intervention reveals its true extent. The crisis limits new lending and reduces the financial system's ability to mobilize resources. It is also likely to encourage credit misallocation and upward pressures on interest rates and inflation. Although full awareness of the extent of this problem is relatively new, it is now accepted that the financial systems of many developing countries exhibit the symptoms of financial distress, and that often the problem is severe. In 1989 the World Bank (1989d, pp. 70-71) concluded that not since the 1930s had so many firms in developing countries been unable to service their domestic debts. Financial distress is insidious, because when it is covered up it damages resource mobilization and allocation and threatens to lead to a full-blown crisis.

Informal financial institutions. As we have already hinted, informal financial institutions may to some degree provide an alternative to the formal sector, indeed, they may have expanded in response to the latter's inadequacies. Although the informal sector remains underresearched, the evidence suggests that it is typically large, broadly based, and a very important source of saving and credit for the groups using

Box 8-2. Four Stages in Bank Mismanagement

The quality of management is an important difference between sound and unsound banks, and in most countries the better-managed financial institutions have succeeded in remaining solvent. Four types of mismanagement commonly occur in the absence of effective regulation and supervision.

• Technical mismanagement. Poor lending policies are the most common form of technical mismanagement and are usually a consequence of deficient internal controls, inadequate credit analysis, or political pressures. Poor lending policies often lead to excessive risk concentration, the result of making a high proportion of loans to a single borrower or to a specific region or industry. Banks sometimes lend excessively to related companies or to their own managers. Mismatching assets and liabilities in terms of currencies, interest rates, or maturities is another common form of technical mismanagement.

• Cosmetic mismanagement. A crossroads for management is reached when a bank experiences losses. Strong supervision or a good board of directors would ensure that the losses are reported and corrective measures taken. Without these, bankers may engage in "cosmetic" mismanagement and try to hide past and current losses. There are many ways to do this. To avoid alerting shareholders to the difficulties, bankers often keep dividends constant despite poorer earnings, and to keep dividends up, bankers may retain a smaller share of income for provisions against loss, thereby sacrificing capital adequacy. If a dividend target exceeds profits, bankers may resort to accounting measures that increase net profits on paper, even if more taxes must be paid as a result. By rescheduling loans, a banker can classify bad loans as good and so avoid making provisions. The capitalization of unpaid interest raises profits by increasing apparent income. The reporting of income can be advanced and the recording of expenditure postponed.

• Desperate management. When losses are too large to be concealed by accounting gimmicks, bankers may adopt more desperate strategies. The most common of these include lending to risky projects at higher loan rates and speculating in stock and real estate markets. Such strategies, however, involve greater risk and may well lead to further losses. The problem then becomes one of cash flow: it gets harder to pay dividends, cover operating costs, and meet depositors' withdrawal demands with the income earned on the remaining good assets. To avoid a liquidity crisis a bank may offer high deposit rates to attract new deposits, but the higher cost of funds eventually compounds the problems.

• Fraud. Fraudulent behavior sometimes causes the initial losses, but once illiquidity appears inevitable, fraud becomes common. As the end approaches, bankers are tempted to grant themselves loans that they are unlikely to repay. Another common fraud is the swinging ownership of companies partly owned by the bank or banker: if a company is profitable, the banker will arrange to buy it from the bank at a low price, and if the company is unprofitable, the banker will sell it to the bank at a high price.

Source: World Bank (1989d, p.77).

it.[1] Informal institutions, such as local moneylenders, rotating credit cooperatives, and community savings and loan associations, tend to be more innovative and responsive to borrowers' needs. They are also more accessible than banks and other formal institutions, particularly in rural areas, and have lower lending costs when dealing with small-scale farmers and business people.

Despite these qualities, however, the extent to which informal institutions can fill the gaps left by the inadequacies of the formal sector is probably quite limited in most cases. The existence of large apparent differences in the effective interest rates charged by formal and informal lenders suggests a limited flow of funds, or highly imperfect arbitrage, between them. Informal institutions in Africa usually seem to operate at the extreme short end of the market, typically offering savings facilities and credits for a one-month term, thus limiting the extent to which they are able to mobilize savings and channel them into genuinely productive investments. The effective annualized interest rate charged to borrowers is often extremely high (although from the lender's point of view it may be much less so because of frequency of default). In terms both of sources of funds and type of borrower, the two sectors seem to cater to separate groups of customers, with limited overlap between them. The financial system is, in other words, dualistic, with the consequential adverse effects on efficiency and investment. If this characterization is correct, the two sets of institutions are complementary rather than competitive and informal arrangements cannot substitute for a well-developed formal sector, particularly when it comes to mobilizing long-term savings and the providing low-cost credit to modern enterprises.

The effects of market failures. Although little systematic evidence on the extent of the market failures described above exists, there is little doubt that they are widespread in the SLICs. We have already mentioned various adverse consequences of this: market failures will reduce the level of formal financial saving; the absence, segmentation, or shallowness of formal markets will prevent savers from hedging to re-

---

1. This discussion is based on Aryeetey (forthcoming), Chipeta and Mkandawire (1991), and other research undertaken for the Nairobi-based African Economic Research Consortium.

duce risk and will discourage saving or drive it to informal or foreign markets; and oligopoly may raise intermediation margins or bring collusion on interest rate controls, both of which depress deposit rates or lead banks to turn away depositors in times of excess liquidity. Insofar as market failures produce volatile real interest rates or symptoms of financial distress, they deter savers by increasing risks.

The inadequacies of financial markets can also contribute to capital flight, a problem that can reach major proportions. Although the emigration of capital from developing countries is primarily a result of people's lack of confidence in their governments' competence and policies (including policies of financial repression) and the tendency of some governments to maintain overvalued exchange rates, the deficiencies of the financial system can provide additional impetus. Capital flight can, for example, reflect insufficient opportunities to diversify risks because of the underdevelopment or inefficiency of financial intermediation. More specifically, it is encouraged by the lack of well-developed bond and securities markets: investors in these could have difficulty in selling assets to move savings overseas without bringing down the value of other investments. Due to oligopoly and segmentation, investors may be unable to participate in profitable projects. The presence of bad debts and financial distress among banks can also lead to capital flight. Investors with poor information, unable to hedge through forward markets or to reduce risk through short-term instruments, may regard domestic investment as excessively risky.

Market failures will also reduce the efficiency of investment. Segmented, incomplete, shallow, or oligopolistic markets limit competition among lenders, reducing opportunities and raising investors' costs, for which informal institutions are likely to be highly imperfect substitutes. Oligopolistic banks may divert credit to uncreditworthy associated companies or projects as box 8-1 on Chile illustrated. Limited information about risk may induce credit allocations based on criteria other than efficiency. Excess credit demand and bad debts may result, further distorting investment allocation, pushing up interest rates, encouraging "evergreening" (new loans in order to roll over bad debts), and denying investment funds to other potential borrowers.

The growth and development of the financial sector and of the overall economy are related to the degree of financial depth, the volume of financial saving, and the efficiency of investment. Since market failures have negative effects on all three variables, they also reduce growth and development. In addition, lower levels of financial saving (and therefore of intermediated investment) and less efficient investment are likely to reduce the profitability of financial institutions, deterring the specialization or diversification that create new types of financial institutions and perpetuating market failures and financial underdevelopment.

These are not failings to be lightly shrugged off. They call for a policy response, to which we shall return later. Next, however, we consider some failings of the state.

Policy Weaknesses

In considering the state's failings, the notion of financial repression is of central importance (see McKinnon 1973 and Shaw 1973 for the classic statements of this concept and its intellectual underpinnings, and Fry 1988, especially chapter 1, for an excellent recent exposition and analysis). This refers to policy actions that hold interest rates below market-clearing levels, introduce nonmarket considerations into decisions on credit allocation, and in other ways directly frustrate the development and efficiency of the financial sector. Box 8-3 provides an example of financial repression drawn from Nigerian experiences.

Direct state controls over interest rate levels, bank asset structures, and credit allocations are the most common instruments of financial repression, and their effects are often aggravated by domestic price inflation. The maintenance of overvalued currencies, exchange controls, and tax policies are also frequently cited as contributing to financial repression, and box 8-3 illustrates a variety of other ways in which the authorities can intervene. The regulation of interest rates is arguably the most common and important of these.

The interest-rate question: theory. Governments commonly impose ceilings on the interest that may be charged for loans. Sometimes they also specify ceilings for deposits, but in any case, ceilings on lending rates restrict the interest that banks can offer depositors if they are to

Box 8-3. Financial Repression in Nigeria, 1970-85

During 1970-85, Nigeria exhibited the characteristic policies of financial repression: interest rate controls, bank deposit and credit controls, and directed investment. Administered interest rates were kept at 3 to 6 percent during 1970-81, while inflation averaged 16 percent. Only in 1972 were real interest rates positive for savings deposits. In 1982-83 they were raised to 7.25 percent and in 1984-85 to 9.5 percent, but this enabled positive real rates to be recorded only in 1985.

Between 1962 and 1970, the government fixed credit ceilings and interest rate ranges, and allocated 35 percent of each bank's loans to indigenous firms. The international oil price rise created huge domestic liquidity, and the government became a net lender to the banks. Banks were so awash with funds that some turned depositors away. The government rejected interest rate rises to restrict credit, and turned to credit allocation and control.

By the mid-1970s the central bank was setting the share of loans and advances that each bank should make to each of sixteen different sectors of the economy, and lower interest rate ceilings for agricultural and other priority project areas. It also set targets for banks to increase branches in rural areas, and by 1980 even insisted that banks administer a car loan program for federal employees. In addition, the government indigenization program ultimately insisted that 60 percent of equity in foreign-owned banks should be owned by Nigerians, and that Nigerians should manage the banks. An unforeseen side-effect of this was to concentrate power in commercial banks (which came to hold 80 percent of financial system deposits), and in three banks holding 60 percent of bank deposits.

Repression pushed savers to look for other assets that provided a greater and safer return. Total and financial savings grew because many Nigerians, flush with oil funds, increased their saving despite low interest rates, but capital flight grew much more rapidly during a period of relative economic growth. Meanwhile the cost of funds for investment was higher than necessary because oligopolistic and inefficient banks were able to insist on high intermediation costs, with a margin of 3 to 4 percent between deposit and loan rates. Banks often could not find sufficient viable projects to fill credit allocation targets, and were not allowed to use funds for more productive projects in more profitable industries. The low interest rates encouraged investment in projects dependent on the economic boom. When the oil price fell after 1981, the effects of repression became clear. Big banks' profits rose, reflecting their ability to corner viable projects, while small and newer state-owned banks, with weaker portfolios due to politically-directed lending, faced growing bad loans and several got into serious difficulties.

Source: Agu (1988); Cole, Wellons, and Yaser (1991); Hanson and Neal (1985).

make a profit from the spread between deposit and lending rates. Governments impose such ceilings for a variety of motives. Some countries have a strong anti-usury tradition, which in Islamic countries extends to outright prohibition of interest charges for loans.[2] Even in the absence of such religious or moral influences, governments have sometimes regarded it as necessary to introduce controls to protect borrowers from being exploited by monopolistic banks and other lenders. No less commonly, they hold down interest rates to encourage investment and stimulate development.

Some theory will help us explore the possible consequences of interest controls. First, we should introduce a by now familiar distinction between nominal and real variables. Interest rates are denominated in nominal terms. If a bank deposit of US$100 pays interest at 10 percent, then after a year the deposit will be worth US$110 in nominal terms. In the presence of inflation its real value will be less, however. If inflation is running at, say, 5 percent per year, then the real value of the deposit after a year will be only about US$105 and the real interest rate will be only some 5 percent. If inflation were at 15 percent, the deposit would be worth less in purchasing power terms after a year than it was originally and the real interest rate would be negative, -5 percent.[3]

Since many developing countries do not merely regulate interest rates, but are plagued by inflation, real rates (hereafter denoted by R*) are often negative, as table 8-1 shows.

---

2. Islamic banking exists nonetheless! This is because such banks have been inventive in finding ways of charging for their loans that are deemed to conform to Islamic teachings against the charging of interest (see Khan 1986; Iqbal and Mirakhor 1987).

3. The exact formula for calculating the real interest rate (R*) is as follows, where R is the nominal interest rate and P is the rate of inflation, and where all variables are expressed in proportional rather than percentage form:

$$R^* = (1+R)/(1+P)$$

Solving for the first example given in the text gives us:

$$(1+0.1)/(1+0.05) = 1.0476, \text{ or } R^* = 4.76\%$$

As we shall see shortly, the inflation term should strictly speaking be expressed in terms of expected inflation, although past inflation is often used as a proxy for expected inflation.

Table 8-1. Comparative Statistics on Real Interest Rates, 1985

Region	Inflation rate	Real deposit rate[a]	Average real financial return[b]
East Asia	5.4	5.5	2.4
Latin America	76.7	-4.5	-8.9
South Asia	6.3	3.4	-0.1
Sub-Saharan Africa	17.4	-3.5	-8.8
Industrial countries	6.4	2.0	-0.2

a. Average real rate on bank deposit accounts.
b. Weighted average real return on financial assets.
Source: Neal (1988, table 2).

It is no surprise that R*s are negatively correlated with inflation, with low-inflation Asia offering generally positive rates of return. Perhaps the most significant figures for our purposes are the entries for Sub-Saharan Africa, for this contains a high proportion of SLICs. Africa is revealed as experiencing substantial inflation and as offering its savers substantially negative R*s. Does this matter?

Part of the answer to that question depends on how we think savers behave. Here a distinction is essential between total and financial saving, where the latter refers to that part of total saving that is channeled through banks and other financial institutions. The most important influences on total household saving include the stock of past saving, income levels, and the population's age structure. In addition, corporations will contribute much of an economy's saving in the form of undistributed profits, as might the government in the form of surpluses on the current account of its budget. Given the importance of these factors, we should not expect total saving to be very sensitive to changes in interest rates.

However, the case is different when it comes to financial saving. Households and corporations can save either with these institutions, or by hoarding currency, acquiring real assets (such as land, property, jewelry, and cattle), or investing abroad (if they can get their money out of the country). Since there is much substitutability between these alternatives, it is reasonable to expect that financial saving will go up with the interest reward being offered as people switch out of currency and real assets and recall capital from overseas.

What about the influence of inflation? Modern theory makes an important distinction between changes that are anticipated and can be built into present decisions and unexpected changes. If we regard savers as rational decisionmakers, and if past experience has taught them to expect inflation, we must expect them to discount the nominal interest rate on offer by the expected rate of inflation and to make their saving decisions on this basis. In other words, we expect the real rather than the nominal interest rate to be the key variable, except when no inflation is expected. In this case, we can presume that the negative R*s shown for Africa and Latin America in table 8-1 will discourage financial saving.

The likely effects of a government-imposed interest ceiling can now be illustrated, as in figure 8-1, which relates to saving and investment intermediated by the financial system. We draw in an upward-sloping schedule, S', to represent financial saving, on the premise that this will be responsive to changes in R*. We also draw in a savings demand, or investment (I), schedule. In a freely operating market, the real rate would settle at r^q, and the volume of saving and investment at i^q. Now assume that the government imposes a ceiling on interest rates that (with a given inflation rate) implies a real rate of only r^1. (For simplicity we shall ignore the spread between bank deposit and lending rates and assume that savers and borrowers face the same rate. Relaxing this assumption does not affect the thrust of the argument.) At this rate the investment demand for savings is i^2, but the quantity of savings available through the financial system falls to i^1. As investment is constrained by the availability of financial savings, only i^1 amount of investment will actually occur, so the effect of an interest control that may well have been intended to boost investment actually reduces it.

The impact on investment is not only on its quantity, however. There will also be a quality, or productivity, effect. If the quantity of saving and investment is confined to i^1, we can see from figure 8-1

Figure 8-1. Saving and Investment Effects of Interest Controls

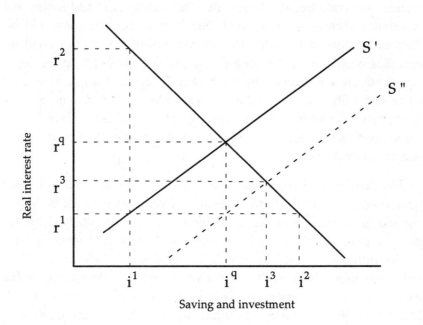

that the market clearing interest rate would be r^2, and only projects offering investors a better real return than r^2 would be undertaken. With interest rates pegged at r^1, however, there is an excess investment demand of i^1-i^2, and the question arises how the lending houses will make credit decisions in this situation, for now any project offering a real return greater than r^1 will be profitable. As we suggested earlier, in this situation they are likely to favor large existing customers, companies in which they have a financial interest, and friends. Bribes may pass between loan applicants and bank officials. In the absence of this, projects perceived as risky will be avoided. In short, the bundle of investments favored in such an excess demand situation is likely to offer substantially lower real returns on average and at the margin than would hold in a market clearing solution. Note that this effect occurs even if saving is interest inelastic.

Figure 8-1 is drawn for a moment in time, with income levels given. We can take the analysis a little further by imagining the results of a government decision to scrap the interest ceiling, r^1, and to allow the market to operate freely. The real rate then settles at r^q and saving and investment increase from i^1 to i^q. The increase in investment will induce an increase in the rate of economic growth that, in turn, will induce additional saving, shifting the savings-supply curve to the right, represented in the diagram by the broken S" curve. Unless there is an equivalent shift in the I-schedule the consequence of this is not merely to increase the volume of investment, by i^q -i^3, but also to bring down the interest rate, to r^3, reducing the initial upward effect of the decision to scrap the control.

The interest rate question: evidence. Theory thus teaches us that interest controls are likely to have adverse consequences for both saving and investment, and hence for the economy as a whole. How far do these predictions take us in the real world? Empirical investigations of the influence of R* on saving have proved less than decisive. Different studies have produced contrasting results, depending on the data used, statistical methods, country sample, and the period studied. Many have limited country coverage and have to use unreliable data (notably on total saving and expected inflation). Measured effects vary tremendously for different countries, making cross-country averages an inadequate basis for policy recommendations. Moreover, few researchers have studied SLICs.

However, recent studies have reached consensus that if higher R*s have any effect on total saving, it is positive, but relatively small (which is why figure 8-1 was confined to financial saving). Only if previous rates were very negative and consumers do not face severe liquidity constraints is there much scope for increasing total saving by raising interest rates.[4] The measured response varies so much among nations

---

4. Thus Khatkhate (1988), whose study includes twenty low-income nations, concludes that the real interest rate by itself has little or no impact on total saving. Fry (1988, chapter 6) finds a 1 percent real interest rate rise likely to raise the aggregate saving rate by only 0.1 percent, with even this effect disappearing as the real rate reaches competitive free-market equilibrium. However, Fry studies Asian countries (only two low-income), and Gupta (1987) argues that Asian results do not apply elsewhere: positive interest rates have statistically positive effects on total saving in Asia, but no significant influence in Latin America. Leite and Makonnen (1986) similarly found real interest rates to have no statistically significant direct positive effect on total saving in franc zone African countries. In a study based on

that arriving at any strong general conclusion is impossible. Though on balance R* is likely to have a marginally positive impact on total saving, its effect is neither large enough nor reliable enough to make raising interest rates an efficient way of trying to increase total savings.

We have already mentioned one reason for this: the level of, and changes in, disposable income and past savings performance are the main determinants of saving, and these influences tend to swamp the price effects. In addition, consumer behavior in some developing countries is dominated by liquidity constraints, which prevent people from postponing consumption and increasing saving. When Rossi (1988) screened out this constraint, she then found a positive correlation between R* and total saving in all regions except Sub-Saharan Africa and East Asia.

Studies of the influence of R* on financial saving have obtained stronger results. Investigators usually approach this relationship by measuring the influence of R* on the rate of financial deepening, as proxied by the ratio of liquid liabilities (M3) to GNP. Findings reported by the World Bank (1989d, pp. 27-28) are typical of the results of a substantial number of other studies.[5] This found substantial financialization: the M3/GNP ratio rose by 0.75 percent for each 1 percent increase in nominal deposit rates. The report also found that financial savings fell by 1.7 percent for every 1 percent rise in the inflation rate. In other words, much of the correlation between R* and financial deepening depends on the degree to which inflation is re-

African case studies, Nissanke (1990) finds interest rate liberalizations by themselves to have had little impact on savings mobilization. Various other studies also find no significant correlation. See Arrieta (1988) for a useful evaluation of some of these studies.

5. Though Khatkhate (1988) finds no influence in the 1970s, Cho and Khatkhate (1989) find influence considerable in Asia. Gupta (1984, 1987) finds that R* raises financial savings. Lanyi and Saracoglu (1983) conclude that positive R*s stimulate growth of financial assets. Fry (1988, pp. 156-158) finds that a 1 percent R* rise raises demand for financial assets by 0.8 percent in the short run and by 1.4 percent in the long run. It also increases the M3/GNP ratio by 0.4 to 0.7 percent (the higher figure applies to countries with a lower initial ratio). Most of this result came from household switches from real to financial assets: 75 to 85 percent of higher financial saving came from substitution out of other savings, and only 15 to 25 percent from a rise in total saving.

duced. Lower inflation makes more contribution to financial deepening than nominal interest rate rises.

Gelb (1989) obtains a similar result using a more accurate gauge of financialization: the sensitivity to R* of the ratio of M3 to total savings. He finds that a 1 percent rise in R* increases financialization by 0.7 percent. These findings are important because they suggest that it is the financialization of savings rather than financial deepening that forms the key link between interest rates and growth. Raising R* by raising nominal rates or (especially) reducing inflation is therefore likely to channel more savings into investment via financial intermediation.[6]

What about the effects of interest controls on the quantity and productivity of investment that we predicted earlier? While evidence on the volume of investment is ambiguous, empirical studies do support the hypothesis that R* influences investment productivity rather strongly. Thus, lower R*s lowered investment efficiency (as measured by the incremental output-capital ratio) in samples of twelve Asian countries (Fry 1988, pp. 148, 422) and of sixty-nine developing countries (Khatkhate 1988). Gelb (1989, p.21) concluded that more efficient investment explained most of the positive relationship that he found between R* and growth. Other studies of the impact of R* on economic growth have produced mixed results, however.[7]

---

6. Studies of the determinants of capital flight disagree over the influence of interest rate repression. Several studies have found that legal capital flight is due largely to wider macroeconomic developments, that differentials between domestic and international interest rates are not a statistically significant factor, and that most of the effect of low R*s is due to the associated inflation rather than directly through repression (see Conesa 1987; Cuddington 1986, 1987; Dornbusch 1985, 1987; Fry 1988; Lessard and Williamson 1987). Other researchers, however, do find that interest differentials matter and that interest rates below market clearing levels drive capital overseas in search of higher returns (see Dooley 1986; Eaton 1989; Khan and ul Haque 1985).

7. Lanyi and Saracoglu (1983) find tentative support for a negative effect of interest repression on growth, but show many countries where it did not apply. Fry (1988 pp. 151-152) found that for Asian countries a 1 percent rise in R* toward (i.e., not above) the "competitive free-market equilibrium level" was associated with a 0.5 percent rise in economic growth. However, Arrieta's 1988 survey article suggests that the evidence is decidedly mixed. Gupta (1987) concludes that R* has had no significant effect on growth in Latin America. Khatkhate (1988) found no association between low R* and low growth.

Overall and notwithstanding our caveats, the predictions of theory stand up quite well. The implication is that financial repression is likely to impair the financialization of saving and lower the quality of investment. That does not necessarily mean that such controls are always and everywhere a mistake. They may stem from religious values rather than economic calculation, or they may be seen as necessitated by market imperfections, but it does mean that the imposition of interest controls is likely to impose substantial economic costs that must be set against—and that could easily be greater that—whatever benefits may accrue.

Other aspects of repression. While interest controls are the most potent source of financial repression, we should also consider some other dimensions. The direction of investment is one such. This takes many forms: requiring banks to lend to specific activities or sectors, central bank rediscounting of credit to key sectors at subsidized interest rates, government ownership of financial institutions, and government guarantees of private sector loans. These policies may restrict investible funds for other sectors (directly, and indirectly by discouraging deposits) in order to finance government deficits or large capital-intensive projects by parastatals. Directed investment through concessional selective credit policies may perversely reduce the credit available to target groups by breeding rent seeking bank behavior and non price credit rationing. This may concentrate credit on the economically advantaged, forcing smaller-scale borrowers to rely on self-financing and informal sector lenders. If funds do reach target groups, they are fungible and may be used for economically unviable projects or for consumption. Even if used as intended, they may encourage excessive capital intensity by subsidizing capital rather than labor. If the state pays subsidies, they may compromise fiscal or monetary restraint. However, the precise method used to direct credit will influence the effects of the controls. In Indonesia in the 1970s, for instance, credit direction is regarded as having brought favorable results (Bolnick 1987). Fry (1988, chapter 16) and World Bank (1989d) present the arguments against directed credit.

Directed investment does not necessarily affect growth or income distribution adversely. In some nations well-run directed credit schemes have improved resource allocation, notably of venture capital to new projects. However, it does tend to undermine the solvency of financial intermediaries. Intermediation becomes more risky and yields lower returns. Moreover, in a regulated market intermediaries may face such a large excess demand for credit that they are not forced by competition to market their product or to select projects on the basis of quality. Both factors increase the potential for bad loans.

Although describing state ownership of financial institutions as an aspect of financial repression as such would not be strictly correct, the way in which state-owned financial institutions sometimes operate can magnify the adverse effects of repression and discourage the emergence of private sector institutions. Thus, government-run development finance institutions and banks are especially prone to high levels of nonperforming assets. This is because their investment decisions are often dictated from outside, subjected to political pressure, vulnerable to business cycle fluctuations, and insufficiently diversified with respect to risk. In general, their record is poor. While they have attracted foreign resources, they have not mobilized domestic savings and have a deteriorating record in allocating investment to productive projects (although housing finance institutions have fared better, notably in mobilizing domestic savings).

Bank deposit controls are another important aspect of financial repression. These consist mainly of requiring commercial banks to maintain high minimum reserve ratios relative to deposit liabilities and to hold government securities. These requirements have the effect of directing a substantial proportion of available funds to the government and the rest of the public sector. They also distort bank interest rate structures. Given the low interest rates they receive on the reserves and bonds, banks enforce wider margins between borrowing and lending rates in order to make profits. Governments impose other forms of taxation on deposits too, such as withholding taxes on interest income, stamp duties on financial transactions, and taxes on loan interest earnings. These reduce incentives for deposits, investment, and intermediation and decrease the overall amount of funds available for investment through the financial system.

The last paragraphs draw attention to a wider feature of financial repression: its association with a diversion of investable resources from the private to the public sectors, often to an extent inconsistent with governments' own stated desire for private sector growth. While such financial crowding-out can occur in a liberalized system, the instruments of financial repression are frequently used as a way to finance the government's budget deficit, or that of the public sector as a whole. One of the effects is to shift the locus of decisions on credit allocation from the boardrooms of financial institutions into the offices of the ministry of finance and the central bank, so that using these powers to give the public sector first bite of the credit cherry becomes temptingly easy. Moreover, artificially low interest rates reduce the cost of large-scale public sector borrowings and the future debt servicing consequences of these. Public ownership of, or control over, major savings institutions adds to the state's ability to divert resources for its own use, leaving the private sector as the residual borrower.

Box 8-4 on Kenya illustrates each of these features. The 1980s records of the franc zone group of African countries provide a further illustration (the following account is based on World Bank 1989c, page 170). Because of restrictions under the zone arrangements on central government borrowings from the banking system, as budgetary pressures built up, governments forced commercial banks to finance expenditures that would normally have been met by government subsidies. At government behest, credits were extended to public enterprises that were not creditworthy, and banks were required to finance payments to commodity farmers in excess of the export value of their crops. These practices seriously undermined the banks' financial position, leading in Benin to an actual collapse. In addition, the accumulation of large arrears in government payments to private contractors, besides representing a form of involuntary lending to the government, also weakened the banks' position by putting private sector borrowers into financial difficulties. As Collier and Mayer (1989, p.8)—authors rather skeptical about pro-market arguments for liberalization—put it: "The concern that financial repression raises is that it has provided inefficient and corrupt governments with easy access to cheap sources of finance."

Box 8-4. Repression and Crowding-Out in Kenya

Even though Kenya's above average economic record is based largely on the dynamism of its private sector, and the government also sees the future growth of the productive system as based on private enterprise, the public sector has claimed a growing share of bank credit since independence, and the evidence suggests that this has been at the expense of the credit needs of private business. Thus, bank credit to the public sector as a proportion of credit to the private sector rose from 22 percent in 1969-73 to 72 percent in 1984-88. Econometric tests found a direct inverse causal relationship between banking system credit to the public and private sectors: when public sector lending went up this caused (in the sense of preceding) a reduction in lending to the private sector. This relationship was particularly strong when the public sector borrowed from the commercial banks (as distinct from the central bank).

The instruments of financial repression were used to increase public sector access to banking resources. The central bank used its control over the minimum levels and composition of banks' liquid reserves to ensure that the banks held large stocks of treasury bills. The central bank similarly sought to use its control over interest rates to divert money out of bank deposits into holdings by the general public of treasury bonds, although with limited success. Government-owned commercial banks had heavy exposures of loans to parastatal bodies, not all of them very creditworthy. The government also used its authority over the Post Office Savings Bank and National Social Security Fund to require these large-scale collectors of private savings to invest extensively in government paper; sums that might have otherwise been available for on-lending to private borrowers.

Probably the most powerful mechanism of crowding-out, however, was through the use of ceilings on bank credit to the private sector to accommodate the financing needs of the public sector. A type of vicious circle was at work, for such ceilings were necessitated by balance of payments difficulties and inflationary pressures, which in turn were partly the result of public sector deficit financing.

Source: Killick and Mwega (1990).

A Summing-Up

As elsewhere, so in the financial sector: both markets and governments are imperfect. Financial markets are often segmented, incomplete, even nonexistent. In banking and other parts of the financial sector monopoly or oligopoly are frequently occurring market structures. Information is imperfect and costly. Institutions' balance sheets are sometimes fragile, insecurity is considerable, and collapse often averted only by accounting sleight of hand.

Government policies toward the sector, sometimes in response to these weaknesses, are often also seriously flawed and actually make things worse by retarding financial deepening. A combination of inflation and interest rate controls reduces financial saving, and is also likely to affect the quality of investment adversely. Other aspects of financial repression also have unwanted results, though these depend on the methods used, and the whole process is associated with a crowding-out of private sector credit needs by the preemptive demands of governments and parastatal bodies. As box 8-5 shows, repression can have the effect of imposing a large tax on financial intermediation, particularly in countries prone to inflation, with predictable effects on the pace of financial deepening.

As the box suggests, the extent and nature of the problems vary from one country to the next—and we have emphasized the limited extent of available knowledge—but most SLICs probably suffer quite seriously from them. The task to which we now turn, therefore, is to examine what lines of action governments might adopt to address these weaknesses and accelerate financial deepening.

Box 8-5. The Taxation of the Financial System in Five African Countries

---

In chapter 7 we described government policies that lowered agricultural prices relative to other domestic prices as a form of taxation. By direct analogy, we can also think of the policies of financial repression described above as forms of taxation. Chamley and Honohan (1990) have attempted to quantify this for a selection of five African countries. In addition to explicit taxes (like VAT, taxes on profits, stamp duties, and so on) their measurements seek to include the effects of minimum reserve requirements, the inflation tax on currency, interest rate controls, and other instruments of financial repression. Although varying from country to country, their results suggest that such taxation was generally substantial relative to various indicators of the size of economic activity (averages for 1978-8):

Country	Percentage of GDP	Percentage of money supply (M2)	Percentage of government revenue
Côte d'Ivoire	2.1	7.5	6.4
Ghana	4.7	31.8	60.9
Kenya	1.6	5.5	6.2
Nigeria	4.0	16.6	31.2
Zambia	7.1	25.5	39.1

Chamley and Honohan point out that the "revenue" from this taxation is particularly elastic with respect to inflation: the three heaviest taxers listed above have all experienced periods of rapid inflation.

Policies for Financial Deepening

A large proportion of recent writings about financial policies has been on the theme of liberalization, and it is to this that we turn first. We shall then take up the options available to governments to combat financial market failures and promote the sector's diversification.

Liberalization

We have seen that repression takes a number of forms. Liberalization is a possible policy response, meaning a package of measures intended to remove undesirable state-imposed constraints on the free working of financial markets. It encompasses the freeing-up of interest rates, the loosening of deposit and credit controls, and various other measures.

Interest rates again. As interest rate ceilings are associated with negative real rates, which tend to reduce the volume of financial savings and worsen the productivity of new investment, it seems a straightforward policy conclusion that they should be loosened or eliminated. As we shall see shortly, however, matters are not that simple and there are good reasons for proceeding cautiously. First, however, we examine how, if interest rates are to be liberalized, their levels should be determined. Should all controls be dropped so that rates find their market levels? If not, how should the authorities decide the levels at which rates should be set? The answers to these questions bring in a number of the complexities that have to be considered when deciding the best policy response.

It is not enough to recommend that real rates should be positive. Policymakers require more guidelines, and the factors they should take into account include the following:

• **The desired balance between capital inflows and outflows,** taking account of the extent of present and planned capital controls. This implies that, depending on the openness of the economy, domestic rates must be contingent on world interest rates, especially those of countries that have been important past sources and destinations of capital flows.

• **Exchange rate policy.** The sensitivity of the balance between capital inflows and outflows will be at its greatest when the currency is allowed to float freely on the foreign exchanges, for then changes in domestic interest rates may have a large impact on the exchange rate, an impact that the government may not desire. Even in more regulated systems coordinating policies on interest and exchange rates will be important.

- **The probable impact of changed interest rate levels on the financialization of savings and the efficiency of investment,** for we have seen that these are the key transmission mechanisms from interest rate policy to financial sector development and the economy's overall performance.
- **The effect of changes on the government budget deficit,** through domestic public debt interest payments, and on the government's ability to maintain monetary control.
- **The extent of risk that financial market defects will prevent interest rates from rising,** or cause them to rise too far or too rapidly, and the government's short-term ability to overcome these market weaknesses by other measures.
- **The level of nonperforming or dubious assets in the financial system**, the preparedness of the system and of government regulators to avoid or overcome financial distress, and the degree of danger to solvency from interest rate rises.
- **The level of domestic inflation**. If inflation is at all rapid, reducing it is likely to be more beneficial to the financial sector, as well as to overall economic performance, than raising nominal interest rates. As raising nominal rates may contribute to inflation by increasing working capital and other production costs, countries with significant inflation should give priority to counterinflation policies.

These considerations help to define the circumstances when freeing interest rates altogether may be appropriate:

- If existing rates are not substantially negative;
- If destabilizing international capital movements are unlikely;
- If financialization and investment-efficiency responses are expected to be strong;
- If the government's domestic debt servicing obligations are manageable;
- If financial markets are relatively competitive, stable, and free of major imperfections and are not seriously affected by financial distress;
- If inflation is low and not strongly affected by nominal interest rate movements.

This is a daunting list of conditions, but most writers caution that until they have been satisfied, governments should continue to administer nominal rates to control volatility and negative side-effects. In this case the best course of action will often be an administered policy of increasing real rates in stages until they become moderately positive as a preliminary to possible further liberalization.

Related to this is the issue of how to maintain positive real rates in the presence of continuing inflation and changing international or domestic economic conditions. As is the case with the real exchange rate, positive real interest rates are a moving target. The first guideline here should be to minimize domestic economic instability, especially to reduce the level of inflation. Liberalization itself should assist in this task, for the evidence from Asian experiences suggests that financial liberalization helps manage the demand for money and the control of its supply through open market operations. (On this see Tseng and Corker's 1991 study of the monetary policy effects of financial liberalization in nine southeast Asian countries. However, they also found that liberalization was associated with some destabilization of the demand for money, which makes effective monetary policy more difficult.)

Once the domestic economy is stabilized, keeping real returns on savings positive by indexing financial instruments and adjusting nominal rates periodically becomes easier. As with the exchange rate, the best method is small, frequent adjustments, which are politically more acceptable and minimize inflationary and other consequences. These tactics will also permit reconsideration of policy should initial expectations be disappointed.

How much effect the liberalization (that is, raising) of interest rates is likely to have is hard to predict and will depend crucially on country circumstances. Box 8-6 on Malaysia illustrates a relatively successful case, but box 8-1 on Chile and (box 8-8 shown later on Sri Lanka) show problems. As we reported earlier, the wider empirical evidence yields mixed results, suggesting that only if previous rates are strongly negative (and in the absence of severe liquidity constraints on consumers) will there be much likelihood of substantially increasing financial savings simply by raising interest rates.

The evidence suggests that high rates are not likely to have any strong deterrent effect on capital flight, nor to attract much foreign savings. The effects of interest reforms on the quantity of investment

---

Box 8-6. Effects of Interest Reforms in Malaysia

Malaysia's relatively successful financial sector reforms in 1978-83 centered on liberalizing interest rates. From October 1978 commercial banks determined their own rates on deposits and loans. In 1981 the central bank stopped controlling lending rates, and by 1983 commercial banks had replaced rates linked to the government prime rate with rates based on the cost of funds, plus a margin depending on loan maturity, borrower standing and security, and the nature of the project. However, the central bank continued to impose ceilings on lending rates for small businesses and housing projects, and it actually increased directed credit programs. Liberalization was therefore gradual and selective.

Nominal rates rose only marginally, but real rates increased substantially to positive levels because inflation went down. Real lending rates changed little before 1981, but deposit rates (and lending rates after 1981) moved slowly upwards. The consequences of liberalization were almost all positive. The financial sector grew rapidly: ratios of M2 and M3 to GNP doubled and financialized savings rose by 50 percent, leaving Malaysia with greater financial depth than other nations with similar per capita GNP. Competition in the financial system increased. Small banks reacted to lower liquidity by increasing rates to compete with larger banks, and their share of deposits rose sharply in 1978-81. Branches proliferated and although the profit rate in the banking sector fell slightly, it remained attractive. Nonbank financial institutions and foreign banks increased their presence and market shares. Competition made interest rates more sensitive to market forces and widened opportunities for financial savings.

Domestic financial markets became better integrated, with informal market premiums falling and finance company rates moving closer to those of banks. Integration with international markets also increased: domestic interest rates became more sensitive to differentials with foreign rates, but the nonbank public had little access to foreign markets so sensitivity was limited. The term structure of deposit rates also improved, offering sufficient returns to increase long-term deposits. Commercial banks saw a gradual increase in long-term deposits and loans, especially after 1982, as inflation fell. However, overall long-term credit stagnated because the securities market was saturated with issues of government bonds, and the share of development finance institutions in total credit stayed small. Intermediation margins also widened slightly due to limited initial competition, the cost of branch expansion, and the widening of credit controls, but they later stabilized.

The success of Malaysian interest rate reform reflected the already fairly liberalized financial system, the government's gradual approach, and its implementation of complementary anti-inflationary policies.

Source: Cho and Khatkhate (1989).

are also disputed, and Cho and Khatkhate (1989) indicate that rate liberalization does not increase the availability of long-term credit, especially if rates are unstable. (Fry 1988, pp. 143-47 concludes that the effects on investment re much greater than those on saving. Most other sources conclude that investment is more likely to be encouraged than saving, but not by much.) The strongest supporting evidence for positive real rates is their effect on the quality of investment (Gelb 1989; Khatkhate 1988).

Credit controls. Earlier we criticized state interventions in the credit allocation decisions of financial institutions on the grounds that these were likely to be used to favor the public sector in times of overall tightness in credit availability, that they tended to reduce the productivity of new investment, and that were liable to reduce banks' ability to offer attractive deposit rates to savers. On such considerations the case for abandoning the direction of investment appears clear. It should free investable funds for other sectors, both directly and indirectly, by increasing the attractiveness of deposits and reducing rent seeking and credit rationing behavior by banks, and, by freeing funds for projects with higher returns and lower risks, it should reduce the danger of nonperforming loans.

Because the bulk of the literature treats the loosening of interest rates as a proxy for liberalization, there has been less investigation of the results of other elements of the freeing-up of the financial system. We have found no empirical studies of the separate effects of ending the direction of investment on the quantity of savings and investment or on the quality of investment. Moreover, given evidence that imperfect financial markets are liable to cause banks to ration credit and discriminate against certain types of borrowers, even without repression, beneficial effects should not be taken for granted.

However, there is strong empirical evidence in support of the reform of directed credit and state-owned financial institutions. To the extent that governments regard intervention as desirable, they should direct or subsidize credit to narrowly defined groups and for specific purposes such as research or exporting, and even then only when they have good reasons to believe that the assistance will reach the intended recipients. Macroeconomic distortions can be minimized by increasing credit to priority sectors (instead of subsidizing interest rates) and by limited central bank rediscounting to shift some of the subsidy cost from the lending institutions (for more details of such measures and their effects see World Bank 1989d and Fry 1988, chapter 17, section 3).

Strengthening Markets

We earlier identified a variety of ways in which financial markets fall short of the competitive ideal in SLIC conditions, so we turn next to consider ways by which the efficiency of these markets may be raised.

One of the weaknesses identified earlier was that capital markets tend to be shallow. To redress this encouraging the growth of stock exchanges and bond markets would be desirable, but this may be problematic. In their early years such markets may be unable to compete with indirect markets subsidized by deposit insurance, a central bank low interest rediscount facility, and tax or regulatory discrimination against equity finance. Removal of these forms of discrimination can help, therefore, as can the creation of a proper legal framework for the operation of these markets and for safeguarding the interests of savers.

One way to strengthen segmented and incomplete markets may be by encouraging commercial banks to invest in expanded networks of branches, perhaps by favorable tax treatment of such investments. Evidence suggests that branch proximity may raise financial savings rates by up to 5 percent over twenty years for each 10 percent reduction in the population of the catchment area. The effect is especially strong in rural areas, where savings are diverted from informal markets and nonfinancial forms of savings. However, government encouragement of more branches should not override considerations of cost efficiency. Branch proliferation is no panacea. Measures to boost the efficiency of management, to improve investment decisions by increasing the flow of information about small investors, and to encourage semiformal and informal markets if formal institutions see no opportunity for profit may also be desirable.

The problem of oligopoly in banking systems can also be tackled by more effective regulation and by promoting new financial institutions to foster competition (see Galbis 1986, pp. 134-140). Thus, more specialized savings and other institutions can be fostered that can compete with the banks. Regulation of lending may be difficult if it is in the holding company's interest to allow some subsidiaries to collapse because of bad debt. Strong and sophisticated supervision of holding companies will be needed in such situations. In the interim, competition may have to be simulated by setting deposit rates at approximately their free-market levels and by issuing government bonds with attractive yields. Existing institutions may also be "educated" by fostering markets in short-term financial claims, such as treasury bills and interbank money markets.

However, governments need to exercise care in introducing pro-competition policies. Earlier chapters have pointed out that monopoly can have benefits, as can the scale economies that it permits in small economies. Regulators must therefore balance the benefits from concentration against the risks that it brings. Furthermore, policies to increase competition on financial markets can bring perverse and destabilizing results if the necessary pre-conditions are not met. This is particularly so if existing banks have made large numbers of dubious or bad loans.

There will often be a strong case for limiting ties between financial and nonfinancial companies and among financial companies, and for requiring divestiture where the public interest makes this desirable. Obligatory limits on lending to individual borrowers should be extended to credits to companies with interrelated interests. Limits should also restrict insider transactions (loans to people influential in, or connected with, the lender), and interlocking directorships and other relationships among directors, officers, and shareholders. Strict limits are needed on the shares, bonds, and real estate that financial institutions may purchase to reduce the dangers for the rest of the economy if they run into difficulty. Scrutiny of transactions should include mandatory disclosure before transactions take place.

We saw earlier how oligopoly is often associated with conditions of financial distress among banks, in which nominal interest rates are bid up to artificially high levels, a high proportion of bad or doubtful loans exists, credit allocation decisions are distorted, and insolvency threatens. To forestall such effects interest rate levels and monetary targets need to take account of interest financing needs if they are to avoid unnecessary destabilization. Supervisory authorities should act before banks become insolvent, which requires better information flows than usually occur in low-income countries. They should limit bank loans to risky firms and concentration of loans on one borrower; strengthen accounting and auditing (possibly commissioning external auditors) to stop fraud; reform bankruptcy and tax laws to require banks to write down nonperforming assets; push banks to collect doubtful debts and sell the marketable assets of bad debtors; and penalize, or change, bad management (for more discussion of these issues, especially the key role of adequate and timely information, see World Bank (1989d, pp. 80-82).

These measures should clear the decks for recapitalizing banks and restructuring firms where necessary. This is a labor-intensive and skilled task, and may require a new agency independent of the central bank. The government may need to close, subsidize, or buy shares in some institutions, preferably in transparent ways (though this may be impossible without loss of public confidence in the banking system). If a large number of institutions is involved, in-depth analysis of their future potential is needed to identify priorities for public assistance. Without restructuring of distressed banks and companies, financial distress can easily frustrate liberalization.

All these market failures require government intervention, mostly of a regulatory nature, and box 8-7 sets out a framework of bank regulation with a focus on the needs generated by liberalization policies. Pending such a framework, market failures may necessitate temporary residual control of interest rates to guard against speculative demand for credit and prevent interest rates from rising too high, before adequate bank supervision and regulation procedures can be introduced.

In small, poor economies regulatory provisions often fall short of the standards suggested in box 8-7 and require reforms of organization and powers. Organization can be divided into two main strands: analysis by off-site supervisors of reports submitted by banks, and frequent on-site inspection to check the accuracy of these reports and to follow up problems identified. In turn, this often requires

---

Box 8-7. A Framework for Bank Regulation

Bank supervisors often have the multiple obligations of ensuring the soundness of banking practices and compliance with monetary policy, and foreign exchange, and other macroeconomic regulations. There is much to be said for allowing them to concentrate more on their supervisory responsibilities. In carrying out this responsibility they should focus on assessing the quality of assets, accounting procedures, and management controls. This, in turn, requires certain standard gauges:

- *Adequate capital to assets ratios.* These are needed to exert discipline on lending, while leaving enough flexibility to permit the solution of financial distress and the absorption of losses. Regulators should set minimum guidelines for assets and off-balance-sheet items (for example, guarantees and lines of credit). These should vary with the degree of risk of the asset. They should apply equally to government-owned institutions to reduce expectations of or actual bail-outs through government guarantees.
- *Realistic asset classification and provisioning.* Supervisors need to be able to require banks to make realistic provisions for potential losses or problem assets, to write off or provide for actual losses, and to prevent accounting for interest as if it has been paid on nonperforming loans.
- *Long-term liquidity ratios.* Most countries already require banks to maintain minimum prudential cash or liquidity ratios so that they can repay depositors' funds if these are called (though this ratio is more often used as an instrument of monetary policy). However, liquidity risk arises when banks borrow short-term and lend long-term and short-term interest rates rise faster than long-term rates. This points in favor of careful monitoring of the whole interest rate structure.
- *Portfolio concentration limits.* Limits as a percentage of capital should prevent excessive lending to a single borrower, group of related borrowers, or particular industry, especially when combined with the supervision of holding companies described below. These limits should be set at prudent levels, well below 50 percent of capital (especially if capital is being increased).
- *Audit standards.* Supervisors should require external audits of banks and set minimum standards for the scope, content, and frequency of audits and related financial disclosures.

Note: See also World Bank (1989d, especially p.92).

improved staffing, training, and remuneration. Closely related to this is the need for political support. To be effective, central banks or other regulatory authorities must be given clear goals and responsibilities, adequate resources, and independence from political pressures. Equally, it is vital to ensure the independence from private business interests of those who design and enforce regulations to avoid conflicts of interest and abuse of regulations.

Powers need to be both strong and subtle. Licensing should screen out owners and managers with inadequate qualifications, financial backing, or moral standing, but not be so restrictive as to suppress competition or encourage oligopoly. Further, all existing guidelines require continual monitoring to ensure that they are met. In many countries enforcement powers are blunt: unless breaches are criminal or violate banking statutes, supervisors can only cancel the banking license. In these situations, the authorities should have intermediate powers, for example, to impose fines, suspend dividends, deny requests for new branches or activities, issue cease and desist orders, remove managers or directors, and hold directors legally responsible for losses.

Many financial market failures are too intractable to be overcome by regulation, even in developed countries. The ability of governments and central banks to undertake the various measures suggested above honestly and efficiently varies greatly between countries. In addition, excessive regulation may distort and delay investment, and drive banks and companies to collude in noncompliance. For these reasons, what the authorities should attempt must depend on specific country circumstances. Once in place, regulatory frameworks need to be monitored for changes in financial and market conditions and for the effectiveness of each regulation so that changes can be made as necessary.

In addition to supervising financial institutions, governments have a vital role in gathering and disseminating information on all types of financial transactions to allow financial institutions to identify creditworthy borrowers and viable projects, and to help savers and investors assess which financial institutions are the most efficient and appropriate for their needs.

Promoting Financial Diversification

We have noted how deepening is accompanied by diversification of the financial system as the requirements of the rest of the economy for savings and credit vehicles become more complex, and as more specialized agencies spring up to meet these developing needs. The success of financial liberalization is also apt to be strongly influenced by the degree of diversification of financial markets. The deepening of markets will, by increasing the effectiveness of existing institutions and promoting new ones, combat underspecialization, segmentation, and oligopoly.

In addition to the commercial banks, we need to ask what types of institutions might have a specially valuable contribution to make in SLICs starting with fairly rudimentary financial systems. Merchant and investment banks can be an important prerequisite for the development of other institutions, but are scarce in many low-income countries. Though in general they neither mobilize savings nor invest their own funds, they can play key roles in all types of investment: acting as brokers, especially in securities and money markets; providing advisory services to domestic and foreign companies, commercial banks, and other investors; managing investment portfolios, including investment trusts; and arranging venture capital and leasing deals. Their willingness to participate in high-risk, high-yield investment makes them a vital complement to commercial banks. However, they are management-intensive, require scarce skills, and depend on the existence of other institutions.

Insurance companies and pension funds are potentially important in mobilizing savings for long-term investment. They are growing rapidly in many SLICs, but are likely to require relatively deep financial (especially securities) markets to achieve attractive returns. They are also likely to be cautious and to avoid higher-risk investment. Housing finance companies (building societies) lend long, and therefore provide the valuable service of transforming what might be short-term savings into long-term investments, mainly residential housing. They too are cautious investors, but they almost certainly mobilize additional savings rather than diverting them from higher-risk uses.

Securities markets (or stock exchanges) are important in only a few low-income countries. Like investment banks, they are a key requisite for the development and efficient functioning of other institutions: they enable companies to raise capital directly by share issues and provide savers and finance houses with an often profitable outlet for funds; they may help public enterprises to go public and raise capital or to be privatized; and they can increase the gearing ratios of public and private companies, improving prospects for their solvency and that of creditor banks. Their main disadvantage is their vulnerability to speculative swings and manipulation, which necessitates close regulation. Well-functioning stock markets are attractive to foreign investors, yielding high returns on a diversified portfolio (see IFC 1987, 1988 for a fuller discussion of this topic). However, securities markets in SLICs often suffer from a short supply of shares and a small number of quoted companies. To some extent they also suffer from lack of demand: domestic financial institutions desiring equity investments often do not exist.

Post office savings banks have the advantages of catering to the needs of very small-scale savers and of accessibility, especially in rural areas, because of the existence of a large network of post offices. They are also cheap to administer because post offices fulfill other functions, thereby permitting economies of scale. However, their record in savings mobilization has been poor, due partly to unattractive interest rates imposed by the financial repression discussed earlier. Moreover, they are not usually allowed to lend to the private sector, being required instead to channel savings to the government, although there is no intrinsic reason why they should not invest in the private sector, subject to prudential safeguards. Savings and credit banks are more likely to avoid capture by the state, allowing them to lend to private borrowers.

Semiformal institutions, such as credit cooperatives and unions and group lending schemes, can be valuable means of mobilizing rural savings and sources of credit for small farmers, although they operate on a small scale, and in some cases have poor loan repayment records. The Grameen Bank in Bangladesh is a widely-cited example of success in mobilizing savings from groups previously regarded as unreachable, investing without formal collateral in small-scale productive projects at lower interest rates than moneylenders.[8] Cooperatives have an even better record in increasing savers' access to financial services, and thereby stimulating saving. Their costs are often low because they use volunteer labor and reduce risk through group accountability. In addition, unlike informal institutions, their often nationwide federated structure gives them access to formal financial markets, and can therefore diversify assets and intermediate between regions.

What can governments do to promote financial diversification along these lines? To a large extent we must expect such institutions to come into being autonomously as the demand for them emerges and supporting services from elsewhere in the financial system come into existence. Nonetheless, governments can do a good deal. Provision of appropriate legal and tax frameworks within which these institutions can operate and of adequate supervision to safeguard the interests of savers and borrowers are themselves crucial contributions, and ones that are often lacking. Of course, ending financial repression and the devices that governments employ to capture a disproportionate share of credit can also make a major contribution.

The practices the government follows with regard to the trading of its own bills and bonds can also exert a strong influence on the vigor with which secondary markets develop in these assets. Governments can also sometimes help by providing start-up capital and security, for example, for credit unions, and by providing accounting and other extension services for semiformal bodies.

Sequencing and Speed

Financial liberalization is like an airplane: of considerable potential utility, but dangerous in inexperienced hands. Flown in the wrong conditions or at the wrong speed it can go seriously awry. Premature liberalization in the wrong environment or without safeguards and institutional diversity may have little positive effect on saving and investment; may bring severe side-effects, including the risk of a finan-

---

8. On this see Hossain (1988); Sadeque (1986); World Bank (1989d, p.177). Seibel and Shrestha (1988) have also suggested the small businessmen's informal self-help bank in Nepal as a model, and the World Bank (1989d, p.117) cites successes in Ghana, Malawi, and Zimbabwe. Leonard (1986) suggests ways of making semiformal and informal institutions more efficient and of integrating them with the commercial banking sector.

cial crisis; and may cause adverse consequences for monetary control and economic stability. In particular, we must stress the dangers of embarking upon financial liberalization under conditions of macroeconomic imbalances or substantial financial distress. Unless a reasonable degree of macroeconomic stability has first been achieved, liberalization is most unlikely to be effective and can easily make matters worse. Similarly, in conditions of undiversified and shallow financial markets that are displaying symptoms of financial distress, and where market failures abound, liberalization must be cautious, even though this may itself retard financial deepening. Until policies for regulation, competition, and institutional promotion are in place, residual interest rate, deposit, and credit controls are likely to be needed. Once such complementary policies begin to take effect, however, more rapid and comprehensive liberalization will become possible.

Absence of the necessary preconditions helps to explain why the results have frequently been disappointing, although Asia has provided some successful examples.[9] Box 8-8 illustrates some of the pitfalls encountered in Sri Lanka. Occasionally the consequences of premature liberalization have been near-disastrous, as in Chile for a time and in Turkey in the late-1980s. (See Aricali and Rodrik 1989 who conclude that: "The Turkish experience . . . demonstrates the inherent destabilizing nature of financial deregulation and capital account liberalization when the economy is still gripped by inflation, fiscal crisis, and continuous real depreciation.") There are manyreasons why practical realities do not live up to theoretical expectations. Among the most important obstacles are continuing weaknesses in financial markets and lack of complementary macroeconomic policies.

---

9. Fry (1988, chapter 13) concludes that liberalization has had no substantial impact on national saving or capital flight; Gupta (1987) that it had an effect in Asia, but not in Latin America; and Dooley and Mathieson (1987) that it has rarely produced a more efficient market-oriented financial system.

Box 8-8. Financial Liberalization in Sri Lanka, 1977-86

Until 1977 Sri Lanka had experienced prolonged economic stagnation. Inflation was at 14 percent, due in part to a fiscal deficit of almost 8 percent of GNP. The balance of payments was precarious, even with tight exchange and trade controls. Its financial sector was fairly well developed, with a variety of institutions, but commercial banks held 35 percent of financial assets. The financial sector was repressed, with negative real interest rates and subsidized credit to priority sectors. Its growth had fallen sharply during 1968-75.

Financial liberalization started in 1977 and centered on reducing controls on interest rates. The bank rate was raised from 8.5 to 10 percent, but remained negative in real terms. Deposit rates were raised more sharply, becoming strongly positive. This was largely due to harsh government restriction of monetary expansion: the central bank tightly restricted the banks' access to its credit, and charged a 5 percent interest premium for loans over the access ceiling. Government intervention also continued on interest rates and credit subsidies, though the latter were slightly scaled down. The government also encouraged competition by allowing foreign banks and deposit taking nonbanks (for example, finance companies). In other words, financial reform was relatively mild and gradual, and government intervention was not abandoned, merely redesigned to encourage some market freedom.

Complementary policies were also introduced. The exchange rate was devalued, trade reform replaced quantitative restrictions with a simplified tariff structure, and exchange controls were diluted. Many prices were decontrolled, food subsidies were reduced and targeted at the poor, and policies in other sectors were liberalized.

However, this partial liberalization did not produce many of the expected positive effects. Although real deposit interest rates remained generally positive, the level and structure of interest rates were not market determined. The monetary authorities guided interest rates by changing the treasury bill rate and adjusting rates charged by state-owned commercial banks. Lending rates were barely positive because banks continued to lend to more risky borrowers due to political ties and other factors.

The liberalization also did not increase financial deepening: M2/GNP and M3/GNP ratios barely increased between 1977 and 1986. There was a strong rise in domestic saving, but this did not translate into improved allocation of capital. Long-term credit and the equity market received some stimulus from liberalization. However, the former remained constrained by a shortage of bankable projects and other factors. Much of the new credit went into short-term working capital due to rapid expansion of domestic demand, continued high inflation, and some speculative demand that raised the inventory/output ratio of companies. There was minimal increased competition

---

Box 8-8. (continued)

---

for long-term capital. Partly as a result of this, high interest rates also brought a rapid rise in bad debts, necessitating new supervisory and legal machinery. Only strict adherence to prudential regulations and the continued existence of some selective subsidized credit prevented banking collapse.

The complementary liberalization of other policies also caused problems. Price decontrol and agricultural and industrial liberalization caused a huge rise in demand for working capital, while trade liberalization increased the supply of goods on which to spend short-term loans. A rapid expansion of public investment created soaring domestic aggregate demand. As a result, inflation rose, turning real interest rates negative, and the real exchange rate appreciated, making foreign long-term borrowing more attractive. This experience pointed up the importance of careful sequencing of complementary measures if financial liberalization is to have its full potential value.

Source: Cho and Khatkhate (1989); Khatkhate (1982); Roe (1982, 1988).

To deal first with macroeconomic policy, we should recall from earlier sections that (a) inflation is a major source of the negative real interest rates that characterize repression, and that (b) governments often use repression as a way to capture more credit than would otherwise come their way in order to finance large budget deficits. What must be stressed here is that liberalization is unlikely to bring many benefits unless accompanied by fiscal measures to reduce budget deficits and the public sector's appetite for credit. Severe liquidity problems for firms and individuals make excess private sector demand for credit the usual situation in SLICs. This makes demand for credit interest-inelastic. Because the same liquidity constraints also make saving (and therefore credit) supply-inelastic, disruptively large interest rate movements may be necessary to achieve a liberalized equilibrium. In such conditions, liberalization in the face of continuing large-scale deficit financing is likely to push nominal interest rates to very high levels, because total demand for credit will exceed supply and high nominal rates will be necessary if real rates are to become positive in the face of continuing inflation. In consequence, private investment will be discouraged and the fragile solvency of some banks may be threatened. Thus, successful liberalization requires fiscal discipline, avoidance of the crowding-out of private credit needs, and the prevention of rapid inflation. The full benefits are also unlikely to be achieved unless the exchange rate is flexible, but fairly stable, and liberalizing capital markets while maintaining an overvalued exchange rate is an open invitation to capital flight.

The poor synchronization of product and financial market liberalization (suddenly raising prices after long-standing distortions) may also cause an artificial excess increase in credit demand. Product and financial markets adjust at different speeds, usually with longer lags in product markets. Similarly, since the basic determinants of saving are likely to include income, past saving habits, and growth in the export sector (due to a higher propensity to save in that sector), policies should seek to increase, or at least maintain, the level and stability of income, persuade people to change their saving habits, and boost the export sector.

This need for complementary policies does not imply an overall "quick-fix" reform of all policies to achieve comprehensive liberalization. This would be likely to exacerbate economic problems, by creating uncertainties and generating multiple, potentially conflicting, price signals. Gradual change is usually preferable, carefully monitored and sequenced with other measures. At the same time, policies must be flexible. Financial markets can change rapidly and their institutions have proved adept at frustrating the wishes of central banks. Flexibility is therefore needed to ensure both that outmoded regulations do not get in the way of desirable financial developments and that desirable levels of supervision and monetary control remain in place.

Turning to market imperfections, segmented and incomplete financial markets are liable to undermine liberalization by continuing to use various credit rationing devices. In the face of oligopolistic banking structures, liberalization may merely increase competition among banks for savings to channel to other enterprises to which they are connected, or the banks may respond by agreeing collectively not to engage in interest rate competition.

We should stress the dangers of liberalizing in the face of financial distress. Where banks are holding major proportions of questionable loans in their portfolios and have weak balance sheets, financial liberalization is apt to worsen the situation, especially if accompanied by similar reforms in other sectors of the economy. Such reforms have the effect of substantially altering relative prices. Faced with the need to adapt to these and to greater competitive pressures, the ability of weak firms to honor their debt servicing obligations is further reduced. Debtors in difficulty will be impelled to seek yet further credits, and fragile banks will feel forced to meet these requests to prevent default. The consequence may be to push interest rates above true equilibrium levels, choking off sound investments and reducing the supply of loans to others, thereby undermining the viability even of sound businesses. In short, the authorities must address financial distress by the types of restructuring and other measures outlined earlier before financial liberalization can proceed far.

More generally, the implication of these observations is that liberalization needs to be preceded and accompanied by measures that will strengthen financial markets and increase competition within them. This is desirable, in any case, if the financial sector is to play its role in promoting the economy's efficiency, flexibility, and growth.

A final point to stress is the importance of tailoring financial policies to specific country conditions and on the basis of careful preparatory research. Our knowledge of the workings of financial systems, and the variables influenced by them, has many gray areas, particularly in SLICs. Although we have pointed to general lessons of experience, it would be an easy mistake to build a program on assumptions inappropriately imported from other countries. Each country's institutions and the problems of its financial sector will be unique.

Summary and Conclusion

This chapter started by discussing the importance of financial deepening for raising the economy's adaptability, chiefly through its effects on saving and investment. In common with earlier chapters, we found weaknesses in both financial markets and government policies. Among the most common market failures are that financial markets tend to be segmented, incomplete, and shallow. Businesses and other users of financial services do not have access to the range of services from which they could benefit, and the costs of the services are often high. Dualism is common, implying failures to attract and invest savings efficiently. Competition within the sector is often limited, with commercial banking commonly oligopolistic. Information flows are often poor, which has particularly adverse effects on the efficiency of investment decisions. Banks' balance sheets are often fragile, with an unhealthy proportion of poorly performing loans, creating an ever-present danger of crisis. At the same time, informal financial institutions, while they provide valuable services in their own spheres, do not offer satisfactory substitutes for the failings of the formal part of the sector.

Although partly a response to market failures, state interventions often make things worse. Financial repression characterizes some of the common failings of policy interventions, holding interest rates below market clearing levels, introducing nonmarket considerations into credit allocation decisions, and in other ways frustrating the development of the financial sector. We concluded that keeping interest rates negative in real terms is likely to reduce the financialization of saving and the productivity of investment. Interventions to influence the allocation of credit may also reduce the quality of investment, and state-owned financial agencies have a generally poor record in savings mobilization and the quality of their investments. We noted the strong connection between financial repression and the crowding-out by the state of the private sector's credit needs. We showed that repression has the effect of imposing a heavy burden of taxation on the sector.

As regards policies to overcome these weaknesses and promote financial deepening, liberalization requires moving toward more positive real interest rates, reducing or changing the form of intervention in credit allocation, reforming financial public enterprises, and so on. Among measures for strengthening markets, we suggested that establishing an adequate legal and regulatory framework was central. We also described the importance of dealing with financial distress and suggested promoting the diversification of financial institutions through the development of merchant and investment banks, insurance companies, pension funds and building societies, securities markets, savings banks, and various semiformal institutions. We stressed the value of appropriate legal, tax, and supervisory frameworks, as well as of dismantling of the instruments of repression, in promoting diversification.

Finally, we pointed out the importance of sequencing and policy interactions. Major market failures in an undiversified financial sector undermine liberalization. Measures to reduce market failure and promote diversification will facilitate liberalization, just as liberalization will strengthen and diversify the markets. We urged caution in proceeding with liberalization. Various conditions should be satisfied prior to liberalization, particularly with regard to financial distress. We stressed the potential dangers of financial liberalization in the face of major macroeconomic imbalances, and the importance of strengthening the budget so as to reduce the government's deficit financing needs.

These findings have reinforced a number of the themes emerging from this book. One is the importance—and delicacy—of striking a balance between the workings of market forces and the policy interventions of the state, with both sets of forces subject to large imperfections. We still envisage a large role for the state, but the thrust of our recommendations has been to urge a change in the nature of policy interventions, away from the use of controls and other devices that interfere with the operations of markets in favor of measures that operate through markets. Specifically, we have favored strengthening the legal and supervisory framework as against direct controls over interest rates and credit allocations.

However, striking this balance is clearly difficult. It can only be attempted in concrete situations, with the best combination depending on a careful assessment of country circumstances. It is also likely to change over time. Initially, starting with a small undiversified financial sector subject to many market imperfections, the balance may be struck more in favor of supervision and of caution in liberalization, always assuming the authorities have the ability to supervise. However, as the system deepens and market imperfections fade, the balance is likely to shift in favor of allowing markets greater freedom.

The final theme to re-emerge is the central importance of the general macroeconomic environment and of avoiding large imbalances. So important is this that much of financial liberalization must await the strengthening of public finances and the management of the macroeconomy.

A Note on Further Reading: Three works provide exceptionally good coverage of the subject matter of this chapter: Cho and Khatkhate (1989); Fry (1988); and World Bank (1989d), which is on the theme of financial systems and development. The winter 1989 (vol. 5, no. 4) issue of the *Oxford Review of Economic Policy* is on the theme of finance and economic development and contains a recommended collection of papers. The contributions by Fry and McKinnon are particularly recommended.

9

THE WIDER CONTEXT OF ADJUSTMENT POLICIES

The preceding chapters have focused on defining the need for structural adaptation, exploring the nature of an adaptive economy, and examining the role that economic policies can play to promote adaptability. In this and the next chapter we shall try to place adjustment policies in their wider context, and in so doing tie up some of the loose ends that have been left dangling.

The Global Economic Context

So far we have largely concentrated on adjustment in one country, even though the economies with which we are particularly concerned are heavily reliant on world trade and payments. Here we examine whether adjustment in one country is feasible, and explore whether the global economic environment is consistent with the adjustment efforts of individual developing countries.

Limitations of Adjustment in One Country

Obviously if a country is to achieve its objectives efficiently, its economic policies must be internally consistent. This is no less true for the world economy as a whole. The limitation of designing adjustment in one country is that developments elsewhere, and the actions—or failures to act—of other governments, may frustrate the intentions of a national government. The open-economy approach to adjustment advocated in this book provides another example, for the export promotion efforts of individual countries must, in sum, be consistent with the expansion of world markets for their goods. Similarly, the amount of international finance needed in support of adjustment efforts and its supply must be in balance. Unfortunately, in the absence of effective international policy coordination, such global consistency is not assured.

Chapter 2 has already described the powerful influence of global economic conditions on small low-income countries. This influence is chiefly transmitted through conditions on world markets for goods, services and capital, and is exerted particularly strongly through movements in terms of trade, capital flows, and world interest rates. We also saw that various major trade and financial variables have exhibited severe instability in the past decade.

That discussion showed the types of international shocks and trends to which developing countries are vulnerable. This vulnerability increases the desirability of having flexible economies and policies. Does this mean that these external influences have to be treated as givens, as brute facts to be adjusted to? In some degree, yes. We showed, for example, that much of the adverse long-run trend in primary product prices was a result of fundamental changes in the structure of world demand. There is not much that policy can do about that. In other areas a good deal more could be done, as some of the adverse conditions developing countries face are the result of industrial countries' policies and the policies of the multilateral institutions they control. In principle, those policies could be changed.

The rules and policies that have regulated the international economy in recent decades have been far from even-handed in their effects on rich and poor nations. A number of asymmetries exist, with the resulting injustices leading to—now largely abandoned—developing country calls for a "new international economic order". The chief asymmetry that concerns us here relates to adjustment itself. If we view the global economy overall, total imports must add up to total exports, and if one group of countries has a balance of payments deficit this must, arithmetically, be matched by an equivalent surplus in the rest of the world.[1] In this case if the payments imbalances are to be removed, both deficit and surplus countries must take corrective responses, for if the latter protect their surpluses, the corrective actions of those in deficit will be frustrated. One of the weaknesses of the present-day

1. Unfortunately, world payments statistics do not add up this way because of errors, omissions, and differences in measurement in national statistics. By 1988 this statistical discrepancy was no less than US $78 billion in the IMF's balance of payments reporting. However, the principle referred to in the text remains intact, and the statistical discrepancies in no way justify the asymmetry.

world economic system, however, is that adjustment has come to be viewed primarily as something to be undertaken by deficit countries, with no equivalent pressure for action on surplus countries.[2]

The essential problem here is one of unequal bargaining strength, for while countries with deficits that they cannot finance have little option but to take corrective action, there is no equivalent force acting upon surplus countries. Thus, the IMF's official historian (de Vries 1987, p.284) has noted that:

> Since 1977 only developing [country] members have used the Fund's re-
> sources and there is an understandable perception of asymmetry between de-
> veloping and industrial country members in that the conditionality applied
> to the use of the Fund's resources has significantly affected developing
> members, while surveillance [of policies] under Article IV . . . seems to have
> had little practical effect on the large industrial members.

One consequence of this is that it tends to impart a deflationary bias to the world economy, with austerity policies in deficit countries unmatched by expansionary policies in persistent surplus countries, such as Germany, and with a high proportion of the costs of this bias thrust upon people in developing countries, who are ill able to afford them. Creditor responses to the debt crisis after 1982 could be interpreted in a similar way, with the rules of debt renegotiation being written by the creditor countries in only thinly disguised pursuit of their own national interests, again leaving a distribution of the costs of renegotiation skewed to the disadvantage of the debtor nations. Only at the end of the decade were more even-handed debt initiatives starting to be introduced.

Another consequence of asymmetry was a marked discrepancy in the degree of policy rectitude expected of different country groupings. We have already drawn attention to this in chapter 7 concerning agricultural pricing policies, with industrial country governments urging the merits of the border-pricing principle on developing countries while flagrantly departing from it themselves. Box 8-1 on energy pricing provides another example. More generally, one of the less inspirational features of the international scene in the 1980s was

---

2. Deficit countries whose currencies are widely used as an international means of payments are, however, exempt from these pressures to adjust so long as the rest of the world is willing to continue to accept more of these currencies, and in that way finance the payments deficits. The United States is the chief beneficiary.

the U.S. government preaching through the IMF and elsewhere that developing country governments must bring their budgets under control and reduce macroeconomic imbalances, while at home it was running large and widening budgetary and payments deficits. This is not to deny that genuine adjustment has been occurring in OECD countries, for instance, major changes in the efficiency of energy consumption followed the oil shocks of 1973-74 and 1979-80. Too often, however, the response has been defensive, in the sense described in chapter 4 and as illustrated in box 9-1, seeking to slow down the pace of change, and thereby to reduce its social and political costs. The metal processing industries provide an example both of defensiveness and of the costs this imposes on developing countries, for in this industry reluctance to close down uneconomic plants has contributed to low worldwide utilization rates and depressed world markets for metals. (See Carnegie 1986, p.16, who comments that in the industrial countries unions, communities, and governments have supported measures to continue uneconomic operations from a desire to maintain employment and export income, thereby further depressing the world markets on which many developing countries depend.)

Another feature of the 1980s was the retreat from international cooperation. The "conservative revolution" that occurred in the major industrial countries brought into power governments that demonstrated a willingness to place (often rather short-term) national interests above international cooperation, and to put their faith in the virtues of world trade and capital market mechanisms over the more interventionist approaches to international economic coordination pursued in earlier decades. (Although some disillusionment with international markets set in as the decade advanced, and toward the end governments exhibited renewed interest in international management of major currency exchange rates.)

In consequence, the machinery for international policy coordination—a role intended to be filled by the IMF—was marginalized. One aspect of this was the refusal of major OECD governments to heed the IMF's advice on policy coordination. Another was the emergence of a less favorable balance between financing and adjustment than existed in the preceding decades, which imposed avoidable costs and added further to deflation. At the same time, the relevance of the General

Agreement on Tariffs and Trade (GATT) was reduced as the result of a burgeoning of nontariff trade barriers.

Box 9-1. Double Standards on Energy Pricing

When Western aid agencies provide loans or grants for energy projects in developing countries, they usually specify that recipient governments should follow pricing policies that (a) ensure the agency's financial viability by yielding a positive rate of return on assets, and (b) are conducive to economic efficiency by being based on border prices. As with industrial country agriculture so with energy pricing, however, it is often a different matter when it comes to the industrial countries' own policies.

For example, the succession of Conservative administrations that governed the United Kingdom throughout the 1980s espoused stout adherence to market solutions, and through their aid to developing countries were advocates of applying the type of policy described above. In their policies toward public sector energy pricing in the United Kingdom, however, they required the Central Electricity Generating Board (CEGB)—then the principal agency in the electricity supply industry—to purchase coal from the nationalized British Coal Corporation at prices that in 1982-87 were only on one occasion less than 25 percent above world market prices and that averaged over 30 percent more. Moreover, for much of the period the CEGB was not permitted to import more than 1 percent of its total coal needs.

The basic problem was that the British coal industry, despite the closure of uneconomic pits and considerable improvements in productivity and cost structures, was not competitive internationally in this period. Had the CEGB been permitted to buy freely at international prices, the coal industry would have been hard hit and many additional mines would have had to be closed down. This would have had grave effects in the communities based around uneconomic mines and would have caused additional job losses in a period of already high unemployment, often in regions where unemployment was particularly severe.

In short, the British government consistently overrode viability and efficiency rules by policies designed to minimize the social and political costs that would be incurred by a more drastic pace of restructuring in the coal mining industry. In doing so it probably had strong public support and may have been justified in welfare terms. To avoid the criticism of applying double standards, however, it needed to be no less understanding of similar actions by governments in developing countries, an understanding that was not always evident.

Source: Based on MacKerron, 1988.

What Might be Done?

To go in depth into such questions as the desirability of greater international policy coordination and of the reform of international trading and monetary arrangements would take us too far afield. Evidently, removing the asymmetries just described would help considerably in increasing the consistency of the global environment with economic adaptation by developing countries. However, the inequality in bargaining strength that underlies the asymmetries is intractable, and there are no grounds at present for expecting any radical systemic reforms of international trade and financial arrangements. Probably the most that one can hope for is agreement on more narrowly defined reforms. Which of the possibilities on the agenda might be particularly relevant to the concerns of this volume?

Starting with trade policy, the essential task is to introduce policy changes that would (a) get rid of avoidable shocks and trends in the system, thereby reducing the required scale of adjustment; and (b) promote developing country adjustment by improving the countries' ability to increase export earnings. We can think of (a) as relating particularly to the condition of primary product markets and (b) as specially concerned with improving the access of developing country manufactured exports to industrial countries.

As regards commodity markets, we have already suggested that little can be done about the underlying changes in the composition of demand. If we adopt the relatively long-term perspective taken in this study and accept chapter 2's suggestion of an underlying tendency for the real prices of primary products to decline, such devices as international commodity agreements and export compensation schemes are unlikely to provide a solution, as they are intended to reduce or cushion the shock of short-term fluctuations. In principle, forming producer cartels to raise prices by restricting supply might be possible, as the Organization of Petroleum Exporting Countries (OPEC) did so successfully for a while. However, rather special conditions have to be satisfied if such arrangements are to be both practicable and beneficial to their members over the longer term. Despite its dramatic successes, even OPEC's supply management eventually proved unsustainable and it was unable to prevent real oil prices returning most of the way back to where they had started in 1973, until the 1990 Gulf crisis pushed them up again. Supply management provides no solution to a long-run deterioration in demand, although it can help in an emergency situation.

Some things could be done, however. One would be to reduce industrial country protection of agriculture, which has a depressing effect on certain of the commodity markets on which developing countries are major sellers, notably for sugar and some cereals. Another would be to strengthen and liberalize existing compensation schemes to provide a more adequate buffer against short-term fluctuations in commodity prices and to give producing countries more time to adjust and diversify their exports.

The price signals coming from commodity markets have, however, been telling producing countries to reduce their dependence on primary products and to diversify their exports. It is important that this message does not get seriously diluted. A more suitable line of approach, therefore, is to work on the structure of industrial country protectionism, which normally increases as one moves up the production chain, with low protection on most unprocessed commodities that do not compete with local producers, more protection for semiprocessed items, and yet higher barriers for fully processed goods. This structure could almost have been designed to prevent export diversification by commodity exporting countries. In a sense, it was.

Another desirable change would be to reduce pressures on producers that contribute to the tendency to oversupply on most commodity markets. Many of them suffer from serious balance of payments difficulties, often associated with major debt burdens, so that measures by industrial creditor countries to provide debt relief and balance of payments support would reduce the frantic scramble to expand traditional exports.

A more specific suggestion along these lines relates to what has become known as "the fallacy of composition." This arises from the generally export-led nature of the adjustment programs associated with the IMF and the World Bank, and concerns the aggregate effect on world commodity markets of measures designed at the single country level. The countries in question face acute payments difficulties. The quickest way to increase their export earnings is likely to be through greater production of their traditional exports, in which they already have a revealed comparative advantage. Hence, targeting export promotion policies in this way would appear to make sense, and in any case, there will often be no obvious alternative. However, if a substantial number of countries supplying a given commodity all act in the same manner, the net effect may be to increase supplies and depress prices so much as to give low, even negative, returns from the export expansion. This is a kind of market failure, with atomistic, country-level decisionmaking failing to result in a collectively optimal outcome.

To what extent this is a real problem is unclear, for it has been little researched. One study (Koester, Schafer, and Valdes 1990), which was confined to African producers, suggests that the position differs greatly among products. Of the six commodities studied, the fallacy argument seemed serious only for cocoa, with returns to additional investments in that crop likely to be negative. For the other five, the prospective returns from an Africa-wide export expansion are shown to be positive in varying degrees. The effect of bringing other commodity-exporting regions into the analysis would, of course, be to increase the probabilities of immiserization. The World Bank's economists tend to respond to the fallacy argument by pointing out that Africa supplies a small part of world totals for most commodities, reducing the likely price depressing effects of expansion. However, one cannot simply look at the African dimension; the argument has to be tested at the global level. More research is needed here and, in the meantime, the World Bank should make a more systematic effort to safeguard against the danger that the programs it supports will lead to self-defeating depression of commodity markets.

Turning to the question of market access for developing country manufactured exports, the background to this is a serious increase in industrial country protectionism against this type of "import penetration." That such an increase has occurred is widely acknowledged, although being precise is difficult because most of it has taken the form of a proliferation of nontariff barriers (NTBs), which are not readily amenable to quantification. These NTBs have probably been applied in ways that discriminate against exports from developing countries, chiefly manufactures. According to UNCTAD, in 1988

NTBs affected nearly 30 percent of all imports by Western industrial countries of manufactures from developing countries, against 17 percent of imports from each other (UNCTAD 1988a).[3] Both proportions were higher than in 1981, although only marginally so in the case of NTBs against imports from developing countries.

Given the extent to which the newly industrializing countries (NICs) have already stretched industrial country tolerance of this type of import penetration and the resulting spread of protectionism, many are skeptical about the practicability—other developing countries— promoting dynamic manufacturing export industries (see Weiss 1988, pp. 300-306, for a balanced discussion of this issue). Against this skepticism, we should note that the protective barriers have not prevented the continuing rapid expansion of manufactured exports from developing countries. The quantity of these rose at an annual rate of 12 percent during 1980-89, three times as fast as manufactured exports from developed countries, so that by the end of the decade the volume of such developing country exports was approaching three times the level of ten years earlier. Note also that increased export earnings by developing countries add to their spending on goods from the industrial world, which might ease protectionist pressures, and that sales by developing countries still make up only a small proportion of total trade in manufactures. Finally, the SLICs are extremely small players in this game, so they should be able to expand their manufactured exports a great deal without causing more than the smallest ripple in the ocean of world trade. Nonetheless, industrial country producers have proved vigilant against the products of even tiny exporters, such as Mauritius, so smallness provides no guarantee of favorable treatment.

This book was completed before the Uruguay Round of trade negotiations under the GATT was concluded. Its outcome will be of crucial importance. In the meantime the obvious point should be restated: there is a clear contradiction in the industrial world advocating vigorous adjustment policies in developing countries while simultane-

---

3. The statistics quoted relate to manufactures other than chemicals. The (then) socialist countries were the most heavily discriminated against, however, with NTBs covering 40 percent of manufactured imports from them. For a useful general survey of trends in protection since 1974 see Page (1987).

ously denying the access to its markets necessary if the adjustment efforts are to succeed.

Turning now to financial flows, we have already seen that the 1980s witnessed a decline in net capital flows to SLICs, and have referred to the difficulties created for them by the rise in world real interest rates. We must draw particular attention here to the debt problems many SLICs face, indicators of which are set out in table 9-1. The comparisons are between 1982, when the world first became conscious of the debt problem, and the latest year for which firm figures are available.

The table shows that both the stock of debt and the flow of debt service payments nearly doubled over this short period, despite the many debt reschedulings and a number of debt relief initiatives. It also shows a large reduction in net financial flows (new loans minus debt servicing payments) during this period, and that in 1989 all the debt ratios were substantially worse than at the time the crisis broke in 1982.

Table 9-1. Debt Indicators for Indebted Low-Income Countries, 1982 and 1989

Indicator	1982	1988
Values (US$ billions)		
Total outstanding debt	100.8	196.4
Total debt servicing payments	10.1	18.7
of which		
Interest payments	5.3	7.6
Net transfers[a]	7.6	-0.2
Ratios (percent)		
Total debt/GNP	33.8	87.6
Total debt servicing/exports	18.1	32.1
Interest payments/exports	9.4	13.5
Interest payments/GNP	1.8	3.1

Note: An aggregation of data for low-income countries classified in the World Bank's *World Debt Tables*, 1989-90 and 1990-91, vol. 1, as severely and moderately indebted. This therefore excludes a number of low-income countries that are not classified as indebted. See this source for definition of concepts used and country classifications.

a. Excluding grants.

Source: World Bank debt tables.

What is the relevance of this to the process of structural adaptation? First, debt servicing obligations add to the foreign exchange constraint by claiming resources that could otherwise finance imports, with the consequences already discussed in chapter 2.[4] Second, apart from the resulting shortages of imported producer goods, the debt overhang discourages the investment necessary for structural adaptation in a number of other ways: by absorbing domestic savings (in 1989 interest payments on external debt probably absorbed about 15 percent of domestic saving in low-income countries[5]). By reducing the incentive to invest because a proportion of any returns must be devoted to debt servicing, in effect acting as a tax on investment; and by introducing additional uncertainties into economic life and adding to the perceived riskiness of investment. The large burden of debt servicing on the national exchequer increases budgetary difficulties, making it harder for the government to achieve the macroeconomic stability necessary for successful adjustment. Policymakers are diverted from longer-term problems of adaptation.

A vicious circle comes into play: import strangulation holds back export growth, thus perpetuating import shortages; the uncertainties created by the debt situation and debt renegotiation processes further discourage investment, which in turn holds back the restructuring necessary if economies are to "grow out of debt"; and depressed export earnings, import volumes, and economic activity reduce government revenues, further decreasing the government's ability to balance the budget and stabilize the economy.

The implication of this analysis is that the debt overhang, and the limited steps taken by creditor countries to provide debt relief in the 1980s, were inconsistent with successful adjustment by those low-income countries that were heavily indebted. Although important moves to reduce the debt burden took place at the end of the decade, and debt ratios improved during 1988-90, there was still tension between

4. For a discussion of Sub-Saharan Africa's debt problems and their consequences see Greene and Khan (1990). Selowsky and van der Tak (1986) provide an excellent analysis of the macroeconomic implications of debt servicing, even though they are chiefly concerned with more advanced Latin American-type debtor countries.

5. The World Bank (1991, table 9), estimates gross domestic saving for all low-income countries other than China and India at 18 percent of GDP in 1989, against the interest payments of 2.8 percent of GNP in 1988 shown in table 9-1.

creditor governments' policies on debt relief and their stated objective of permitting "adjustment with growth" in indebted countries.[6]

There was also evidence that adjustment programs supported by the IMF and the World Bank were being underfunded. This is illustrated for Zambia in box 9-2, and the authors of the article upon which the box is based argue along similar lines for Malawi, Mauritius, Uganda, and Zaire. But why is aid necessary to support policy reforms? For the most part, the relevant policy changes do not absorb large amounts either of foreign exchange or of government revenues. Indeed, they are often intended to save or increase both types of finance. Since adjustment policies are in the interests of the country where they are being adopted, why should outside supporting finance be necessary?

In the light of the above discussion, the case for financial support can be made in terms of easing the period of transition, reducing the costs of adjustment, and reinforcing the political sustainability of the process. Particularly in low-income countries, responses to changes in relative prices and other policy stimuli are liable to be slow and initially small, so the transition is likely to be lengthy. Saving is likely to be low in poor countries experiencing economic difficulties, but structural change necessitates major investments in the productive system and its supporting infrastructure. Aid and other forms of foreign capital can permit higher investment levels by supplementing domestic saving.

Countries faced with severe shortages of foreign exchange will somehow need to finance the transition until responses to the policies begin to strengthen the balance of payments. During that transition imports will be needed to provide raw materials and spare parts to the productive system, to provide incentive goods to consumers, and to

---

6. In 1988 ten major creditor countries agreed on a menu of options for providing greater debt relief to low-income Sub-Saharan African countries than previous policies had permitted, under what became known as the Toronto Agreement, but the total savings to the debtors were expected to be less than 1 percent of 1989 debt. For an account of this and other initiatives see ODI (1990). Mistry (1988) provides a more substantial analysis of the African debt problem. However, at the time of finalizing this book, the Paris Club of major creditor governments was discussing important proposals for more radical debt relief for low-income African countries under the so-called Trinidad Terms. These could provide substantially greater relief.

combined with the economic and financial difficulties in which many developing countries found themselves in the 1980s, led to a very rapid spread in the influence of these two international financial institutions (hereafter, the IFIs) over economic policy reform in developing countries. Thus, as at June 1991 the IMF had programs in no fewer than thirty-seven developing countries, with a special concentration in Sub-Saharan Africa, where it had programs in about two-thirds of the countries. Directly comparable figures are not available for the Bank, but a measure of its involvement in policy change is provided by the statistic that in 1986-88 it made thirty-eight structural adjustment or sectoral adjustment loans to low-income African countries alone, involving 70 percent of all such countries. The geographical coverage of IFI conditionality has thus become extensive, and its effects are therefore a matter of considerable importance.

Although conditionality remains controversial and generates resentment from time to time, it is hard to deny that those who provide assistance can legitimately take an active interest in the design of the recipient country's policies. If this book has any general message, it is that policies matter. The wisdom or otherwise of a government's economic policy decisions is liable to have a crucial influence on the subsequent performance of the country's economy. The importance of the overall policy environment, which as we have seen strongly influences the effectiveness of policies for the exchange rate, agriculture, manufacturing, and the financial sector, has been a recurring theme of previous chapters.

One could argue that the policy environment is the single most important determinant of the economic effectiveness of aid and debt relief and that this entitles aid and creditor representatives to a seat at the policymaking table (for a survey of the literature on the developmental effectiveness of aid to Africa, which elaborates on this theme, see Killick (1991b) and the literature cited there.) In the absence of policy conditions, the danger is that financial assistance can be—and in some cases has been—used to defer needed action, to buy time in the hope that some favorable turn of events will remove the need for unpalatable action. Moreover, besides providing financial support, IFI involvement can help through the provision of advice and technical assistance in the preparation of adjustment measures. It can also provide the government with a useful scapegoat upon whom it can deflect the blame for unpopular measures.

Chapter 3 discussed the extent to which the IFIs' view of adjustment coincided with the approach adopted in this book, and concluded that their programs could be thought of as an important subset of our own meaning of the concept, more confined in time and coverage, but addressed to some of the most important problems of economic adaptation. Although serious problems do exist, the general thrust of the adjustment policies advocated by the IFIs is similar to, or at least consistent with, the policies advocated in this volume. We therefore view the IFIs as a force trying to change policies in usually sensible directions.

This consideration is reinforced by the absence of any intellectually persuasive approach to economic adjustment that is radically different from that advocated by the IFIs, as distinct from reformist suggestions for improving present approaches. It is true that a group of neostructuralist economists has been developing a critique of orthodox approaches and has sought to work out a more thorough-going alternative. However, their efforts relate more to short-term stabilization than to long-term adaptation; are more concerned with relatively advanced Latin American-type economies than with the SLICs; and, in any case, have not achieved general acceptance as a viable alternative model (see, for example, Taylor 1988b and the set of country studies linked to that volume and Kahler 1990 for an excellent survey of orthodoxy and its alternatives).

Of greater potential relevance for our purposes is the work of the Economic Commission for Africa (ECA 1989), which seeks to develop an "African alternative framework" for the design of adjustment programs. This framework shares the premise that structural transformation is necessary, but is highly critical of IFI approaches, and therefore aims to provide a different approach to the task. Unfortunately, it has so far only offered a conceptual framework within which country programs might be designed that leaves a rather large number of questions unanswered. Further, it appears to be predicated on major political changes within Africa, so how much would be left of the approach given existing political systems is uncertain, and it is ambiguous about the importance of domestic and external balance as part of the adjustment process. In short, the commission has not so far convinced many others of the coherence and practicability of its alternative.

Another approach is to look at the experiences of countries that have sought to develop their own heterodox approaches, of which Argentina (the Austral Plan), Brazil (the Cruzado Plan), and Peru are examples. Unfortunately, this offers little encouragement to those searching for an alternative to orthodoxy. While these programs were undermined by the reluctance of creditor countries to provide supporting finance, each collapsed in some chaos, and each has since been recognized as having been seriously flawed. The experiences of African governments that have in the past sought to work out their own approaches are also discouraging, for example, in Ethiopia, Tanzania, and Zambia.

We conclude, in short, that IFI and other donor conditionality in structural adjustment programs is legitimate and generally tries to move policies in sensible directions, and that in any case no convincing alternative approach is available. At the same time, however, the practice of conditionality entails major problems and doubts about its effectiveness.

Does Conditionality Work?

Any conclusive evaluation of the effectiveness of adjustment programs encounters large methodological pitfalls. Comparing results during the program period with performance in preceding years is unsatisfactory because of the influence of changing world economic conditions and of the additional financial inflows that the program triggers, because of numerous and varying time lags between policy changes and their effects, and because we do not know what policies would have been in place in the absence of the program. Comparing results with the targets set by the program's architects can similarly do no more than give us some pointers, for the additional reasons that the targets themselves may have been unrealistic, arbitrary, or designed to achieve results by influencing expectations. Another method economists have sometimes applied is to compare the results obtained for a group of countries pursuing adjustment programs with a control group of nonprogram countries. The central difficulty with this approach is selecting a control group that is truly comparable.

The essential problem in program assessment is that of the counterfactual: how can we judge what would have happened in the program's absence? Other difficulties include how to disentangle the program's effects from the effects of the credits provided in support of IFI programs, and how to handle different degrees of program implementation across countries? There is also the quandary of deciding the period over which a program should be assessed: do we look simply at results during the program, or during some longer period? It thus turns out that one of the limitations of adjustment packages is the difficulty of learning from experience.

Of course, we are not completely in the dark, for each of the approaches mentioned provides some pointers. Most studies of the impact of IMF programs find that they improve the balance of payments, but that they have little revealed ability to further the objectives of reducing inflation and stimulating economic growth (for a survey of the literature and additional testing see Killick, Malik, and Manuel 1991; Killick and Malik 1991; also Khan 1990).

More relevant to our present purposes are the effects of World Bank structural adjustment programs. The Bank has published two major evaluations. The first of these (World Bank 1989a) used the control group method without, unfortunately, employing much refinement to ensure true comparability. It was thus properly tentative in its conclusions. It found that, on average, program countries had moderately better economic performance than nonprogram countries in terms of economic growth and internal balance.[7] The differential in performance was greater for countries that had implemented a succession of programs. However, the study also found that adjustment was not being sustained in a number of countries, especially as regards the internal macroeconomic balance. Differential results were weaker in Africa and in heavily indebted countries, where the problems were

---

7. Just how moderately better can be judged from the following results, which show the percentage of performance indicators that improved during the program period:

Program countries	54
Countries with 3+ adjustment loans	63
Control group (nonprogram countries)	46

greater and there were difficulties with program implementation. Three-quarters of all adjustment loans had loan installment releases delayed because of noncompliance with policy conditions, and about 40 percent of all conditions had not been fully implemented by the end of the program period.

Results obtained in independent research by Mosley, Harrigan, and Toye (1991) underlined the inconclusive nature of the Bank's results. Using a smaller sample of countries, but a wider range of methodologies, they found that Bank programs had no measurable effect on real GDP, positive effects on export growth and the balance of payments, and negative effects on investment levels. They also found a rather lower rate of implementation of program policies than the Bank did. Work by Faini and his associates (1991) similarly found no statistically significant program impact on economic growth and lower investment ratios (however, Peter Montiel in Thomas and others (1991) contests the validity of the results in the latter study and suggests they may be the consequence of sampling errors.)

The second evaluation (World Bank 1990a), which used different, improved methods and country classifications, was similarly unable to report strong results. In terms of statistical significance, the strongest before and after comparison, after controlling for the effects of greater inflows of assistance and various other factors, was for an improvement in saving ratios during 1985-88 as contrasted with the preceding four years, but for a decline in investment ratios by comparison with the 1970s. Comparing the two subperiods of the 1980s, adjusting countries also tended to grow somewhat faster in the latter part of the decade, and showed a (statistically nonsignificant) tendency for export volumes to grow faster. The results of such tests are not reported separately for low-income countries, but the growth effect appeared to be stronger in their case, while saving and export effects were weaker, and the (undesired) decline in investment more marked. The report claims an improving implementation record during the 1980s, with an average of 77 percent of all policy conditions substantially implemented by the end of the loan period, and with better results for the key conditions, although comparable figures in the earlier report were slightly higher.[8]

One way of trying to overcome some of the methodological difficulties is to undertake in-depth country studies, although generalizing from them is dangerous. A study by World Bank staff (Nooter and Stacy 1990) used this approach to study adjustment programs in seven African countries, but this too yielded only weak results (p.14):

> Only three of the seven countries under review (Ghana, Guinea and Madagascar) appear to have adopted adjustment programs which are broad and deep enough to constitute effective, growth oriented adjustment programs. Even in these cases, further adjustment measures will be necessary. Since the seven countries under review are considered by the Africa Region [of the Bank] to have the most effective programs in the region, it can be assumed that the adjustment programs not reviewed are also not yet fully comprehensive (with the exceptions of Gambia and Mauritius).

To sum up, we cannot provide strong evidence that IFI-supported adjustment programs achieve their objectives. The indications are that when implemented, they help in some degree, but that the results are less than dramatic, particularly in SLICs. Indeed, few countries can convincingly claim that adjustment programs have made a decisive difference, particularly in Africa and Latin America, although some have made encouraging progress. Moreover, even fewer countries can say that improvements have become self-sustaining, so that they will achieve consistently better results over a period of years.

Given this rather indecisive evidence on whether adjustment works, the question arises, if not why not?

---

8. Substantially stronger results are claimed in a further Bank evaluation confined to experiences in Sub-Saharan Africa (World Bank 1989b). This too uses a control group method, but simply on the basis of comparisons between countries with "strong" reform programs and countries with "weak" or no reform programs, with no other attempt to ensure comparability. The findings claim some tendency for faster GDP and agricultural growth in the strongly reforming countries, superior export and investment records, and a better record on the growth of private consumption. Savings performance, however, was better in the nonreforming group. The findings of this study are, however, difficult to reconcile with the Bank's other evaluations, just reported, and are subject to several of the methodological difficulties mentioned earlier, particularly as regards the choice of control group, the difficulty of differentiating between the effects of program finance and program policies, and the absence of tests for statistical significance in the results obtained. It also contains a larger than usual degree of subjectivism.

Sources of Weakness

The answers to this question can be roughly divided into three types: difficulties created by a hostile global environment, more or less technical considerations relating to the design of economic policy packages, and relationships between aid agencies and recipient governments. The first part of this chapter dealt with the first of these. The other two require some elaboration.

Technical considerations. As earlier chapters have demonstrated, the design of policy packages to foster economic adaptation is no simple matter. We have drawn attention to the centrality of tradeoffs in policymaking and the difficult choices they can pose. We have stressed the importance of viewing economic policies as a system, the complex interactions that occur between policy and target variables (including time lags between policy decisions and their effects), and how indirect effects can be quite different from the direct impact of a policy change. We have stressed the need to consider carefully the desirable sequence in which actions should be taken. We have pointed out the sensitivity of results to the particularities of economic structures, the need to tailor policies to the specific circumstances of the problem in hand, and the resulting dangers of applying generalized solutions. Finally, we have had to draw attention to deficiencies in our knowledge of how things work and how they might be improved.

In other words, the construction of adjustment programs is a difficult, complex business. This is true generally, not just of IFI-supported programs. However, it does raise questions about the effectiveness of conditionality, for donor agencies will often not have enough experienced personnel with intimate knowledge of local circumstances to be able to design policy conditions or provide advice that are appropriate for local circumstances (not least because the Bank and Fund have for some years been under pressure to keep down their staff numbers, with the result that many of their professionals have become seriously overextended). An almost inevitable result, reinforced by a desire to achieve comparability of treatment across countries, is to resort to a more or less standard approach. This has long been a complaint against the IMF, which faces particular difficulties in varying the content of its programs across countries. There is evidence that Bank programs are more tailored to country circumstances.[9] Even the Bank, however, has limits to its flexibility and faces institutional pressures to use standard recipes. In other words, the inherent limitations on the expertise and freedom of action of the IFIs make it difficult for them to cope with the complexities of devising adjustment packages. Thus, home-produced programs probably stand a better chance of coping with the complexities than programs largely initiated from outside.

Another area of difficulty relates to the reconciliation of the demand management approach of IMF stabilization programs and the supply-oriented thrust of Bank structural adjustment programs. Earlier chapters have hinted at some of the difficulties. Thus, chapter 2 refers to the danger that IMF-type programs that envisage large reductions in imports are liable to erode export supply responses, to say nothing of the costs imposed by way of output forgone. At a more microeconomic level, chapter 7 mentioned the dangers of counterproductive cuts in agricultural services as a result of reductions in government spending incorporated in IMF programs.

To put the case in more general terms, tensions can arise between demand management and supply-oriented programs as a result of differences in the requirements for program success in respect of (a) import levels, (b) volumes and terms of domestic credit, and (c) government expenditures on economic services and/or capital formation. In principle, there is no inevitable contradiction in these requirements. They can be reconciled, depending on the amount of external finance available in support of the programs and, therefore, the time over which macroeconomic balance must be achieved; the respective priorities placed upon the short-term stabilization and longer-term adjustment objectives; and the range of policy instruments available to the government. The first—finance and time—is likely to be a crucial determinant. In a world in which supporting finance is scarce, all too often countries have had to sacrifice longer-term adjustment to short-term stabilization.

---

9. In an unpublished study of a number of Bank structural adjustment programs in Africa, William Kingsmill found considerable variation in the content of these programs, including different approaches to similar problems in different countries, although the broad thrust of the programs was the same. On IMF conditionality see Killick (1984), especially pp. 199-205, on program flexibility.

An implication of this is that the two IFIs may sometimes give differing advice to governments. The dilemmas created for governments become even more acute when they are seeking to execute Fund and Bank programs simultaneously and when these are subject to cross-conditionality (situations in which access to the credits of either IFI depends upon observing the policy conditions of both). In practice, this generally takes the form of the requirement that a government must first agree a program with the Fund before the Bank will agree to a structural adjustment credit (see Commonwealth Secretariat 1986; Griffith Jones 1988). One of the problems with such cross-conditionality is that it assumes away the tensions between short-term stabilization and longer-term structural change. Unfortunately, the tensions are real, as is illustrated for Jamaica in box 9-3.

We should also recall the so-called fallacy of composition problem discussed earlier. Essentially, this draws attention to the difficulties of ensuring that the aggregated results of individual country program targets for export expansion are consistent with overall world trading conditions, and the dangers inherent in putting one program together largely in isolation from programs in place or in preparation elsewhere.

Donor-recipient relationships. A danger is that the very fact of conditionality, and the nature of the donor-recipient relationship that it implies, will undermine program effectiveness (for a trenchant statement of such a viewpoint see the note by Elliot Berg in Thomas and others 1991). Much hinges on the extent to which the IFIs and the government in question genuinely agree about the desirability of the program and its provisions. Where there is a real meeting of minds conditionality is not really necessary (except of a *pro forma* kind to comply with board requirements in Washington) because the government would have undertaken the policy changes anyway. However, if we define conditionality as those actions that the government would not otherwise have undertaken, it is almost tautological to say that the government is not fully persuaded of the desirability of the changes.

One source of difficulty here may be a mismatch of values or objectives. There is a direct link between much of the thrust of the orthodox adjustment programs of the 1980s and the conservative revo-

Box 9-3. Stabilization Versus Adjustment in Jamaica, 1984·

During 1984-85, Jamaica attempted to implement both an IMF stand-by agreement and a World Bank structural adjustment loan. The former concentrated on demand-restraining conditions while the latter focused on increasing supply. However, despite a considerable degree of coordination between the Fund and Bank in preparing the programs, the policies used to comply with the IMF targets largely undermined the Bank's supply-oriented growth aims.

This was particularly true of tight monetary policy, including nominal interest rates above 25 percent. This was intended to restrict the amount of domestic currency available for firms to borrow and use to bid in the foreign exchange auction, and to induce foreign private capital inflows. Both effects were expected to reduce downward pressure on the exchange rate and ease the foreign exchange constraint on growth.

However, such policies put much of the burden of stabilization on to the private sector. In the context of imperfect financial markets and economic uncertainty, foreign capital did not appear while pent-up demand for foreign exchange and psychological factors depreciated the exchange rate rapidly. Although rapid inflation made real interest rates negative, high nominal borrowing rates adversely affected private sector investment because investors saw their expected profits slashed. Commercial bank loans to companies fell sharply, and many firms developed liquidity and cash flow problems due to rising burdens of past debt and inability to borrow for working capital. This was partly because the debt-equity structure of many firms was heavily weighted toward debt, reflecting incentives designed to increase supply implemented under previous World Bank programs. This resulted in an increased bankruptcy rate, especially for smaller firms.

In addition, growing uncertainty about the level of the currency and the high cost of borrowing funds for the exchange auction led many exporters to experience shortages of imported equipment and supplies. Several tried to reorient production away from exports to the domestic market. At the same time, devaluation failed to cut import levels: the current account deficit was twice as large as the IMF target. These adverse effects on investment and the balance of payments fed through into output performance and were a principal cause of a fall in GDP by 5 percent during 1984-85.

Source: Harrigan (1991, pp. 334-44).

lution that occurred in the politics of North America and much of Europe in that decade, particularly the emphasis they gave to reducing state interventions in the economy and to greater reliance on market forces. However, this shift in the political center of gravity affected only some developing countries, so in some cases conditionality embodied policy changes that conflicted with the government's philosophies.

A closely related point concerns the possibility of conflicts between the IFIs' objectives and the government's, even when they share broadly the same philosophy. The IFIs have to satisfy their major shareholders, who often take a lively interest in what loans are made to whom and for what, and who sometimes seek to use their influence on the IFI boards to promote their own foreign policy and/or commercial interests. The IFIs see their loans to any one country in the context of a far larger set of lending activities, so that decisions about policy changes in one country are influenced by what is being done elsewhere. Indeed, in the context of the fallacy of composition above we have urged that this should be so. The lending decisions of the World Bank, as well as of the regional development banks, are also influenced by the need to maintain their credit rating on world capital markets, on which they raise much of their capital. Moreover, large bureaucracies generate their own internal politics and these too influence the content of conditionality. Thus, the Bank has long acknowledged that some of its earlier structural adjustment loans specified far too many policy changes, but its internal politics have prevented it from remedying this defect as much as its management would like.

Governments and ministers, however, are supposed to concentrate on promoting the national interest. They may also have other worries: how to win (or avoid!) an election, how to keep the army happy, and how to reward supporters and deal with the opposition. In short, government and IFI objectives may not match up, which may lead to disagreements about policies. In addition, disagreements of a more intellectual nature may arise as Berg has pointed out (1991 draft):

> Many of the intellectual or analytical underpinnings of 1980s-style adjustment lending are contested - such fundamentals as the feasibility of export-led growth, the efficacy and beneficence of deregulated markets, and the desirability of market-determined interest rates or exchange rates. It is true . . . that there is more consensus on these ideas now than there was ten years ago. But . . . profound disagreements remain. Similar disagreements remain on less cosmic matters, such as the size and timing of exchange rate adjust-

ments, the desirability of border pricing for basic foods, and the degree and the speed of reducing industrial sector protection. Since consensus is lacking in many countries on important loan conditions, implementation will tend to lack conviction and programs will be easily diluted or derailed.

He goes on to a further source of resistance:

Political and bureaucratic consensus is even more uncommon . . . Agreements negotiated and signed by ministers of finance or planning are implemented by sectoral ministries. Sometimes these ministries are only perfunctorily consulted; often they are in deep disagreement with the spirit and particulars of the reform program.

He indicates yet another difficulty: that conditionality gives the impression that programs are being imposed upon a reluctant government even when they are not. Such a public perception may undermine the program's legitimacy, and therefore the likelihood that it will be successfully implemented and sustained. Even where that does not occur, extensive IFI determination of the content of a program will weaken what the Bank calls the government's sense of ownership of the program, which may well be the most important determinant of its success.[10] Although the IFIs are aware of the danger, the modalities of program negotiation do little to foster government identification with it.

Such circumstances are liable to throw up programs that governments do not regard as their own, and which they will implement only the inescapable minimum. Consequently, some governments have become adept at finding ways that do not formally contravene the agreed policy conditions, but that effectively restore the previous *status quo*. One of the difficulties is that by insisting on major policy changes, the IFIs become important players on the domestic political stage, but without the ability to assemble a coalition of interests sufficient to sustain the reforms, particularly if the economic situation improves and economic pressures diminish. Moreover, their prescriptions may sometimes threaten the government's survival or unity, and/or clash with the bureaucracy's collective or personal interests. In such

---

10. Thus, Mills (1989), reporting on a series of World Bank seminars on adjustment in Africa, states (pp. 9-10) that most participants—chiefly government officials—at all seminars saw African governments as having only a superficial input into the design of structural adjustment programs, for reasons only partly related to limited internal country capacities for program design.

situations, the domestic actors are likely to prevail. Technocratic solutions have limitations, particularly when originated abroad.

This draws attention to a related feature: that countries often adopt IFI-supported adjustment programs during economic crises.[11] Crises may be necessary before governments can take radical policy decisions, but this runs the risk that they will make decisions hastily, on the basis of poor information, with inadequate consultation or consideration of administrative aspects.[12] The chances of implementation are reduced in such circumstances. The policy changes most likely to be carried through successfully are probably those that emerge organically and gradually through existing political and bureaucratic structures. Conditionality-related reforms rarely have these qualities and are thus bound to be fragile, undermined by their crisis-driven nature. This type of consideration may help to explain the relatively successful adjustment experiences of some Asian countries. As a generalization, their past adjustment policies have probably been more home-grown, less crisis-ridden, and less donor-driven, which may well have contributed to program success. If this is so, it reinforces the importance of the ownership factor in adjustment policies and cautions against excessive expectations about what conditionality can achieve.

IFI conditionality also includes a substantial element of bluff that further undermines the process. There is a good deal of signing of apparently tough policy agreements, however, the government knows it will be allowed considerable latitude in their execution. Fund and Bank missions are often under pressure not to return to Washington without an agreement. Both institutions are making new loans to protect the repayment of past credits, to avoid the borrowing countries' moving into arrears with them, or to validate an already negotiated debt rescheduling agreement. Both come under considerable political pressures from the executive directors of major shareholder countries in favor of particular countries. Moreover, once the process has begun,

---

11. In this and the previous paragraph I am heavily influenced by a paper by Grindle and Thomas (1989) and by the proceedings of a 1988 conference on the politics of policy reform organized by the Harvard Institute of International Development.

12. See White (1990) for a perceptive essay on the implementation of policy reform programs. She emphasizes the value for implementation of designing reforms in collaboration with those who will be in charge of executing them.

the IFIs can get locked into a country: their commitment to making a success of the programs they have financed pushes them into providing yet more finance (what we called evergreening in the previous chapter). In these circumstances the threat of fund withdrawal because of noncompliance with a policy condition loses plausibility. As a result, IFI conditionality can in some countries be little more than a paper tiger.

Summing Up. Finally, we should note the limitations inherent in the relatively short time spans of IFI programs. The view taken in this book is that structural adaptation is a continuous process, inseparable from long-run economic development. We have highlighted the considerable time lags that are often involved; the benefits of a steady, persistent adherence to policies that maintain balance in the economy and help it to adapt to changing circumstances; and the potentially heavy costs of a shorter-term, and therefore more draconian, approach to adaptation. The staff of the IFIs are, of course, aware of these factors, but they face institutional and political imperatives (and in the case of the IMF, constitutional limitations on the term of their lending), which in practice make it difficult for the IFIs to take a long-term view. The short- to medium-term nature of their programs diminishes their effectiveness, even when a country has a succession of programs.

Summary

Among the wider contextual issues taken up in this chapter, the first related to the feasibility of adjustment in one country, or the consistency of the global economic environment with national adjustment efforts. We pointed out a number of asymmetries in the system, the double standards sometimes applied by industrial countries, and the retreat during the 1980s from international cooperation. The effect of these distortions was to thrust a disproportionate share of the costs of adjustment on low-income countries. Even if systemic reform of the international system is impracticable, specific policy changes by industrial countries could improve matters, including reform of their policies on market access and protectionism, measures to reduce pressures for continuing oversupply on commodity markets, and greater financing for export compensation schemes.

We drew attention to ways in which the overhang of external debt and shortages of supporting finance in many developing countries undermined their adjustment efforts, and urged donor and creditor countries to come up with more generous, imaginative, and flexible policies with respect to the provision of aid and debt relief.

With financial assistance come policy conditions, however, and we turned to examine some of the issues arising from conditionality, particularly that of the IMF and World Bank. We suggested that the overriding impact of the policy environment on the effectiveness of assistance gave the donors/creditors a legitimate interest in recipient policies, that IFI conditionality generally tried to move policies in a sensible direction, and in any case that no convincing and thorough-going alternative approach was available. However, experience has not provided strong evidence that conditionality is actually very effective in achieving its objectives.

Weaknesses arise from a number of sources. Some of these are technical, for example, relating to the complexities of designing adjustment programs and the difficulty of striking an appropriate balance between the regulation of aggregate demand and the promotion of supply-side reforms. Difficulties in donor-recipient relationships are another source of weakness: they may differ over objectives, the fact of conditionality may weaken a government's sense of ownership of a program, and there are difficulties about the short-to medium-term time horizons of IFI programs. We concluded that conditionality probably has the most effect when IFI intervention tips the domestic policymaking balance in favor of reform, but that in other circumstances it risks being impotent, or actually harmful.

A Note in Further Reading: This chapter draws fairly heavily upon my essay in Bird (1990), and other contributions to that volume are also useful, especially those by Bird himself. The World Bank's (1989a and 1990a) evaluations of the results of its adjustment lending are useful, as is the two-volume study by Mosley, Harrigan, and Toye (1991). See Khan (1990) on the methodological pitfalls of program evaluation.

10

THE COSTS AND POLITICAL MANAGEMENT OF ADJUSTMENT

Having dealt in Chapter 9 with the global context, we turn in this concluding chapter to more domestic contextual issues. We first take up the connections between structural adaptation and poverty and their policy implications. We also look briefly at the implications of adjustment policies for the protection of the environment. Finally, we take further a matter that has already emerged as central to our concerns: the political management of adjustment.

Adaptation, Poverty, and the Environment

How actually do adjustment policies impinge upon poverty and on the environment? We will consider the distributional question first and the costs of adjustment.

Adjustment Costs

When pointing out the frequency with which policymakers have to confront tradeoffs between competing objectives, chapter 5 signaled the existence of adjustment costs against which the benefits had to be set. The literature abounds with references to the costs of adjustment, but discussions of these are often rather loose. It is therefore worth spending a little time to elucidate this subject (see, however, Corden 1989; Huang and Nicholas 1987). Various types of cost may be identified.

First, are what we might term absorption costs. These arise in the common situation where a country's adjustment policies are addressed to improving an unviable balance of payments situation. Faced with a need to reduce a current account deficit, standard theory tells us that the country must reduce absorption (consumption plus investment) relative to income. In principle, a country can achieve this by increasing income while holding absorption constant, but in practice—and in the short term—countries are likely to have to cut back on consumption and/or investment in the public and/or private sectors. Such cuts can be seen as costs that result in lower consumption or investment levels than would otherwise have occurred. In a sense, such costs are unavoidable in that they are part of the economic logic of the balance of payments problem, although they can be minimized by doing everything possible to maximize the growth of income.[1]

In institutional terms, absorption costs arise more commonly in connection with the IMF's stabilization programs, which is one of the reasons why controversy often surrounds them. However, as they actually arise from the circumstances—and policies—that allowed absorption to get too far out of line with incomes in the first place, they might be better thought of as the costs of adverse shocks or past policy weaknesses.

A second category might be termed frictional costs. These refer to losses of output, employment, and consumption resulting from the reallocations of resources from declining to expanding sectors intrinsic to economic adaptation. They arise because markets are imperfect. If they were everywhere perfect, all prices would be flexible, resources would be homogeneous and mobile, and adjustment would be instantaneous. However, many types of labor, capital, and natural resources are specific in their productive employment. An irrigation system cannot be used in factories, a miner cannot instantly be converted into a hotel worker, and agriculture land in a given ecological zone is not necessarily suitable for conversion from cultivation of one crop to another.

Markets are imperfect in other ways too. Prices are often sticky in the downward direction, none more so than in labor markets, which exhibit fierce resistances to cuts in money wages even in the face of an

---

1. The history of attempts to deal with the debt crisis of the heavily-indebted Latin American countries after 1982 can be traced in these terms. The initial effort focused on cutting absorption, and both consumption and investment were reduced. As a result, major improvements in the trade balances of the debtor countries occurred (necessary for the countries to make interest payments on their external debt), but at the cost of severely reduced living standards and investment levels. In the belief that such sacrifices were not sustainable indefinitely and could, in any case, prove counterproductive, from about 1987 international attention switched to adjustment with growth, with the intention of being able to ease up on the absorption variables. The Baker Plan of that year was the catalyst, although only limited improvement was achieved in practice.

industry's decline. Structural adaptation is, therefore, associated with frictional losses of employment and capacity utilization: losses that may be large and persistent. Indeed, most of the discussion of adjustment costs in industrial countries is about the unemployment that results.

A closely related category is what we can call distributional costs. Of course, absorption and frictional costs affect the distribution of income, but distributional consequences would occur even in the absence of these, for adaptation affects the relative sizes of sectors of production, and these employ differing factor proportions. Structural change thus gives rise to differing groups of gainers and losers whose short-term interests can conflict with one another.

Net distributional costs arise when the value society attaches to the losses of those adversely affected exceeds the value placed upon the benefits of the gainers. Much of the discussion of the costs of adjustment is about distributional aspects, in particular, the danger that the poor will be disadvantaged. Implicit here is the idea that a dollar's worth of loss by the poor is not offset by a dollar's gain by the rich, so that different weights are placed on the income changes.

We might further notice the time factor in adjustment costs. Especially in the case of absorption costs, the government is faced with choices between reduced consumption and reduced investment (which boils down to whether consumption is reduced now or in the future). There is an ever-present temptation to push required reductions on to investment. This is especially the case in the public sector, where governments find cutting their current budgets very difficult (because that is likely to require layoffs of civil servants) and cutting back on their own capital spending easier. A similar choice arises with frictional costs: it is tempting to minimize these by slowing down the rate of change and subsidizing industries that otherwise would decline, at the expense of the rest of the economy (as illustrated in box 9-1). In both examples, economic adaptation is retarded and costs are shifted forward to the next generation. Such intergenerational issues are closely related to the choice discussed in chapter 4 between positive and defensive adjustment strategies, where we concluded in favor of a generally positive strategy implied an approach that avoided shifting the costs into the future.

In the low-income countries, however, this can be a harsh doctrine. As we showed in chapter 3, poor countries have inflexible economies. Hence frictional costs are likely to be severe. Starting from already very low living standards, the temptation to shift costs into the future will be large, but the results of doing so will be to retard the very process of change upon which the improvement of living standards ultimately depends.

Dangers to the Poor

An important proposition to emerge from chapter 3 was that a well-functioning market system is conducive to economic flexibility. It can handle large volumes of information in a decentralized way and convert it into appropriate incentive signals, and competitive forces can raise supply elasticities, thereby increasing the economy's responsiveness to changing relative prices. This is a theme that has been further developed in other chapters, and although we have argued for a large and active role for the state, we have seen it as acting more through market signals or as allowing markets to work better.

At the same time, chapter 4 identified the existence of degrees of poverty and income inequality inconsistent with what society regards as equitable as a common market failure. In this case, greater reliance on markets to achieve structural adaptation could be associated with increases in inequalities that further impoverish the poor. A central question that emerges is how are the costs of adjustment to be distributed across society and how can we protect those already living in poverty?

An answer to this, however, presumes that we know who the poor are, how they fit into the national economy, and the extent of their vulnerability (the influence of adjustment measures upon them and their ability to cope with these). In reality, ignorance about these matters is widespread, but such information is essential because the poor are far from being a homogeneous group, and how adjustment policies affect—and can protect—them depends crucially upon the nature of their incomes. One fairly well-established generalization is that the urban population tends to bear many of the short- to medium-term adjustment costs, but in most low-income countries a large majority of the poor live in rural communities. This is illustrated for selected countries in table 10-1, where we see that typically 80 to 90 percent of those classified as living in poverty are in rural areas.

Table 10-1. Rural and Urban Poverty in Low-Income Countries in the 1980s

Country	Rural population (percentage of total)	Rural poor (percentage of total)	Infant mortality (per thousand)		Access to safe water (percentage of population)	
			Rural	Urban	Rural	Urban
Côte d'Ivoire	57	86	121	70	10	30
Ghana	65	80	87	67	39	72
India	77	79	105	57	47	80
Indonesia	73	91	74	57	36	46
Kenya	80	96	59	57	21	61

Source: World Bank (1990b, table 2.2).

Nonetheless, the urban poor may be particularly vulnerable to adjustment policies as a result of public sector job retrenchments, other frictional unemployment, and possible losses of food subsidies and other welfare provisions. Among the rural poor much will depend on their access to land; whether those with land are producing cash crops (likely to benefit from higher producer prices) or local foods (whose relative prices may not go up at all as a result of adjustment policies), and whether they are net sellers or buyers of food; and the extent to which they are integrated into the modern market economy. Much of the evidence suggests that households headed by women are particularly at risk because women have often had fewer educational opportunities, are confined by cultural *mores* and active discrimination to less lucrative work, sometimes face legal or customary restraints on the ownership and inheritance of wealth, and are discriminated against in the provision of government services. (Lewis 1988 provides a valuable assessment of the lessons of experience in identifying and assisting the poor; see the article in his volume by Buvinic and Lycette).

The heterogeneous nature of the poor and the varying ways in which they fit into the overall economy makes generalizing about the impact of adjustment programs upon them impossible. Typically, some of the poor will lose and some will gain. Thomas and Weidmann (1988,p.69) cite the policy reforms in Zambia in 1983-87, which reversed the previous heavy taxation of agriculture and shifted relative prices in favor of the rural economy, as an example of an adjustment program beneficial to the poorer segments of the population. It is hence no surprise that the World Bank (1990a) evaluation of experiences with adjustment lending, reported earlier, concluded that changes in living conditions did not appear to be systematically related to adjustment programs in either direction. Significantly, the organization that has done most to urge the need to protect the poor in adjustment programs, UNICEF, is cautious about blaming such programs for worsening poverty, although it does regard them as having been a contributory element (see Cornia, Jolly, and Stewart 1987 for a general statement of the UNICEF view, especially p.288, and Cornia, Jolly, and Stewart 1988 for a set of ten country case studies). Against this, one must presume that planned adjustment of the type supported by the Bank has greater potential for protecting or benefiting the poor than unplanned adjustment forced upon reluctant governments by an economic crisis. As UNICEF has pointed out, however, until the late 1980s few programs incorporated specific provisions to safeguard the poor, who thus stood to suffer as a result of heedless neglect.

As already suggested, one danger that affects the urban poor is particular job losses, resulting from the recessionary effects of reductions in absorption, from job cut-backs in the public sector, or from the decline of industries adversely affected by shifts in relative prices. Another danger arises from the cut-backs in government spending that are often associated with attempts to reduce absorption and budget deficits. Many argue that when faced with the need to cut, governments tend to give low priority to social and economic services and favor military and administrative expenditures.[2] This indeed is what

---

2. The United Nations Development Program (UNDP 1990 pp.76-78) draws particular attention to the expansion of military spending in low-income countries. This grew at 7.5 percent per year in real terms in the least developed countries in

has happened in a number of the heavily indebted countries of Latin America, but the same trend is less evident for low-income countries. Thus, the World Bank (1990b, table 7.5) found that when African governments had to prune their budgets social spending was cut less than other categories (although there were nonetheless large real reductions in social spending), and this is consistent with other evidence.[3]

This is less than fully reassuring, however. For one thing, much of the burden of cuts falls upon the economic services provided by the state and its investment in the economy's infrastructure, and the poor are liable to lose from these reductions. Second, the government may tend to cut back on food subsidies, as these often place severe burdens on the budget.[4] General food subsidies are an inefficient way to help the poor because those who could afford to pay market prices capture many of the benefits, and the effect may be to depress prices paid to farmers, who themselves may be poor. Nonetheless, some of the poor do gain from subsidies, particularly in the towns, and can be badly affected by cuts.

There is also a serious danger that the quality of social services will be reduced during times of budgetary stringency, even when the share of social spending is protected. The thing that governments find hardest to ax is jobs. Pressures to avoid reducing the civil service are strong, and this leads instead to pruning the supporting expenditures

---

1960-86, much faster than total GNP, so that it increased its share from 2.1 to 3.8 percent and, of course, much larger proportions of total government spending.

3. Thus, Hicks (1991) studied the data for twenty-four developing countries in which government expenditures had been cut and found that social expenditures and defense were relatively protected compared with expenditures on infrastructure and economic services. However, capital expenditures were the main victims of expenditure reductions, underlining the earlier signaling of intergenerational aspects of this question. See also Hicks and Kubisch (1984).

4. Zambia provides a case in point. In 1986 subsidies on maize meal alone accounted for 16 percent of the government's total budget deficit, but government attempts to cut back on these caused riots and led to the abandonment of an adjustment program, supported by the IFIs (see Thomas and Weidemann, 1988).

that make civil servants productive: drugs for clinics, books for schools, transport for social workers.[5]

The poor may also lose from any slow-down in economic growth that results from adjustment efforts. In the broadest terms, the position of the poor is determined by the overall level of income achieved in an economy and the way it is distributed. In the presence of large inequalities, many people can continue to live in severe poverty even in countries with relatively high average incomes. With a more equal distribution widespread poverty can be avoided even with moderate per capita incomes (see table 10-2). The position of the poor can hence be improved by increasing incomes in general, by redistributing income in favor of the poor, or some combination of the two.

Table 10-2. Per Capita GNP and Selected Social Indicators

Country	GNP per capita (US$)	Life expectancy (years)	Adult literacy (%)	Infant mortality (per 1,000 live births)
Modest GNP per capita with high human development:				
Sri Lanka	400	71	87	32
Jamaica	940	74	82	18
Costa Rica	1,610	75	93	18
High GNP per capita with modest human development:				
Brazil	2,020	65	78	62
Oman	5,810	57	30	40
Saudi Arabia	6,200	64	55	70

*Source:*UNDP (1990, table 1.1).

---

5. Cameroon provides an extreme example of this: the share of salaries in total government recurrent spending rose to 99 percent during a fiscal crunch in 1985-87 (World Bank 1990b, p.117).

In the long run, however, and in countries starting from low average incomes, continuing to improve the position of the poor becomes impossible without overall economic growth, because there are severe limits upon the extent to which the state can redistribute income and wealth without running into evasive action on the part of the relatively well-to-do and without eroding incentives to save and invest. Similarly with the costs of adjustment: these are likely to be smaller and better tolerated when the overall economy is growing than in conditions of stagnation. For example, in the face of changes in the structure of production, it makes a great deal of difference to employment prospects if a shift from one industry to another is absolute—involving the actual decline of the disfavored industry—or merely relative, meaning that it will grow more slowly than the favored industry. The danger of adverse budgetary cuts will also be less if the country can maintain a reasonable pace of economic growth, for growth, in turn, will increase government revenues, reducing budgetary pressures.

So, while growth is far from being a sufficient condition for the long-run alleviation of poverty, in low-income countries it is a necessary condition. Hence, any economic slow-down makes protecting the poor harder.

Adjustment, then, endangers the poor in a number of ways: by job losses, reduced subsidies and government services, and the adverse effects of economic slow-down. This danger is made all the greater by political considerations. The politics of adjustment is the subject of the final section of this chapter, so we confine ourselves here to pointing out the frequent tension between the distribution of political power and a desire to provide special protection to those living in poverty. For the poor are usually unorganized, and rarely powerful. It is the relatively well-to-do who command political clout, and it is their opposition that the government will desire to buy off or to manage in some other way. The politics of compensating those who lose from adjustment rarely favors the poor, which places them even more at risk.

However, viewing structural adjustment as a zero-sum game in which gains are necessarily offset by losses would be quite wrong. Although it may sometimes seem that way in the short term, the large long-term gains that can be won from successful adaptation can scarcely be exaggerated. In a historical perspective, adjustment is a massively positive-sum game. In the end, the losers are those who do not adapt, but in the meantime the most vulnerable must be protected.

We should similarly not overlook the risks to the poor of postponing adjustment or of resisting the adaptation of the economy. In the face of imbalances governments have often tried to repress the problems by using import and price controls, heavy implicit taxation of agriculture, and an undiscriminating protection of industry. Such defensive responses have often been associated with the emergence of large scarcity rents (including corruption) and capital flight, which distort the distribution of income to the advantage of a favored few, erosion of real agricultural incomes and of the government's own tax base, and general economic slow-down. All these developments are likely to be bad news for the poor. Protection of the vulnerable requires orderly adjustment, which incorporates poverty-alleviation measures, and is most unlikely to be achieved when adjustment is forced upon a reluctant government by the brute force of events.

Next, let us consider specifically what might be included in adjustment policies to safeguard the position of those living in poverty.

Protecting the Poor

All governments, in whatever kind of society, find it difficult to reach the poorest effectively. They exist on the margins of the economy, they are unorganized and poorly educated, they are often suspicious of the state and its officials, and ignorance about them is widespread. Protecting the poor from the costs of adjustment is, therefore, very difficult. This is so even in the presence of a strong political commitment, a condition that is often not satisfied. Only efforts based upon careful planning and determined implementation are likely to be effective. Often a necessary starting point is to find out more about the economic and social characteristics of the vulnerable and how they fit into the economy. Only when the government can identify the target groups and trace how different policy instruments affect them shall it be able to provide effective assistance, and safeguard against the danger that benefits intended for the poor get captured by the not-so-poor. Sometimes a major research effort will be needed to gather and analyze the necessary information.[6]

Assuming the necessary political commitment and knowledge base exist, we can identify five broad approaches to helping the poor in adjustment programs (the following is based closely on Demery and Addison 1987):

- Increasing their access to productive assets, for example, land;
- Raising the returns they can achieve from the productive assets they already possess, for example, by providing extension advice;
- Improving their employment opportunities;
- Improving their access to education and health services;
- Supplementing their resources with transfers, for example, through food subsidies.

The government can bring various levels of policy into play in executing such a package. Macroeconomic policy can be given a greater orientation toward maintaining economic growth than is often the case, especially with shorter-term stabilization efforts. A role exists for what have been called meso-level measures (Cornia, Jolly, and Stewart 1987, p.291), that is, policies that mediate between macro measures and the poor. These would, for example, safeguard the position of the social services during periods of budgetary stringency. Sectoral policies can be used, to safeguard, say, against inappropriately capital-intensive production methods and to create employment, or to provide special help to smallholder farmers and those operating in the economy's informal sector. At a more microeconomic level, policies within sectors can be changed to help the poor, for example, to ensure that they are not discriminated against in the provision of public education and health services, or to target special public works or nutritional programs on the poor.

---

6. Calls for more research as a preliminary to further action can, of course, be used as a device to postpone substantive action indefinitely. However, when basic information simply does not exist it is difficult to see how an effective package of measures to protect the poor can be put in place, although some things can probably be done right away. Glewwe and van der Gaag (1990) have shown how the size and composition of the poor can vary greatly according to the definition employed.

Following UNICEF recommendations we can add certain additional broad principles. One is that measures to protect the poor are much more likely to be effective if they are built into the original design of an adjustment program than if they are treated separately or added as an afterthought. This is among the lessons to be derived from the highly successful Korean experience sketched in box 10-1. Another is that raising the productivities and incomes of the poor is central to any strategy for improving their material well-being, for we have already suggested the existence of rather severe limits to governments' abilities to redistribute existing income and, in any case, productivity-raising measures lessen the danger that the poor will become dependent on special help. One aspect of this task is to try to find ways of increasing the participation of the poor in sectors of production that can be expected to grow in the process of structural adaptation.

Box 10-1 Protecting the Poor from Adjustment Costs in the Republic of Korea

In consequence of a mixture of adverse international and domestic developments, Korea's previously fast-growing economy went into a recession in 1979-80, causing average incomes to decline by a tenth and even larger regressions among the poor. Their diets worsened and social progress was threatened in a number of ways.

The government responded in 1980 with a stabilization-adjustment package that sought to stabilize prices, liberalize trade and the economy, and encourage structural change toward technology-intensive industries. At the same time it incorporated measures to safeguard the poor. These included a medical assistance program targeted at the lowest income groups; public works programs to provide work for the poor during the crisis; a program of transfers also targeted on the poor, including provision of food, assistance for fuel, and increased educational subsidies; and increased public spending on education and low-cost housing.

The package was broadly successful both in its overall economic objectives and in protecting the poor. Indeed, the percentage of absolutely poor and the infant mortality rate continued to decline at historical rates despite the recession and restructuring. Success at the macro level in restoring economic growth itself helped to improve the position of the poor.

Source: Suh and Williamson in Cornia, Jolly, and Stewart (1988, chapter 8).

A further principle is that efforts to protect the poor are more likely to succeed when a wider range of government departments and other agencies (including nongovernmental organizations) is involved in program design than the usual concentration upon the ministries of finance and planning, even though coordination problems multiply as more are brought in. Another lesson of experience is that attempts to protect the poor are more likely to succeed if the pace of adjustment can be fairly gradual, for as we have suggested earlier, adjustment costs are a rising function of the speed of change. This plea for a more gradual approach underlies the case for more growth-oriented programs, because growth is almost certain to suffer with "sharp shock" approaches, but for more gradual adjustment to be feasible, more external financial support will be necessary to finance the intervening period before a viable macroeconomic balance is restored, and that takes us back to the whole question of access to world savings. A final general principle is that programs should incorporate mechanisms to monitor their impact on the poor and the effectiveness of the safeguards designed to protect them.

We turn now to take up a few more specific policy possibilities. Since most of the poor live in rural areas one obvious possibility is to use agricultural policies for poverty alleviation. Lele (in Lewis 1988, chapter 3, p.29) has put the case trenchantly:

> In Africa, growth in agricultural production is essential for poverty alleviation; technical change in agriculture is essential for growth; appropriate balance in the availability and deployment of physical, human and institutional capital is essential for technical change to occur; and it is the lack of such balance in the accumulation and use of different forms of capital that explains the persistence of poverty.

Such policies would need to be focused on the needs of smallholder farmers and the landless and, depending on country circumstances, could include land reforms that would redistribute land from large estates to those with little or none; policies to discourage labor-replacing technologies and to favor employment creation; improved producer prices; and improved provision of research, extension, marketing, and other public support services to the target groups, including greater attention to the problems of those farming land that is marginal or with an unreliable climate.

At the same time, we need to be conscious of the limitations of this approach. Sectoral policy is a blunt instrument for aiding poverty groups. For example, smallholders may benefit rather little from improved producer prices, with most of the gains going to more prosperous producers, because the truly poor may produce little or no marketable surplus, having to concentrate largely on growing enough food for the family to eat. We should also recall from chapter 7 that it is easier to manipulate the producer prices of export crops than of foodstuffs, whereas the poorest farmers are likely to concentrate largely on foods. Remember too that many of the poorest households are net purchasers of food and could be hard hit if improved producer prices spilled over into higher consumer prices. We should similarly not underestimate the difficulties, political and other, of executing meaningful land reform programs. Examples abound of apparently radical land reforms coming to little as a result of resistance from those who stand to lose, and there is today some skepticism about the feasibility of meaningful land reform in other than exceptional circumstances. Something of the same could be said of attempts to reorient government support services in favor of poor smallholders.

These considerations caution against relying too much on agricultural policy, and this caution is reinforced by the importance of nonfarming sources of income for the well-being of the rural poor. Figure 10-1 illustrates for Botswana what is a general feature, namely, a negative correlation between the income of rural households and the proportion of income derived from off-farm activities, with transfer payments (typically from household members who have migrated to the towns) of special importance to the poor. In the longer term, access to education (and, to a lesser extent, health services) is of fundamental importance to raising the incomes of the poor.

We have referred already to the unemployment that can arise from fiscal retrenchments and other aspects of adjustment programs. Those affected can easily find themselves members of "the new poor," suddenly deprived of what they had previously regarded as a dependable major source of income. A frequent palliative is to make redundancy payments to those who have lost their jobs and to offer retraining schemes. Some countries have devised special (temporary) employ-

Figure 10-1. Distribution of Income by Source in Rural Botswana, 1985

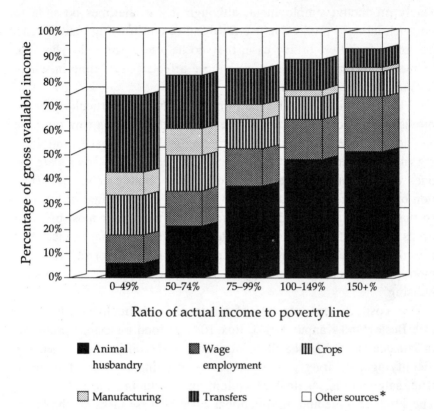

Ratio of actual income to poverty line

| ■ Animal husbandry | ▦ Wage employment | ⦀ Crops |
| ▨ Manufacturing | ⦀ Transfers | ☐ Other sources* |

Notes: The poverty line varies with household.
* Other covers trading and vending; services and construction; hunting and fishing; gathering; and property.
Source: Watanabe and Mueller (1984).

ment programs as a further response, of which the emergency employment programs introduced in Chile in 1975-84 have some-times been cited as promising models (see Demery and Addison 1987, pp.22-23; World Bank 1990b). At their peak these provided employ-ment to a full 13 percent of the labor force, even though the total cost was only 1.4 percent of GNP. This was made possible by paying wages at below market rates, which had the further advantage that only the poor were interested in taking up such work. Such schemes can often have the disadvantage (as in Chile) that they do not offer genuinely productive employment, although it is sometimes possible to put such labor to productive use repairing or constructing roads, dams, and other facilities. In any case, they do help to cushion the shock of increased unemployment and give those affected more time in which to find alternative employment.

What else might be achieved through the budget, particularly in the provision of social services? In the face of an often narrow tax base and acute budgetary difficulties, targeting is the key, that is, introducing safeguards to ensure that those most in need of the services are the ones who actually receive them. This implies both precise identification of target groups and the design (or often the redesign) of services so that they actually reach these groups and meet their most pressing needs. The latter stipulation necessitates a shift away from services that disproportionately favor the urban middle class in favor of providing more primary health and education, rural water supplies, and low-cost housing.

The cost-efficient targeting of services is a difficult task, however (see Besley and Kanpur 1988). Box 10-2 on food assistance programs in Jamaica and Sri Lanka illustrates some of the difficulties, especially identifying the target group accurately, keeping records of it up to date, safeguarding against deception, and excluding the not-so-poor. The administrative and informational costs of these tasks can be large. Another possible difficulty is avoiding a poverty trap, that is, creating disincentives for the poor to raise their earnings, which leads to long-term dependence on social support, if they find themselves no better off (perhaps worse off) if higher incomes reduce their eligibility for anti-poverty relief. There are also the political difficulties, already mentioned, of excluding the relatively affluent. However, these difficulties do not mean that targeting is invariably impractical, as boxes 10-1 and 10-2 make clear. One resort that governments are increasingly using is to channel assistance through nongovernmental organizations.

We should also mention two often taboo topics. With the ending of the Cold War at the beginning of the 1990s, many people in the major military nations hoped for a "peace dividend," including the possibility of diverting resources from now excessive military budgets into

---

Box 10-2. Targeted Food Programs in Jamaica and Sri Lanka

Jamaica and Sri Lanka are among the countries that have introduced food assistance programs targeted on poverty groups. Jamaica, for example, responded to problems created for those below the poverty line by policy reforms introduced in the early 1980s. The government decided that the budgetary situation dictated that a general subsidy on various foods would have to be abandoned. At the same time, heavy dependence on food imports meant that devaluations raised food prices, and at a time when the real purchasing power of low-income families was tending to decline because of increasing unemployment. The government thus introduced a Food Aid Programme that included provisions for the feeding of school children, food supplementation through health clinics, and the distribution of stamps targeted on the elderly and very poor which could be used for the purchase of food. Sri Lanka also introduced a food stamp scheme to replace an insupportably expensive universal budgetary subsidy on various basic foodstuffs (see box 5-1).

Both programs were highly successful in reducing the claim of food subsidies on the exchequer. In Sri Lanka the cost of the subsidies declined from 5 percent of GDP in 1975-79 to a little over 1 percent in 1984; in Jamaica the reduction was from a peak of 6 percent in 1977 to under 1 percent by the mid-1980s. But were they successful in protecting the poor? In some degree they clearly were, but there were problems too. One of these concerned identification of the target groups. In Sri Lanka the group was identified by the size and incomes of households at a particular time without provision for striking out those who subsequently increased their real incomes or for adding new low-income families. Moreover, the face value of the stamps was not increased in line with prices, so their real value became eroded. In consequence, some who benefited could have managed without while others who needed help slipped through the net. This contributed to declines in real incomes among the poorest fifth of the population and in their nutritional standards.

There were similar problems in Jamaica. Thus, all schoolchildren benefited from the school feeding program, whatever the incomes of their parents, while some of the children of the poor secured no relief because they did not attend school. Despite these difficulties, however, there is no doubt that the poor received greater protection from these schemes in the face of very large general subsidy reductions than they would have done in the absence of special provisions.

Source: Besley and Kanpur (1988); Cornia, Jolly, and Stewart (1988, chapters 5 and 7); Demery and Addison (1987); World Bank (1990b, chapters 6 and 7).

more constructive social uses. Similar questions could be asked about the military budgets of a good number of developing countries. In a large number of them the cost of spending on the armed services exceeds the combined size of the education and health budgets, and the military justification for this is often far from clear (see UNDP 1990, pp.76-78 and 162-163).

Progressive taxation (that is, based on ability to pay) is the second subject that has become somewhat taboo in recent years because of the adverse effects that this can have on incentives, as well as a less well-defined belief that taxation has become generally too high relative to total incomes. While suggesting that in the SLICs' circumstances progressive taxation can bring about more than a small reduction in income inequalities would be wrong, ignoring the fact that reluctance to tax can prevent governments from helping the poor adequately would be equally wrong. So too a heedless (but fashionable) shift from direct to indirect taxation, which can easily be regressive and impose serious additional burdens on the poor, can be harmful.

Reference to progressive taxation does, however, bring us to the existence of tradeoffs between measures to protect the poor and other objectives of adjustment policy. In the case of taxation, the tradeoff is between raising revenues necessary for social and economic expenditures that benefit the poor and the potential disincentive (or tax evasion) effects of higher marginal tax rates on work, saving, and investment. Some, like the UNICEF team, are inclined to deny that tradeoffs are a major problem (Cornia, Jolly, and Stewart 1987, p.290):

> A strategy which protects the vulnerable during adjustment not only raises human welfare but is also economically efficient. Many studies have shown that investment in human resources is at least as vital for economic growth, and exhibits as high returns, as physical investment. All the main elements of the strategy [for protecting the poor] have been shown to yield positive economic returns - for example, worker productivity rises with improved nutrition; small-scale producers in both agriculture and industry have been shown to be as efficient, and often more efficient, than large producers. The most important factor explaining the great economic success of the East Asian countries is agreed to be the very high levels of human capital, resulting from comprehensive education and health systems.

Others are less sanguine. We have already mentioned the potentially high administrative and informational costs of targeted welfare programs, for example, and the choice that may have to be made between maintaining government social or economic services, and while it is true that some small-scale manufacturing and farming is economically efficient, this is less likely to be true of small-scale production by the very poor. Reaching poor, uneducated, subsistence farmers with extension and other public services can be both expensive and unproductive. Similarly, the literature on informal sector manufacturing does not support the contention that the type of enterprise run by the very poor can be induced to grow and modernize with only modest investments in assistance. On the contrary, they are liable to be among the victims of successful structural adaptation. We should also bear in mind a lesson from the industrial countries already touched upon in chapter 4 and illustrated in box 9-1, that attempts to alleviate the social costs of adjustment often tend to preserve existing structures of employment and production and to slow down structural change.

In short, the problem of tradeoffs is often a real one. This is not a reason for inaction, however, but for the careful design of programs so as to minimize the costs and maximize the benefits.

Adjustment and the Environment

In addition to concerns about the impact of adjustment policies on the poor, mounting public concern is being expressed about the effects of past policies on the quality of the environment and the sustainability of past approaches to economic development. We first took up environmental considerations in chapter 2 when discussing adaptation to global warming. There, however, we were taking such change as exogenous, beyond the direct control of national policymakers, and asking how they could help the economy adapt to it. Now we ask how adjustment policies themselves affect the environment. The answer offered is necessarily conjectural, however, for this subject came onto the international agenda only late in the 1980s, and little research has been published to date.

From an economic perspective we can view environmental issues largely in terms of: (a) market failures, chiefly in the form of external diseconomies, when pollution and other environmental damage is not reflected in producers' cost structures and is instead borne by the wider community; (b) state failures, when government interventions (or failures to intervene) make things worse, as dramatized by the appalling environmental record of the former Communist governments of various Eastern European countries; and (c) myopic intertemporal choices that fail to give due weight to the future and result in unsustainable forms of development.

Against this background we can offer the following suggestions. These relate particularly to the influence of a stable macroeconomic environment, which we have emphasized at a number of points as being important for efficient adaptation.

- **Economic stabilization** will, more or less by definition, reduce uncertainty, thereby helping to foster confidence in the future. The odds are weighted against future generations when economic instability creates uncertainties so large as to undermine belief that postponement of consumption will actually benefit the future. For example, saving—hence investment in the future—will tend to be discouraged by high inflation. Future environmental costs will be heavily discounted; the bias will be in favor of consumption now.

- **Macroeconomic stability** is also good for the efficient working of markets. In turn, this increases the possibilities of avoiding environmental diseconomies by manipulating prices through the use of taxes (for example, on the principle of making polluters pay the true cost of their output), because economic agents are better able to make rational decisions, and demand and supply elasticities will be larger (with price signals clearer, and more dependable).

- Successful **macroeconomic management** will reduce the risk of situations in which people experience periods of declining living standards, which cause them to place a very heavy premium on the present as against the future. This could be related to the present-day situation of a country like Brazil, which is asked to defer short-term gains in favor of preserving the Amazon forest while its people continue to suffer major hardships because of the huge claims made upon national savings and export earnings by the cost of servicing its external debts.

- **Economic stability** creates a policymaking climate more conducive to decisions favoring the future. The crisis-driven, day-to-day nature of policymaking in unstable economies is strongly antithetical to policy choices in favor of long-run environmental protection and planning. This will be particularly so if economic imbalances induce political instability, further shortening politicians' time horizons.

To the extent that they are valid, these propositions strongly favor the stabilization and structural adjustment programs many developing countries adopted in the 1980s. Given the special importance for environmental protection of addressing the problem of state failures and of improving governments' abilities to intervene effectively in this area, the focus of these programs on rationalizing policymaking processes was potentially very valuable.

The positive thrust of the above is consistent with the conclusions of a study by Hansen (1991) based on an examination of eighty-three adjustment programs supported by the World Bank and ten by the Asian Development Bank. His chief findings include the following:

- Reductions in government spending incorporated in these (and associated IMF) programs could have both harmful and beneficial environmental effects, with no reason to believe that they were, on balance, damaging to the environment.
- Measures to increase farmers' prices, commonly included in these programs, can also have mixed effects. In the case of tree crops, the effect is likely to be favorable, but when price increases favor annual cash crops or foodstuffs farmer practices determine the net effect. The measures could raise farmers' incentives and abilities to conserve the soil, but they could equally lead to a damaging intensification of cultivation and erosion.
- Measures to reduce subsidies for agricultural inputs tend to benefit the environment by reducing excessive applications of fertilizers and insecticides, and by discouraging mechanization and the wasteful use of irrigation water, although the end result also depends on complementary measures.
- The common inclusion in adjustment programs of measures to raise energy prices also tends to be environmentally beneficial, promoting conservation of fossil fuels and reducing emissions, although this effect is undermined if it triggers a substitution by fuelwood harvested from common land.

To these points we can add that the measures to protect the poor discussed in the previous section are also liable to have positive environmental effects. Their very struggle for survival in the face of ever-growing numbers tends to make the poor degraders of the environment through overcropping, overgrazing, and denuding forest land. Measures that help the poor and reduce the pressures on them thus also make an indirect contribution to protecting the environment.

Against this positive evaluation, however, we should set some qualifications. First, the relative shift in production in favor of tradable goods (chiefly made in the agricultural, mining, and manufacturing sectors) and away from nontradables (principally various service activities) usually incorporated in adjustment programs is liable to be environmentally damaging due to intensified cultivation, accelerated depletion of nonrenewable assets, and greater industrial pollution. Nontradable services are more environmentally friendly as they typically require only limited material inputs. In relation to this, note the strong connection between successful adjustment in developing countries and their success in exporting manufactured goods, as in the east and southeast Asian examples. More generally, this study has emphasized industrialization as one of the enabling components of structural transformation, and there is a strong conflict between this and environmental concerns about greenhouse gases and other forms of industrial pollution.

Second, the short- to medium-term nature of IFI programs (and the shortages of supporting finance that underlie this) can be detrimental by creating pressures for quick results, especially in export industries. Environmental concerns are liable to be thrust aside in the concern to meet Fund or Bank conditions and targets, of which the accelerated depletion of Ghana's tropical forests provides an example.

Third, in the 1980s much of the policy advice and conditionality of the IMF, the World Bank, and bilateral aid donors pushed in the direction of disengaging the state from the economy, playing down the role of planning and urging privatization and deregulation. Given the often deplorable past record of many interventions, this orientation was fully understandable, but the externalities problem requires substantial state interventions on behalf of the environment, and the long-term nature of environmental tasks requires the adoption of planning in some form, although not necessarily 1970s-style development planning. Although structural adjustment programs do tackle government failures, they have not necessarily had a focus that is ideal for addressing neglect of environmental protection.

This leads on to a political-economy point. A shift in the way that economies are run away from state interventions and towards greater reliance on private enterprise is not neutral with respect to how political systems will work. Dissimilar economic systems possess different pressure groups and varying distributions of power. A shift in favor of markets and private enterprise will tend both to create a greater decentralization of power and (to use a crude shorthand) to redistribute it in the direction of capitalists. This, in turn, will make it politically more difficult for governments to act against private sector polluters, a consideration that helps to explain the reluctance of various OECD governments to take firm action against industrial polluters.

Managing Change

Politics has been floating just beneath the surface of this study, as the previous paragraph reminds us. Let us now give it an airing.

Politics is central to structural adaptation. One of the most frequently recurring themes from earlier chapters is the crucial importance of the overall policy environment. We saw this in chapter 6, which showed that effective exchange rate policy was contingent upon a much wider range of policy actions, with government ability to manage a coordinated set of measures as a key determinant. We saw it in chapter 7 when discussing the influence of the overall policy environment on industrial efficiency and when describing the conditions that had to be satisfied for export processing zones to stand a chance of success. We saw it in chapter 8 when setting out the fiscal and macroeconomic preconditions for successful financial liberalization. It was for reasons such as this that we urged in chapter 5 the importance of viewing economic policies in the round, as an integrated system, as contrasted with a policy by policy approach.

Policies, then, are of crucial importance. So, therefore, are the political processes from which policy choices emerge. This being so, the issue raised in chapter 4 of how we should view the state as an economic agent takes center stage. Should we think of the state as motivated by a desire to find the most effective ways to promote the general good of society? Or is it more realistic to view it as promoting special, rather than general, interests, or even as being predatory upon the economy? Clearly, the view we take of the desirable role of policies to promote adaptation hinges closely on how we answer that question. This arose, for example, in chapter 7, when we considered the scope for industrial protection policies. Do we trust the government to confine itself to such protection as can be economically justified? In taking a view on such questions, however, we need to understand the reasons for political resistance to change to identify the scope for positive action and what types of action might be most effectual.

Politics as an Obstacle

The influence of political systems on long-run patterns of growth and change was among the issues Kuznets (1966, pp.445-453) explored in the 1960s. Comparing the political structures of developing and developed countries, he saw the former as unstable, ineffectual, and ambiguous about the merits of modernization; less representative, less tolerant of interest groups, with power more concentrated and more personalized. Kuznets noted that modern economic growth was achieved in the nineteenth and twentieth centuries by countries that by the 1960s had political structures quite different from those then prevailing in the developing countries. He went beyond that to suggest that the characteristics just noted constitute formidable obstacles to economic progress in many developing countries: "Political instability and nonrepresentativeness of the regimes, combined with an authoritarian structure dominated by personalist leaders and backed by familial and ethnic ties and the police, are hardly favourable conditions for economic growth" (p.453). The influence of traditional values on governments and their resulting ambiguity about the desirability of modernization observed by Kuznets is a situation that was illustrated in the 1980s by the spread of an Islamic fundamentalism that appeared to reject much of the modernization model (although box 3-2 offers a more nuanced perspective).

Happily, fewer developing countries today have political systems with the characteristics Kuznets observed. Much has happened since the 1960s, particularly in Latin America. Moreover, there is no suggestion of some mechanistic connection running from political modernization to economic development. Nevertheless, enough resonances remain between Kuznets' observations and the contemporary scene for us to take his comments seriously, and enough developing countries have experienced adjustment difficulties that emanate from the political system for his warning to be underlined (see Sandbrook 1986 for an exploration along these lines applied to Sub-Saharan Africa that examines the implications of patrimonial government for economic management). Indeed, a much more recent upsurge of concern about a crisis of governance in Africa and elsewhere underlines some of his worries. Thus, according to the Khartoum Declaration of the Economic Commission for Africa (1989, p.7):

> The political context for promoting healthy human development [in Africa] has been marred, for more than two decades, by instability, war, intolerance, restrictions on the freedom and human rights of individuals and groups as well as overconcentration of power with attendant restrictions on popular participation in decision making.

Next the World Bank (1989a, pp.60-61) has this to say:

> Underlying the litany of Africa's development problems is a crisis of governance . . . Because the countervailing power has been lacking, state officials in many countries have served their own interests without fear of being called to account. In self-defense individuals have built up personal networks of influence rather than hold the all-powerful state accountable for its systemic failures. In this way politics becomes personalized, and patronage becomes essential to maintain power. The leadership assumes broad discretionary power and loses its legitimacy. Information is controlled, and voluntary associations are co-opted or disbanded.

Authoritarian, nondemocratic systems of personal rule quickly lose legitimacy—public acceptance of the government's right to govern—and such loss of legitimacy seriously undermines the state's ability to adopt, and even more to sustain, adjustment policies. Despite the appearance of hardness and their often ruthless suppression of opposition, such regimes are often quite weak, in the sense of being unwilling or unable to implement measures that may incur unpopularity.

Even if a democratic and modernizing government is in power, that is far from being the end of the matter. Another factor bearing upon its ability to undertake policy reforms will be its strength relative to other centers of power in society. Many developing societies are fragmented, with power widely dispersed and limited social cohesion. Various groups will be forces to be reckoned with, even by apparently authoritarian governments. Special interest groups are usually conservative, resistant to change, and defensive of the existing privileges of their constituents, whether they represent employers, organized labor, landowners, or some other group.

This draws attention to the strength of the forces of inertia. Existing policies should not be viewed as accidental, nor as the outcome of purely technocratic considerations. They also reflect the distribution of power and influence. Thus, the bias toward urban dwellers—and the resulting difficulties of shifting relative prices in favor of agriculture—reflects the greater power and potential for creating trouble of those living in the towns. Similarly, this chapter drew attention to the delicacy of reorienting policies in favor of politically weak poverty groups, of the difficulties of enforcing effective land reforms in the face of opposition from large landowners, and of instituting antipollution measures in the face of a powerful industrial lobby. Discussion of the politics of environmental protection also drew attention to a considerably broader point: that the general thrust of our recommendations to rely more upon market forces pushes in the direction of a greater decentralization of economic decisions, which will alter the balance between the state and society in ways that state institutions and agents are likely to resist. We are reminded again of the difficulties of using the instrumentalities of the state to change policies in a less statist direction.

Policies based on the distribution of power often have great inertial force. They cannot be changed easily because those who benefit from them are influential enough to block reform. Among the potential beneficiaries are state employees, the very bureaucrats who must execute policy reforms. Unless treated with care, they can be a potent obstacle to change. Such resistance helps to explain why the World Bank has encountered difficulty in promoting the reform of institutions, for it is precisely this type of change that can pose a special threat to administrators' privileges or comfortable routines.

Bureaucratic obstacles may also arise for the simple reason that in a good many countries civil servants' pay and conditions are appallingly bad, with governments preferring to maintain an excessively large civil service that they are unable to remunerate adequately (for an excellent discussion of this problem, possible solutions, and country illustrations see Klitgaard 1989). In such circumstances, the best civil servants leave for more adequately rewarded jobs elsewhere. The rest become demoralized, moonlight on second jobs so that they are often not in their government offices, or use corruption to augment their official incomes. This problem of inadequate incentives is compounded by an even more common weakness of civil services: lack of connection between individuals' performance and their reward or promotion. A government's ability to execute reforms with a depleted and demoralized civil service is severely limited, while budgetary pressures and the unpopularity of laying people off may prevent it from restoring adequate incentives.

We should also recall an observation made earlier. On the one hand, conditions of economic crisis may be politically necessary before the government can take, and the public will support, necessary action. On the other hand, policies adopted under crisis conditions are less likely to have been carefully prepared, to be well chosen, and to include adequate provisions for implementation.

Countervailing Forces and the Cost-Benefit Balance

All this seems to make policy change impossible. Yet somehow changes do occur, progress is made. How can this be? An answer can be sketched along the following lines.

A kind of cost-benefit logic is at work. A proposed change of policies to facilitate structural adaptation—say a rationalization of industrial protection—will generate costs and benefits, both economic and political. In terms of the political system, the way these are distributed within society will be of crucial importance. If most of the benefits are expected to accrue to the poor, the unorganized, or those supporting the opposition, while the costs are expected to be concentrated on powerful groups of government supporters, the cost-benefit calculation is unlikely to encourage the government to "do the right thing." However, if the industrial sector is widely regarded as grossly inefficient, if this is seriously penalizing much of the population and if the sector is stagnating, then the net balance of costs and benefits could point to a different resolution.

In other words, much depends on the initial situation, how bad things have become, how widely the existence of a problem is publicly recognized, and who is blamed for the mess. There are times when things have to get worse before they can get better. If the ruling group is sufficiently repressive, the opposition unorganized, and the populace demoralized, things may have to get very bad indeed, as the histories of such countries as Ghana, Haiti, and Zaire demonstrate. In such situations change is only possible through the installation of a new government riding to power on a wave of popular discontent. A more likely scenario, however, is that, however reluctantly, the incumbent government will come to see change as being in its own interests, to avoid unchecked economic deterioration generating such widespread public disaffection that it is swept from power. Ultimately, it cannot be in the interests of the government to allow the economy and the machinery of the state to collapse (see Beckman 1988; Fearon 1988, pp.136-137).

The business community may play a key role, for this is usually a very influential group. Continuing with the industrial protection example, in normal times industrialists can be relied upon to resist the reform of protection, but if the condition of the manufacturing sector becomes parlous enough they too may come to favor change, and are likely to be in a position to exert pressure on the government to take action. The urban wage labor force may occupy an even more strategic position. Governments are often particularly nervous of this group because of its ability to mount highly visible, sometimes riotous, protests in major cities. Often it will be a force against change, but again that may alter if things get bad enough.

This tendency for a deteriorating balance of economic costs over benefits to set up countervailing pressures for political change is a strong finding of the most substantial study so far undertaken of the politics of adjustment (Nelson 1989, pp.11-12).[7]

> Among those governments pursuing particularly far-reaching programs of economic reorientation in the 1980s (plus a few cases from the 1970s), most share important political features. Consider Chile after 1973, Sri Lanka from 1977 to the early 1980s, Turkey and Jamaica since 1980, Ghana since 1983, and the Philippines since 1986. All of these countries had suffered long periods - in Ghana's case, two decades - of economic stagnation or decline or of deepening financial crisis, coupled with increasingly widespread political alienation and/or polarization and violence. In each, in the years noted . . . a new government took office, elected with overwhelming majorities in Sri Lanka, Jamaica and the Philippines; and taking power

---

7. See also Nelson (1990) for additional country materials.

in military coups but with considerable or sweeping public support in Chile, Turkey and Ghana. In all of these countries, there was clearly widespread support - indeed *demand* - for major changes, although there were deep divisions in every case regarding the nature of the needed reforms.

What her last sentence implies, however, is that successful reform is likely to need more than a past history of economic decline. She goes on (p.12) to write of a reform syndrome:

> Leaders firmly committed to major change, widespread public acceptance or demand for such change, new governments with strong centralized authority, and a disabled opposition constituted the political context for determined adjustment efforts.

Nelson emphasized the quality of leadership.[8] This includes a willingness on the part of heads of government and their colleagues to influence and prepare public opinion and to initiate change, shrewdness in the phasing of policy changes to avoid upsetting too many groups at once and to keep potential opposition groups isolated from each other, and a willingness to offer compensation to those who may lose from the reforms and who could make political trouble. Her reference to the desirability of a strong centralized government is perhaps more problematical, for we have suggested at a number of points that authoritarian governments are apt to lose legitimacy and hence the ability to sustain pro-adaptation policies over time. Box 10-3 on Ghana illustrates most features of the reform syndrome.

This provides an extreme illustration of the message with which we close: the enormous superiority of a steady, long-term adherence to policies that promote continuous adaptation. A process that first has to generate a major economic crisis (with all the human suffering that creates) before it is possible to introduce the draconian measures that by then have become unavoidable is an extremely high-cost path to

---

8. Consistent with this, Horowitz (1989, p.207) suggests that there is more scope for the exercise of political leadership in developing country conditions, where the strength of the central government may be greater compared to that of organized interest groups than in the more highly articulated societies of the industrial world. Support for this proposition comes from a study of agricultural policy change in India by Varshney (1989), who argues that the state had considerable degrees of freedom to initiate changes (a) because existing policies were widely agreed to be failing, and (b) because interest groups had not coalesced in defense of the *status quo* or in favor of particular solutions.

Box 10-3. The Reform Syndrome in Ghana

On the last day of 1981 a group of military officers headed by Flight Lieutenant Jerry Rawlings seized power for a second time, overthrowing a civilian government to which Rawlings had transferred power two years earlier. By instinct and conviction Rawlings was a radical populist, espousing the doctrines of Ghana's first president, Kwame Nkrumah, and skeptical of the economic orthodoxies associated with the IMF and World Bank. The economy, however, had been in decline for most years since the early 1960s, and twenty years later was in a desperate condition, with triple-digit inflation, a grossly inflated exchange rate (the black market rate reached thirty times the official rate), acute shortages of all types of imports, an industrial sector nearly at a standstill, a crumbling infrastructure, a massive hemorrhage of educated manpower out of the country, and per capita incomes a third lower than in 1970. It represented a classic case of an economy whose inherent structural inflexibility had been worsened by years of mismanagement and resistance to adjustment by a succession of governments.

A drought, widespread bush fires, and an enforced mass return of Ghanaian migrants from Nigeria turned a crisis into a catastrophe. Rawlings and his advisers began to realize that the measures they had in place could not cope with this situation and how desperately they needed the financial support of the IFIs. Moreover, the depths to which the economy had descended—and the privations this was forcing upon the mass of Ghanaians—created a desperation of opinion that was willing to accept any change that would offer the prospect of economic recovery. In 1983 the government therefore turned for help to the IMF and World Bank. Since that time it has executed a succession of conventional adjustment programs. These have included a huge effective devaluation of the currency, the cedi, from C2.75 to the dollar in 1982 to well over C300 by mid-1990. They also included greatly increased producer prices for cocoa farmers and other exporters; measures to reduce government spending and to bring it under better control; the reform (and in a few cases, privatization) of public enterprises, including large-scale reductions in the hugely inflated payroll of the Cocoa Marketing Board; rehabilitation of the infrastructure; and the partial liberalization of imports and of the financial system.

This set of policies marked a sharp break both with the tradition of post-Independence economic policies and with Rawlings' own predilections. Nevertheless, his government has been consistent in its adherence to the course it adopted in 1983, and by 1990 could point to a major economic recovery as a result. Their fortitude was, however, made easier by a highly centralized and authoritarian style of government. The human rights record

Box 10-3. (continued)

of the government was initially bad and has remained poor. The media are kept under strict government control. Political parties and other forms of organized opposition are banned. There is no clear timetable for a return to civilian rule.

The Ghanaian case thus incorporates all the ingredients of Nelson's description of the reform syndrome: leaders firmly committed to major change; widespread public acceptance of the need for this; a strong, centralist new government; and a disabled opposition. By the beginning of the 1990s some cracks were beginning to show, however. In particular, there seemed to be a contradiction between the broadly decentralizing thrust of post-1983 economic policies and the continuing centralist style of government. Rightly or wrongly, it was widely believed that most of the benefits of the recovery of the economy were being concentrated on a limited number of the population. There was uncertainty about how much popular support the Rawlings administration retained and about future political developments, and this was contributing to a sluggish response by private investment to the improved framework of economic policies. The sustainability of the reforms still appeared fragile.

Note: Interested readers should refer to a comparative study of the politics of adjustment in Ghana, Nigeria, and Zambia by Callaghy in Nelson (1990, chapter 7).

adjustment. Governments that finally take the risk of grasping the reform nettle deserve credit, but the governments—and political systems—that deserve the highest praise are those that throughout recognize the need for change and adaptation, and which, by so doing, avoid the trauma of an economic collapse as a necessary prelude to adjustment.

Summary

The last two chapters have examined the wider context within which economic adaptation occurs. Having examined the international context in chapter 9, we have here concentrated on the domestic context. The first issue concerned the impact of adjustment measures on the poor. Adjustment costs were classified into absorption costs (the losses of output and income associated with reductions in consumption and/or investment necessary to restore macroeconomic balance), fric-

tional costs (resulting from shifts of resources from declining to expanding sectors), and distributional costs (when adjustment is associated with a change in poverty and inequality regarded by society as
undesirable). We also noted an intergenerational element, when adjustment costs are shifted on to future generations, for example, by
cutting back on investment rather than consumption.

Adjustment endangers the poor in a number of ways: through job
losses, cut-backs in state spending on food subsidies and social services, and the adverse effects of an economic slow-down. Moreover,
the poor are rarely politically powerful, which increases their vulnerability. Even when they wish to, most governments helping the truly
poor difficult, but this can be done by measures that increase their access to productive assets, raise the returns from the assets they already
possess, improve their employment opportunities, improve their access
to education and health services, and supplement their resources by
transfers. Policy can be brought into play at all levels, and one fundamental principle is that measures to protect the vulnerable need to be
integral to the design of adjustment programs rather than being added
on as supplementaries. A number of more specific measures were discussed: job creation schemes, the targeting of food subsidies and other
social provisions, use of the peace dividend from reduced military
spending, and progressive taxation. However, tradeoffs do exist between measures to protect the poor and the adjustment of the economy, which emphasizes the need for careful policy planning.

Consideration of the environmental effects of policies of adaptation
suggested that adjustment was a generally positive factor, particularly
by creating an economic environment favorable to longer-sighted decisions. However, this overall judgment had to be qualified in a number of respects: a shift in favor of tradables, particularly in the direction of industrialization; the thrust of programs in the 1980s toward a
relative disengagement of the state; and a probable resulting shift of
political power toward capitalists were all identified as having potentially adverse environmental consequences.

Finally, we turned to examine the politics of adjustment, which is
central to the whole process. It is easy to see political realities as barriers to adjustment. Governments that have become insecure, corrupted,
and repressive are unlikely either to give much priority to economic

adaptation or to have the legitimacy necessary for adjustment policies to be executed and sustained. Existing policies—however ill-chosen—often have large inertial power because those who benefit from them become powerful enough to block change. The civil service can itself be a major obstacle, sometimes because of grossly inadequate pay and conditions.

Change is not impossible, however. A cost-benefit logic is at work, in which the economic deterioration that results from resistance to adaptation throws up a countervailing public discontent that will either impel the government to act or replace it with a more reform-minded successor. When combined with leadership and a strong government, public acceptance of the need for change can render politically feasible policy shifts that would formerly have been judged suicidal. If things get bad enough, economic flexibility has more friends than enemies, but a sustained encouragement of flexibility is a policy stance far superior to a situation in which an economic crisis is a pre-condition of decisive action.

A Note on Further Reading: On adjustment and poverty, the best succinct treatment is Demery and Addison (1987). The World Bank's *World Development Report 1990* also contains valuable material, especially chapters 7 and 8. The seminal contributions by the UNICEF team are in Cornia, Jolly, and Stewart (1987, 1988). By far the best sources on the politics of adjustment are Nelson (ed.), 1989 and 1990, but Roemer and Perkins (1991) contains a useful collection of papers, including Grindle and Thomas' illuminating essay, also published separately in 1989. Lindenberg and Ramirez (1989) are unusual in providing a textbook treatment of the political management of adjustment.

REFERENCES

Agu, C.C. 1988. "Interest Rates Policy in Nigeria and its Attendant Distortions." *Savings and Development* (Milan) 12(1): 19-34.

Allison, Graham T. 1971. *Essence of Decision: Explaining the Cuban Missile Crisis*. Boston, Massachusetts: Little Brown.

Ardeni, Pier Giorgio, and Brian Wright. 1990. *The Long-Term Behavior of Commodity Prices*. Working Paper WPS 358. Washington, D.C.: World Bank.

Aricali, T., and D. Rodrik, eds. 1989. *The Political Economy of Turkey: Debt, Adjustment and Sustainability*. London: Macmillan.

Arndt, H.W. 1988. "Market Failure and Underdevelopment." *World Development* 16(2).

Arrieta, G.M.G. 1988. "Interest Rates, Savings and Growth in LDCs: An Assessment of Recent Empirical Research." *World Development* 16(5).

Arrow, Kenneth J. 1987. "Planning and Uncertainty." *International Journal of Development Planning Literature* 2(2).

Aryeetey, Ernest. Forthcoming. "The Relationship Between the Formal and Informal Sectors of the Financial Market in Ghana." (Nairobi, African Economic Research Consortium.) *Research Report*.

ATI, Hassan A.A. 1988. "The Process of Famine: Causes and Consequences in Sudan." *Development and Change* 19(2).

Bacha, Edmar L. 1990. "A Three-Gap Model of Foreign Transfers and the GDP Growth Rate in Developing Countries." *Journal of Development Economics* (32).

Balassa, Bela. 1988. "The Interaction of Factor and Product Market Distortions in Developing Countries." *World Development* 16(4).

Bates, Robert H. 1981. *Markets and States in Tropical Africa*. Berkeley, California: University of California Press.

Beckman, Bjorn. 1988. "The Post-Colonial State: Crisis and Reconstruction." *IDS Bulletin* 19(4).

Beeman, W. 1983. "Patterns of Religion and Economic Development in Iran from the Qajar Period to the Islamic Revolution of 1978-79." In James Finn, ed., *Global Economics and Religion*. New Brunswick: Transaction Books.

Behara, Meenakshi, and C.P. Chandrasekhar. 1988. *India in an Era of Liberalisation.* London: Euromoney Publications.

Bennett, M.K. 1954. *The World's Food.* New York: Harper and Row.

Besley, Tim, and Ravi Kanbur. 1988. *"The principles of targeting."* DERC Working Paper 85. Coventry, U.K.: University of Warwick.

Bevan, D.L., P. Collier, and J.W. Gunning. 1990. "Economic Policy in Countries Prone to Temporary Trade Shocks." In Maurice Scott and Deepak Lal, eds., *Public Policy and Economic Development.* Oxford, U.K.: Clarendon Press.

Bevan, D.L., A. Bigsten, P. Collier, and J.W. Gunning. 1986. *East African Lessons on Economic Liberalisation.* London: Trade Policy Research Centre.

——————. 1987. "Peasant Supply Response in Rationed Economies." *World Development* 15(4).

Beynon, J.G. 1989. "Pricism v. Structuralism in Sub-Saharan African Agriculture." *Journal of Agricultural Economics* 40(3).

Bhagwat, A., and Y. Onitsuka. 1974. "Export-Import Responses to Devaluation: Experience of the Non-Industrial Countries in the 1960s." *IMF Staff Papers* 21(2).

Bhagwati, Jagdish N. 1978. *Anatomy and Consequences of Exchange Control Regimes.* Cambridge, Massachusetts: Ballinger.

——————. 1982. "Directly Unproductive Profitseeking (DUP) Activities." *Journal of Political Economy* 90 (October).

——————. 1987. "Outward Orientation: Trade Issues." In Vittorio Corbo, Morris Goldstein, and Mohsin Khan, eds., *Growth-Oriented Adjustment Programs*, pp.257-90. Washington, D.C.: IMF and World Bank.

Bhagwati, Jagdish N., and T.N. Srinivasan. 1983. *Lectures on International Trade.* Cambridge, Massachusetts: MIT Press.

Bhatia, Rattan J. 1985. *The West African Monetary Union: An Analytical Review.* Occasional Paper no. 35. Washington D.C.: International Monetary Fund.

Bigsten, Arne. 1983. *Income Distribution and Development: Theory, Evidence and Policy.* London: Heinemann.

Binswanger, Hans. 1990. "The Policy Response of Agriculture." In the *Proceedings of the World Bank Annual Conference on Development Economics.* Washington, D.C.: World Bank.

Bird, Graham. 1984. "Balance of payments policy." In T. Killick, ed. *The Quest for Economic Stabilization: The IMF and the Third World.* London: Overseas Development Institute and Gower Publishing.

_____. 1990. *The International Financial Regime.* London: Academic Press and Surrey University Press.

Bliss, Christopher. 1989. "Trade and Development." In Hollis Chenery and T.N. Srinivasan eds., *Handbook of Development Economics,* vol. II, chapter 23. Amsterdam: North-Holland.

Bolnick, Bruce R. 1987. "Financial Liberalisation with Imperfect Markets: Indonesia during the 1970s." *Economic Development and Cultural Change* 35 (3): 581-600.

Bond, Marion E. 1987. "An Econometric Study of Primary Product Exports from Developing Country Regions to the World." *IMF Staff Papers* 34(2).

Bond, Marion E., and Elizabeth Milne. 1987. "Export Diversification in Developing Countries: Recent Trends and Policy Impact." In *Staff Studies for the World Economic Outlook.* Washington, D.C.: International Monetary Fund.

Branson, William H. 1983. "Economic Structure and Policy for External Balance." *IMF Staff Papers* 30(1).

Braybrooke, D., and C.E. Lindblom. 1963. *A Strategy of Decision.* New York: Free Press.

Bruton, Henry. 1987. "Technology Choice and Factor Proportions Problems in LDCs." In Normal Gemmell, ed., Surveys in Development Economics. Oxford, U.K.: Basil Blackwell.

Campbell, Burnham O. 1988. "The Little Dragons have Different Tales." *World Economy* 11(2).

Canlas, M., M. Miranda, and J. Putzel. 1988. *Land, Poverty and Politics in the Philippines.* London, U.K.: Catholic Institute for International Relations.

Carnegie, R.H. 1986. *Outlook for Mineral Commodities.* New York: Group of Thirty.

Chamley, Christophe, and Patrick Honohan. 1990. "Taxation of Financial Intermediation: Measurement Principles and Application to Five African Countries." Washington, D.C.: World Bank. Processed.

Chenery, Hollis B. 1979. *Structural Change and Development Policy.* New York: Oxford University Press.

_____. (1988); "Structural transformation: a program of research," in G. Ranis and T.P. Schultz (eds.), chapter 3.

Chenery, Hollis, Sherman Robinson, and Moshe Syrquin. 1986. *Industrialization and Growth: A Comparative Study.* New York: Oxford University Press.

Chenery, Hollis, and T.N. Srinivasan, eds. 1988, 1989. *Handbook of Development Economics,* two volumes: I, 1988; II, 1989. Amsterdam: North-Holland.

Chhibber, Ajay. 1989. "The Aggregate Supply Response: A Survey." In Simon Commander, ed., *Structural Adjustment and Agriculture,* chapter 4. London: James Currey and Overseas Development Institute.

Chipeta, C., and M. Mkandawire. 1991. *Informal Financial Markets and Macroeconomic Adjustment in Malawi.*" AERC Research Paper no. 3. Nairobi: African Economic Research Consortium.

Cho, Yoon Je, and Deena Khatkhate. 1989. *Lessons of Financial Liberalization in Asia.* Discussion Paper no. 50. Washington, D.C.: World Bank.

Clements, Kenneth W., Frederick E. Suhm, and Henri Theil. 1979. "A Cross-Country Tabulation of Income Elasticities of Demand." *Economic Letters* (3): 199-202.

Cody, John, Helen Hughes, and David Wall. 1980. *Policies for Industrial Progress in Developing Countries.* New York: Oxford University Press.

Cole, David C., Philip A. Wellons, and Betty Slade Yaser. 1991. "Financial Systems Reforms: Concepts and Cases." In Michael Roemer and Dwight H. Perkins, eds., *Reforming Economic Systems in Developing Countries.* Cambridge, Massachusetts: Harvard University Press.

Collier, Paul, and Colin Mayer. 1989. "The Assessment: Financial Liberalization, Financial Systems, and Economic Growth." *Oxford Review of Economic Policy* 5(4).

Commonwealth Secretariat. 1986. *Co-Operation Without Cross-Conditionality: An Issue in International Lending.* London.

Conesa, Eduardo R. 1987. *The Causes of Capital Flight from Latin America.* Washington, D.C.: Inter-American Development Bank.

Cooper, R. N. 1971. "Currency Devaluation in Developing Countries." In G. Ranis, ed., *Government and Economic Development.* New Haven, Connecticut: Yale University Press.

Corden, W. Max. 1974. *Trade Policy and Economic Welfare.* Oxford, U.K.: Oxford University Press.

_____. 1987. "The Relevance for Developing Countries of Recent Developments in Macroeconomic Theory." World Bank *Research Observer* 2(2).

_____. 1989. "Macroeconomic Adjustment in Developing Countries." *World Bank Research Observer* 4(1).

Cornia, G.A., R. Jolly, and F. Stewart eds. 1987. *Adjustment with a Human Face: Protecting the Vulnerable and Promoting Growth.* Oxford, U.K.: Oxford University Press and UNICEF.

_____. 1987. *Adjustment with a Human Face: Protecting the Vulnerable and Promoting Growth.* Oxford, U.K.: Oxford University Press and UNICEF.

Cuddington, John T. 1986. *Capital Flight: Issues, Estimates and Explanations.* Essay in International Finance no. 58. Princeton, New Jersey: Princeton University.

_____. 1987. "Macroeconomic Determinants of Capital Flight: An Econometric Investigation." In Donald R. Lessard and John Williamson, eds., *Capital Flight and Third World Debt.* Washington, D.C.: Institute for International Economics.

_____. 1989. "Commodity Export Booms in Developing Countries." *World Bank Research Observer* 4(2).

Dearlove, John, and Gordon White. 1987. "The Retreat of the State? Editorial Introduction." *IDS Bulletin* 18(3).

de Grauwe, Paul. 1988. "Exchange Rate Variability and the Slowdown in the Growth of International Trade." *IMF Staff Papers* 35(1).

de Macedo, Jorge Braga. 1986. "Collective Pegging to a Single Currency: The West African Monetary Union." Sebastian Edwards and Liaquat Ahamed, eds., *Economic Adjustment and Exchange Rates in Developing Countries,* chapter 10. Cambridge, Massachusetts: MIT Press.

de Melo, Jaime, and Sherman Robinson. 1990. "Productivity and Externalities: Models of Export-Led Growth." Working Paper WPS 387. Washington D.C.: World Bank.

Demery, Lionel, and Tony Addison. 1987. *Alleviation of Poverty under Structural Adjustment.* Washington D.C.: World Bank.

Devarajan, S. and J. de Melo, (1987). "Adjustment with a fixed exchange rate: Cameroon, Côte d'Ivoire and Senegal." *World Bank Economic Review,* 1(3).

de Vries, Margaret Garritsen. 1987. *Balance of Payments Adjustment, 1945 to 1986: The IMF Experience.* Washington D.C.: International Monetary Fund.

Diakosavvas, Dimitris. 1989. *"Government Expenditure on Agriculture and Agricultural Performance in Developing Countries."* New Series Discussion Paper no. 3. Bradford, U.K.: University of Bradford, Development Project Planning Centre.

Diaz-Alejandro, Carlos. 1985. "Good-Bye Financial Repression, Hello Financial Crash." *Journal of Development Economics* 19(1-2): 1-24.

Donges, J.B. 1976. "A Comparative Survey of Industrialisation Policies in 15 Semi-Industrialised Countries." *Weltwirtschaftliches Archiv* 112(4).

Donovan, Donal J. 1981. "Real Responses Associated with Exchange Rate Action in Selected Upper Credit Tranche Stabilization Programs." *IMF Staff Papers* 28(4).

Dooley, Michael. 1986. *"Country-Specific Risk Premiums, Capital Flight and Net Investment Income Payments in Selected Developing Countries."* Discussion Paper DM 86/17. Washington D.C.: International Monetary Fund.

Dooley, M. and S. Mathieson, 1987. "Financial Liberalization in Developing Countries." *Finance and Development* 24(1) (March).

Dornbusch, Rudiger M. 1985. "External Debt, Budget Deficits and Disequilibrium Exchange Rates." In Gordon W. Smith, and John T. Cuddington, eds., *International Debt and the Developing Countries.* Washington, D.C.: World Bank.

——————. 1987. "Comment." In Donald R. Lessard and John Williamson, eds., *Capital Flight and Third World Debt.* Washington, D.C.: Institute for International Economics.

Dornbusch, R., and F. Leslie C.H. Helmers. 1988. *Open Economy: Tools for Policy Makers in Developing Countries.* New York: Oxford University Press and World Bank.

Drucker, Peter F. 1988. "Low Wages No Longer Give Competitive Edge." *The Newsletter* (International Center for Economic Growth, San Fransisco) 1(4).

Eaton, Jonathan. 1989. "Foreign Public Capital Flows." In Hollis Chenery and T.N. Srinivasan, eds., *Handbook of Development Economics*, vol. II, chapter 25. Amsterdam: North-Holland.

ECA (Economic Commission for Africa). 1989. *African Alternative Framework.* Ref. E/ECA/CM 15/6/Rev.3. Addis Ababa.

Edwards, Sebastian. 1987. "Sequencing Economic Liberalization in Developing Countries." *Finance and Development* 24(1).

_____. 1989a. "Exchange Rate Misalignment in Developing Countries." *World Bank Research Observer* 4(1).

_____. 1989b. *Real Exchange Rates, Devaluation and Adjustment.* Cambridge, Massachusetts: MIT Press.

Elias, J.V. 1985. *"Government Expenditure on Agriculture in Latin America."* Research Report no. 23. Washington, D.C.: International Food Policy Research Institute.

Elkan, Walter. 1988. "Entrepreneurs and Entrepreneurship in Africa." *World Bank Research Observer* 3(2).

Faini, Riccardo, Fernando Clavijo and Abdel Senhadji-SemlalI, . 1989. *"The Fallacy of Composition Argument: Does Demand Matter for LDCs' Manufactures Exports?"* Oxford, U.K.: Queen Elizabeth House. Development Studies Working Paper No. 7.

Faini, Riccardo, Jaime de Melo, Abdel Senhadji-Semlali, and Julie Stanton. 1989. *"Growth-Oriented Adjustment Programs: A Statistical Analysis."* Oxford, U.K.: Queen Elizabeth House.

_____. 1991. "Macro Performance Under Structural Adjustment." In Vinod Thomas, Ajay Chhibber, Mansoor Dailami, and Jaime de Melo, eds., *Restructuring Economies in Distress.* Washington, D.C.: World Bank.

Fearon, James D. 1988. "International Financial Institutions and Economic Policy Reform." *Journal of Modern African Studies* 26(1).

Findlay, Ronald. 1988. "Trade, Development and the State." In Gustav Ranis and Paul T. Schultz, eds., *The State of Development Economics: Progress and Perspectives*, chapter 4. Oxford, U.K.: Basil Blackwell.

Finke, Renata, Mercedes C. Rosalsky, and Henri Theil. 1983. "A New Cross-Country Tabulation of Income-Elasticities of Demand." *Economic Letters* (12): 391-396.

Fones-Sundell, M. 1987. *"Role of Price Policy in Stimulating Agricultural Production in Africa."* Issue Paper no. 2. Uppsala: Swedish University of Agricultural Sciences.

Fosu, A.K. 1990. "Exports and Economic Growth: The African Case." *World Development* 18(6).

Frankel, J., and M.L. Mussa. 1985. "Asset Markets, Exchange Rates and the Balance of Payments." In R.W. Jones and P.B. Kenen, eds., *Handbook of International Economics,* vol. II. Amsterdam: North-Holland.

Fry, Maxwell J. 1988. *Money, Interest and Banking in Economic Development.* Baltimore, Maryland: Johns Hopkins University Press.

Galbis, Vicente. 1986. "Financial Sector Liberalisation under Oligopolistic Conditions and a Bank Holding Company Structure." *Savings and Development* 10(2) 117-141.

Galvez, Julio, and James Tybout. 1985. "Microeconomic Adjustments in Chile During 1977-81: The Importance of Being a Grupo." *World Development* 13,8 (August): 969-993.

Gelb, Alan H. 1989. *Financial Policies, Growth and Efficiency.*" PPR Working Paper No. 202. Washington, D.C.: World Bank.

Glewwe, Paul, and Jacques van der Gaag. 1990. "Identifying the Poor in Developing Countries: Do Different Definitions Matter?" *World Development* 18(6).

Goldsmith, Raymond W. 1969. *Financial Structure and Development.* New Haven and London: Yale University Press.

_____. 1983. *The Financial Development of India, Japan and the United States.* New Haven, Connecticut and London: Yale University Press.

_____. 1985. *Comparative National Balance Sheets.* Chicago, Illinois and London: Chicago University Press.

Gray, Clive S. 1991. "Antitrust as a Component of Policy Reform: What Relevance for Economic Development?" In Dwight H. Perkins and Michael Roemer, eds., *Reforming Economic Systems in Developing Countries*, chapter 15. Cambridge, Massachusetts: Harvard Institute for International Development.

Green, R. H. 1989. "Articulating Stabilization Programmes and Structural Adjustment: Sub-Saharan Africa." In Simon Commander, ed., *Structural Adjustment and Agriculture.* London: James Currey and Overseas Development Institute.

Greene, Joshua E., and Mohsin S. Khan. 1990. *"The African Debt Crisis."* Special Paper No. 3. Nairobi, Kenya: African Economic Research Consortium.

Griffith-Jones, Stephany. 1988. "Cross Conditionality and the Spread of Obligatory Adjustment." Brighton, U.K.: University of Sussex, Institute of Development Studies. Processed.

Grilli, E. R., and M.C. Yang. 1988. "Primary Commodity Prices, Manufactured Goods Prices and the Terms of Trade of Developing Countries: What the Long Run Shows." *World Bank Economic Review* 2(1).

Grindle, Merilee S., and John W. Thomas. 1989. "Policy Makers, Policy Choices, and Policy Outcomes: The Political Economy of Reform in

Developing Countries." *Policy Sciences* 22 (3-4). Also in Roemer and Perkins (1991).

Grosh, Barbara. 1990. "Public, Quasi-Public and Private Manufacturing Firms in Kenya: A Surprising Case of Cliché Gone Astray." *Development Policy Review* 8(1).

Gulhati, Ravi, and Raj Nallari. 1988. "Reform of Foreign Aid Policies: The Issue of Inter-Country Allocation in Africa." *World Development* 16(10).

Gupta, Kanhaya L. 1984. *Finance and Economic Growth in Developing Countries*. London: Croom Helm.

_____. 1987. "Aggregate Savings, Financial Intermediation and Interest Rate." *Review of Economics and Statistics* 69(2) 303-311.

Hagen, Everett. 1962. *On the Theory of Social Change: How Economic Growth Begins*. Homewood, Illinois: R. Dorsey.

Hallwood, P., and R. MacDonald. 1986. *International Monetary Theory, Evidence and Institutions*. Oxford, U.K.: Basil Blackwell.

Hansen, Stein. 1991. "Macroeconomic Policies: Incidence on the Environment." In James T. Winpenny, ed., *Development Research: The Environmental Challenge*. London: Overseas Development Institute.

Hanson, James A., and Craig R. Neal. 1985. *Interest Rate Policies in Selected Developing Countries, 1970-82*. Staff Working Paper No. 753. Washington D.C.: World Bank.

Harrigan, Jane. 1991. "Jamaica." In Paul Mosley, Jane Harrigan, and John Toye, eds., *Aid and Power: The World Bank and Policy Based Lending*, vol. 2, chapter 17. London: Routledge.

Helleiner, Gerald K. 1986. "Outward Orientation, Import Instability and African Economic Growth: An Empirical Investigation." In Sanjaya Lall and Frances Stewart, eds., *Theory and Reality in Development*. London: Macmillan.

Helleiner, Gerald K. 1990. "Trade Strategy in Medium-Term Adjustment." *World Development* 18(6).

Hicks, Normal L. 1991. "Expenditure Reductions in Developing Countries Revisited." *Journal of International Development* 3(1).

Hicks, Norman, and Anne Kubisch. 1984. "Cutting Government Expenditures in LDCs." *Finance and Development* 21(3).

Hirschman, Albert O. 1982. "The Rise and Decline of Development Economics." In Gersovitz, Diaz-Alejandro, Ranis, and Rosenzweig, eds., *The*

Theory and Experience of Economic Development. London: Allen and Unwin.

Horowitz, Donald L. 1989. "Is There a Third-World Policy Process?" *Policy Sciences* 22 (3-4).

Hossain, Mahabub. 1988. *Credit for Alleviation of Rural Poverty: The Grameen Bank in Bangladesh.* Washington, D.C.: International Food Policy Research Institute.

Howell, John, ed. 1985. *Recurrent Costs and Agricultural Development.* London: Overseas Development Institute.

Huang, Yukon, and Peter Nicholas. 1987. *The Social Costs of Adjustment.* LPD Discussion Paper No. 1987-6. Washington, D.C.: World Bank.

Hugon, Philippe. 1988. "The Impact of Adjustment Policy in Madagascar." *IDS Bulletin* 19(1).

Hussain, M. Nureldin, and A.P. Thirlwall. 1984. "The IMF Supply-Side Approach to Devaluation: An Assessment with Reference to the Sudan." *Oxford Bulletin of Economics and Statistics* 46(2).

IFC (International Finance Corporation). 1987. *Global Investing - the Emerging Markets.* Washington, D.C.: IFC Council of Institutional Investors.

_____. 1988. *Emerging Stock Markets Factbook 1988 Edition.* Washington, D. C.

ILO-UNCTC (International Labour Organisation and U.N. Centre on Transnational Corporations). 1988. *Economic and Social Effects of Multinational Enterprises in Export Processing Zones.* Geneva: ILO.

IMF (International Monetary Fund). 1990. *World Economic Outlook.* Washington, D.C. April.

_____. 1991. *World Economic Outlook.* Washington, D.C. May.

Iqbal, Zubair, and Abbas Mirakhor. 1987. *Islamic Banking.* Washington, D.C.: International Monetary Fund.

Jackson, Robert H., and Carl G. Rosberg. 1984. "Personal Rule: Theory and Practice in Africa." *Comparative Politics* 16(4).

Jamal, Vali. 1988. "Getting The Crisis Right: Missing Perspectives on Africa." *International Labour Review* 127(6).

Jayawardena, L., A. Maasland, and P. N. Radakrishnan. 1987. *Sri Lanka.* Country Study No. 15. Helsinki, Finland: WIDER.

Jebuni, C.D., J. LOVE, and D.J.C. Forsyth. 1988. "Market Structure and LDCS' Manufactured Export Performance." *World Development* 16(2).

Johnson, G.G., Jean Clement, Sena Eken, Roger Pownall, Robert L. Sheehy and Emmanuel J. Zervoudakis. 1985. *Formulation of Exchange Rate Policies in Adjustment Programs*. Occasional Paper No. 36. Washington, D.C.: International Monetary Fund.

Jones, Leroy P. 1975. *Public Enterprise and Economic Development: The Korean Case*. Seoul: Korea Development Institute.

Joshi, Vijay. 1990. "Exchange Rate Regimes in Developing Countries." In Marice Scott and Deepak Lal, eds., *Public Policy and Economic Development*. Oxford, U.K.: Clarendon Press.

Jung, Woo S. 1986. "Financial Development and Economic Growth: International Evidence." *Economic Development and Cultural Change* 34(2).

Kahler, Miles. 1990. "Orthodoxy and its Alternatives: Explaining Approaches to Stabilization and Adjustment." In Joan M. Nelson, ed., *Economic Crisis and Policy Choice: The Politics of Choice in the Third World,* chapter 2. Princeton, New Jersey: Princeton University Press.

Kaldor, N. 1972. "The Irrelevance of Equilibrium Economics." *Economic Journal* 82(328).

Khan, Mohsin. 1974. "Import and Export Demand in Developing Countries." *IMF Staff Papers* 21(3).

_____. 1986. "Islamic Interest-Free Banking: A Theoretical Analysis." *IMF Staff Papers* 33(1).

_____. 1990. "The Macroeconomic Effects of Fund-Supported Adjustment Programs." *IMF Staff Papers* 37(2).

_____. (1988); "Import Compression and Export Performance in Developing Countries." *Review of Economics and Statistics* (May).

Khan, Mohsin S., and Nadeem Ul Haque. 1985. "Foreign Borrowing and Capital Flight: A Formal Analysis." *IMF Staff Papers* 32(4): 606-28.

Khatkhate, Deena R. 1982. "The Anatomy of Financial Retardation in Less Developed Countries: The Case of Sri Lanka, 1951-76." *World Development* 10(9).

_____. 1988. "Assessing the Impact of Interest Rates in Less Developed Countries." *World Development* 16(5): 577-588.

Killick, Tony. 1973. "Price Controls in Africa - The Ghanaian Experience." *Journal of Modern African Studies* 11(3) (September).

_____. 1981. *Policy Economics*. London, U.K.: Heinemann.

_____. 1983. "The Role of the Public Sector in the Industrialisation of African Developing Countries." *Industry and Development* (7).

_____. ed. 1984. *The Quest for Economic Stabilisation: The IMF and the Third World*. London: Overseas Development Institute and Gower Publishing Company.

_____. 1989. *A Reaction Too Far: Economic Theory and the Role of the State in Developing Countries*. London: Overseas Development Institute.

_____. 1991. "Policy-making Under Extreme Uncertainty: Developing Country Responses to Global Warming." *Journal of International Development* 3(5).

_____. 1991b. "The Developmental Effectiveness of Aid to Africa." In Husain, I., and J. Underwood, eds., *African External Finance in the 1990s*. Washington, D.C.: World Bank.

Killick, Tony, with Moazzam Malik. 1991. *Country Experiences with IMF Programmes*. ODI Working Paper No. 48. London: Overseas Development Institute.

Killick, Tony, and F.M. Mwega. 1990. *Monetary Policy in Kenya, 1967-88*. Working Paper No. 39. London: Overseas Development Institute.

Killick, Tony, Moazzam Malik, and Marcus Manuel. 1991. "What Can We Know About the Effects of IMF Programmes?" ODI Working Paper No. 47. London: Overseas Development Institute.

Kirkpatrick, C.H., N. Lee, and F.I. Nixson. 1984. *Industrial Structure and Policy in Less Developed Countries*. London: Allen and Unwin.

Klitgaard, Robert. 1989. "Incentive Myopia." *World Development* 17(4).

Koester, Ulrich, Hartwig Schafer, and Alberto Valdes. 1990. *Demand-Side Constraints and Structural Adjustment in Sub-Saharan African Countries*. Washington, D.C.: International Food Policy Research Institute..

Krueger, Anne O. 1974. "The Political Economy of the Rent-Seeking Society." *American Economic Review* 64. (June).

_____. 1978. *Liberalization Attempts and Consequences*. New York: Ballinger.

Krueger, Anne O., Maurice Schiff, and Alberto Valdes. 1988. "Agricultural Incentives in Developing Countries: Measuring the Effects of Sectoral and Economywide Policies." *World Bank Economic Review* 2(3).

Krugman, Paul, and Lance Taylor. 1978. "Contractionary Effects of Devaluation." *Journal of International Economics* (August).

Krugman, Paul R. 1987. "Is Free Trade Passé?" *Journal of Economic Perspectives* 1(2).

Kubo, Yuji, Jaime de Melo, Sherman Robinson, and Moshe Syrquin. 1986. "Interdependence and Industrial Structure." In Hollis Cheney, Sherman Robinson, and Moshe Syrquin, eds., *Industrialization and Growth: A Comparative Study*. New York: Oxford University Press.

Kuznets, Simon. 1965. *Economic Growth and Structure*. London: Heinemann.

_____. 1966. *Modern Economic Growth: Rate, Structure and Spread*. New Haven, Connecticut: Yale University Press.

Kydd, Jonathan. 1988. "Policy Reform and Adjustment in an Economy Under Siege: Malawi, 1980-87." *IDS Bulletin* 19(1).

Lächler, Ulrich. 1988. "Credibility and the Dynamics of Disinflation in Open Economies." *Journal of Development Economics* 28(3).

Laker, John F. 1981. "Fiscal Proxies for Devaluation: A General Review." *IMF Staff Papers* 28(1).

Lal, Deepak. 1983. *The Poverty of Development Economics*. London: Institute of Economic Affairs.

_____. 1984. "The Political Economy of the Predatory State." Discussion Paper 84-12. London, U.K.: University College.

Lall, Sanjaya. 1987. "Long-Term Perspectives on Sub-Saharan Africa: Industry." Washington, D.C.: World Bank. Processed.

_____. 1989. "Human Resources, Development and Industrialisation, with Special Reference to Sub-Saharan Africa." *Journal of Development Planning* (19).

_____. Forthcoming. "Explaining Industrial Success in the Developing World." In V.N. Balasubramanyam and S. Lall, eds., *Current Issues in Development Economics*. London: Macmillan.

Lall, S., A. Khanna, and I. Alikhani. 1987. "Determinants of Manufactured Export Performance in Low-Income Africa: Kenya and Tanzania." *World Development* 15(9).

Lamb, Geoffrey. 1987. *Managing Economic Policy Change: Institutional Dimensions*. Discussion Paper No. 14. Washington, D.C.: World Bank.

Lanyi, Anthony, and Rusdu Saracoglu. 1983. *Interest Rate Policies in Developing Countries*. Occasional Paper No. 22. Washington, D.C.: International Monetary Fund .

Leibenstein, Harvey. 1966. "Allocative Efficiency Vs. X-efficiency." *American Economic Review* 56 (June).

_____. 1976. *Beyond Economic Man*. Cambridge, Massachussetts: Harvard University Press.

_____. 1987. *Inside the Firm: The Inefficiencies of Hierarchy*. Harvard University Press.

Leite, Sergo Pereira, and Dawit Makonnen. 1986. "Saving and Interest Rates in the BCEAO Countries: An Empirical Analysis." *Savings and Development* 10(3): 219-232.

Lele, Uma. 1988. "Comparative Advantage and Structural Transformation: A Review of Africa's Economic Development Experience." In Gustav Ranis and T. Paul Schultz, eds., *The State of Development Economics: Progress and Perspectives*. Oxford, U.K.: Basil Blackwell.

_____. Forthcoming. *Agricultural Growth, Domestic Policy and External Assistance to Africa: Lessons of a Quarter Century*. Washington, D.C.: World Bank.

Leonard, David K. 1986. "Putting the Farmer in Control: Building Agricultural Institutions." In Robert J. Berg and Jennifer Seymour Whitaker, eds., *Strategies for African Development*. Berkeley and Los Angeles: University of California Press.

Lessard, Donald R., and John Williamson, eds., 1987. *Capital Flight and Third World Debt*. Washington, D.C.: Institute for International Economics.

Lewis, John P., ed., 1988. *Strengthening the Poor: What Have We Learned?* Washington, D.C.: Overseas Development Council and Transaction Books.

Lieberman, Ira. 1990. *Industrial Restructuring: Policy and Practice*. Policy and Research Series No. 9. Washington, D.C.: World Bank.

Lindenberg, Marc, and Noel Ramirez. 1989. *Managing Adjustment in Developing Countries*. San Francisco, California: ICS Press.

Lipton, Michael. 1977. *Why Poor People Stay Poor: Urban Bias in World Development*. London: Temple Smith.

_____. 1987. "Limits of Price Policy for Agriculture: Which Way for the World Bank?" *Development Policy Review* 5(2). See also the interchange between Lipton and Anandarup Ray, 1988, same journal, 6(2).

Liqing, Xu. Forthcoming. "Reform, Development and Efficiency—A Case Study of Industrial Development in Changzhou City." *China Programme Working Paper*. London: London School of Economics.

Little, Ian, Tibor Scitovsky, and Maurice Scott. 1970. *Industry and Trade in Some Developing Countries*. London: Oxford University Press.

Lizondo, J. Saul, and Peter J. Montiel. 1989. "Contractionary Devaluation in Developing Countries: An Analytical Overview." *IMF Staff Papers* 36(1).

Lopez-Claros, Augusto. 1988. *The Search for Efficiency in the Adjustment Process: Spain in the 1980s*. Occasional Paper No. 57. Washington, D.C.: International Monetary Fund.

MacBean, A.L., and D.T. Nguyen. 1987. *Commodity Policies: Problems and Prospects*. London: Croom Helm.

Mackerron, Gordon. 1988. "Energy Pricing: Industrialised Country Pricing Versus Criteria for Developing Countries." In Ian Brown and others eds., *Energy Pricing: Regulation, Subsidies and Distortion*. Discussion Paper No. 38. Guildford, U.K.: University of Surrey, Energy Economics Centre.

Maizels, Alfred. 1992. *Commodities in Crisis*. Oxford, U.K.: Clarendon Press.

McKinnon, Ronald I. 1973. *Money and Capital in Economic Development*. Washington, D.C.: Brookings Institution.

Meier, Gerald M., and William F. Steel, eds., 1989. *Industrial Adjustment in Sub-Saharan Africa*. New York: Oxford University Press.

Mills, Cadman A. 1989. *Structural Adjustment in Sub-Saharan Africa*. Economic Development Institute (EDI) Policy Seminar Report No. 18. Washington, D.C.: World Bank.

Millward, R. 1988. "Measured Sources of Inefficiency in the Performance of Private and Public Enterprises in LDCS." In Paul Cook and Colin Kirkpatrick, eds., *Privatisation in Less Developed Countries,* chapter 6. Brighton, U.K.: Wheatsheaf Books.

Mirakhor, Abbas, and Peter Montiel. 1987. "Import Intensity of Output Growth in Developing Countries, 1970-85." In *Staff Studies for World Economic Outlook*. Washington: IMF.

Mistry, Percy. 1988. *African Debt: The Case for Relief for Sub-Saharan Africa*. Oxford, U.K.: Oxford International Associates.

Montiel, Peter. 1988. *Empirical Analysis of High-Inflation Episodes in Argentina, Brazil and Israel*. Working Paper 86/68. Washington, D.C.: International Monetary Fund.

Moran, C. 1990. "Imports under a Foreign Exchange Constraint." *World Bank Economic Review* 3(2).

Morris, Cynthia Taft, and Irma Adelman. 1988. *Comparative Patterns of Economic Development, 1850-1914.* Baltimore and London: Johns Hopkins University Press.

Moschos, Demetrios. 1989. "Export Expansion, Growth and the Level of Economic Development: An Empirical Analysis." *Journal of Development Economics* 30(1).

Mosley, Paul, Jane Harrigan, and John Toye. 1991. *Aid and Power: The World Bank and Policy-Based Lending.* 2 vol. London: Routledge.

Mussa, Michael. 1987. "Macroeconomic Policy and Trade Liberalization: Some Guidelines." *World Bank Research Observer* 2(1).

Nashashibi, Karim. 1980. "A Supply Framework for Exchange Reform in Developing Countries: The Experience of Sudan." *IMF Staff Papers* 27(1).

Neal, Craig R. 1988. "Macro-Financial Indicators for 117 Developing and Industrial Countries." Washington, D.C.: World Bank. Processed.

Nelson, Joan M., ed. 1989. *Fragile Coalitions: The Politics of Economic Adjustment.* Washington: Overseas Development Council and Transaction Books.

_____. Ed. 1990. *Economic Crisis and Policy Choice: The Politics of Adjustment in the Third World.* Princeton, New Jersey: Princeton University Press.

_____. Ed. Forthcoming. *The Politics of Economic Adjustment in Developing Nations.* Washington, D.C.: Overseas Development Council.

Nissanke, Machiko. 1990. "Mobilising Domestic Resources for African Development and Diversification." Oxford, U.K.: International Development Centre. Processed.

Nooter, Robert H., and Roy A. Stacy. 1990. "Progress on Adjustment in Sub-Saharan Africa." Washington, D.C.: World Bank. Processed.

Obuagu, Chibuzo S.A. 1989. "Import Substitution Industrialisation: What Lessons Have We Learned in Nigeria?" *Scandinavian Journal of Development Alternatives* VIII(4).

ODI (Overseas Development Institute). 1987. *Coping with African Drought.* ODI Briefing Paper. London.

_____. 1988. *Commodity Prices: Investing in Decline?* ODI Briefing Paper. London.

_____. 1989. *Labour Standards or Double Standards? Worker Rights and Trade Policy.* ODI Briefing Paper. London.

_____. 1990. *Recent Initiatives on Developing Country Debt.* ODI Briefing Paper. London.

OECD (Organisation for Economic Co-Operation and Development). 1983. *Positive Adjustment Policies: Managing Structural Change.* Paris: OECD.

Olson, Mancur. 1982. *The Rise and Decline of Nations: Economic Growth, Stagflation, and Social Rigidities.* New Haven, Connecticut: Yale University Press.

Ostrom, Vincent, David Feeny, and Hartmut Picht, eds., 1988. *Rethinking Institutional Analysis and Development.* San Francisco, California: International Center for Economic Growth.

Otani, I., and D. Villanueva. 1990. "Long-Term Growth in Developing Countries and Its Determinants: An Empirical Analysis." *World Development* 18(6).

Page, Sheila. 1987. "The Rise in Protection Since 1974." *Oxford Review of Economic Policy* 3(1).

Perkins, Dwight H., and Moshe Syrquin. 1989. "Large Countries: The Influence of Size." In Hollis Chenery and T.N. Srinivasan, eds., *Handbook of Development Economics,* vol. II, chapter 32. Amsterdam: North-Holland.

Pfefferman, Guy. 1985. "Overvalued Exchange Rates and Development." *Finance and Development* 22(1).

Please, Stanley. 1984. *The Hobbled Giant: Essays on the World Bank.* Boulder and London: Westview Press.

Pratten, Cliff. 1988. *A Survey of Economies of Scale.* Economic Papers no. 67. Brussels, Belgium: Commission of the European Communities.

Quirk, Peter J., B.V. Christensen, K.M. Huh, and T. Sasaki. 1987. *Floating Exchange Rates in Developing Countries.* Occasional Paper No. 53. Washington, D.C.: International Monetary Fund.

Rajeswaran, K. 1986. *Performance Aspects of Mansa Batteries Ltd, Mansa, Zambia.* TECO Publication No. 7. Helsinki, Finland: University of Helsinki, Institute of Development Studies.

Ram, Rati. 1987. "Exports and Economic Growth in Developing Countries: Evidence from Time-Series and Cross-Section Data." *Economic Development and Cultural Change* 36(1).

_____. 1988. "Economic Development and Income Inequality: Further Evidence on the U-Curve Hypothesis." *World Development* 16(11).

Reisen, Helmut, and Axel Van Trotsenburg. 1988. *Developing Country Debt: The Budgetary and Transfer Problem.* Paris: OECD.

Remmer, Karen. 1986. "The Politics of Economic Stabilisation: IMF Standby Programs in Latin America, 1954-84." *Comparative Politics* 19(1).

Republic of Zimbabwe. 1986. *Report of the Commission of Inquiry into Taxation* Harare.

Riddell, Roger C., ed. 1990. *Manufacturing Africa.* London: James Currey and ODI.

Roberts, John. 1989. "Liberalizing Foreign Exchange Rates in Sub-Saharan Africa." *Development Policy Review* 7(2).

Rodinson, Maxime. 1974. *Islam and Capitalism.* Translated by Brian Pearce. London: Allen Lane.

Roe, Alan R. 1982. "High Interest Rates: A New Conventional Wisdom for Development Policy? Some Conclusions from the Sri Lankan Experience." *World Development* 10(3): 211-222.

_____. 1988. *The Financial Sector in Stabilisation Programmes.* Discussion Paper No. 77. Warwick, U.K.: University of Warwick, Development Economics Research Centre.

Roemer, Michael. 1979. "Resource-Based Industrialization in the Developing Countries." *Journal of Development Economics* 6.

_____. 1988. *Macroeconomic Reform in Developing Countries.* Development Discussion Paper No. 266. Cambridge, Massachusetts: Harvard Institute for International Development.

Roemer, Michael, and Dwight H. Perkins. 1991. *Reforming Economic Systems in Developing Countries.* Cambridge, Massachusetts: Harvard University Press.

Rossi, Nicola. 1988. "Government Spending, the Real Interest Rate and the Behavior of Liquidity-Constrained Consumers in Developing Countries." *IMF Staff Papers* 35(1): 104-140.

Ruddle, Kenneth, and Walther Manshard. 1981. *Renewable Natural Resources and the Environment.* Dublin, Ireland: Tycooly International.

Rwegasira, Delphin G. 1984. "Exchange Rates and the Management of the External Sector in Sub-Saharan Africa." *Journal of Modern African Studies* 22(3).

Sachs, Jeffrey D. 1987. "Trade and Exchange Rate Policies in Growth-Oriented Adjustment Policies." In Vittorio Corbo, Morris Goldstein, and Mohsin

Khan, eds., *Growth-Oriented Adjustment Programs*. Washington, D.C.: International Monetary Fund and World Bank.

Sadeque, Syed. 1986. "The Rural Financial Market and the Grameen Bank Project in Bangladesh." *Savings and Development* (Milan) 10(2): 181-96.

Sandbrook, Richard. 1985. *The Politics of Africa's Economic Stagnation*. Cambridge, U.K.: Cambridge University Press.

_____. 1986. "The State and Economic Stagnation in Tropical Africa." *World Development* 14(3).

Sapsford, D. 1985. "The Statistical Debate on the Net Barter Terms of Trade Between Primary Commodities and Manufactures." *Economic Journal* 379.

Schultz, Theodore W. 1975. "The Value of the Ability to Deal with Disequilibria." *Journal of Economic Literature* XIII(3).

Schydlowsky, Daniel M. 1982. "Alternative Approaches to Short-Term Economic Management in Developing Countries." In T. Killick, ed., *Adjustment and Financing in the Developing World*. Washington, D.C.: International Monetary Fund and Overseas Development Institute.

Seibel, Hans Dieter, and Bishnu P. Shrestha. 1988. "Dhikuti: The Small Businessmen's Informal Self-Help Bank in Nepal." *Savings and Development* 12(2): 183-200.

Selowsky, Marcelo, and Herman G. Van Der Tak. 1986. "The Debt Problem and Growth." *World Development* 14(9).

Shapiro, Helen, and Lance Taylor. 1990. "The State and Industrial Strategy." *World Development* 18(6).

Sharpley, Jennifer. 1981. "Resource Transfers between Agricultural and Non-Agricultural Sectors, 1964-77." In Tony Killick, ed., *Papers on the Kenyan Economy*. Nairobi and London: Heinemann Educational Books.

Shaw, Edward S. 1973. *Financial Deepening in Economic Development*. New York: Oxford University Press.

Shaw, G.K. 1984. *Rational Expectations: An Elementary Exposition*. Brighton, U.K.: Wheatsheaf Books.

Sheahan, John. 1980. "Market-Oriented Economic Policies and Political Repression in Latin America." *Economic Development and Cultural Change* 28(2).

Singh, Shamsher. 1983. *Sub-Saharan Agriculture: Synthesis and Trade Prospects*." Staff Working Paper No. 608. Washington, D.C.: World Bank.

Spraos, John. 1983. *Inequalising Trade*. Oxford: Oxford University Press and UNCTAD.

Spulber, N., and I. Horowitz. 1976. *Quantitative Economic Policy and Planning*. New York: Norton.

Steel, William F., and Jonathan W. Evans. 1984. *Industrialization in Sub-Saharan Africa: Strategies and Performance*. Technical Paper No. 25. Washington, D.C.: World Bank.

Stiglitz, Joseph E. 1986. *Economics of the Public Sector*. New York: Norton.

_____. 1988. "Economic Organisation, Information and Development", in Chenery and Srinivasan, *op. cit.*, Vol. 1, Chapter 5.

Streeten, Paul. 1987. *What Price Food?* London: Macmillan.

Sutcliffe, R.B. 1971. *Industry and Development*. London: Addison-Wesley.

Syrquin, Moshe. 1988. "Patterns of structural change." In Hollis Chenery and T.N. Srinivasan, eds., *Handbook of Development Economics*, vol. I, chapter 7. Amsterdam: North Holland.

Syrquin, Moshe, and Hollis Chenery. 1989. "Three Decades of Industrialisation." *World Bank Economic Review* 3(2).

Tanzi, Vito. 1988. *The Impact of Macroeconomic Policies on the Level of Taxation in Developing Countries*. IMF Working Paper 88/95. Washington, D.C.: International Monetary Fund.

Taylor, Lance. 1988a. *Economic Openness - Problems to the Century's End*. WIDER Working Paper No. 41. Helsinki, Finland: World Institute for Development Economics Research.

_____. 1988b. *Varieties of Stabilisation Experience*. Oxford, U.K.: Oxford University Press.

Theil, Henri, and James L. Seale. 1987. "Income Elasticities at Different Price Vectors." *Economics Letters* (24): 261-265.

Thiesenhusen, W.C. 1989. `Recent Progress Towards Agrarian Reform in the Philippines." *Land Reform* (1/2).

Thomas, Scott and Wesley Weidemann. 1988. "The Impact of Zambia's Economic Policy Reform Programme in the Agricultural Sector." *Development Policy Review* 6(1).

Thomas, Vinod, Ajay Chhibber, Mansoor Dailami, and Jaime de Melo. 1991. *Restructuring Economies in Distress*. Washington, D.C.: World Bank.

Timmer, C. Peter. 1988. "The Agricultural Transformation." In Hollis Chenery and T.N. Srinivasan, eds., *Handbook of Development Economics*, vol. I. Amsterdam: North-Holland.

_____. 1989. "Food Price Policy: The Rationale for Government Intervention." *Food Policy* 14(1).

Tinbergen, Jan. 1955. *On the Theory of Economic Policy*. Amsterdam, Netherlands: North-Holland.

_____. 1967. *Development Planning*. London, U.K.: Weidenfeld and Nicolson.

Tseng, Wanda, and Robert Corker. 1991. *Financial Liberalisation, Money Demand and Monetary Policy in Asian Countries*. Occasional Paper No. 84. Washington, D.C.: International Monetary Fund.

Tullock, Gordon. 1980. "Efficient Rent Seeking." In J. Buchanan, R. Tollison, and G. Tullock, eds., *Towards a Theory of the Rent-Seeking Society*. Texas: A and M University Press.

United Nations. 1987. *World Economic Survey. 1987*. New York.

_____. 1990. *World Economic Survey. 1990*. New York.

UNCTAD, (United Nations Conference on Trade and Development). 1988a. *Problems of Protectionism and Structural Adjustment: Statistical and Information Annex*. Geneva. Ref. TD/B/1196/Add.I.

_____. *Trade and Development Report, 1988*. New York: United Nations.

_____. 1989. Trade and Development Report. New York: United Nations.

UNDP (United Nations Development Programme). 1990. *Human Development Report, 1990*. New York: Oxford University Press.

UNIDO (United Nations Industrial Development Organization). 1988. *Nepal: Industrialisation, International Linkages and Basic Needs*. Vienna.

_____. 1989a. *Bangladesh: Strengthening the Indigenous Base for Industrial Growth* (April). Vienna: UNIDO.

_____. 1989B; *New Technologies and Global Industrialisation* (November). Vienna: UNIDO.

Varshney, Ashutosh. 1989. "Ideas, Interests and Institutions in Policy Change: Transformation of India's Agricultural Strategy in the Mid-1960s." *Policy Sciences* 22 (3-4).

Von Pischke, John D., Dale W. Adams, and Gordon Donald, eds., 1983. *Rural Financial Markets in Developing Countries*. Baltimore, Maryland: Johns Hopkins University Press for the World Bank.

Warr, Peter G. 1989. "Export Processing Zones: The Economics of Enclave Manufacturing." *World Bank Research Observer* 4(1).

Watanabe, B., and E. Mueller. 1984. "A Poverty Profile for Rural Botswana." *World Development* 12(2).

Weiss, John. 1988. *Industry in Developing Countries*. London: Croom Helm.

Wellisz, Stanislaw, and Ronald Findlay. 1988. "The State and the Invisible Hand." *World Bank Research Observer* 3(1).

Wheeler, David. 1984. "Sources of Stagnation in Sub-Saharan Africa." *World Development* 12(1).

White, Louise G. 1990. "Implementing Economic Policy Reforms: Policies and Opportunities for Donors." *World Development* 18(1).

Wickham, Peter. 1985. "The Choice of Exchange Rate Regime in Developing Countries: A Survey of the Literature." *IMF Staff Papers* 32(2).

Wolf, Martin. 1986. "Timing and Sequencing of Trade Liberalisation in Developing Countries." *Asian Development Review* 4(2).

World Bank 1981. *Accelerated Development in Sub-Saharan Africa "The Berg Report"*. Washington, D.C.

_____. 1986. *World Development Report 1986*. Washington, D.C.

_____. 1987. *World Development Report, 1987*. Washington, D.C.

_____. 1988a. *Adjustment Lending: An Evaluation of Ten Years of Experience*. Washington, D.C.

_____. 1988b. *World Development Report 1988*. Washington, D.C.

_____. 1989d. *World Development Report 1989*. Washington, D.C.

_____. 1989c. *Sub-Saharan Africa: From Crisis to Sustainable Growth*. Washington, D.C.

_____. 1989a. *Adjustment Lending: An Evaluation of Ten Years of Experience*. Washington, D.C.

_____. 1989b. *Africa's Adjustment and Growth in the 1980s*. Washington, D.C.

_____. 1990a. *Adjustment Lending Policies for Sustainable Growth*. Policy and Research Series No. 14. Washington, D.C.

_____. 1990b. *World Development Report, 1990*. Washington, D.C.

_____. 1991. *World Development Report, 1991.* Washington, D.C.

World Resources Institute, and International Institute for Environment and Development. 1986. *World Resources, 1986.* New York: Basic Books.

INDEX

(Page numbers in italics indicate material in tables, figures, or boxes.)